Laos' Path Towards the ASEAN Economic Community

Context, Sustainable Development and Challenges

Kham Vorapheth

Laos' Path Towards the ASEAN Economic Community

Context, Sustainable Development and Challenges

L'Harmattan

Works by the Same Author

Chine : le monde des Affaires, Éditions L'Harmattan, 1997.

Asie du Sud-Est : art du commerce et culture. Les enjeux pour gagner à l'international, Éditions L'Harmattan, 1998.

Commerce et Colonisation en Indochine (1860–1945) : les maisons de commerce françaises, un siècle d'aventure humaine, Éditions Les Indes Savantes, 2004.

Patrons, réussissez votre Chine ! Éditions L'Harmattan, 2006.

La redéfinition de la stratégie politique et économique du Laos (1975-2006), Éditions Les Indes Savantes, 2007.

Forces et fragilités de la Chine, les incertitudes du grand Dragon, Éditions L'Harmattan, 2009.

L'ASEAN de A à Z, Éditions L'Harmattan, 2011.

Le Laos contemporain : parcours et développement d'une nation, Éditions L'Harmattan, 2013.

Contemporary Laos, Development Path and Outlook of a Nation, English Translation Version, Published by White Lotus Press, Bangkok, 2015.

5-7, rue de l'École-Polytechnique – 75005 Paris

www.editions-harmattan.fr

ISBN : 978-2-343-14240-1
EAN : 9782343142401

Contents

Abbreviations

ADB: Asian Development Bank (headquartered in Manila)
AEBF: Asia-Europe Business Forum
AEC: Asean Economic Community
AFTA: Asian Free Trade Association
APEC: Asia-Pacific Economic Cooperation
ARF: ASEAN Regional Forum
ASDSP : Association de Soutien au Développement des Sociétés Paysannes
AIIB: Asian Infrastructure Investment Bank (headquartered in Beijing)
ASEAN: Association of Southeast Asian Nations (headquartered in Jakarta)
ASEM: Asia-Europe Meeting
BCEL : Banque pour le Commerce Exterieur Lao
BOL: Bank of Lao PDR
BOOT: Build, Own, Operate, and Transfer
CLMV: Cambodia, Lao PDR, Myanmar, and Viet Nam
ECCIL: European Chamber of Commerce and Industry in Laos
EDL: Électricité du Laos
FAO: Food and Agriculture Organization of the United Nations
ERIA: Economic Research Institute for ASEAN and East Asia
EU: European Union
FDI: Foreign Direct Investment
FTA: Free Trade Agreement
GDP: Gross Domestic Product
GMS: Great Mekong Sub-Region
IMF: International Monetary Fund
IPP: Independent Power Producer
IPR: Intellectual Property Rights
ITC: Information Technology and Communication

JETRO: Japan External Trade Organization
JICA: Japan International Cooperation Agency
LDC: Least Developed Country
LNCCI: Lao National Chamber of Commerce and Industry
LPDR: Lao People's Democratic Republic
LPRP: Lao People Revolutionary Party
LSX: Lao Stock Exchange
MAF: Ministry of Agriculture and Forestry (of the Lao PDR)
MFA: Ministry of Foreign Affairs (of the Lao PDR)
MDG: Millennium Development Goals
MOF: Ministry of Finance (of the Lao PDR)
MOIC: Ministry of Industry and Commerce (of the Lao PDR)
MPI: Ministry of Planning and Investment (of Lao PDR)
MRC: Mekong River Commission
NEM: New Economic Mechanism
NGO: Non-Government Organization
NUOL: National University of Laos
OBOR: One Belt, One Road
ODA: Official development assistance
OECD: Organization for Economic Co-operation and Development
PPP: Public Private Partnership
RCEP: Regional Comprehensive Partnership Agreement
SEZ: Special Economic Zone
SDG: Sustainable Development Goals
SME: Small and medium-sized enterprises
SOE: State-owned enterprise
UN: United Nations
US: United States
UXO: Unexploded ordnance
WHO: World Health Organization
WTO: World Trade Organization (headquartered in Geneva)

Foreword

For a small and landlocked Laos, the launching of the ASEAN Economic Community (AEC) in 2015 not only marked a milestone in regional economic integration in Southeast Asia but offers great economic potential and more opportunities for the country to have access to an economy of scale. The AEC is a highly integrated market consisting of 625 million consumers with a combined purchasing power of USD 2.3 trillion and ASEAN Member States already account for more than half of Laos' total foreign trade.

Nevertheless, the AEC also comes with challenges for the country's public and private sectors. Among other top priorities, Laos will have to be in compliance with ASEAN agreements among other international norms and regulations. Lao business sector has to cope with increasing trade liberalization and strong competition from more advanced ASEAN economies. At present, Laos' main exports are energy and mineral resources, both sectors require capital-intensive but have limited effects on local employment. The vast majority of Lao businesses are small and medium-sized enterprises (SMEs). Strengthening SME development would therefore enable Laos to integrate more inclusively and sustainably into the AEC.

The publishing of this book on Laos' Path Towards the ASEAN Economic Community by Mr. Kham Vorapheth is highly valuable and timely. The author had published several books and articles on Asia and its transformation which have been well accepted by general public and scholars as well. This book follows closely with the previous one ASEAN de A à Z, which was published in French, are useful introduction to ASEAN and Asia in general.

I therefore sincerely welcome this book and hope that it would be a useful and reliable tool for the public in discovering the Lao People's Democratic Republic and its geo-politic environment.

YONG CHANTHALANGSY

Ambassador of Lao PDR to France,
Former General Director of Foreign
Affairs Institute of the Ministry of
Foreign Affairs, Lao PDR

Abstract

Over the last thirty years, Laos has made steady progress in implementing economic reforms and building the institutions necessary for a market economy, culminating in accession to Asean in 1997 and to the World Trade Organization (WTO) in 2013. The purpose of this book is first to outline the Laos' economic transformation from 1986 to present and then to examine the positioning of Laos in the ASEAN Economic Community (AEC) and how the Lao government embarked on turning the geographical "constraint" into an "opportunity" by launching the catchword, as part of its development vision: "transforming the landlocked to the land-linked country". It also proposes to explore how the AEC will impact Laos and how the country is expected to benefit from the free flow of goods, services, investments, and skilled labor, the freer movement of capital across the region, and the regional integration.

This book highlights in what way Laos can respond to these economic changes, including the implication for its processing industries, market prospect, obstacles, threats, competitiveness. Today, the New Digital Economy and the Green Economy open opportunities to Laos' growing private sector and businesses, which is reflected in the government's socioeconomic development strategy until 2025 and the Vision 2030 that the book takes under consideration. The book also reviews identified challenges to Laos' economic development in the years to come, projects Laos' standing in the future, and concludes by briefly summarizing the experiences in several topics that this country can consider from other successful countries. To achieve the sustainable economic development within the framework of the AEC, including narrowing the development gap, at the end of the book some concrete recommendations are proposed and challenges highlighted.

Introduction

Upon coming to power in 1975, the Lao People's Revolutionary Party (LPRP) transformed the economy along socialist lines. They nationalized industry and financial institutions and encouraged the formation of agricultural. Following peasant opposition and collapsing production, the party was forced to modify its hard line first in 1979, and then again in 1986 to embark on a reform program known as the New Economic Mechanism (NEM). The changes to the system have contributed to a significant transformation of Laos' economy towards a market system based on private ownership. The market economy is opening therefore to international competition and consequently has led to the accessible of the country to the outside world.

Today, thirty years after the economic reform, steady transformation has resulted in a relatively strong annual growth rate, followed by the birth of state capitalism and the emergence of small and medium-sized enterprises. Laos is becoming a lower-middle-income, landlocked country with a population of less than 7 million. It has achieved high and persistent economic growth with real gross domestic product (GDP) averaging about 7.5% per annum from 2008 to 2016. In 2017, the GDP growth rate decreased slightly to 7% compared to the previous years. Though the GDP is among the highest in Asean, Laos remains the poorest state amid the association members, with 73 percent of its population living on two dollars a day. Laos, now integrated into the regional community, aims to become a valuable partner in joining the ASEAN Economic Community (AEC), the crossroads of major transport and communication axes through the three regional corridors crossing the country. Much of the growth has been the result of foreign direct investment, which has transformed Laos into a provider of natural resources, consisting mainly of energy and minerals. The manufacturing sector has performed well, construction and industry sectors have grown steady since 2006 thanks to the country's large stock of natural resources and hydropower potential, while the tourist industry has seen a boom of tourist arrivals and has played a significant role in the development of the Lao economy.

Laos has begun the implementation of the 8th National Socioeconomic Development Plan (2016–2020), with the objective of Least Development Country (LDC) graduation at its center. At the same time, the Lao government has formulated the 10-Year Development Strategy (2016–2025) and the Vision 2030 (2016–2030) plan focusing on industrialization and sustainable development. Laos sees the ASEAN Economic Community as an opportunity to achieve its socioeconomic goals faster, but it also perceives constraints and challenges in numerous aspects. In view of the changing developments to the economic and industrial landscapes, this book aims first to outline Laos' economic transformation and its remarkable achievements over the past three decades, then to conduct a factual look at the present evolution of the Lao state in the frame of its long-term strategic development goals, provide various perspectives, and raise different questions such as: Where does Laos stand in the AEC? What are the benefits and impacts for Laos in joining the AEC? Can Laos follow the pace of the AEC? How does Laos intend to organize and to attain the Sustainable Growth Development Strategy and the Vision 2030 in the AEC perspective? What are the main challenges the country is going to face? What is a projection for Laos in the future?

This book also attempts to make some recommendations that can hopefully contribute to the further development and growth of Laos and that can complement recommendations made in other proposed strategies drawn up by Laos' research and economic institutes, donor countries, international institutions, and experts.

After the general introduction, this book is structured as follows: Chapter 1 sets out the general context of Laos: historic and politic background, socialist production experience and the economic reform, new state-building after the liberation war, and the socioeconomic state of Laos today. Chapter 2 gives an overview of the economic transformation in Laos over the last thirty years, with its achievements and its shortfalls; the economic success was largely due to the government's energy policy which focused on the intensive exploitation of its natural resources. Chapter 3 provides a quick overview of Laos' statistics compared to the overall levels of Asean member states.

Chapter 4 examines the positioning of Laos in the AEC. This part analyses what the AEC means for Laos, and what benefit and impact it has for Laos, including immediate obstacles, challenges, and all the implications. Chapter 5 discusses the Laos market prospect in the AEC, in particular the evaluation of the potential sectors, the attractiveness for businesses, the emergence and role of the private sector, and the business environment and investment climate. Chapter 6 evaluates the impact of the AEC towards Laos business outlook. It analyses key business success and explores the niche markets that can boost local industry. The exposure of China to Lao's economy is a significant factor considered here. Chapter 7 describes the government's strategic development of the 8th National Socioeconomic Development Plan (NSEDP), the growth strategy path to achieve the Vision 2030, and the Sustainable Goals Development (SGD). Notably, it illustrates the importance of inter-connectivity for Laos within the Asean, and raises future challenges in economic growth development. Chapter 8 wonders how to achieve the objectives and targets of the Sustainable development and Vision 2030 and particularly the external and internal forces that could affect the growth. It underlines how important the regional integration and connectivity is for Laos. Chapter 9 proposes to examine the twelve future key challenges the country has to face. Chapter 10 briefly features a projection for Laos in the future. What follows is an attempt to foresee the factors that can influence the change along with the geopolitics game in the region. Lastly, Chapter 11 illustrates a few experiences in various topics from successful countries that Laos might consider.

The author hopes that this book will be a valuable resource for companies, business people, and all those interested in Laos' sustainable growth development in the AEC context, including students, to find ways in which they can share in the dividend generated by Laos' dynamic growth while making their own contribution to the economy's transformation. This would represent a win-win for business and national interests as Laos strives to maintain steady significant development, shift to the low to middle end of the value chain, and progress towards becoming a high-middle nation by 2030.

This book has benefited from many fruitful discussions and informal interviews with economic experts from international organizations, Lao officials, as well as Lao and foreign business executives, the Lao National Chamber of Commerce and Industry, and the European Chamber of

Commerce and Industry. Several interviews also have been carried out with professional associations, small and medium-sized enterprise owners, and business people. The author thanks them all, as all in their own way have contributed directly or indirectly to the enrichment of this book by their input.

The book is the result of the analysis outcome from the author and the observation of Laos' current economic context, and it also derived largely from various literature and articles on the AEC, reports from ASEAN Secretary publishing and statistics, published documents from various ministries of the Lao government, reports from the World Bank, IMF, ADB, OECD, articles in the Vientiane Times, and the KPL News. Any mis-interpretations and deficiencies, of course, remain fully the author own.

The author is deeply indebted to Dr. Surin Pitsuwan, former ASEAN Secretary-General from 2008 to 2012, with whom he had the chance to discuss several issues regarding the AEC's prospects, and would like to express his posthumous gratitude to Mr. Surin for his enthusiastic support for this book. Many will also say that among the heads of Asean in its 50-year of history, Surin was the most effective and formidable.

The author also wishes to thank H.E. Yong Chanthalangsy, Ambassador of the Lao PDR to France and General Director of Foreign Affairs Institute of the Ministry of Foreign Affairs for his support and prefacing this book.

Lastly, a special thanks to Scott Onak, for the proofreading and the editing of this book, including putting the text into good English for English speaking people.

Paris, February 2018.

Lao PDR Map

Names in Vietnam are shown without diacritical marks.
CHINA
BURMA
VIETNAM
THAILAND
CAMBODIA
Gulf of Tonkin
BOKÉO
LOUANG-NAMTHA
OUDÔMXAI
HOUAPHAN
VIANGCHAN
XAISÔMBOUN*
BOLIKHAMXAI
VIANGCHAN*
KHAMMOUAN
SALAVAN
XÉKONG
CHAMPASAK
Vientiane
Louangphrabang
Phôngsali
Hanoi
Hai Phong
Vinh
Hue
Nong Khai
Udon Thani
Khon Kaen
Savannakhét
Pakxé
Laos
International boundary
Province (khouèng) boundary
National capital
Province (khouèng) capital
Railroad
Road
A province has the same name as its capital except where noted.
*Kamphèng Nakhon Viangchan (municipality) and Khétphisét Xaisômboun (special zone) each has status equal to that of a province.
0 50 100 Kilometers
0 50 100 Miles
Lambert Conformal Conic Projection, SP 15°00' N/21°30' N
802411AI (C00140) 7-03

AEC

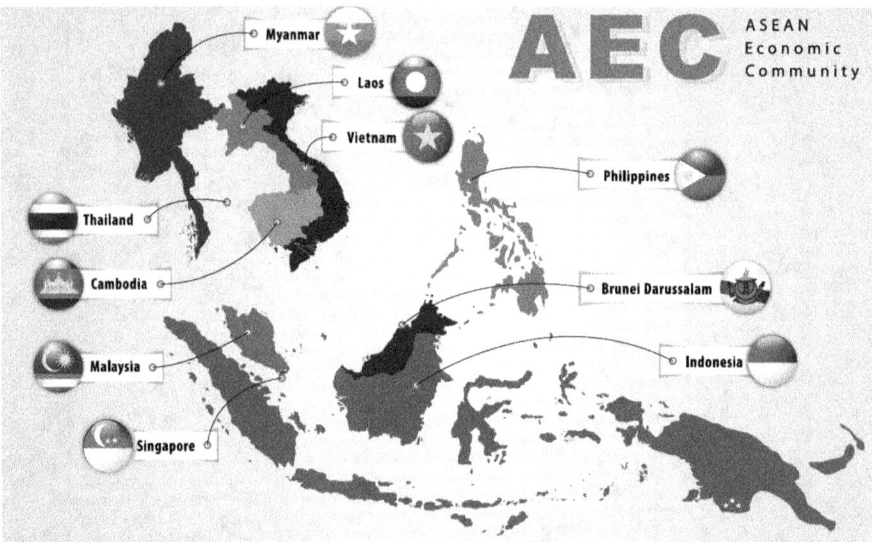
AEC
ASEAN
Economic
Community
Myanmar
Laos
Vietnam
Philippines
Thailand
Cambodia
Brunei Darussalam
Malaysia
Indonesia
Singapore

GMS Economic Corridors

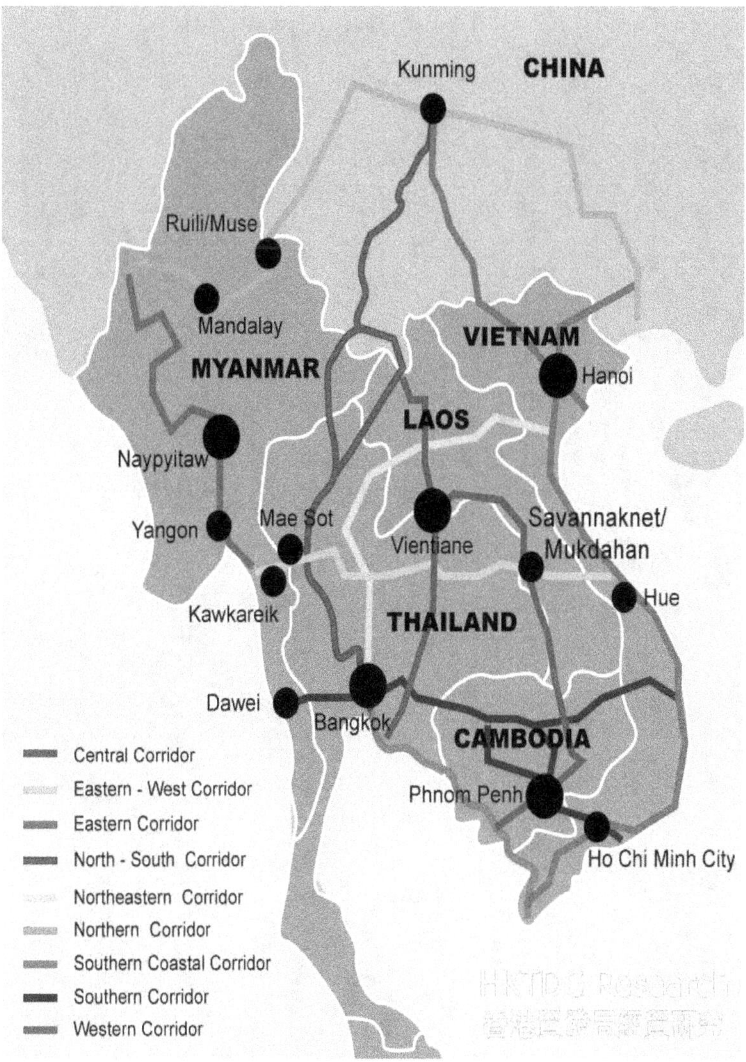

CHAPTER 1

The General Context

1.1 Geography and People

Laos is the only landlocked Southeast Asian country. With an area of 236,800 square kilometers and almost half of the length of the Mekong River flowing through it, two-thirds of the country is mountainous (northern) and cannot be cultivated; thus, its geographic circumstances constrain both the quantity and quality of agriculture and cause difficulties to the development of trade, social infrastructure, and transportation and communication links. The country has a tropical monsoon climate with a rainy season from May to October. Laos is located in the center of energetic and prospering regions of Southeast Asia that are endowed with huge potential to support a strategic resource base, and shares borders with five neighboring countries: China, Cambodia, Vietnam, Thailand, and Myanmar. The country is divided into three main regions: northern, central, and southern.

The total population of Laos according to the last 2015 census is 6,472,400, of which 3,237,600 are women and 3,254,800 are men, the majority of whom live in valleys of the Mekong River and its tributaries. The population density was found to have increased slightly from 23 to 29 people per square kilometer, which is low compared to other countries in the region. The majority of the population is mostly young, with 57.5 percent of the total at the age of below 25. Compared to Vietnam, Thailand, and Cambodia, Laos has the largest youth composition of a population, and this number will continue to increase. The growing urbanization rate currently stands at 27 percent, but Lao society as a whole remains irresistibly rural. The census showed that 15 percent of people live in Savannakhet province, 13 percent in Vientiane, 11 percent in Champassak province, and 7 percent in Luang Prabang province. Since 2014, Xaysomboun, a newly created province, has the smallest population, accounting for just 1 percent of the national total population. The survey also revealed an increase in the number of households, with 1.2 million recorded. However, the average size of households dropped from 5.8 people in 2005 to 5.3 people in 2015. Vientiane, the capital, has about 820,000 residents and the highest population density at 209 people per square kilometer, while Xaysomboun and Xieng Khuang provinces have the lowest density at about 10 people per square kilometer. Village infrastructure was shown to have developed significantly with 80 percent of all villages now having road access and electricity, while 90 percent of villages have a primary school. The country is made up of 49 different ethnic groups: 68 percent of Lao Loum (low land), 22 percent of Lao Theung (upland), 9 percent of Lao Soung (highland) including the Hmongs and Yao, and 1 percent of Vietnamese and Chinese. Over 65 percent of the population are Buddhists.

From the north to the south, there are eighteen provinces: Phongsali, Luang Namtha, Oudomxay, Bokeo, Luang Prabang, Huaphanh, Xayabouri, Xieng Khuang, Vientiane Province, Vientiane Municipality, Xaysomboun, Bolikhamxay, Khammouan, Savannakhet, Saravan, Sekong, Champassak, and Attapeu. Despite being endowed with abundant natural resources for agriculture, forestry, mineral and hydro-power development, Laos remains one of the poorest nations of the Southeast Asian region. Its economy is at the early stage of growth, which remains heavily reliant on agricultural production. Today about 70 percent of the population depends on agricultural livelihoods and the agriculture sector accounts for more than 23 percent of the GDP.

1.2 A Brief Review of History and Politics

Laos' long history dates back to the founding of its first kingdom in 1353 by King Chao Fa Ngum. It was then known as Lane Xang (the land of a million elephants). For Lao people today Chao Fa Ngum was a Lao hero who fought to unify and protect the country. He was the first king to unify the Kingdom of Lane Xang into a single territory and also the first king to bring Buddhism to Laos, after which the teachings of the Buddha were disseminated nationwide. Rituals, donations, performances, almsgiving, and other activities were held in January 2017 to celebrate the fourteenth anniversary of the Chao Fa Ngum statue in Vientiane, attended by hundreds of people[1].

The kingdom of Lane Xang reached its period of greatest glory and influence during the years 1633-90. Later succession struggles led Lane Xang to break into three smaller kingdoms (Luang Prabang, Vientiane, and Champassak), which became easy prey for Vietnam, Burma, and Siam. This was the end of the longest period of unity in the history of Laos.

Laos in the nineteenth century was experiencing a dramatic situation: war, looting, and invasions from its neighbors. Chao Anou was the last king of the former Lao kingdom of Lane Xang. He ruled from 1805 to 1828 in Vientiane, and from 1826 to 1828 he rebelled against Siam in an attempt to gain independence. He was defeated by the Siamese troops and held captive while the Siamese King Rama III ordered Vientiane completely destroyed. Chao Anou died as a prisoner in Bangkok in 1829. The weakened three kingdoms then came initially under the Siamese tutelage and later French protectorate[2]. The Lao government recently opened a new park and monument on the Mekong River in Vientiane to celebrate the 450th anniversary of Vientiane as the capital of Laos and to honor Chao Anou. One interesting note to mention is that the statue of Chao Anou turns its back towards Laos and looks once again over the Mekong River into Thailand, where more than 25 million former Lao, nowadays Thais, are living in Thailand's Northeastern Isaan provinces.

Under French colonialism, Laos suffered neglect. Admittedly, when France settled in Indochina, their interest in what would become the protectorate of Laos was not so much driven by economic or strategic considerations, especially after they discovered that the upper Mekong River was unnavigable and prevented it from being utilized to penetrate China, a fact that disappointed many traders at that time. To a large extent, the attractiveness of Laos was instead the result of individual initiatives of romantic adventurers like Henri Mouhot[3] and Auguste Pavie[4]. Considering that the former Kingdom of a Million Elephants was so sparsely populated, landlocked, a political entity with too many internal contradictions, and a human desert, one then understands why Laos was neglected, forgotten by the Indochinese colonies, and why so little effort was made to develop this country. Laos as a hinterland offered vast, fertile land and natural resources for French Indochina. To administer the country, the colonial authorities encouraged a large influx of Vietnamese immigrants to Laos to supplement the lack of labor and skilled personnel. What economic legacies were left by France during this period? As a matter of fact, few infrastructure works, schools, office buildings, hospitals, or factories were built. No railway emerged, although a line from Tan Ap in Vietnam to Thakhek on the Mekong River in Laos was planned. Construction of the Tan Ap–Thakhek line, which would have linked the longest navigable reach of the Mekong River to the sea, was halted in 1934 due to lack of funds on the Lao side. The Banque de l'Indochine decided not to open an office in Thakhek in 1927, and only after the Second World War established itself in Laos, which demonstrated that Laos offered little interest to bankers and businesses. Laos was the quintessential land of disappointment for colonial businesses[5].

The Second World War shifted the balance of power between the countries of Indochina and their colonizers. Following the collapse of Japan on August 15, 1945, backed by the movement Lao Pen Lao, Prince Phetsarath[6] played a dominant role in Lao politics before and after Japanese occupation, declared the unity of the kingdom through the integration of the southern provinces with the Kingdom of Luang Prabang, and on October 12 he declared the independence of Laos with the formation of a government, bringing together Lao nationalists of all tendencies under the name Lao Issara[7]. The aim of Lao Issara was to fight against French colonialism and to establish Lao sovereignty.

Following the defeat of the French army at Dien Bien Phu in May 1954, an international conference in Geneva two months later ratified the division of Vietnam into two Vietnamese states: the Democratic Republic of Vietnam (North Vietnam), with a communist government, and the State of Vietnam (South Vietnam; later renamed the Republic of Vietnam), pro-Western and under increasing American influence. Regarding Laos, the Geneva conference simultaneously confirmed the constitutional monarchy that had been established by the French in 1947 and also officially recognized the Pathet Lao[8], a communist guerrilla force established in Laos in 1950, whose military forces were allowed to gather in the provinces of Phongsali and Houaphanh in the northeast of the country.

The two Geneva Accords signed in 1954 and 1962, followed by the constitution of the national unity government, did not permit to end the "liberation" war. The royalist Lao regime was gradually drawn into the maelstrom of the U.S. war in Vietnam. Although the Pathet Lao joined forces with the Democratic Republic of Vietnam, the two parties were united by a fighting alliance for independence, freedom, and national liberation.

The Lao economy (Royal government) became war-torn, suffering from extreme dependence on foreign aid. Extensive U.S. bombing of northern, northeastern, and eastern Laos from 1964 to 1973 seriously disrupted the rural economy. The U.S. dropped more than two million tons of ordnance on Laos during 580,000 bombing missions – equal to a planeload of bombs every 8 minutes, 24 hours a day, for 9 years – making Laos the most heavily bombed country per capita in history[9]. The bombings were part of the U.S. Secret War in Laos to support the Royal Lao Government against the Pathet Lao revolutionary forces and to interdict traffic along the Ho Chi Minh Trail[10]. The bombings destroyed many villages and the civil war saw considerable displacement, hundreds of thousands of Lao civilians during the nine-year period.

The Paris Peace Accords signed on January 23, 1973, between the United States and the North Vietnamese government had an immediate impact on Laos. A cease-fire was signed on February 21, 1973 (known as the Vientiane Treaty), between "the party of Vientiane" and the Lao Patriotic Front (LPF), thereby ending the civil war. A few months later, an interim National Assembly was set up. On April 3, 1974, Prince Souphanouvong[11] returned to Vientiane; after the signing of the Vientiane Treaty, an interim government of national unity was established on April 5, 1974, with Prince Souvanna Phouma[12] as prime minister and Phoumi Vongvichit as deputy prime minister. Prince Souphanouvong meanwhile served as chairman of the Political Consultative Council, at the same hierarchical level as the prime minister's office. The LPF had taken advantage of its position of strength and extended its influence across the country. The area controlled by the LPF at that time constituted nearly two-thirds of the kingdom's territory, mostly mountainous and infertile, which contained half of the country's total population. As areas were abandoned by the Royal Army and occupied by the PLA, the LPF and the Lao People's Revolutionary Party were quick to set up administrative and military regions and take over effective administration.

After the "Thirty Years of Liberation Struggles," Laos changed its form of political organization. On December 1 and 2, 1975, the National Assembly, the legitimate legislative body of the new power resulting from the general elections of November 23, 1975, met; it was attended by 264 people and was chaired by Prince Souphanouvong, president of the Lao Patriotic Front, and Kaysone Phomvihane[13], general secretary of the Lao People Revolutionary Party (LPRP). The people's representatives, or members of Parliament, endorsed a statement abolishing the monarchy and establishing the new regime. On December 2, the monarchy was abolished, and the first republic in the history of Laos was proclaimed under the official name, the Lao People's Democratic Republic (Lao PDR), a one-party state. As the only party in the political arena, the role and influence of the LPRP was unique, ending a six-century old monarchy and instituting a strict socialist regime closely aligned to Vietnam. Thus, the Lao PDR was established, representing the culmination of a long extended revolutionary war[14]. This event brought peace, stability, and independence to the country from this date to today.

In December 2015, former Secretary General of the Lao People's Revolutionary Party and President of the Lao PDR Choummaly Sayasone delivered his remarks at the official ceremony of the 40th anniversary highlighting the significance of the national day and how the country had developed over the past 40 years. He reiterated that December 2, 1975 was the date when all Lao people were extremely proud to free the nation from foreign imperialists, abolishing obsolete feudalism and establishing the new regime – the regime of the Lao People's Democratic Republic. "Since then our country has enjoyed full independence, sovereignty and full territorial integrity and the multi-ethnic people have become the real self-masters of the nation," Choummaly Sayasone said. He described the development changes that had been made over the past forty years, resulting in the continued growth of the Lao economy and declining rate of poor families.

Forty three years after the seizure of power by the Lao People Revolutionary Party, it is important to understand the major and special contribution of Vietnam in the political, military, economic, and national security areas as well as the increasingly significant position occupied by China, especially in the economic, finance, trade, and large-project sectors. A close relationship has long been cultivated between Laos and Vietnam throughout the "thirty years of liberation struggles" of Indochina and "Vietnam" wars. The Lao government must constantly adjust its geopolitics and take a balanced position in its political and economic decision making vis-à-vis Vietnam and China, its two sister parties. Admittedly, maintaining such a balance requires a great deal of diplomacy for Lao leaders. Laos works to earn the trust of its regional partners and is committed to ensuring that its relations and cooperation with all other nations are accepted and respected. Laos wishes to be an open country rather than a dividing country, and as such the Lao government advocates a policy of building a "multifaceted, multidirectional, and multilevel" relationship with all its partners. Laos's primary achievements have been to embrace the principle of "peace and prosperity for all" and to maintain a position of neutrality among all countries.

Laos changes leadership every five years. Former Vice President Boungnang Vorachith, elected Party Secretary General at the 10th LPRP Congress in January 2016, became the President of the state after the approval of the National Assembly in the first session held on 20–22 April. The then-deputy Prime Minister Thongloun Sisoulith was elected Prime Minister[15]. The new leadership has demonstrated its capabilities that Laos successfully played the role of Asean Chair and hosted the 28th and 29th Asean Summits and related meetings in 2016 after establishing the ASEAN Economic Community on December 31, 2015. Laos has gained authority and credibility since it hosted in 2004 the tenth Asean Summit of heads of state and government, despite the many economic, technical, logistical, and human resource constraints the country has had to face. Furthermore, the country organized the ninth Asia-Europe Meeting (ASEM 9) in November 2012, in Vientiane, bringing together fifty-one heads of state and government of the EU and Asian countries as well as the presidents of the Council of the European Union and the European Commission; the first objective of ASEM 9 was to strengthen relations between Asia and Europe in a spirit of mutual respect and partnership. It is in the interest of the European Commission to promote the intensification of links between Asia and Europe and multilateralism in the international arena. At the same time, Laos also hosted the thirteenth Asia-Europe Business Forum[16] (AEBF).

1.3 From Socialist Production Experience to Market Economy

When the Pathet Lao took power in that country in 1975, the economy was in ruins. Two decades of fighting between royalist and capitalist forces on the one side, and revolutionary forces on the other side, had resulted in great loss of life and widespread destruction of livelihoods and property.

Upon coming to power in 1975, the LPRP nationalized industry and financial institutions and encouraged the formation of agricultural cooperatives; up to 2,500 agricultural cooperatives were established in about a quarter of the country's villages, but often the collectivization was only partial. During that period, the government saw that the performance of the economy was unable to reach the expected goals, and that poverty and frustration gained in all categories of the population. Laos established controls over the economy through the centralized fiscal and socialist government. The first years of socialist management resulted in an economic disaster for the country, with low productivity, no industry, and lack of export. In addition to the disastrous policy of collectivizing agriculture and sending civil servants, military officers, intellectuals, and politicians of the old regime to prisons and reeducation camps, Laos was challenged by a mass exodus of its population to Thailand, the United States, Canada, Europe, and Australia[17]. Also, because of the low level of peasants' political and cultural awareness, lack of capacity in party organization, weak competencies of cadres coming from the liberated zone, and the immaturity of the state sector, there was not enough infrastructure to directly advance to socialism immediately following the foundation of the state. Thus, there was a gap between the ideal and the reality. Economic management was weak due to the lack of expertise and skilled laborers. There was some external assistance, but many projects were not completed at a satisfactory level. This was accentuated by a fall in the level of economy growth. The economy was centrally planned and private ownership very limited. The failure of this experiment led to a rapid reversion to family farming, largely for subsistence until the late 1980s, and with strong government encouragement to achieve provincial self-sufficiency in rice[18]. The country at this time was closely aligned to Vietnam in terms of party policy. The Council for Mutual Economic Assistance (COMECON) countries of the Eastern bloc provided development assistance. The ideological orthodoxy was reflected not only in a commitment to central planning but also in political isolation from the non-socialist world.

Peasant opposition and collapsing production forced the party first to modify its hard line in 1979, then in 1986 to embark on a reform program, which set in motion the transition from a centrally planned economy to a free-market one. Taking into consideration the above, Laos was forced to revise its policies and recognize the need for competition and a certain economic liberalism quite different from the Marxism-Leninism previously advocated. The country had to acknowledge the suitability of a transitional and soothing period but without calling into question the national security concerns and communist ideology.

Fortunately, China provided an example of a socialist market economy beginning in 1978. This example prompted economic reforms in Laos, beginning with the timid reform of rural collectivization programs in 1979 led by Kaysone Phomvihane (then General Secretary of the Party and Prime Minister). This reform movement, launched before a similar reform (Doi Moi) in Vietnam, was approved at the end of the Fourth Congress of the Lao People's Revolutionary Party (LPRP) in 1986 with the adoption of the "New Economic Mechanism (NEM)," and was regarded as a genuine break with the era of communist orthodoxy[19]. Thus, agricultural cooperatives were abandoned, restrictions on internal trade were removed and a free market was introduced for the agricultural harvest.

Following the Party Fourth Congress, Laos began the shift toward a more outward-oriented and market-based economy, under the label of a socialist market economy. The new economic reform was initiated, aimed to move expansion from a centrally-planned economy to a market-oriented one under NEMs, which turned from a political, socialist economic management system into a market-oriented system. The three basic principles included: 1) open market policy, 2) introduction of market economic principles, and 3) private ownership of businesses. The changes have made favorable conditions for economic development. Since then, steady transformation has resulted in a relatively strong annual growth rate, followed by the birth of state capitalism and the emergence of small and medium-size private enterprises. Growth in the Laos economy has been driven by an ongoing transition to a market economy and increased engagement in regional markets, and the country has opened itself to the rest of world and consistently embarked on improving its business environment to make the country more investor-friendly. Prudent macroeconomic policies have contributed to growth, the resource sector has boomed, and the services and industrial sectors have steadily increased their share of non-resource sector in the gross domestic product (GDP).

The collapse of the communist regimes in Central and Eastern Europe and the end of their financial assistance accelerated the reform process in Laos during the first half of the 1990s. The need to find alternative sources of assistance, combined with the ideological vacuum following the fall of the Union of Soviet Socialist Republics (USSR), indebted the Lao leadership to accept the kind of market-oriented reforms advocated by the donor community, especially the International Monetary Fund (IMF) and the World Bank (WB).

Initial progress was rapid, developing one of the most liberal foreign investment packages in the region. This integration into the region's political and economic structures led Laos to be accepted as a member of the Association of Southeast Asian Nations (Asean) in July 1997, and later Laos joined the World Trade Organization (WTO) in February 2013. Today, the market is widely open to international trade and investment; the Lao government has pursued and speeded up policy reforms over the last decade, focusing on promoting economic growth and integration. The government permits both domestic and foreign-owned private companies to operate, but state interference trumps market principles and the playing field is not level. Most state-owned enterprises have been privatized, but others still dominate their respective sectors (electricity, water). Reform agendas in trade and investment facilitation, private sector development, public financial management reform, and public expenditure policy have been driven by an increasing number of well-trained local managers and technical experts, many of whom have been educated in Australia, Japan, Singapore, Thailand, Vietnam, India, and China, and therefore have a more international mindset.

Economically, the regime has continued to experience some of Asean's highest GDP growth rates as a result of market reforms commenced in the mid-1980s and more particularly from 1997 onward. This growth has been accompanied by a gradual shift away from agriculture, which had traditionally fueled growth in Laos. Industry and services now account for a larger share of value added, and average annual growth in these two sectors has outstripped growth in agriculture since the 1990s. While agriculture's share of GDP has fallen over the last decade, it has still grown at about four per cent per annum and has been the key driver in reducing rural poverty. Expanding exports have played a significant role in Laos' growth and the economy is now significantly more open. Foreign direct investment (FDI), while small at less than 1.5 per cent of GDP in 2001, grew 15 percent in 2016. The Lao economy continues to benefit from international aid and from foreign investment in hydropower, mining, infrastructure, and agriculture. Furthermore, to support the country's development, the first Lao stock market, a joint venture between the Lao government and Korean Stock Exchange, was officially opened on October 2010 and confirmed the transition to an economy based on free trade, even if the regime is still officially socialist. The Vientiane Stock Exchange is set to be a source of long-term funding for investment and business.

While maintaining its socialist ideal, Laos has moved from a planned economy, subject first and foremost to communist orthodoxy, to a regulated market economy, externally oriented in order to attract FDI via a form of state capitalism. From a landlocked, self-sufficient, agricultural economy, Laos has opened up significantly, reaching out to its dynamic neighbors. The economic reform has become the most important factor that persuades the economy of Laos to liberalize foreign trade through an open market system, leading to an increase in the regional economic development and global development. As a result, it has witnessed a significant rise in public and private investment and improvement of economic activities.

1.4 Post-Liberation War Reconstruction and New State Building

The Lao People's Revolutionary Party came to power in 1975 as a Marxist-Leninist regime modeled on that of the Democratic Republic of Vietnam and closely controls key ministerial and senior bureaucratic positions at national and provincial levels. The establishment of the republic opened a new chapter in the contemporary history of Laos; it also represented a complete victory for the LPRP and justified the "determination" of its revolutionary leaders and the "thirty years of struggle" under the guidance of the Party[20].

The LPRP plays a central role in the political system. The party-state structure extends throughout the country, from national to provincial, district and village levels. Appointments are made, or at least directed, by higher levels in the party-state structure.

One of the LPRP's first acts in 1976 was to replace the multiparty parliamentary system with a system of "democratic centralism." In theory, each level of the party, from the bottom up, elects delegates to the next level, but in practice those controlling the higher level co-opt the delegates they want. Lacking a constitution since its inception in 1975, Laos eventually adopted one officially in 1991. The role of state power was formally defined by this first constitution, enacted on August 15, 1991, by the president of the republic. The Constitution was revised in 2003 to reflect the country's new economic and political context; thus, in addition to implementing market-oriented policies, the country has enacted laws governing ownership, inheritance, contracts, and foreign and domestic investment. The new Constitution expresses the will of the ruling class; it also defines the socioeconomic and political regime, the defense and security of the country, the fundamental rights and duties of citizens, the organization of the state bureaucracy, and the judicial system of the Lao PDR. This fundamental law establishes the three branches of the People's Democratic Republic of Laos: legislative, executive, and judicial. In addition, it determines other social and political organizations. According to the organization of the state apparatus set by the provisions of the basic law, power is represented by the National Assembly (NA), the government, and the judiciary, itself composed of the People's Supreme Court and the Public Prosecutor General. Elections for the NA take place every five years. Tightly controlled elections have been held since the promulgation of a Constitution, but all candidates are screened by, and the overwhelming majority are, members of the party. According to the Constitution, the LPRP is the "leading nucleus" of the political system. The LPRP selects the candidates to the NA and, through the Assembly approve the Prime Minister and the members of the government after proposals from the state President (who is also the party General Secretary). The Party congresses design the five-year economic plans that set the priorities for the government and shape its economic strategy.

There is no party system in Laos: the sole political party is the LPRP as mentioned above. The ruling party is well institutionalized, stable and deeply rooted in Lao society. Independent organizations were not permitted until recently in Laos, and most interest groups continue to function under, or in close cooperation with, the party and/or state. The party's mass organizations include the Lao Federation of Trade Unions, Lao Women's Union, Lao People's Revolutionary Youth Union and Lao Front for National Construction, which includes representatives of ethnic minorities, religious organizations and professional.

The Lao Constitution outlines also a formal separation of powers between the NA (legislature), the government (executive) and the judiciary, but in fact, all function according to the dictates of the ruling LPRP. The role of the LPRP extends to the judicial system in spite of this being institutionally distinct from the executive branch.

In December 2015, the Constitution was amended for the second time, stipulating that Laos is a democratic state with all powers belonging to the people, by the people, and in the interests of the people[21]. The NA is ranked as the highest state power, apart from the other two state powers of the executive and judicial bodies in the country, and plays a significant role in approving the country's leaders and laws as well as making decisions on all fundamental issues. The rule of law prevails according to the Constitution but not in reality, as widely illustrated by human rights organizations, in particular Amnesty International. The amended Constitution defines a clearer role for the NA, the President of Laos and the Prime Minister, with the president permitted to hold office for not more than two consecutive terms. Under the Constitution, provincial people's assemblies are established to consider and approve major issues in these localities as well as oversee the performance of local authorities, following the "Three Builds" directive of the Politburo implemented since 2013[22]. Taking into consideration that provinces play today a key role in the country's economic and social development, provincial administrations and cadres are accountable and responsive to local economic stakeholders.

Today, the NA, while also dominated by LPRP members, has become a channel for discussion. Foreign observers of Lao politics have noted that the NA has evolved from a traditional role as simply a "recordkeeping room" to a body with its own identity that has substantially improved certain laws.

The 10th LPRP Congress was held in Vientiane from January 18 to 22, 2016 and was attended by 685 delegates, representing the 252,879 Party members nationwide. The Congress elected the 10th Party Central Committee comprising 69 members and eight alternative members, which constitutes the core leadership body in guiding the Party, state, armed forces, and Lao people nationwide. A number of changes have been made by the new government to ensure the efficiency and effectiveness of its administration. Restructuring government bodies to avoid duplication and overlapping among the various sectors has already begun, including a crackdown on corruption and unapproved and so-called 'ghost' development projects, public debt, revenue shortfall, and budget leaks.

1.5 Laos Enters a New Era

1.5.1 Strategic and Geopolitical Positioning

Laos today is a crossroads at the center of various axes and corridors of development that are structured around China, Vietnam, and Thailand. With regional integration, the country has moved indeed from a buffer state to a central position. This new role is bolstered by Asean membership but also by Laos's contribution to the Great Mekong Sub-Region[23] (GMS), leading to the construction of transportation corridors financed by the Asian Development Bank, FDI, Lao private investment, and government spending. Over sixty years after independence and under forty three years of socialist rule, Laos has transformed gradually its status from a landlocked country to a land-linked country, a state that has found a way to open up via the high-speed rail Laos-China project (Vientiane- Boten) under construction and two other railway projects under consideration both to connect to Vietnamese borders. Indeed, Laos occupies a strategic position on the main transit routes designated by the GMS program, namely the North-South corridor connecting the cities of Yunnan and Sichuan Provinces in China with Bangkok on one hand, and the East-West corridor linking the cities of the eastern and western coasts of the Indochinese Peninsula on the other. Laos is perfectly positioned as a driver of Asean connectivity. And the GMS program is transforming the Mekong River countries into a "new frontier of Asian economic growth." The ADB and Asean for their part support the strategy of creating economic corridors as a way of promoting regional connectivity. Laos, as an interconnection node, is gearing up for greater regional connectivity and international interaction.

The country's progress vis-à-vis the transformation between the mid-1980s and today reflects changes both in the leadership's approach to economic policy making and in the global political economy, as well as the government's continued ability to maintain political stability.

Laos has turned all the disadvantages of a small state into numerous benefits; the country has particularly taken advantage of significant financial aid from foreign donors earmarked for economic growth and social development, and has benefited from training programs and scholarships granted by Western countries for Lao students and cadres. New transportation infrastructure projects—roads, railways, and airports—are essential to Laos's development. In addition, the country has taken advantage of its human resources (tourism, supported by a substantial architectural and anthropological heritage) as well as its natural resources (mining, forestry, agriculture, and water).

Despite rapid changes in the global and regional situation, Laos has been able to maintain social peace and security while undertaking the tasks of building and developing the country. The positive results obtained by cooperation today within the AEC, and with international and regional institutions and some Non-Government Organizations (NGOs), have helped strengthen the confidence of other countries in Laos's government policies and consolidate the country's role on the regional and international scene. Indeed, the country hosted two of the region's most important annual gatherings—the ASEAN Summit and the East Asia Summit—in its capital, Vientiane, in 2016. President Barack Obama, who led the U.S. delegation, made history by becoming the first sitting U.S. president to visit the country. "Remain a good neighbor and promote win-win cooperation" has become the watchword of the Lao government's political strategy. Given Laos's deficit in terms of human resources, training, management of its cadres, experience in organization, and information technologies, Laos seeks assistance provided primarily by Vietnam and China, then by Thailand, Singapore, Malaysia, Japan, and South Korea. The diversification of support from Asean and Asean Plus Three[24] allows for alternatives to exclusive assistance from Vietnam and China, and thus permits the country to assert its national identity.

As observed in the current context, Laos works to earn the trust of its partners and is committed to ensuring that its relations and cooperation with all other nations are accepted and respected. Laos wishes to be an open country rather than a dividing country, and as such the Lao government advocates a policy of building a "multifaceted, multidirectional, and multilevel" relationship with all its partners. Laos's primary achievements have been to embrace the principle of "peace and prosperity for all" and to maintain a position of neutrality among all countries. The geopolitics of Laos and its history have landed the country in a very particular position; indeed, the political stability and development of Laos depend on the country's ability to maintain a balanced relationship between its larger neighbors.

1.5.2 Boosting Diplomatic Relations and Strengthening International Cooperation

Laos' emergence from international isolation has been marked through improved and expanded relations with nations such as Australia, France, Japan, Sweden, Switzerland, Luxembourg, and India. Trade relations with the United States were normalized in 2004.

Laos has been lauded recently for its proven ability to host international events and to communicate with nations around the world. During the Asean Summits and related summits, Laos issued a number of joint statements to foster greater cooperation both within Asean and between Asean and its dialogue partners, and notably has established Dialogue Partnerships with ten parties: Australia, Canada, China, the European Union, India, Japan, New Zealand, the Republic of Korea, Russia, and the United States. In order to broaden and deepen the engagement among parties and to enhance parties' participation in economic development of the region, the leaders of sixteen participating countries established the Regional Comprehensive Economic Partnership (RCEP). The RCEP was built upon the existing Asean+1 Free Trade Agreement (FTA) with the spirit to strengthen economic linkages and enhance trade and investment related activities, as well as contribute to minimizing the development gap among the parties. More countries are keen to be Dialogue Partners, including from as far away as Latin America and Europe.

Moreover, Laos pursues a consistent foreign policy of peace, independence, friendship and cooperation with all nations around the world based on the principles of mutual respect, a win-win approach, and non-interference in internal affairs. As a result of the proactive implementation of its foreign policy in recent years, Laos has currently established diplomatic relations with Laos has diplomatic relations with 140 countries and has 39 diplomatic representative offices, 26 of which are embassies, three are permanent representative offices to the United Nations in New York, Geneva, and Jakarta, nine are general consulates, and 15 honorary consulates abroad. The country has embassies in 27 nations, and nine general consulates. It has also established and strengthened bilateral relations with 130 countries around the world including the European Union[25].

The Lao government widely opened development and economic cooperation with foreign countries, enhancing the effectiveness and efficiency of the cooperation with friendly countries and strategic partners to contribute to its socio-economic development. Cooperation within the United Nations has expanded regularly. Indeed, the most outstanding achievement has been the endorsement by Laos of the United Nations Development Assistance Framework 2011–2016 (UNDAF), which mostly aimed at strengthening governance, legislation, health, education, unexploded ordnance (UXO) clearance, agriculture and nutrition, environmental protection, trade, and humanitarian assistance. Furthermore, Laos has also participated in the Free Trade Areas of Asean–China, Asean–Japan, Asean–Republic of Korea, Asean–India and Asean–Australia, New Zealand, and recently Asean-Hong Kong.

In addition, cooperation with international institutions has become intensive, with the Lao government organizing consultations and the development of cooperation strategies such as those with ADB, the World Bank (WB), IMF, the United Nations Program Development (UNPD), and the International Fund for Agriculture Development (IFAD) to set out the programs/projects in need of Official Development Assistance (ODA) that reflect the local needs in each sector. Laos and ADB have been in partnership for a long time. ADB is one of Laos's largest multilateral financiers, providing US$1.94 billion in loans since 1966. Since starting operations in Laos, ADB has responded to the country's changing development priorities—from an early emphasis on agriculture in the 1980s, to roads and transportation in the 1990s, and to education, energy, and regional integration in the 2000s. ADB assistance to Laos is consistent with the rapidly evolving development needs of a lower-middle-income country[26] .

Laos also has cooperated within the framework of the Greater Mekong Sub-Region in many programs: the Action Plan for Flood and Drought Control and Management has been developed to establish the National Early Warning Center under the ADB-GMS Program; under the Asean Sub-committee, the Meteorology and Geography Program (SCMG) has been implemented, including installation of the early warning system on natural disaster and activities on disaster risk mitigation; the capacity for monitoring sanitary and phyto-sanitary (SPS) procedures in the GMS has been strengthened to facilitate trade, with the Ministry of Agriculture and Forestry being the lead agency that covers three countries, Laos, Vietnam, and Cambodia; and also priorities have been determined for the economic and social sectors, health, service, eco-system, ethnic cultural tourism, and environmental assessment in the golden quadrangle area in the tourism sector. Importantly, there is the Cooperation Framework in the Mekong Agreement on Sustainable Development in the Mekong River Basin; particularly, attention has been focused on improving the weather forecast and flood early warning system in the Mekong River basin[27].

The accession of Laos to WTO in 2013 after 15 years of preparation and trade negotiations was the latest in a series of steps towards achieving economic integration. The milestone in its integration agenda was the implementation of the AEC at the end of 2015.

1.6 Where Does Laos Stand Today?

1.6.1 Global Integration: After joining the World Trade Organization in 2013, Laos is now entering into regional economic integration, in particular with the ASEAN Economic Community (AEC) since the end of 2015. Laos is expected to benefit from the free movement of goods, services, investment, skilled labor, and freer flow of capital.

1.6.2 Economic Situation: Strong and stable economic growth, averaging almost 7.5 percent per annum since 2007. The Lao economy remains robust. With the implementation of the AEC, the gradual recovery of the global economy, and dynamic regional demand, Laos' economic outlook continues to be encouraging, with the economy projected by the government to grow over the coming years on average at about 8 percent a year. However, the realistic figure should be around 7 percent. A major driver of GDP growth has been foreign direct investment (FDI), particularly from China, Vietnam, and Thailand, and particularly in the hydropower and mining industries. Expansion in the agriculture, construction and manufacturing sectors has also helped to drive growth since 2012.

Despite the continuing growth of the economy, Laos still faces a lot of challenges. Its macro-economy is not strong and it remains vulnerable to external impacts. The government is striving to meet national revenue collection targets as approved by the National Assembly for 2017 despite challenges and shortfalls recorded in previous years. Over recent years, the government has stayed true to fighting corruption, preventing officials from misappropriating funds as well as educating them to be responsible. The Ministry of Finance is introducing more modern technology to collect taxes; taxes collected electronically will be extensively utilized[28]. The government also stressed the need to improve the business environment and promote private sector investment in Laos to serve as new sources of revenue in the future.

Backed by the World and Asian Development Banks, the government has thus committed itself to a long-term poverty reduction program aimed at lifting the country out of its least-developed country status by 2020.

1.6.3 Lao Market: Laos' domestic market is tiny and fragmented. Businesses are dominated by micro-enterprises and SMEs in all fields: commercial, agriculture, handicrafts, and light industry. Eighty percent of consumer products and almost 100 percent of construction material, mechanic, electronic and electrical equipment are imported. The market capitalization represents about 12 percent of 2017 GDP, with seven enterprises listed in the Lao Stock Exchange: EDL-Gen, BCEL, LWPC, PTL, SVN, Phousi Construction and Development Group, and Lao Cement.

Laos has made considerable progress in moving from a command to market-based economy and has steadily moved to liberalize foreign trade. Laos supplies 85 percent of the electricity produced to Thailand. Electricity, mining, agriculture, and tourism provide main revenues to the state's coffer.

1.6.4 Macroeconomic Context: Inflation was reduced to an average of 15 percent between 2000 and 2003 and has remained under 10 percent since 2007. Since falling to zero in 2009, in the wake of the global financial crisis, annual inflation has fluctuated between 4.3% and 2 percent in 2017. The Central Bank oversees a managed floating exchange rate, aimed at maintaining nominal exchange rate stability against major currencies (US$, Euro and Bath). The government is aware of the importance of keeping inflation under control and the need for macroeconomic factors to remain stable.

For the past few years, Laos' external public and publicly guaranteed (PPG) debt has risen, due mainly to higher borrowing from Thailand and

China and sovereign bond issuance in the Thai market. The rise in debt was in part driven by heavy investment in power generation projects[29].

1.6.5 Business Environment: Laos permits both domestic and foreign-owned private companies to operate, and most state-owned enterprises have been privatized, but those the government considers to be of strategic importance remain in state hands, including electricity and water. The most significant constraints to expansion for enterprises in Laos are tax administration, access to finance, and most importantly workforce skill. The taxation system discourages formalization of businesses and the growth of small enterprises into medium-sized firms. Chronic lack of labor force is a crucial issue for businesses; large firms tend to be more constrained by the availability of skilled and unskilled labor.

The revised Constitution for the second time in 2016 allowed more flexibility and facilities to foreign direct investment. Despite this improvement in the ease of doing business, Laos still lags far behind its neighboring countries (Thailand, Vietnam, and Cambodia); 70 percent of its commerce is cross-border trade.

1.6.6 Private Sector: The private sector plays an increasingly important role in Laos as a driver of change and engine of economic growth. The sector now accounts for over 80 percent of the country's GDP.

The fact is that Lao enterprises and SMEs are still weak in terms of competencies, fragile in terms of financial capacity, insufficient in government support, and not properly organized and structured to compete and to partner with other Asean businesses.

Today, Lao enterprises and particularly SMEs do not have access to finance or with unsustainable conditions; moreover, their products are not up to Asean standards yet. In addition, Lao enterprises are lacking in market information and ignore marketing research and long-term strategy vision. Regarding the issue of logistics, it does not favor exchanges and trade for the moment with neighboring countries, and Laos faces high transport costs. The future Laos-China railway under construction.

Despite the fact that many jobs will be created by SMEs and that these companies contribute to the long-term national economic growth, the government still privileges power plant projects and large commercial plantations (bananas, cassava, rubber, and eucalyptus) and pushes for improved and expanded commercial crop production for export to the detriment of small farmers. This translates the priority given to the agriculture sector now focused heavily on the cultivation of rice, which is destined for export. Many farmers, instead of cultivating the crop and harvesting the land, sell out their land to foreign investors. This practice is denounced by many Lao people; as a matter of fact it destroys the traditional peasants' spirit which has always cultivated the land.

1.6.7 Competiveness, Connectivity, and Diversification: With the support of the World Bank, efforts to diversify Laos' source of growth beyond natural resources--in other words, to emphasize the processing industry, agribusiness, ecotourism, and handicraft--has been undertaken by the Lao government to bolster Laos' competitiveness and connectivity among its neighbors to better integrate the country regionally and internationally. Furthermore, Laos deploys its efforts to leverage its natural resources sustainably and equitably. Today, the country has become much more closely integrated into the regional and global economy as measured by a substantial increase in trade in goods and services. All the World Bank Group's Country Partnership Strategy (CPS) outcome indicators for strengthened government capacity to support growth diversification and competitiveness are broadly on track, although implementation of the modernized automated customs system and the Enterprise and Investment Promotion Laws face challenges.

1.6.8 Risk Management: Laos is rich in natural capital. Forests, agricultural land, water and hydropower potential, and mineral resources comprise more than half the country's total wealth. While there have been important benefits to the rapid growth in natural resource based economic activities, there are also significant risks, especially in hydropower and mining; however, the government is building the capacity to manage hydro and mining development financing risk.

1.6.9 Education: Although the Lao government has made significant progress, the average Lao person has 10.8 years of schooling, according to HDI Report in 2017. Laos has failed to make education a national priority and the quality of education at all three levels (primary, secondary, and tertiary) remains low. Education attracts significant funds from foreign donors, the European Union (EU) has agreed in 2017 to approve more than 570 billion kip (62 million EUR) to help Laos achieve Sustainable Development Goals (SDGs), especially in education, and to support education development in Laos by 2018-2020. The assistance will improve educational standards as well as the administration and management for the education sectors in Laos. Investment in research and development is nonexistent at the moment. Vocational schools and training provided by professional schools are insufficient. Apprenticeship system is almost non-existent.

1.6.10 Strategic Partnership: Laos maintains privileged and balanced relationships with Vietnam and China. Laos continues to entertain good relations with its neighbors, Asean members, and Western powers, both for internal security reasons and to ensure the continued flow of foreign aid and investment.

In summary, the Lao government is giving priority to human resource and socioeconomic development so that the country can benefit fully from regional integration. The energy policy implemented which is driving growth of the country will be pursued. Political stability, security and social order have been maintained to facilitate national development and poverty reduction. At present, Laos is making all efforts to develop the country in line with the new policy of the government in order to reduce its poverty and become a modern country. In this context, it is likely that the Lao government is upbeat to continue its efforts to increase capacity to maximize benefits from the economic integration within the AEC.

Notes

---

[1] Fa Ngum, (born 1316-died 1374), founder and first king of the Lao kingdom of Lane Xang who created the first unified state of the Lao people The statue of King Fa Ngum with a small army of 3 elephants was erected in 2003 in Vientiane to commemorate the establishment of the Kingdom of Lane Xang in the 14th century.

[2] Laos was placed under French protectorate in 1887 through the action of Auguste Pavie at the request of King Oun Kham to escape the tutelage of Siam, whose army had occupied Luang Prabang.

[3] Henry Mouhot was a French naturalist and explorer, born in Montbéliard in 1826 and died in Luang Prabang in 1891. He is known for the "discovery" of Angkor, the ancient capital of the Khmer Empire.

[4] Auguste Pavie was an explorer, diplomat, and French civil servant, born in Dinan in 1847 and died in 1925 in Thourie.

[5] See Contemporary Laos, page 7, Kham Vorapheth.

[6] Prince Phetsarath Ratanavongsa (born 1890 – died 1959) was the 1st Prime Minister of Laos from 8 April to 20 October 1945, and was the first and last vice-king of the Kingdom of Laos. Phetsarath played a dominant role in Lao politics before and after the Japanese occupation. He was the leader of the Lao Issara movement.

[7] Lao nationalist movement namely "Free Lao".

[8] The Pathet Lao means "Country of Lao people" was a communist political movement and organization in Laos, founded in 1950. The movement joined with the Viet Minh, the Communist-oriented Vietnamese nationalist organization, in armed resistance to French rule in Indochina.

[9] Ho Chi Minh trail: an iconic path symbolic of Laos-Vietnam's shared struggle. The Ho Chi Minh trail is a revolutionary path traverses Lao territory over hundreds of kilometers tracing the country's rugged eastern spine in the Annamite Cordillera that helps to form the border with neighboring Vietnam. The rugged road allowed North Vietnamese soldiers to fight and eventually reunite their country which had been colonized and later divided into North and South. The trail is one of the most tangible physical icons of the friendly relations and special solidarity between Laos and Vietnam.

[10] Laos: Barack Obama regrets 'biggest bombing in history', BBC News Asia, 7/09/2016.

[11] Souphanouvong (born in Luang Prabang, died in1995in Vientiane). Leader of the revolutionary Pathet Lao movement and first president of Communist-governed Laos, Lao People's Democratic Republic. Souphanouvong, was half- brother of the Lao premier Souvanna Phouma.

[12] Souvanna Phouma, (born in 1901, Luang Prabang, died in 1984, Vientiane), premier of Laos known for having sought, throughout several terms in office, to maintain Laotian neutrality in Southeast Asian affairs. He was half-brother of prince Souphanouvong. Souvanna Phouma retained the premiership until December 1975, when the People's Democratic Republic of Laos was established. He remained an adviser to the government until his death.

[13] Kaysone Phomvihane (born in 1920 – died in 1992) was the leader of the Lao People's Revolutionary Party from 1955 until his death in 1992. He also served as the first Prime Minister of the Lao People's Democratic Republic from 1975 to 1991 and then as President from 1991 to 1992. He established in January 20, 1949 the Lao People's Liberation Army (LPLA) and became minister of defense of Resistance Government (of the Neo Lao Issara) from 1950. He was the top policer maker and strong man of the Lao PDR.

[14] See Contemporary Laos, by the author.

[15] Thongloun Sisoulith, former vice-prime minister has been elected prime minister at the 10th Party Congress in 2016. He was born in 1945 in Houaphanh province, and was further educated in the Soviet Union.

[16] This Forum brought together business leaders who shared the goal of strengthening trade and investment relations between Asia and Europe. The AEBF traditionally convenes in parallel with the ASEM Summit and develops recommendations that are addressed to the Asian and European Leaders.

[17] NGOs and UNHCR estimated about 320,000 people or 10 % of the population have left Laos after 1975; see http://www.unhcr.org/3ebf9bad0.pdf,The State of The World's Refugees 2000.

[18] The first Five-Year Plan was implemented from 1981-1985 under the purview of Saly Vongkhamsao, minister of the economy and planning, with priority being given to food self-sufficiency. Rice production gradually improved beginning in 1984.

[19] Laos opened to a new era, taking a step toward Western liberalism with its second Five-Year Plan (1986-1990). The politburo adopted the New Economic Mechanism, intending to move the country from a central planning system to a free market system. Credit for this economic opening goes to Kaysone Phomvihane.

[20]« Kaysone's Vision Remains the Cornerstone of Modern Laos", Vientiane Times, 13/12/2012; see also Contemporary Laos, book from the author.

[21] The "Three Builds" directive of the Politburo in order to allow for the "transformation of the provinces into strategic units, districts into global units, and villages into development units.

[22] This is to allow for "the transformation of the provinces into strategic units, districts into global units, and villages into development units.

[23] The Greater Mekong Sub-region was launched in 1992 by the five Mekong countries— Laos, Vietnam, Cambodia,
Thailand, and Myanmar—as well as the southern Chinese provinces of Yunnan and Guangxi that are crossed by this 4,200-kilometer-long river before it flows out into the South China Sea. Laos, a country without sea access, is bordered by Thailand to the southwest (with a 1,754-kilometer common border), Vietnam to the east (2,130 kilometers, mainly along the Annamese Cordillera), Myanmar to the west (235 kilometers), China to the north (423 kilometers), and Cambodia to the south

[24] ASEAN + China, Japan, and South Korea.

[25] Laos enjoying increasing success in foreign affairs, Vientiane Times, 28/12/2017.

[26] Asian Development Bank and Lao PDR: Fact Sheet, ADB publication, April 2016.

[27] 8th Five-Year National Socioeconomic Development Plan (2016–2020).

[28] Government striving to collect revenue as planned, Vientiane Times, 27/06/2017.

[29] IMF Country Report, Laos, February 2017.

CHAPTER 2

Economic Transformation in Laos Over the Past Thirty Years

2.1 From Post-Reforms to Regional Economic Integration

Following a period of socialist orthodoxy that constrained commercial activity, nationalization of the economy, and agrarian collectivization under state control, Laos adopted a more pragmatic line by 1979. The first Five-Year Plan was implemented from 1981 to 1985 under the purview of Saly Vongkhamsao, Minister of the Economy and Planning, with priority being given to food self-sufficiency. As a result, the situation gradually improved beginning in 1984, particularly with rice production and small industries. Since 1986, with economic reforms from a planned to a market economy started, the regime has engaged in a "New Economic Mechanism" resulting in a gradual opening of the country's markets, including establishing partnerships with international institutions and western countries, without jeopardizing the existing political system. Since then, Laos has survived to a great extent thanks to subsidies from various donor countries. Importantly, economic reform and international institution aid programs have improved the national economy and the living conditions of the Lao people[30].

The Lao government's main concern was to ensure macroeconomic stability and therefore reinforce its credentials as a stable investment destination. As a result, it took measures to tighten monetary policy and sustained fiscal discipline to address the source of inflation. Consequently, significant gains made in economic growth and social sectors over the past thirty years have paved the way for continual improvement in human and economic development in the country. Laos had almost no industrial production outside the Vientiane area in 1994; its main agricultural crop was rice, with corn, tobacco, and coffee also grown. The country's industrial restructuring then began at a rapid pace from 1996.

Given that Laos has left behind its early socialist production status, how should we characterize the current period of continuing change? In this section, we use the term "economic transformation" to describe the current context. This economic transformation represents a visible change in the level and nature of economic activities from 1986 to present. Over the past thirty years, the Lao economy has proven its rapid change. Politically the country has opened up after the privatization program, which played a major role in the country's development, ratifying six out of the nine core human rights treaties, creating a more encouraging legal environment for civil society, and actively pursuing regional and global integration.

The period from 2006–2016 undeniably constituted the golden age in the modern economic history of Laos. Foreign direct investment (FDI) increased over 7.8 percent per year, largely due to the robust nature of the mining, electricity, and infrastructure sectors. The investments were mainly driven by new large investment projects, such as mining, non-resource industries (food and beverage, agro-processing industries, and manufacturing), agriculture, services, ongoing construction of mega-hydropower plants, and an historic railway project between Laos and China. Growth remained strong. Macroeconomic performance and the individual dynamics of the period suggest that Laos was committed to a notable resurgence, overcoming previous decades marked by a succession of destructive wars (colonial, revolutionary, and liberation) and inappropriate economic choices.

Laos has made significant progress to becoming more integrated both internally and with the regional and international trading system. Nevertheless, Laos remains a country with an underdeveloped infrastructure, particularly in rural areas; it has a basic, but improving, road system, and limited external and internal land-line telecommunications. Yet hydropower plants along with public investment infrastructure, especially roads, have fostered growth in agriculture, transport, and tourism. Emphasizing the policy shift towards establishing a rules-based system for governing trade and private sector development, Laos was preparing for years for the Asean single market, the Asean Economic Community (AEC), coming in force since January 1st, 2016. Laos' economic growth has more recently been among the fastest and most dynamic in Southeast Asia and averaged nearly 8% per year for the last decade (2010-2016), a rather positive sign. This performance is the empirical manifestation of sweeping institutional reforms carried on since the mid-1980s.

To support such growth, Laos relies heavily on natural resources (i.e., agriculture, forestry, energy, and mining) and a heritage of natural agricultural production. Although agriculture, service, and entry customs sectors were unable to generate the planned revenue, the power industry sector has driven growth in the national economy. Laos has vast hydropower resources and aims to be a regional energy power supplier, the "battery" of Asean. Besides this, there is at present an increasing investment in processing industries in the special and specific economic zones (SEZs). The World Bank annual ratings in 2017 showed Laos was ranked 141th among 190 economies on the ease of doing business scale. Laos' ranking deteriorated to 141 in 2017 from 139 in 2016. Under the index, the nation averaged 153.70 from 2008 until 2017, reaching an all-time high of 136 in 2015 and a record low of 167 in 2009. The country is still highly dependent on official development assistance (ODA), especially for infrastructure development.

During the last 7th NSEDP, Laos received from donors an average of US$500 million per year, and in 2016 about US$622 million. Laos is the poorest Southeast Asian state, with 73 percent of its population living on two dollars a day. However, the living conditions and incomes of Lao people have been improved gradually from the average gross domestic product (GDP) per capita of US$114 in 1985 to US$2,341 in 2016 and US$2,472 in 2017[31]. An urban middle class is beginning to emerge. National security and social order have been firmly maintained. Political stability has been solidly upheld and the multi-ethnic Lao people have enjoyed a better life today. At the eighth Party Congress in 2006 the Party formulated a policy on poverty alleviation, with the country's goal to work harder to fulfil all of its United Nations Millennium Development Goals (MDGs) by 2015. Thus, household poverty has steadily declined. There are now 32 districts classified as poor out of the 148 countrywide, compared to 47 in 2010, according to a report from the Lao National Committee for Rural Development and Poverty Eradication. In 2010, about 20.4 percent of Lao families were classified as poor, while the number of low income families dropped in 2014 to 10.57 percent; this figure dropped to 9 percent in 2015, to 6.5 percent in 2016, and to further 5.8 percent in 2017.

Supported by the World and Asian Development Banks, the Lao government has thus committed itself to a long-term poverty reduction program, improving public health, and upgrading its national education system. It is interesting to note that between 1990 and 2016, Laos' HDI value increased from 0.397 to 0.586, an increase of 47.6 percent. Laos made progress also in each of the HDI indicators. Between 1990 and 2015, Laos' life expectancy at birth increased by 13 years, mean years of schooling increased by 2.1 years, and expected years of schooling increased by 4.1 years. Laos' gross national income (GNI between 1990 (US$190) and 2017 (US$ 2,251)[32].

Laos' economy is dependent on capital-intensive natural resource exports. It has benefited from high-profile FDI in hydropower dams along the Mekong River and its tributaries, copper and gold mining, logging, and construction, although some projects in these industries have drawn criticism for their environmental impacts. In order to boost its economy, the government committed to raising the country's profile among foreign investors and has developed Special Economic Zones (SEZ) with large tax incentives given to investors.

Over the past decade, Laos gained international recognition. The country succeeded in its role of assuming the rotating Asean Presidency and successfully hosted in 2004 and in 2016 Asean Summits and other related summits and meetings. "All the achievements have improved the livelihoods of the Lao people and elevated the role and influence of the Lao PDR in the regional and international arena," President Bounnhang Vorachit said, as he delivered his well-wishing message on the occasion of Lao New Year 2560[33].

The economic context of Laos is changing; there is nowhere in the world where the impact of transformation has been as tangible and rapid. The reforms process launched thirty years ago continues to attract infrastructure development projects and accompanies the recent creation of larger industrial and manufacturing sectors that are to play today a more prominent role within the AEC and beyond. The reforms that have been initiated have profoundly changed the legal, economic, societal, and cultural landscape of the country, along with the overexploitation of natural resources.

The factual economic transformation of Laos can be dated from 1997 onward when the country joined Asean. Over the past twenty years, Laos has achieved a respectable track record of economic liberalization and integration, experienced sustained growth, transformed the Lao economy, and forged the entrepreneurial mindset among the inhabitants[34]. The Lao government aims to develop the country from "landlocked to land-linked", supported by the Great Mekong Sub-region (GMS) programs and the Asian Development Bank (ADB). In spite of the recent progress made in its economy, Laos relies extensively on foreign aid to relieve its budget deficit and develop its infrastructure. Today, one can observe that international donors assisting Laos have made a positive evaluation of the country's prospects regarding its economic transformation. Lao's partners in the region and beyond have likewise intensified their involvement in the country, not only through increased trade or investment but also through more generous aid and grants to the country. Interestingly, political stability, security, and social order have been contributed to facilitate national development and poverty reduction. Besides, Laos has adopted its eighth socio-economic development plan for 2016-2020 (8th NSEDP), which seeks to achieve the MDGs.

Additionally, a series of liberal supporting measures have been introduced over the past thirty years: the elimination of microeconomic constraints limiting private production; legislation to encourage foreign direct investment, including a legal framework of commercial, trade and labor laws; closer attention to macroeconomic stability (improved budgetary and monetary policy, reduced state subsidies, civil service cuts, and a new tax framework); and the privatization of most state-owned enterprises (SOEs), with the exception of about 20 that were designated as "strategic." Since the early 2000s, these measures were producing their desired economic effect of improving resource allocation and spurring economic growth. As investment has steadily picked up, especially in hydropower, mining, plantation agriculture, and tourism, economic growth has surged remarkably since 2006. Subsequently, steady transformation has resulted in a relatively strong annual growth rate, followed by the birth of state capitalism and the emergence of individual enterprises, family enterprises, and small and medium-sized private enterprises (SMEs). Nevertheless, the country continues to face a number of challenges in the form of a revenue shortfall, public debt deficits, and financial leaks. To remedy the fiscal deficit, the country has implemented a value-added tax system since 2010, in order to increase revenues from taxes, royalties, dividends from the exports of products, and other electricity and mining projects.

Notably, the private sector plays an increasingly important role today in Laos as a driver of transformation and an engine of economic growth. The sector now accounts for over 80 percent of the country's GDP. Although the government still controls the main industrial sectors through SOEs, since 1997 it has placed an increasing emphasis on encouraging private enterprises to spur growth, employment, and poverty reduction. Market forces are the main determinant of prices and the government has granted most SOEs increased decision-making authority while cutting subsidies to SOEs substantially. Moreover, import barriers have been eased and replaced with tariffs, and private sector firms have been granted direct access to imports and credit. Farmers are permitted to own land and market their crops, and reforms have been implemented to make it easier to start a business and to encourage investment.

During her first visit to Laos on March 2016, Christine Lagarde, Managing Director of the International Monetary Fund (IMF), lauded Laos' economic achievements while cautioning that more work is needed to consolidate as the nation transitions from a low-income country. She also stated that "the growth in Laos has been impressive" and advocated for Laos "to keep momentum of fiscal consolidation, diversify the economy, while distributing the benefits more widely[35]." At the same time, "the achievements over the past twenty years represent a leap in progress for the Lao people," Prime Minister Thongloun Sisoulith was quoted as saying in the magazine Foreign Affairs. [36]

With the entry into the World Trade Organization (WTO) and the AEC coming into effect, Laos has truly gotten a foothold in the capitalist world. This opening of the Lao market promotes and increases foreign investment. Foreign insurance companies and banks already operating in Laos will reinforce their presence in the country. Airlines are currently developing new routes between Laos and many countries of the region (Thailand, Myanmar, China, Vietnam, South Korea, Japan, Singapore, and Malaysia). Globalization has also allowed for the movement of Lao people abroad, especially students for study and exchange programs with different universities in Australia, Japan, Singapore, Thailand, Vietnam, China, and Europe.

2.2. Achievements of Socioeconomic Performance

The accomplishments of Laos' economic reform over the past thirty years are not negligible. Table 1 gives the historic evolution of the GDP growth rate from 1985 to 2017. Tables 1 and 2 below show the real GDP nominal growth in value and the evolution of the GDP per capita. In this connection and for the following arguments, it is interesting to point out the continued increase of the foreign direct investment, the dynamic trade with regional and international partners, the improvement of foreign exchange reserves, and the reasonable retention of public debts.

In order to ensure a stable economic environment, management of the government budget has been cautious since 2000. The government has been running a moderate and decreasing fiscal deficit from 5.7 percent of GDP in 2003 to 2 percent GDP in 2008. This has been driven mainly by an increase in resources and non-resource revenues. From 2011 to 2017, the fiscal deficit was an average of 3.2 percent of GDP per year, which was an improvement compared to the early 2000s[37].

Clearly, economic reform policies after 1986 were aimed at relaxing the state monopoly of industry and commerce, promoting foreign direct investment, introducing free market principles, focusing on Mekong River hydropower exports and relying on mining exploitation, enhancing economic growth beyond the resources sector, developing a friendly business environment, encouraging private sector and processing industry improvement, strengthening the private sector development, fostering the special and specific economic zones, undertaking infrastructure works, boosting the SMEs, assuring a sustainable economic growth, and reducing poverty and inequality in the country. Now that Laos has been in the AEC for two years, the following sections highlight a brief overview of different components of Laos' socioeconomic transformation over the past thirty years and describe its recent results achieved both in economic and social sectors. At the end of this section, weaknesses and shortcomings of Laos' economic development are also reported.

2.2.1 GDP Rapid Growth Based on Capital Intensive Investments in the Natural Resources Sector

Looking back to the years before 1975, the living conditions of all Lao people were very poor. The Lao People's Revolutionary Party (LPRP) set two important strategic tasks for the revival of Laos: national protection and economic development. The most prominent feature of the country's development since 1976 has been the continuous growth of the economy guided by the Five-Year Socioeconomic Plan.

The reform process has witnessed a significant rise in public and private investment and improvement of economic activities, which contributed to average real gross domestic product growth rates of around 4.5 percent per annum from 1986 to 1990. GDP growth was recorded at 6.4 percent per year from 1991 to 1995 and then at an average of 6.2 percent per year in the period from 1996 to 2000. The adoption of a stabilization program since 2001 and the implementation of several reform programs in public expenditure management, banking, SOEs, forestry, trade and the private sector all contributed to the strong growth. Between 2001 and 2005, annual GDP was reported at 6.2 percent; from 2006 to 2010, GDP grew at an average of 7.9 percent per year and then from 2011 to 2013, GDP growth accelerated to an average of 8.2 percent per year, placing Laos among the fastest growing economies in Asia (see Figure 1). During the period 2014 to 2017, the Lao economy has shown notable resilience, with the annual GDP growth averaging 7.4 percent. GDP growth in 2017 was reported at 6.8 percent compared to 6.9 percent of the previous year and 7.5 percent of 2015. However, according to the Ministry of Finance, the country's economy is still robust and relatively stable. The economic will continue to grow to at least 7 percent in 2018, since many new megaprojects that have been delayed in past years have now commenced[38]. Despite the global uncertainty, Laos ranked among the top 10 fastest growing economies in the world in 2017. According to the World Bank, Cambodia, Laos, and Myanmar, which are among Asia's least developed countries, are projected to have the most rapid expansion in Asia from 2017 to 2019, sustaining growth rates of close to 7 percent[39].

Moreover, the development projects economic reform launched continues to attract infrastructure and is accompanying the creation of larger manufacturing, commercial agriculture, and tourism sectors, which have played a more prominent role within Asean economies, and importantly, the large inflows of FDI in the hydropower and mining sectors have significantly contributed to growth, particularly since 2006.

Figure 1: GDP Growth Rate Evolution in Laos, 1985-2017

(Growth in %)

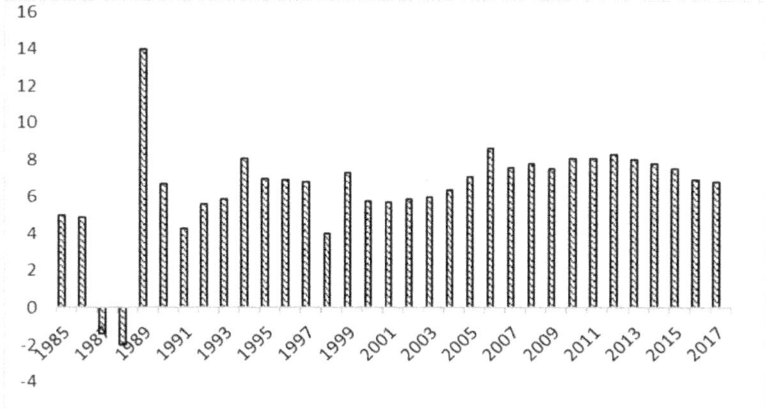

Source: World Bank 2016; NSEDP Achievements 2011-2015; Ministry of Finance Estimation for 2017.

However, increasing reliance on natural resources means that growth will progressively be more sensitive to the volatility of commodity prices and could impede development of other sectors. The Lao government is aware of such risk and manages prudently its resources in the present day. Non-resource sectors have also contributed to overall growth and FDI has increased significantly over the past decade in this sector.

During the last twenty years, Laos made slow but steady progress in implementing reforms and building the institutions necessary for a market economy, culminating in accession to the WTO, and gained the confidence of investors and market. The country aimed at improving the social and economic well-being of Lao people by consistently building itself a market-orientated economy. The national economy has seen continuing growth and has been developing constantly.

Table 1: Economic Growth (Nominal), 1986-2006

(GDP in billions US$, GDP per capita in dollars)

	1986	1988	1990	1992	1994	1997	1999	2000	2002	2004	2005	2006
GDP	1.8	0.6	0.9	1.2	1.5	1.8	1.4	1.6	1.7	2.5	2.7	3.5
GDP Per Capita	149	128	152	230	255	289	310	303	314	451	507	596

Source: Laos's Economic Statistics and Indicators from Economy Watch and Penn World Table; World Bank Data.

Table 2: Economic Growth (Nominal), 2007-2017

(GDP in billions US$, GDP per capita in dollars)

	2007	2008	2009	2010	2011	2012	2013	2014	2015	2016	2017*
GDP	4.2	5.3	5.6	6.8	8.3	9.3	10.3	11.2	12.3	13.7	14.6
GDP Per Capita	694	857	856	1,105	1,320	1,454	1,588	1,692	1,857	2,341	2,472

*Source: Lao National Statistics Bureau, 7th NSEDP. * Ministry of Finance Estimation.*

The GDP per capita showed steady growth as illustrated in Tables 1 and 2, boosted by the resource sector and its related activities but also sustained by accommodative macroeconomic policies on both the fiscal and monetary fronts. In 2016, however, the Lao GDP per capita was among the lowest in Asean with Myanmar and Cambodia.

2.2.2 Contribution to GDP Growth by Sector

The Lao economy has been getting industrialized particularly since 1997, as it became more open to the world economy and to investors. There has been a gradual change from agriculture–forestry to industry in line with the directions of the Five-Year Plan. The agriculture–forestry sector decreased from 70.7 percent of GDP in 1985 to 15,73 percent in 2017; the industry sector, however, increased from 18.4 percent in 1985 to 30.79 percent in 2017; while the service sector increased strongly from 10.9 percent in 1985 to 41.83 percent in 2017[40]. The revenue from import tariffs increased by 9 percent and accounted for 11.65 percent of GDP in 2017. Therefore, the economic structure gradually changed towards modernization and industrialization as shown in Figure 2. The agriculture share decreased continually from 1990, and meanwhile industry (including mining, construction, electricity, water, and gas) and services shares increased sharply; these two sectors have been growing fast over the past decade. Major FDI-funded energy projects have boosted domestic economic activity such as construction and transport.

A recent slowdown in mining, mainly gold, has been more than offset by a surge in logging for exports to neighboring countries. While gradually declining in terms of its contribution to GDP in recent years, agriculture continues to play a major role. The production volumes continue to grow and provide input to regional and global value chains. Nevertheless, the urban sector is playing also an increasingly important role in the economy's growth. Vientiane City, the provincial capital towns, and other secondary towns gain increasing access to national and international markets with the development of highway networks; additionally, more reliable power networks and improved digital telecommunication are supporting this urban economic growth.

The non-resources sector, including construction, services sector, including tourism, and trade are important for sustainable broad-based growth. The contribution of the GDP to non-resource sector growth has exceeded today those of natural and manufacturing sectors (see Figure 3). The non-resources sector is also traditionally more stable than the natural resource sector, and provides more direct employment due to their higher labor intensity.

Table 3 shows that the agriculture and forestry sectors experienced little growth but remained stable at around three to four percent since the beginning of the early 2000s.

Figure 2: Economic Structure GDP, Composition by Sector

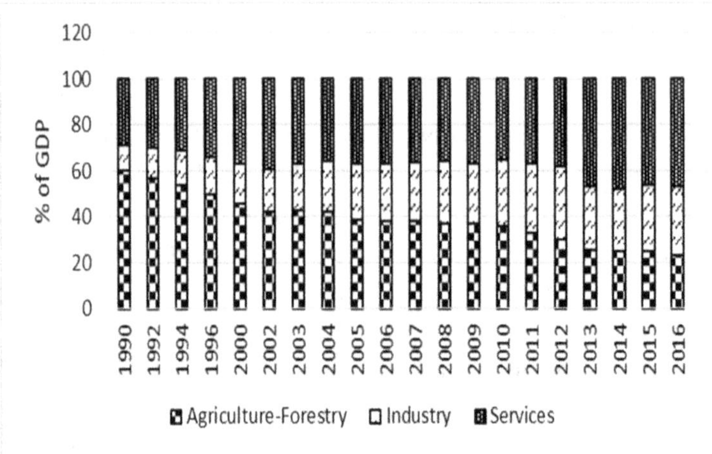

Source: World Bank, Ministry of Investment and Planning 2016.

Table 3: Evolution Sector Growth as to percent GDP

Sector	1996-2000 (% average by year)	2001-2005 (% average per year)	2006-2010 (% average by year)	2011-2017 (% average by year)
Agriculture & Forestry	2.9	3.0	3.4	3.1
Industry	8.1	11.1	12.6	13
Services	5.2	6.7	8.4	9.3

Source: The World Bank, 5th, 6th, 7th, 8th NSEDP.

Figure 3: Contribution of GDP to Resources and Non-Resources

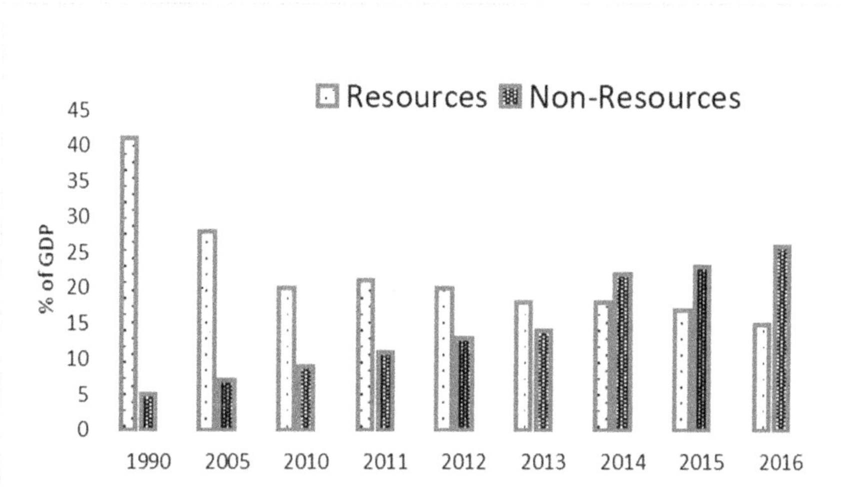

Source: World Bank Data; IMF; Ministry of Planning and Investment 2016.

Figure 4: Contribution to Growth: by Industry

(Percentage points)

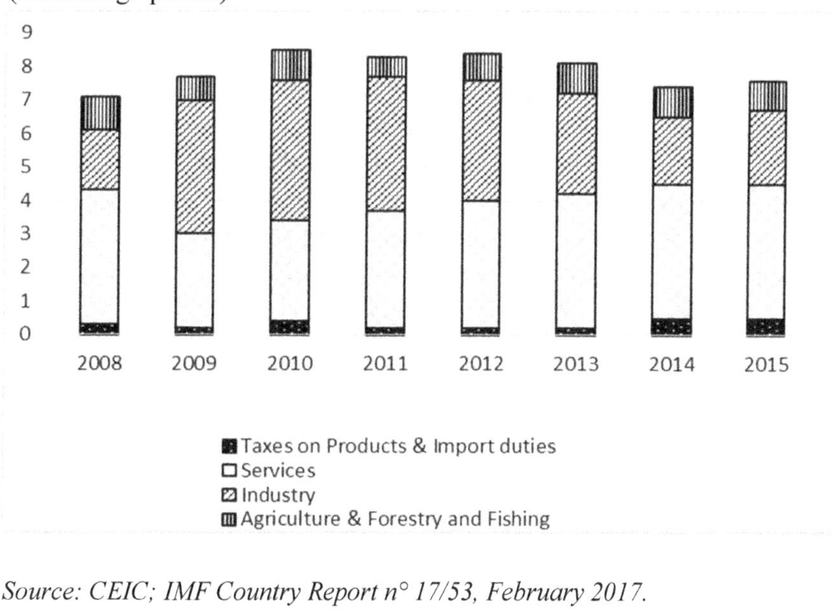

Source: CEIC; IMF Country Report n° 17/53, February 2017.

Figures 3 and 4 show that the non-resources and manufacturing sectors grew consistently since 2014. The growth in garment exports was due to the EU relaxation of the raw material sourcing requirement and increased orders by key garment producers. The service sector also showed signs of improvement, particularly the transport and tourism sectors (hotels and restaurants), and retail trading. Agriculture (fishery, livestock, and crops) benefited from the recent increase in regional demand and higher food prices.

2.2.3 Rapid Growth of Foreign Direct Investment (FDI) in an Open, Post-Reform Economy

As early as 1976, the new Lao state, following the Soviet model, laid the foundations for a collective, planned, and controlled economy where agriculture, small crafts industry, and trade functioned as state enterprises and cooperatives. Trade hardly existed then, or was conducted in the form of barter. Foreign investments were almost nonexistent. Through economic aid programs from the Soviet Union and its socialist allies as well as various international financial institutions during the 1976–1983 period, Laos was able to survive through the most difficult moments of its modern existence.

After the adoption of the New Economic Mechanism or Chintanakan Mai in 1986 as part of the second Five-Year Plan (1986-1990), Laos moved from a central planning system to a free market system. Credit for this economic opening goes to Kaysone Phomvihane, then Prime Minister. The Investment Code (law on foreign investment promotion) was promulgated in 1988 in the wake of the Fourth Party Congress, followed by the first Structural Adjustment Program adopted in 1989 with the support of the International Monetary Fund (IMF) and the World Bank. The Fifth Party Congress in 1991 was devoted to the consolidation of the accumulated economic reforms. With the third Five-Year Plan (1991–1995), the government decided to facilitate the country's transition to a market economy by promoting the development of infrastructure and undertaking reforms to encourage the private sector. At the same time, the first Constitution of the republican regime was proclaimed in 1991, recognizing private property, a great leap forward in the transformation of the political system of the country. The successive Five-Year Plans reaffirmed the reform policy, including opening up the domestic market to FDI, and encouraged the development of Small and Medium

Enterprises (SMEs) and national enterprises. The Government has been pursuing a national policy of FDI promotion to attract more investors: greater openness to foreign investment and foreign trade, freedom of prices on the domestic market, the reestablishment of family farms, the sale of state units' production, and the marketing campaign all contributed to stable economic growth. Because FDI is considered to be a significant capital source to support social economic development in Laos, it has become a crucial factor to stimulate economic growth.

As a result, more than a hundred state enterprises have been privatized, macroeconomic fundamentals have improved significantly, foreign direct investment have increased, and foreign companies have been able to hold up to 100 percent of their capital following a review of investment laws. Therefore, FDI inflows to Laos have shown a tremendous increase from $US 58.5 million in 1991 to $US 1.5 billion in 2016. This was because of incentive investment policies, which have been offered by the government in order to attract foreign investors, such as a low profit tax, import tariff exemption for machinery and equipment, and a longer land concession. Although FDI inflows have a high concentration on hydropower and mining sectors, the two sectors account for 70% of total FDI during the period 1990-2011. Meanwhile, FDI from the services and agriculture sectors also increased rapidly during the same period. Major important sources of FDI inflows to Laos are from neighboring countries, namely Vietnam, China, and Thailand. The three countries account for 80% of total FDI inflows to Laos.

According to the World Bank data for Laos from 1985 to 2016, the average value of FDI for Laos during that period was US$0.17 billion with a minimum of US$0.01 billion in 1985 and a maximum of US$1.5 billion in 2016[41]. The country achieved high and persistent economic growth, much of which was the result of FDI, the major driver of GDP growth. This has led to the transformation of Laos into a provider of natural resources in the region, consisting mainly of energy, minerals, timber, and cash crops. A mining "boom" began in 2005 with the start of exploitation at the Sepon mine (copper cathode and gold) followed by the commissioning of the Phu Bia mine (copper concentrate and gold). This has changed the country from a largely agrarian society into a mobile, upward-oriented economy.

Figure 5 shows the evolution of FDI from 1985 to 2016. The FDI growth as a percentage of GDP has increased from 4.5 percent in 1985 to 10.5 percent in 2017 as shown in Figure 6, according to the World Bank data for Laos from 1985 to 2016, and the Ministry of Planning and Investment. Given the several mega-infrastructure projects (including the Laos-China 427 km railway under construction and the forthcoming Savannakhet-Lao Bao 225 km railway to be financed by the Malaysian investor Giant Consolidated Limited), hydropower plants, processing industries, hotels, resorts, and commercial agriculture current and upcoming projects, Lao authorities and experts predict that FDI could exceed 11 percent of GDP during the 8th NSEDP (2016-2020). The railway aims to boost investment, trade, tourism and people-to-people exchanges between Laos and China and within the region. Notably, China-Asean and intra-Asean economic integration are also expected to provide a further boost to FDI inflows.

Figure 5: Foreign Direct Investment, 1985-2016

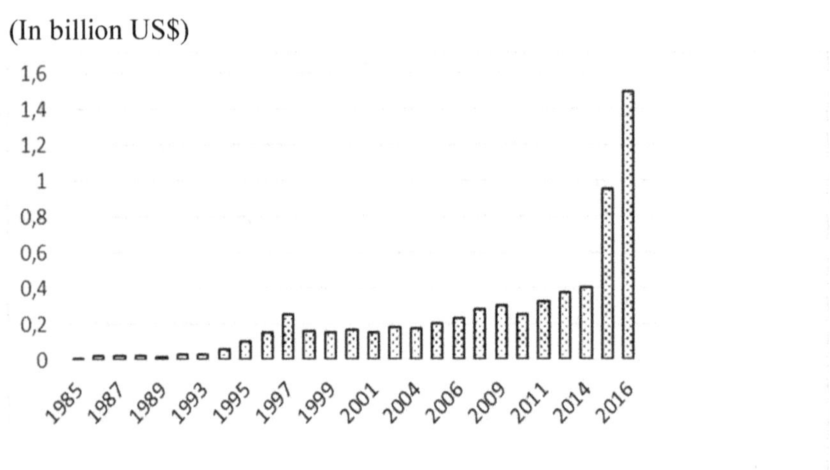

Source: The World Bank; the Global Economy.com.

Figure 6 below shows that Laos' FDI registered steady growth to the country's nominal GDP since 2002, compared with a record low of 0.3% in 2002, after negative growth in 1985, 1986, and 1988.

Figure 6: Foreign Direct Investment as percent of GDP, 1985-2017

(In billion US$)

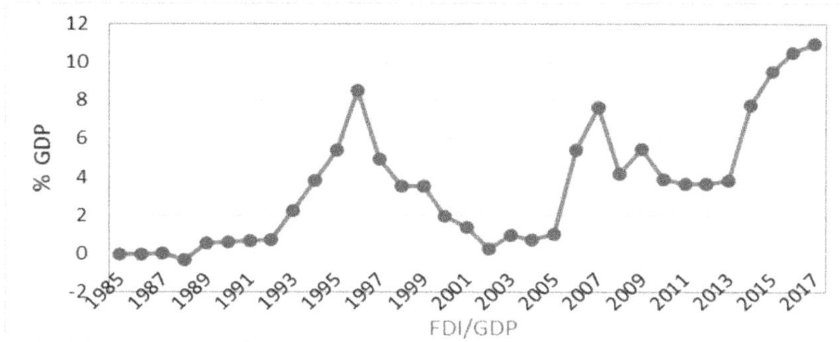

Source: World Bank; Ministry of Planning and Investment 2016 and Estimation 2017; www.theglobaleconomy.com/Laos.

Figure 7: Foreign Direct Investment: By Sector, 2007-2015

(In million US$)

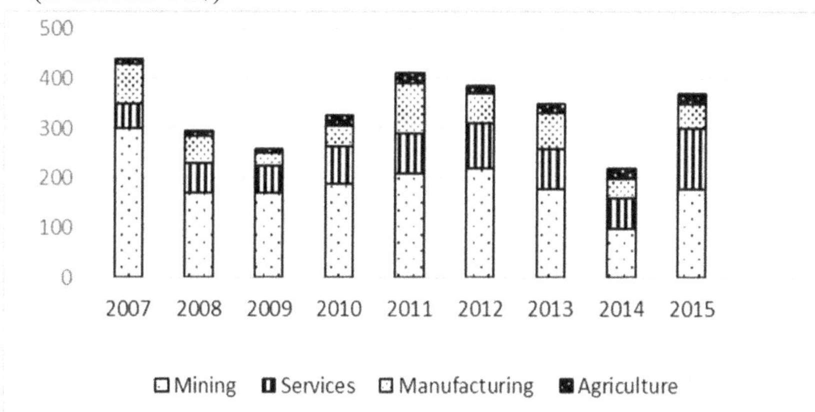

Source: Ministry of Planning and Investment; WB, Economic Monitor 2016.

Over the last thirty years of restructuring (1989-2015), about US$21.9 billion of FDI including joint ventures was invested in 1,957 investment projects. The sectors attracting the most investment include electricity, mining, agricultural development, and services (Figure 7). The major investment inflows in 2016 are from Asean countries, China, Japan, and South Korea. Foreign investments have considerably contributed to Lao economic development and merchandise production[42]. Thus, this has raised the variety of products manufactured, job creation, and local development. Besides, the government has given support to strengthen the private sector. During the 7th NSEDP (2011-2015), the country enjoyed broadened international cooperation, continued and stable economic growth, which has resulted in increased employment and quality of FDI. The government has endeavored to create an enabling environment for investors. The landmark decision has been the opening of the one-door investment service starting from October 1, 2011, which helps facilitate fast and transparent investment. This has attracted approved FDI of about US$9.5 billion between 2011 and 2015[43]. Currently, the foreign investment represents 53 countries and goes to 15 fields, mostly mining, electricity, agriculture, and services. More recently, private foreign and national investments in agriculture, especially large-scale commercial plantations, have increased considerably. Furthermore, garments and tourism dominate the non-resources sector (Figure 8). China investment in Laos accounts for about 40 % of total foreign investments (Figure 9)[44]. Since 2010, Laos was able to attract investments in real estate development, trade, and manufacturing, which made a great change for the national industry diversification.

Figure 8: Foreign Direct Investment in Private Sector

(Percent of GDP)

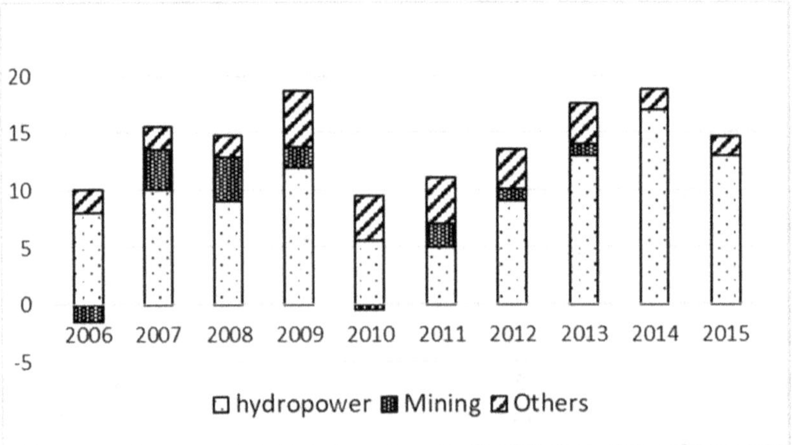

Source: IMF country Report, February 2016.

Despite the fact that the Lao economy remains the smallest in Southeast Asia, it has been drawing the attention of foreign investors for a number of reasons, including its abundant natural resources, low-cost labor force, and proximity to China and the fast-growing markets of Asean. Indeed, with strong forecasts for growth, investors see Laos as a new production base following the improvement of the country's infrastructure, legal framework, and the availability of competitive electricity cost. According to the Ministry of Industry and Commerce, after China, the largest foreign investors in Laos as of 2016 are Thailand, Vietnam, South Korea, Japan, France, Malaysia, Australia, USA, and India.

From 1989 to 2017, China and Thailand became the dominant foreign investors in Laos, with the total accumulated investment value of US$6.5 billion with Chinese companies operating in Laos[45] and US$5.2 billion for Thailand, followed by Vietnam with so far a total investment of about US$5 billion through 276 projects[46].

China's investment soared to over US$1.3 billion in 2017 compared to US$1 billion the previous year, while Vietnam's investment decreased by US$45 million in 2016 after registering US$466 million in 2015[47]. However, Vietnam investment reached US$120 million in 2017. Undeniably, both China and Vietnam are considered to have a privileged relationship to Laos. They also have a similar economic policy and political system, which might be a reason affecting a rapid increase of investments from the two countries. Chinese investments have covered over 850 projects in 14 sectors, mostly hydropower, agriculture, industry, real estate development, construction, handicraft, and services. Several Vietnamese investment projects in Laos that had been delayed for many years have now been revitalized, including shopping center, airport, and commercial building construction projects, giving new hope that the two countries will boost their economic cooperation (Figure 9).

In addition, FDI from South Korea and Japan have shown a great improvement. The accumulated FDI value of the two countries increased from $US196 million and US$24 million during the period 1990-2000 to US$1.1 billion and US$620 million during the period 2001-2016. On top of the power plants, South Korean firms are also investing in services such as banking and tourism. The accumulated Korean FDI in Laos is estimated over US$800 in 2017[48].

With regard to Australia, this country and Laos are long-standing regional partners and share a strong and diverse relationship underpinned by deepening economic ties including aid programs, trade, and investment. From 1999 to 2000, the total investment accumulated value of Australia in Laos was

US$202 million, while it increased to around US$400 during the period of 2001-2016. France is the sixth largest foreign investor in Laos and the biggest European investor during the preceding decade, with a total accumulated investment value over US$510 million. As to the US, investment is still in the moderate stage; currently, American companies play almost no role in Laos. From 2005-2010, US investment in Laos reached more than US$32 million and increased to US$42 million in 2011-2015. Currently the US ranks as the tenth largest investor in Laos[49], but the investment may become more important with the presence of GE and Microsoft. More recently, in August 2017, UK Export Finance (UKEF), the United Kingdom's official credit export agency, has added Laos to its list of supported countries, with a total country limit of £200m (US$260 million). According to the British Embassy, this is a major milestone for UK-Laos trade and investment links. This step shows British confidence in the growing trade relationship between Laos and the UK and provides security for British companies wishing to do business in Laos. The United Kingdom is already the tenth biggest investor in Laos in 2017 and UKEF's decision will further boost commercial ties[50].

Figure 9: Foreign Direct Investment: By Country (Percent of total)

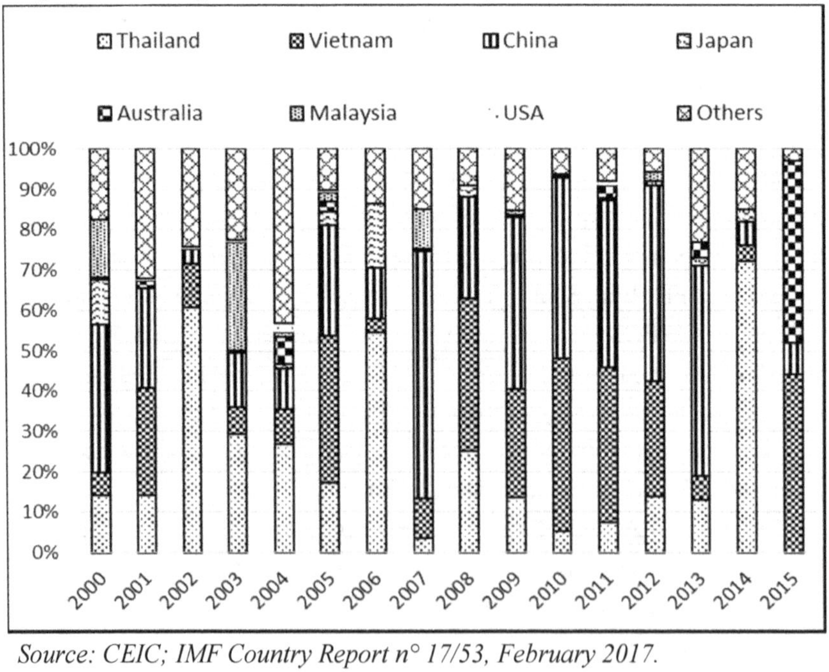

Source: CEIC; IMF Country Report n° 17/53, February 2017.

To finance its infrastructure development, the Lao government was looking for US$18 billion from foreign investors, donors, ODA, grants, and bilateral assistance during the period 2011–2015, which ensured economic growth of 8 percent until the end of the 7th Five-Year Plan. Likewise, an estimated US$27 billion -- equivalent to 30 percent of national GDP -- is required to implement the 8th NSEDP (2016-2020). In 2017, ODA granted US$960 to Laos. Investment in infrastructure remains robust, providing support to economic growth. A mix of state investments, loans, and private investments is expected to provide the necessary funding. The biggest contribution -- about 55 percent – is to come from private domestic and foreign investors[51]. Indeed, the increased private investment boosted the Lao economy over the last decade, with mining and hydropower accounting for 80 percent of total FDI. Currently, Lao private investment in the non-resources sector is small in terms of value and has been stagnant at around 5 percent of GDP, three times less than FDI[52]. At present, domestic and foreign private investment account for over 50 percent of total investment in the country.

The reality today is that investment is flooding into the country from China, Vietnam, Thailand, Japan, and newer investors such as Malaysia and South Korea. As a result, Laos relies less on Western investments as much as it used to.

2.2.4 Trade Is Increasing and Concentrated with Regional Partners

Prior to the LDRP taking power, Laos had a severe trade imbalance with exports being only a tiny fraction of imports. While Laos still imports much more than it exports, the ratio of exports to imports has steadily improved. In 1976, the first year of the new regime, Lao exports were only adequate to cover 12 percent of imports.

Until 1989 major trading partners were from nonconvertible currency areas: mainly China, the Soviet Union, and Vietnam; Laos also traded with Bulgaria, Czechoslovakia, Mongolia, and Poland. The nonconvertible currency area accounted for over half of all imports. Three Asean countries, Malaysia, Singapore, and Thailand, accounted for 65 percent of Laos' exports to the convertible currency area in 1987, up from 43 percent in 1978. Following the easing of some trade restrictions in 1988 and the improvement of relations with Thailand, the pattern of trade began to shift in favor of the convertible currency area[53]. Also, after having improved relations with China at the end of December 1989, trade with China grew by 40 percent in 1990. The United States accounted for less than 1 percent of imports from the convertible currency area in 1987, although Laos' first trade mission to the United States in 1991 signaled its eagerness to expand trade. Later, Laos gained Normal Trade Relations status with the US in 2004 and applied for Generalized System of Preferences trade benefits in 2013.

Following the disintegration of the Soviet Union, trade in 1991 with the nonconvertible area accounted for just 2 to 3 percent of total imports and total exports. Since then, major trading partners from the convertible currency area were Britain, France, Japan, Malaysia, Singapore, and Thailand; the trade volume increased to about 51 percent by 1991. Of these, Malaysia, Singapore, and Thailand accounted for roughly 45 percent of imports from 1970 to 1978; their share increased to about 51 percent by 1987. Similarly, Japan's share of imports from the convertible currency area increased from 7 percent in 1978 to 19 percent in 1987.

In the midst of the 1990s there was considerable diversification of Lao exports. Laos' largest export earner was timber and furniture, followed by garments, raw logs, electricity, manufactured products, coffee, agricultural products, gold re-export, and motorcycle assembly. Imports are comprised primarily of consumer goods, capital goods, and industrial inputs. Approximately 52 percent of Laos' imports were from neighboring Thailand, while only 22 percent of its exports went to Thailand, reflecting a strong negative trade balance with that country. In contrast, 42.7 percent of Laos' exports went to Vietnam, while only 3.9 percent of its imports were from that country. Thus, Laos had an extremely favorable trade balance with Vietnam. Other leading export destinations for Laos were in order of importance (after Vietnam and Thailand): France, Germany, and the UK[54]. Since Laos did not have at that time most favored nation status with the United States, it was difficult to export to the U.S.

In 1999, exports of US$271 million were sufficient to cover 55 percent of imports, which stood at US$497 million. To decrease its dependence on international aid and to reduce poverty, the Lao government expanded its exports. That was the primary rationale for its long-term plan to build more hydropower plants to sell electricity to its neighbors, an area in which Laos has a clear comparative advantage. The export of textiles such as clothing and garments was also for Laos an important revenue. Being in economic transition, the Lao export sector is narrowly based on natural resources (copper, gold, hydropower, timber, and agriculture) that account for over 70 percent of exports through customs. In 2016, due to a slump in coffee prices on the world market[55], the sale price of Lao coffee and export volumes have been declining in recent years; however, coffee remains a key commercial export crop in Laos.

As a landlocked country, Laos had a relatively closed economy and engaged in trade with only a few neighboring countries. The country consistently ran trade deficits due to its underdeveloped infrastructure and undiversified export base during that time. The country mainly imported oil, machinery and equipment, vehicles, iron and steel, telecommunication equipment, beverages, and cement. Until 1997 Laos' trade deficit was financed by two primary sources: international aid and electricity and mining exports. Aid was primarily provided by Japan, Australia, and Sweden. Given the Asian financial crisis in 1997, the government also turned to both China and Vietnam for important economic assistance. Lao trade was more integrated, but more exports were from natural resources. Yet the nature of imports and exports did not change much in 2017; electricity and mining products remained predominant. Figure 10 shows the import and export values from 1975 to 2017; for the first time in 2016 Laos recorded a trade surplus of US$320 million after deficits for many years. Overall, the trade balance recorded a deficit of more than US$1.6 billion. The main causal factor was an important increase in imports of intermediate goods and capital goods, while exports also increased, driven by mineral products, timber, garments, beverages, and tobacco.

Today, the government has improved mechanisms for international trade, especially through the establishment of information centers in the form of websites to provide information and facilitate the import-export of goods by business sector, resulting in an increased trend in import value.

Trade is important to the Lao economy; the value of exports and imports taken together equals 70 percent of GDP (see Figures 11 and 12). Although Laos is implementing a process to broadly open its economy, the country maintains restrictions for the import of certain goods such as chemical products, weapons, and some medications. Timber and weapons cannot be exported. Besides, the weakness of the financial sector and a lack of transparency in administrative procedures limit the development of trade.

Laos exports to and imports from many countries around the world and has signed a Trade and Investment Framework Agreement with countries in Asia, Europe, and the Americas. But while the trade value between Laos and Asean countries is also growing, the value of trade between Laos, Europe, and America is stable. The two-way trade between Laos and the European Union (EU) remains healthy, with Germany continuing to be Laos' top trading partner in the bloc after buying products worth US$43.3 million in the first nine months of 2017, mostly garments[56].Trade with the US remains minor; its value between Laos and the US reached US$14 million in 2005 and increased to US$88 million in 2016. The US ranks as the twelfth export market and tenth import market with Laos[57]. Large quantities of goods are exported to and imported from neighboring countries, especially Thailand and Vietnam. These countries remain Laos' top trading partners within Asean. Mining and electricity exports currently account for more than two thirds of total exports.

Figure 10: Trade Balance in Million US$, 1975-2017

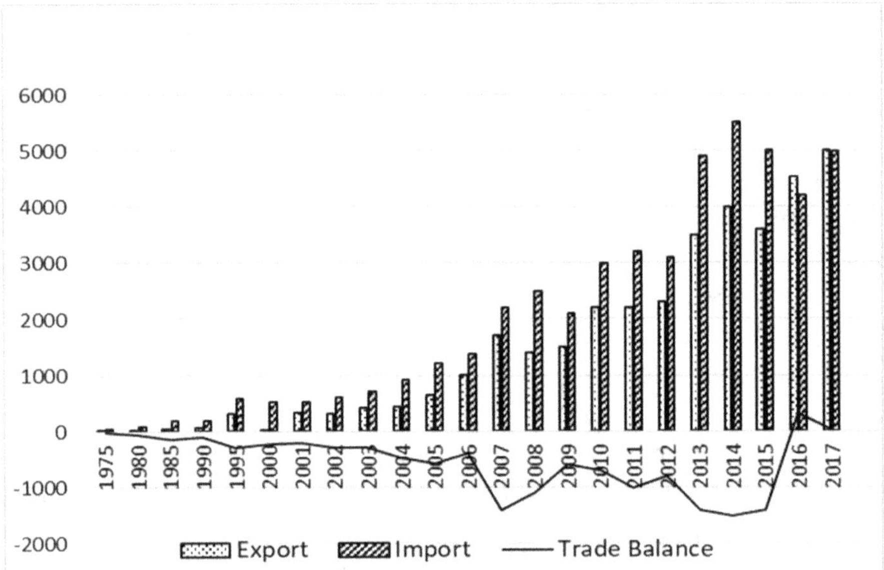

Source: Ministry of Commerce and Industry; WB, Lao Economic Monitor FY15-16. Estimation for 2017.

Laos imported almost much more than it exported in 2014, which translated into an important trade deficit; the deficit reached US$1.5 billion in net imports, as compared to the trade balance in 1995 when the country still had a negative trade balance of US$304 million in net imports. In 2017, the exports and imports increased by 11 percent or a trade surplus of US$261 compared to the surplus of US$360 million in 2016[58]. Import growth was driven by capital and consumption goods imports, some of which were related to the investment in hydropower projects. However, this trend could be reversed in the coming years due to the strong and steady growth of exports and the completion of infrastructure projects. During the 8th NSEDP, imports are expected to grow faster due to the high demand for consumption goods and the goods required for the large construction projects. Although the export of minerals can be volatile, the export of hydroelectric energy has the advantage of being stable.

Figure 11: Merchandise Exports, 2010-2015 (in million US$)

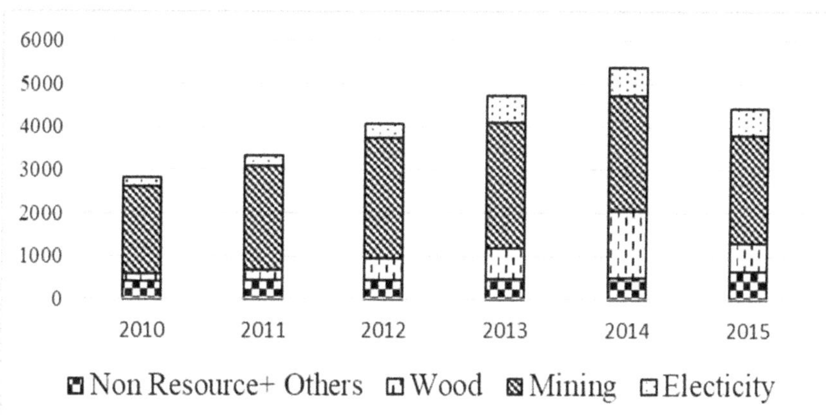

Source: Ministry of Commerce and Industry; WB, Lao Economic Monitor FY15-16.

Figure 12: Merchandise Imports, 2010-2015 (in million US$)

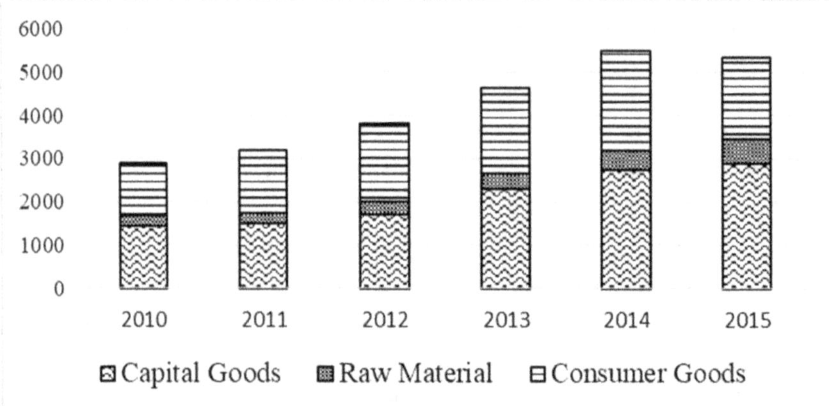

Source: Ministry of Commerce and Industry; WB, Lao Economic Monitor FY15-16

Laos began selling rice with an annual purchasing contract of 20,000 tons of organic rice a year to China, starting in 2016[59]. So far, about 3,700 tons of sticky rice and non-glutinous rice have partially been shipped. Additionally, exports of agricultural products among others are growing steadily in recent years. Laos remains relatively a net food exporting country. Figure 13 shows trade between Laos and its three top partners. The top exporting provinces are Champassak, Saravan and Attapeu, which sell electricity, coffee, sweetcorn, cassava, rubber, sugar, and cattle carcasses

Thailand continuing to be Laos' top trading partner. The two-way trade between Thailand and Laos reached US$4.8 billion in 2017, the highest among Asean member trade partners. Thailand and Laos have agreed to draw up a five-year master plan to double the value of bilateral trade and investment to US$10 billion (Bt344 billion) by 2021. The two countries will collaborate to develop both trade and investment by focusing on logistics, energy, tourism, border trade, industry and the capital market, and also develop small and medium-sized enterprises in both countries, according to the announcement by the Deputy Prime Minister Somkid Jatusripitak of Thailand and the Lao Deputy Prime Minister and Finance Minister Somdee Duangdee in a meeting in Vientiane[60]. This target should likely be reached. Up to 98 percent of total trade value was from border trade today. Moreover, Thailand recently increased its purchase of electricity from 7,000 to 9,000 megawatts from Laos.

The exchanges between the two countries have always been dynamic and enjoy a long tradition of cooperation.

According to the Laos Ministry of Planning and Investment, trade between Laos and China has been increasing significantly annually. However, sluggish global demand for Chinese exports in 2017 is squeezing Chinese importation demand, which therefore includes the demand for minerals from Laos. Most of this bilateral trade moves between Laos and Yunnan province. Trade between the two jumped from US$203 million in 2010 to US$1.37 billion in 2015, while the total volume between Laos-China was US$2.3 billion[61] in 2016. The trade between the two countries in 2017 is expected to US$2.8 billion (Figure 13). According to a Laos-China Cooperation Committee report, China is now Laos' second largest trading partner[62].

With regard to trade with Vietnam, over the past 50 years, and especially 35 years spent implementing the Vietnam-Laos Friendship and Cooperation Treaty, the traditional friendship, special solidarity, and comprehensive cooperation between the two countries have become ever more closely and widely developed in all areas, including politics, diplomacy, defense-security, education-training, economics, trade, investment, and science-technology. Thus, two-way trade between the two countries has continuously increased. The two countries reached bilateral trade of US$1 billion USD in 2013, US$1.4 billion in 2014, and US$1.6 billion in 2015. However, the value of bilateral trade in 2016 was recorded at only US$801 million, fell by half compared to the previous year, following the Lao government's orders for some mining exploration projects to be stopped and to ban the export of logs and timbers overseas[63]. In 2017, Vietnam ranks third in terms of trade with Laos. The total value of imports and exports is expected to US$1.17 billion, of which exports account for US$621 million and imports for US$554 million. The two countries have set a two-way trade target of US$4 billion by 2020.

Figure 13: Comparison Two-Way Trade Laos with China-Thailand-Vietnam, 2011-2017

(In billion US$)

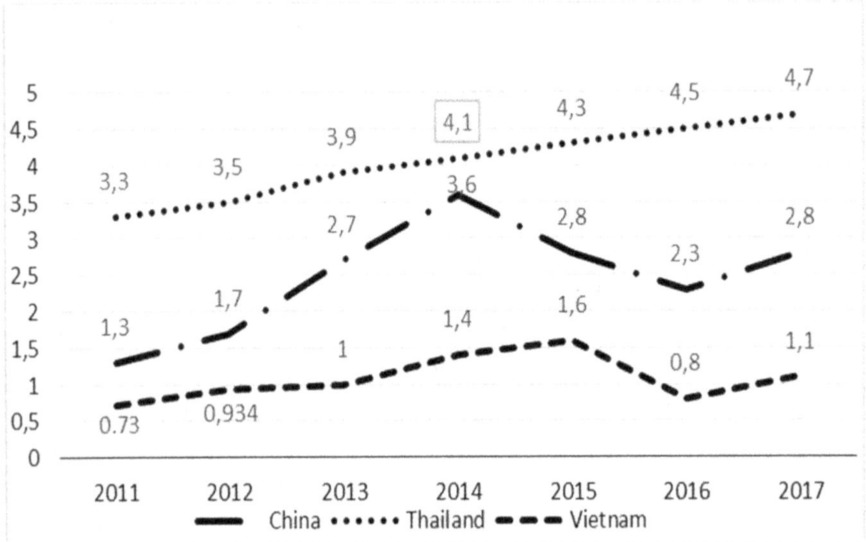

Source: The World Bank, Ministry of Planning and Investment.

The value of the two-way trade between Laos-Japan in 2016 attained US$231 million, while it reached US$88 million between Laos-Korea[64]. According to the Economic Complexity Index (ECI)[65], Laos is the 115th largest export economy in the world and the 132nd most complex economy.

Figure 14 shows the shares in percentage of Laos' total exports and imports with Asean member countries, extra-Asean countries (namely Australia, Canada, China, EU, India, Japan, South Korea, New Zealand, Pakistan, Russia, and the US), and the rest of the world during 2014 and 2015. However, exports to extra-Asean countries were as important as those of intra-Asean, while imports of Laos from extra-Asean countries were less significant. This demonstrates that Laos has taken benefits from regional integration.

Figure 14: Share of Laos Total Exports and Imports in Percentage

Share of Laos Total Exports

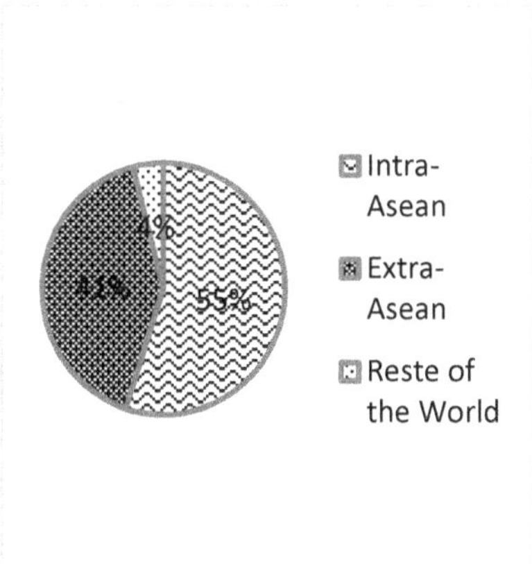

Share of Laos Total Imports

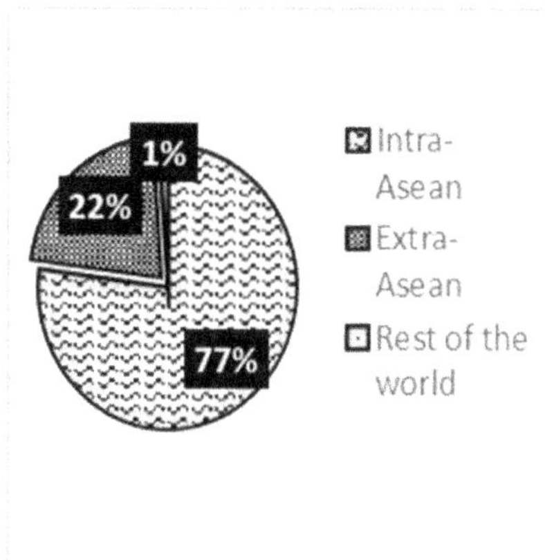

Source: WB, Lao Economic Monitor FY15-16.

Notably, there is still room for Laos to gain more share in exporting its products outside the Asean markets.

2.2.5 Foreign Exchanges Reserves Remain Low but Increasing Gradually

Regarding the level of its foreign reserves, the Lao government is concerned about its unbalance. Foreign exchange reserve coverage remains low as compared with the prudential benchmark, due to strong investment inflows and foreign borrowing. Nevertheless, the reserves cover remained a thin buffer at around 2.2 months of imports throughout the 2000s. Therefore, building up foreign reserves to increase buffers against shocks remains critical to macroeconomic stability for Laos and is the country's high priority. Yet, the Lao authorities are improving their external debts and managing their prudent financial balance policy, which are currently part of the Public Finance Management Modernization Program.

Until 1996 the foreign exchange reserves of Laos were insignificant. Figure 15 shows foreign exchange reserves including gold from the World Bank data from 1986 to 2016. Although the country has made significant progress in the last ten years, indeed foreign exchange reserves are insufficient, making the country vulnerable to external shocks. The present foreign exchange reserves (notably Thai baht and US dollar) are enough to pay for importing goods and services for 4.14 months (lower than the target of five months), according to the Bank of Lao PDR and IMF Report in early August 2017. In short, the financial status of the banking system is relatively stable. In addition, rising imports of capital goods for infrastructure projects will mean that the current account deficit remains large.

Figure 15: Foreign Exchange Reserves

(In billion US$)

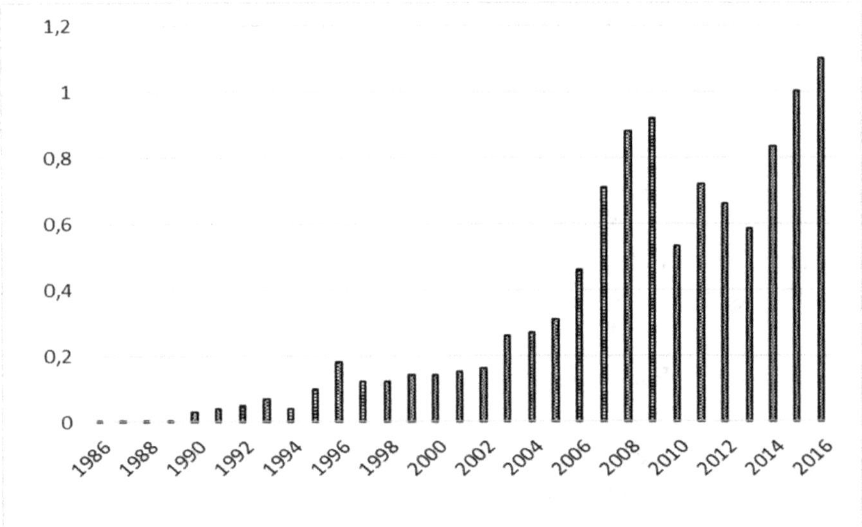

Source: The World Bank; the Global Economy.com; 8th NSEDP;

2.2.6 Continued Economic Growth and Inflation Contained

The Lao government has a policy to stabilize the currency exchange rate in order to create confidence in the business sector, keep product prices steady, and boost the economy. After annual inflation hit 110% in 1998-1999 during the Asian crisis, the government embarked upon a macroeconomic stabilization program. The inflation rate has seen many fluctuations, dropping from 30.3 percent in 1985 to 19.6 percent in 1990 and 11.2 percent in 1995. It increased again to 23.5 percent in 2000, mainly due to a rise in global commodities prices. However, during the period 2003-2017, inflation declined from 15.5 percent to 2 percent due to the pass-through of lower international fuel prices and a strengthening of the currency[66].

Lao monetary policy over the past decade indicates that the government was aware of the importance of keeping inflation under control. The main factors affecting inflation included prices of consumables, housing, electricity, water and fuel, restaurants and hotels, clothing and footwear, and goods and services[67].

The exchange rates fluctuated considerably between 1995 and 2000. The value of the Lao kip depreciated greatly by 83 percent during this period against the US dollar, starting from 923 kip to the US$ 1 in 1995 to 7,848 kip to the US$ 1 in the year 2000. The main reasons for the free fall of the Lao currency were the lenient monetary policy and the monetary financing of some budgetary expenditure. However, the Lao kip has begun to appreciate and stabilize gradually since 2005[68]. The central bank of the Lao PDR oversees a managed floating exchange rate aimed at maintaining nominal exchange rate stability against major currencies. The official exchange rate tracks the free-market rate, a policy that the government maintains.

The appreciation of the kip since 2012 reached more than 30 percent, which has undermined the competitiveness for Laos' tradable exports and cheapened consumer imports, and therefore contributes to the pressure on the external balance. However, since 2016, the kip has depreciated 1 and 5 percent against the Thai baht and the US dollar respectively, which has made import goods more expensive for Lao people.

2.2.7 Public Debt Has Risen Steadily but Moderately

Although the government ran fiscal deficits from 2008-2014, the country's external debt position has improved in recent years, but Laos continues to face a high risk of debt distress. Laos' nominal debt stock increased by US$1.16[69] billion in 1999 to US$6.5 billion in 2016. While the debt ratio reached 54 percent of GDP at the end of 2016, from 82 percent at the end of 1999, this was higher than the IMF's indicative threshold of 40 percent, and the Joint IMF-World Bank Debt Sustainability Analysis (DSA) concluded that the country's risk of debt distress was "moderate".

It should be noted that around 70% of debt in Laos was held by multilateral creditors, mainly the ADB and International Development Association (IDA), until 2010. Slightly more than 25 percent was held by bilateral creditors, mainly Russia (lesser amount today), China, and Japan. New emerging market creditors were increasing their presence in Laos with bilateral debt to total debt growing significantly. The remaining 5 percent was from external debt incurred by public entities (hydropower development plants) including to finance equity stakes, and funding provided by multilateral and bilateral credits to the government[70]. The biggest bilateral creditor was Russia, which accounted for almost 80 percent of the stock bilateral debt at the end of 2003. But the trend has changed from 2011 onwards with ADB and IDA portions reduced somewhat, while Thailand, Vietnam, South Korea, Malaysia, and particularly China creditors increased sharply. Out of public external debt, China accounts for about 44 percent in 2015 compared to 35 percent three years ago[71].

Admittedly, Laos' external public debt and publicly guaranteed debt stock remains at elevated levels; nonetheless, the debt profile (percent of debt in share GDP, exports of government revenue) has improved in recent years due to robust economic growth and currency appreciation, more favorable debt indicators in recent years, supported by a strong and more stable macroeconomic environment, and favorable external conditions (AEC, China inflow investment, and increased intra-Asean trade).

The data reached an all-time high of US$ 6.0 billion in December 2016 and a record low of US$ 769.6 million at end-1996 (Figure 16). For the time being, external debt covers government debt only.

Figure 16: Laos External Debt, 1996-2016

(In million US$)

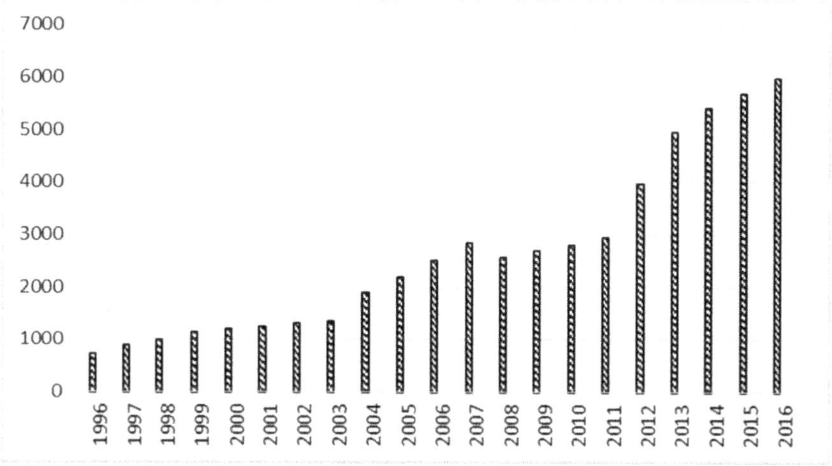

Source: WWW.CEICDATA.com/Bank of the Lao PDR

Figure 17: Outstanding External Debt (percent Total Debt)

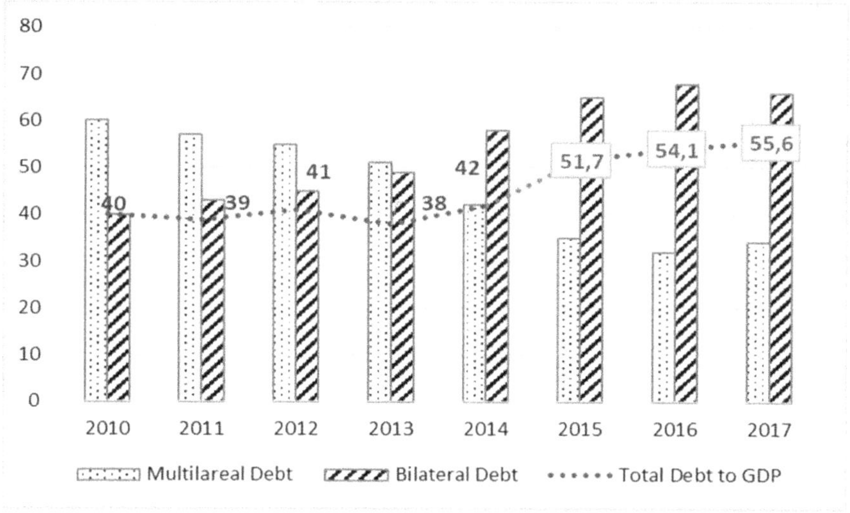

Source: Annual Economic Report 2014; The World Bank, Lao Economic Monitor, 2016; 2017 is the World Bank projection.

Figure 16 above shows Laos' outstanding external debt; notably since 2015, bilateral represented more than double of multilateral debt. This was the result of the substantial loans contracted with foreign countries for Lao infrastructure development. However, the total debt to GDP was on average below 60 percent, considered as acceptable by international institutions.

2.3 Key Sector Achievements

After the Lao government recognized the failure of agricultural collectivization, the period 1976–1979 was marked by the moderation of socialist dogma, with economic realism finally prevailing. A year after the beginning of reforms were enacted, by 1980 rice, timber, and electricity production had increased slightly. The organization of the industrial sector prior to economic reform was aligned on the state. Between 1979 and 1984, most state-owned enterprises incurred huge losses and industrial sector output decreased by 10 percent. At the same time, gross industrial production began to shift slightly to the private sector: private industrial output as a percentage of gross industrial output doubled to 8 percent between 1980 and 1983, whereas state output decreased slightly from 93 percent to 89 percent. In the early 1980s, a slow increase in the number of private enterprises began, reflecting both the government's newly relaxed policy on the private sector and the private sector's greater efficiency along with profitability compared to that of the state sector. The processing industry, mining, construction, handicraft, and tourism industry are the fastest and most noticeable growing sectors; however, agriculture's growth is slow (Figure 18).

Figure 18: Contribution GDP Growth by sector

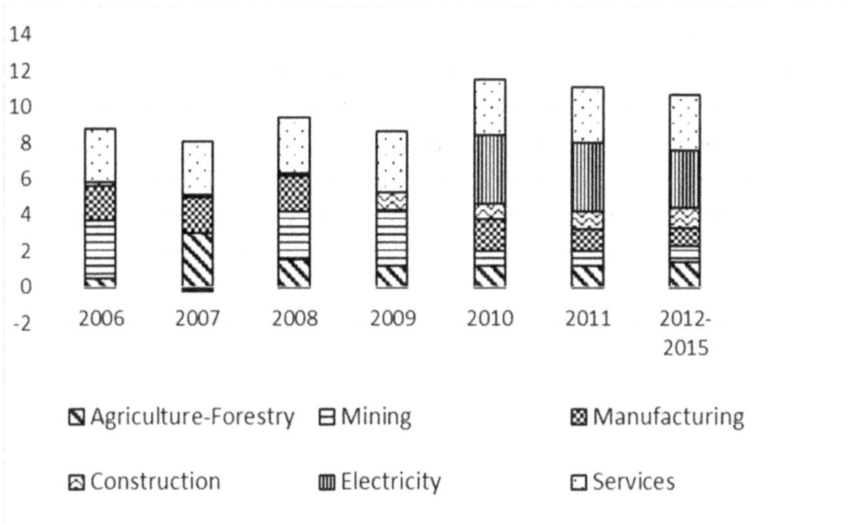

Source: Ministry of Planning and Investment, WB Country Report 2015.

2.3.1 Industry Sector Moving Up Rapidly

After the reform and privatization of SOEs were implemented in 1986, the industrial sector's contribution (including construction) to GDP varied, according to the World Bank, from about 10 percent in 1984 to about 17 percent in 1993. Throughout the 1980s, the World Bank estimated an average annual growth rate of 3.4 percent between 1980 and 1989, despite negative growth in the drought years of 1987 and 1988 during which exports of hydroelectricity were substantially lowered. By 1990 the growth rate had leveled off from a surge of nearly 32.0 percent in 1989 to about 12.7 percent in 1992. Main activities in the industrial sector included manufacturing, construction, mining, processing agricultural and forestry goods, and hydroelectricity production. During the five-year period 2001-2005 of the 5th NSEDP, the Lao economy maintained rapid and sustained expansion. The economic sectors underwent significant restructuring. This restructuring was concentrated on production capacities, and quality and efficiency, thus contributing to economic growth and meeting the initial requirements for international integration. Industrial production grew at a steady and rapid pace, with the sector-wide average growth reaching 11.3 percent per year. In the industrial sector, several significant activities were implemented during the five-year period, a number of industrial zones were established and there was a general increase in the number of new factories and companies created. During this period, industries related to the manufacturing of construction equipment, mining, and other processing industries as well as the handicraft sector were considerably developed and expanded. The 6th Five-Year Socio-Economic Development Plan (2006-2011) saw remarkable change in Lao's economic transformation; the industrial sector grew at about 12.6 percent per annum. The average share of mineral exploration of the value added in industry was 35.4 percent, the share of the processing industry was 34.3 percent, and electricity 14 percent[72]. Many factories were built in Laos, located in Vientiane Capital City, Vientiane province, Khammouan, Savannakhet, Champassak, Oudomxay, Bokeo, Luang Namtha, Borikhamxay, and Houaxay provinces. Several special and specific economic zones were set up by the government. They became the main driver for growth in the industrial and service sectors, boosting economic growth and generating job opportunities for local people. The prominent factories and plants built during the 6th NSEDP were brewery, soft drinks, food processing, cement, garment, bio-fertilizer, tobacco, furniture, textile and handicraft, steel, mining, cassava powder processing, coffee roasting plant, and bricks.

Throughout the 7th NSEDP, between 2011 and 2015, overall the processing industries made rapid and significant achievements, not only in the development of value added but also in the rapid growth of job creation. The industry sector grew during the period 2011–2015 at an average annual rate of 13.4 percent. The most outstanding sectors were food and beverage processing, construction materials (cement, tiles, steel bars, roof tiles, paint, and other materials), garments, and cigarettes and shoes, among others[73]. At present, the production of alcohol/beer meets 100 percent of the total demand while soft drink, cement, and steel bar production can supply only up to 89 percent, 65 percent, and 25 percent respectively. In 2017, Laos has 16 cement factories (4 under construction), the annual production capacity of existing plants is about 4.4 million tons in response to market demand[74]. Today, new processing industries that have emerged are silk thread and textiles; animal feed; meat processing; Savannakhet Sugar Factory; 26 rubber latex processing plants, 11 of which are medium and 15 are small scale; Dao Heuang coffee; Café Sinouk instant coffee; palm oil; pine resin; and potassium. At present, there are 15 processing factories with an investment value of more than 50 billion kip, including maize drying and jatropha extraction factories, Beer Lao Ltd, Lao Asia-Pacific Brewery Ltd, Lao Indochina Tropicana, cassava processing factory in Sayaboury province, factory potatoes TTL in Borikhamxay province, Dak Tak Rubber Factory and Lao-Vietnam Rubber Factory, Dao Heuang Coffee, Café Sinouk, sugar, and cement factories[75].

From 1986 to present, significant accomplishments in various economic sectors such as agriculture and forestry, energy and mining, infrastructure, telecommunication, and tourism have gradually improved and expanded. These numerous developments are recounted as follows.

2.3.2 Agriculture and Forestry Sector Continues to Play a Major Role

In the early 1980s, the agriculture sector was not developed, with an average growth rate of just 2.9 percent per year. After the liberalization of the agriculture and forestry sector, the government has concentrated on the development of agricultural production, to reorient the agriculture sector from semi-subsistence and subsistence to commercial production to ensure the enhanced supply of raw materials to the processing industries, meet the growing domestic requirements for agricultural products, and rapidly expand agricultural exports.

Although the contribution of the sector to GDP has declined steadily from the 1990s to present, the agriculture and forestry sector is essential to the development of the country. From the period 1996-2000 the sector contributed an estimated average 2 percent of GDP per year to 3.5 percent per year during 2011-2015. The agricultural sector remains predominant and generates, along with the logging industry, more than half of the national GDP.

Nonetheless, agriculture production revitalized since 2000 and tended to grow constantly, and the production of many crops increased significantly. The 5th NSEDP (2001-2005) succeeded in transforming the agriculture sector into a thriving sector based on innovative technologies and practices in high value-added production and processing, catering to domestic and world markets. Over the five years 2001-2005, the value of production in the agriculture sector increased on average by 3.4 percent per year. The introduction of better farming practices and improved technology by investors have brought benefits to the sector. In addition, the construction of irrigation systems for resisting droughts, flooding, and for dry season crop production have become more efficient and vital for farmers across the country.

Throughout the 6th and 7th NSEDP, agriculture and forestry sector grew at average rate of almost 3 to 3.5 percent per year and accounted for 25 percent of the total GDP in 2015. During the Five-Year Plan (2006-2010), agriculture and forestry was one of the sectors that generated a number of significant achievements despite the impacts of natural disasters. Overall, agriculture and forestry production has improved and is able to supply sufficient production for basic domestic needs. Rice yields increased from 2.6 tons per hectare in 1996 to 3.4 tons in 2005. Since 2006, locally grown rice was sufficient for self-consumption and also with some set aside for sale. Land yield rate increased from 3.6 tons per hectare in 2006 to 4 tons per hectare in 2016. Rice production reached 3.14 million tons in the planting season of 2009, of which wet seasonal rice is expected to account for 78 percent, irrigated rice 14.4 percent, and upland rice 7 percent. Production was 4.1 million tons in 2015, equivalent to 97 percent of the 7th Five-Year Plan (2011-2015) target of 4.2 million tons, while in 2016, the rice production reached 4.1 million tons. In 2017, the production is estimated to 4.2 million tons. The government is also trying to improve rice yields by increasing farmers' efficiency, especially in rice production, thereby allowing Laos to become today a small rice exporter. Some 2.1 million tons of rice will be set aside to ensure food security, 400,000 tons will be stockpiled for use in emergencies such as flooding, and 500,000 to 600,000 toes will be sold. It is hoped that farmers can also grow about 400,000 tons of rice for export. Moreover, the Government is planning to irrigate 160,000 hectares of crops on the domestic market. The government is aiming for farmers to plant rice on 90,400 hectares and to harvest 475,600 tons. Laos plans to produce about 5 million tons of rice by 2020 to ensure food security in the country. However, the Ministry of Agriculture and Forestry is concerned that a large number of farmers are growing other crops instead of rice, as these bring in more money and require less water. This could therefore have a negative impact on the rice yield target of the government planning[76].

In 2017, the agriculture and forestry sector contributed to an estimated 15.73 percent of GDP and absorbed an estimated 70 percent of the total workforce. Women farmers are responsible for over half of all agricultural activities. Laos achieved rice self-sufficiency around 2000, a major milestone in the history of the country. Today, 72 percent of the total cultivated area is dedicated to rice. Other important economic crops include coffee, sugarcane, maize, cassava, sweet potato, and industrial tree crops (such as rubber, eucalyptus and acacia). Overall, agriculture and forestry production has improved and is able to supply sufficient production for basic domestic needs.

In the last decade Laos has transformed itself into a provider of natural resources (timber, agricultural products, minerals, and energy) for its wealthier and more populated neighbors China, Vietnam, and Thailand. Laos has emerged as a significant supplier of agricultural commodities (cassava, feed, and corn) and industrial tree crops (rubber, teak, eucalyptus, and acacia). The past few years have seen a proliferation of large-scale land concessions, mostly to Chinese, Thai and Vietnamese investors, to develop export-oriented agriculture and forestry projects.

The move to commercial production was growing strongly in the high-potential areas. Prominent among these were the emphasis on the cultivation of rubber in Luang Namtha province; cashew nuts in Oudomxay and Phongsaly provinces; corn, vegetables, and fruit trees in Vientiane province and Vientiane Capital; seeded-trees for oil extraction and sugarcane in Savannakhet province; and rice in Vientiane province. The number of irrigation schemes has continued to increase from 19,170 in 2000 to 24,695 by the end of 2004. The big change today is the development of agricultural and rural economies that have begun to diversify. A large number of farms have been established and the production of traditional handicrafts has been resumed. The development of traditional handicrafts has generated additional jobs for the local people and contributed to the changes in the rural economic structure as well as the improvement of the population's living conditions.

Apart from rice, production of crops (corn, taro, fruit, and vegetables) has also risen significantly and is able to meet the fundamental consumption needs of the country. Furthermore, cassava production increased six times between 2005 and 2016: from 51,000 tons to 315,000 tons. It is being spread for processing to flour factories in the country and exported to Vietnam and China. Sugarcane production has risen by seven times as well, from 218,000 tons in 2005 to 1,460,000 tons in 2016. In addition, coffee, vegetables, and organic vegetables (cabbage, chayote, coriander, and other vegetables) are grown in Paksong and the Bolaven Plateau, mainly for export. Exports of agricultural products among others have been growing steadily since 2011.

Furthermore, commercial plantations including tobacco, rubber plantations, cotton, and soybeans have constantly expanded. The outstanding crops such as coffee, cassava, soybeans, sesame, peanuts, banana, maize, and sugarcane are grown as commercial crops. These crops have a potential market; in addition, market demand and prices have met farmers' conditions, and they have the support of the government and the private sectors, including enterprises investing in agriculture and agro-processing for export.

The total irrigated area increased from 409,276 hectares in 2010 to 419,267 in 2015, or 52 percent of the 7th Five-Year Plan target (800,000 ha), thus improving crops for the country. Nevertheless, agricultural productivity in Laos today is still less than half of its neighboring countries. In the rice sector, low farm productivity is due to factors such as inadequate access to high-quality seeds and other inputs, limited extension services, inefficient and inadequate irrigation and drainage infrastructure, and regional differences in social and climactic characteristics. Greater productivity would not only improve the livelihoods of the large proportion of farmers, but also free up labor to move into higher-productivity sectors. Organic production in particular is being targeted by the government as a promising niche for exports, though the government strongly encourages farmers and others involved to grow more crops organically to meet market demand. The Bolaven Plateau Coffee Producers' Cooperative has been exporting more than 1,000 tons of organic coffee per year to many foreign counties, which is currently valued at some US$5 million. Indeed, in 2013, Laos exported 30,000 tons of coffee valued at US$72 million. In 2014, total coffee exports dropped to 26,000 tons valued at US$60 million, while 2016 exports fell further to 23,000 tons valued at US$50 million. In 2017, more than 40,000 tons of coffee are harvested for export, an increase of 10,000 tons compared to 2016 and the value of coffee exported by Laos is expected to exceed US$112 million. The main reasons for the surge in sales are the favorable weather and the increasing demand from overseas markets, especially Vietnam, Japan and China, according to the Lao Coffee Association[77].

The forestry sector provides another source of growth, especially in rural areas. The sector is dominated by natural log but it also produces a variety of other woods such as cork, rattan, bamboo, and eucalyptus. Since 2006, eucalyptus tree plantations have started in Savannakhet with plans to build pulp mills to process the wood into paper. The investors are mainly from India and China, and the projects have provided jobs for local people.

In conclusion, Laos remains heavily dependent on agriculture and forestry sector, which has traditionally been dominated by smallholder and subsistence farming with related micro and small and medium enterprises. The growth of the sector has so far remained relatively modest and below its potential.

2.3.3 Hydroelectricity and Mining Pulling Economic Growth

It is worth recalling that in 1975 there was only one hydropower plant in the whole country, the Selabam plant with installed capacity of 5 megawatts, located in Champassak province; at that time only 19,000 families or 3 percent of the total population had access to electricity, whereas today 91 percent of the population can access the power grid. In 2016, the energy and mining sectors grew strongly, with an average growth rate of 14 percent and around 10 percent respectively. Several hydropower plants including the lignite Hongsa power plant have been built during the 7th NSEDP. The energy sector is the major source that pushes up economic growth. According to Dr. Khammany Inthirath, Minister of Energy and Mines, as of 2015 Laos has built 38 power plants at a cost of more than 81.7 trillion kip (US$10 billion) with a total installed capacity of 6,265 megawatts.

At the end of 2017, there are 50 power plants around the country with an installed capacity of about 6,860 megawatts generating about 33,822 gigawatts per hour (GWh) annually (primarily for export); about 36 percent are managed by the government under EDL and EDL-GEN, and the remaining are managed by independent power producers. Currently there are 54 power plants under construction that the government and private energy developers expect to complete by 2020, including 54 more electricity transmission lines and another 16 substations to be built, according to EDL and EDL-GEN planning.

In 2019, commercial operation is expected of the Sayabouri dam on the Lower Mekong River, approximately 30 kilometers east of Sayabouri town in northern Laos, started in 2015. This project is surrounded in controversy due to complaints from downstream riparian and environmentalists. The Sayabouri dam is the first of the 11 dams planned on the lower Mekong; the second dam, the Don Sahong has been under construction since December

2016 on the Mekong River in southern Laos. Laos is aiming for a total installed capacity of about 12,000 megawatts by 2025. The abundant resources of the Mekong River and its tributaries give Laos the potential to produce more than 25,000 megawatts of electricity[78].

Under current arrangements, the generated energy is for both local supply (15 percent) and the remaining for export to Thailand, Vietnam, and Cambodia. The sector also has the potential for development of an electricity grid linking Laos and Singapore, and trading in electricity is possible as Thailand and Malaysia would also benefit from the project. Laos will push for the acceleration of energy integration under the Asean Power Grid (APG) to address the imbalance in the distribution of power-generating resources in the region. APG aims to connect countries with surplus power generation capacity to those who face a deficit. The intention is to link up power lines in the ten Asean nations by 2020. Furthermore, Laos has signed an agreement to provide 100 megawatts of electricity to Malaysia via Thailand's power grid; Singapore and Myanmar also have recently signed agreement to import electricity from Laos. As a matter of fact, Laos can help Asean countries to reduce their use of fossil fuels, which are the main source of greenhouse gas emissions, and importantly can also assist Asean to stabilize its power supply.

From 2013 to 2016, Laos received around US$2.75 billion from electricity sales to Thailand and more than US$23 million to Cambodia, according to the Ministry of Industry and Commerce. The country exported electricity to Vietnam in 2016 for a total value of around US$19.8 million, a figure set to increase from 2017 onwards[79]. The electricity export sales in 2016 was US$1,250 million, the government expects for 2017 to earn US$1,357 million[80].

Major investors today in the energy sector are from Thailand, China, South Korea, France, Vietnam, and Japan. Lao Holding State Enterprise (LHSE) is a state-owned enterprise under the responsibility of the Ministry of Energy and Mining. It represents the Lao government and holds 20 percent to 25 percent of the shares in several hydropower plants. At the present time, the government has authorized LHSE to participate in more than fifteen projects with foreign companies. LHSE recorded revenues of US$35.3 million at the end of 2016, reflecting a growth of 128 percent from 2015[81].

With regard to the mining sector, compared to the 5th NSEDP (2000-2005), the mining industry increased by 33.9 percent during the 6th NSEDP (2006-2010); the sector has implemented several significant activities, such as the exploitation of gold and copper from Lane Xang Mineral (LXML) at Sepon, and zinc in Vientiane province. The sector accounts for 9.5% of GDP. Exploration and production of gold bars during the four years between 2006 and 2009 reached 33.2 tons (in 2006 the production was 12.7 tons, about 9.2 tons in 2007, in 2008 it reached 5.8 tons, and in 2009 the production was 5.5 tons), while in 2015 it reached less than 5 tons (the figures show the decline in production of gold because there have been changes each year in the amount of gold extracted from the gold ore). Within these four years, the production of copper plates was 321,487 tons and copper dust 585,607 tons; the total sale of copper reached US$3,274 million. Since 2003, over 1.2 million ounces of gold and more than 500,000 tons of copper have been produced. In 2016, Sepon produced 78,492 tons of copper cathode.

Additionally, Phu Bia Mining's contribution of copper extraction to the national economy since 2000 has been especially important. In 2008, copper extraction was recorded at 1.1 million tons, a large increase from production figures of 62,621 tons recorded from 2007[82]. Export earnings of US$620 million for 2008 marked a significant increase compared to US$24 million in 2004. However, earnings from copper exports are unstable due to fluctuation of copper prices in the market, and the production has also dropped since 2015. The copper in concentrate production at Phu Kham in 2017 is expected to peak at 72,000 tons and gold in concentrate is expected to 70,000 ounces.

During the 7th NSEDP (2011–2015), the mining sector in general recorded an average annual growth rate of 10 percent, which exceeds the Five-Year Plan target by 184 percent. The production of copper plate was 427,329 tons, gold mixed with silver was 85.94 tons, lignite was 1.60 million tons, anthracite was 876,704 tons, copper dust reached 1.53 million tons, gypsum was 3.93 million tons, and the production of other minerals has also been on an increasing trend. Gross mineral export value is higher than US$8 billion, covering 60 percent of the total exports of the country. LXML has contributed significantly to economic development with over US$1.3 billion in direct revenue in taxes, royalties and dividends paid to the Lao Government since operations commenced in 2003 at Sepon and hundreds of millions of dollars in indirect benefits through local contractors, suppliers, employment, and training. LXML owns 90% and the Lao Government 10% of Sepon mining. With regard to Phu Bia Mining, the company paid US$80 million of dividends to the government in 2017. The Lao government owns a 10 percent share in

Phu Bia Mining and has received over US$600 million in direct contributions since 2008 to the end of 2017[83]. Although the mining trade dips compared to the previous years but it remains the nation's top export income earner.

In 2017, about 74 domestic and foreign companies have been given exploration contracts, 25 of which are at the stage of preparation for exploration and construction of a processing factory, and 49 of which have been extracting, processing, and exporting. Most of these are small and medium-sized businesses. For large-scale projects, such as LXML and Phu Bia Mining Ltd, projects have a production value of over US$ 500 million per year. Important mines for new exploration during that period that have come up include kali salt in Thong Mang, in Vientiane province, and potassium salt in Khammouan province[84]. Thus, the mining sector remains a second source of revenue for the government.

2.3.4 Catching Up on the Infrastructure Development

The road system is not extensive. A rudimentary network begun under French colonial rule and continued from the 1950s has provided a few new roads and communication networks. There were only 12,462 km of roads in Laos in 1976[85]. Generally, Laos has a poor physical infrastructure. The Public Works and Transport sector made great achievements over the past forty years, which has seen huge differences in infrastructure development in comparison to the time before 1975. In spite of limited funding, the government is committed to developing and improving most of the regional transport infrastructure that passes through the country.

The development of the road network and land transport services saw greater achievements than that of other sectors. Being a landlocked country, Laos depends heavily on road transport for trade links both externally and internally.

As a result of ongoing improvements in the road system started during the early 1990s, various new road and infrastructure and upgrading construction projects have been carried out since 1991. The government dedicated large sums of its founding to develop infrastructure including roads and bridges.

Consequently, the total length of the national roads network (paved roads) increased from 5,427 km in 2010 to 5,702 km in 2013 and to about 11,200 km in 2016. The country has nearly 44,500 kilometers of roads (all types) across the country in 2016. The increase was almost four-fold in forty years, including along the North-South and East-West Economic Corridors, providing access to neighboring countries and serving the various provinces, districts, and villages.

The national roads have been upgraded to be Asean Roads that link domestic roads with neighboring countries along the regional economic corridors, such as the improved 2,200 km of the road along the North-South Economic Corridor (the 7th Five-Year Plan target was 920 km) and the 1,280 km along the East-West Economic Corridor. There are now several routes connecting Asean to China, such as Road No. 3 (R3) linking Thailand-Laos-China (called the North-South Corridor) and the central East-West Corridor, Road No. 9, connecting Thailand-Laos-Vietnam.

In 2016, according to the Ministry of Public Works and Transport, 26 percent of the total length of roads are paved with Asian Development Bank lending assistance. At present, eighty-nine districts throughout the country have paved roads.

Meanwhile Laos had its first railway built in 2007, a 3.5-km rail link across the Mekong River between Thanaleng in Laos and Nongkhai in Thailand and operated since 2009. Thanaleng station is the only station of the Bangkok–Thanaleng rail route on the Lao side of the border; the rail link is mainly used for freight traffic. Furthermore, the extension of the Lao-Thai railway began construction in 2016 and will be completed in early 2019; it will stretch 9 km from Thanaleng to a new main station in Khamsavat village in Vientiane's Xaysettha district, 4 km away from That Luang Temple.

Currently, the landmark railway project linking Vientiane with the Laos-China border over a distance of 427 km is under construction and is expected to be completed by 2021.The almost-US$6 billion project should drive economic growth and job creation in Laos. Laos and China set up a joint venture company to oversee the project, with Laos holding 30 percent of the project share and China being responsible for the remainder. For the Lao government, the railway is important in transforming Laos from a landlocked country to a land linked within the region and will attract more foreign investment and tourists. The railway is a part of the "One Belt, One Road Initiative" strategy of China. Laos has an important role in this scheme. Once completed, the railway in Laos will link with the track in Thailand to form part of the regional rail link known as the Kunming-Singapore railway, covering a total distance of about 3,000 km[86]. In addition, the feasibility study for another key railway project linking Laos to Lao Bao (Vietnam) over a length of 217 km has also been completed.

Remarkable achievements over the past twenty years are the four Laos-Thailand friendship bridges crossing the Mekong River in service today: Vientiane Prefecture/Nongkhai, Savannakhet/Mukdahan, Thakhek/Nakhon Phanom, and Ban Houayxay/Chiang Khong. There is also one bridge that spans the Mekong River at Pakse that is entirely in Lao territory from Japanese funding. Most recently, a Myanmar-Laos friendship bridge Shan/Luang Namtha over the Mekong River has been built and open since May 2015.

Concerning air transport services, airports have been built and expanded, including the expansion of Wattay International Airport to accommodate Boeing 747 planes and the expansion of Luang Prabang, Savannakhet, and Pakse International Airports. Meanwhile, Nongkhang airport in Huaphanh province, Xieng khuang, and Attapeu now have their own airports.

Infrastructure improvement therefore is playing an important role in raising living standards nationwide, with many areas benefitting from such changes. Slowly but surely remote regions are gaining in prosperity and moving closer to their development goals and poverty eradication.

2.3.5 Telecommunications Sector Boosted Business and Investment

Regarding the telecommunications sector, between 1986 and 1990 the government developed and strengthened the nation's telecommunications system. Telex, telegraph, fax, and telephone services are available throughout the country. During the period from 1996 to 2000, the telecommunications systems were upgraded and modernized. Then from 2000 to present, the government promoted investment in all segments of business (post, telephones, and Internet), including investment by the private sector in telecommunications systems and infrastructure equipment.

Lao telecommunications infrastructure has been developing quickly and using high technology since early 2010. Internet access and Wi-Fi are readily available in large population centers. The services of telecommunications have significantly developed and expanded, especially in the 2000s. Mobile phones are omnipresent today and 4G Internet has been available since 2012 in Vientiane, then gradually expanded to provincial capitals. Services have been expanded with an optic fiber system of 20,391 km and now comprise a total of 60,813 km covering all 18 provinces and 148 districts and extending services to 90 percent of all villages nationwide. Currently, there are six Internet service providers, both private and state owned, and the number of users is increasing rapidly. The Internet network has connected with networks in foreign countries. Among other networks, Laos has leased and used the Internet network NTT of Japan in order to connect with the undersea cable and link with the international network.

In addition, Laos' first telecommunications satellite (Lao Sat-1) was launched by a LM-3B launch vehicle from the Xi Chang Launch Centre in Sichuan province, China. The satellite was designed, developed, and delivered into orbit by China. The total project amounted to US$259 million and is expected to have a life of about 15 years. The satellite is designed to provide communication links for government work, television transmission, and a range of telecommunication applications in Laos. The Lao government holds a 45 percent stake in the Lao Sat-1 Joint Venture Company, while the Chinese investors hold the remainder stake[87].

Laos is also proud to have its first energy-efficient data center built in Laos, which went online in December 2016 in a project aided by a Japanese group, and which holds promise for modernizing the country's underdeveloped information infrastructure[88]. It is the first center of this model type to be set up outside of Japan. The government said the country had the potential to become a data center hub for Southeast Asia due to its wealth of resources for generating electricity. Similarly Laos needs to improve access to high-speed broadband services for social and economic objectives; indeed, ICT is now a utility, essential to almost everything we do. Digitization is changing business, public services, and the way people live.

In general, post and telecommunications have considerably developed in terms of both quantity and quality using advanced imported high technology. Nevertheless, further investments are required in terms of ICT and digitalization infrastructure to cope with the fast growing demand of the users and business community.

2.3.6 The Booming Tourism Sector Provided Large Revenue to State's Coffer

Laos has been a member of the UN World Tourism Organization (UNWTO) since 1971, which has more than 150 member countries. Since 1990, the number of visitors to Laos has been increasing; the country first opened to tourism in 1990, when it hosted 14,400 visitors. This number reached 346,460 in 1995, 1.1 million in 2005, 2.5 million in 2010, about 4 million in 2014, and 4.6 million recorded in 2015; however, the number of tourist arrivals fell to 4.2 million in 2016. The numbers have multiplied eleven-fold in nineteen years. Laos has had considerable success in developing its tourism industry; the sector increased between 1994 and 2016 at an average of 8 percent per year. The tourism sector has also adopted strategic plans to boost economic growth through its national tourism strategy plan since 1998. Revenue from the tourism industry has increased dramatically and tourism has quickly become a major export industry of Laos. The sector, a major challenge for Laos, as it is one of the country's major sources of foreign exchange, generated annual revenues of approximately US$500 million since 2010 and in 2016 the revenues hit US$720. It constituted about 9 percent of GDP, according to the Ministry of Information, Culture, and Tourism. However, the number of tourist arrivals in 2016 dropped to 4.2 million against 4.6 million the previous year. Again the number of tourists failed to meet the target of 4.7 million set for 2017, reaching only 4.1 million, generating about US$750 million for the government coffer[89]. The government projected that 5.3 million foreign visitors would come to Laos for Visit Laos Year in 2018, about 5.7 million in 2019, about 6 million in 2020, and 8.1 million in 2025.

International flights have increased. To meet the boom in the tourism sector, Laos' tourism infrastructure has been developed in all areas: hotels, guesthouses, restaurants, and road connections to all provinces. Foreign investors already have their eyes on cities like Sam Neua, Phongsaly, Savannakhet, Thakhek, and Pakse, and other attractions like Don Khong, in view of developing and improving the insufficient tourist infrastructure (i.e., road and river transportation, restaurants, and hospitals) in anticipation of the Chinese and Asean tourists who are expected to arrive *en masse*.

The government's goal is to make Laos a destination of worldwide recognition for sustainable tourism and not mass tourism. Indeed, the Land of a "Million Elephants" has encouraged ecotourism to display its natural wealth and ensure sustainability. Lao authorities expect that tourism will bring in more than US$850 million in 2020. These figures will probably be reached in 2018, two years ahead of schedule. However, revenue is forecast to reach US$1.3 billion in 2025 by experts and tourism professionals. The tourism industry is not only seeing rapid growth but is developing partnerships with other countries and international organizations.

2.4 Special and Specific Economic Zones (SEZs) Attract Foreign and Local Enterprises

The government invests in the establishment of special and specific economic zones to boost growth and development. The SEZs have the objective to attract domestic and foreign investments; create a strong foundation for industrialization; contribute to GDP growth, technology transfer, and job creation; and increase government revenue. "Ultimately this is to attain our goal of graduating from Least Developed Country (LDC) status by 2020," says Bouatha Khatthiya, Standing Vice Chair of the National Committee for Special Economic Zones (NCSEZ).

The special economic zones are economic development areas set up to attract large-scale investors. The government is creating new decrees to ensure the sustainable development of SEZs in ways that yield strong benefits. These decrees are aimed at simplifying procedures for investors, making them faster, more transparent and fair, and ensuring that investors have confidence in the country[90]. In the late December of 2017, the government has amended the decree on SEZ to make it more comprehensive and create more confidence among domestic and foreign businesses about investment in these zones. Currently Laos has 12 SEZs covering more than 19,600 hectares. The first established SEZs in Laos were in 2002, starting with the Savan-Seno Special Economic Zone (Savan-Seno SEZ), which was the testing ground for this form of economic development. Since then the number of SEZs in Laos has grown steadily, and the prospects are promising.

Over the last few years, Laos was able to attract a number of multinational companies including Nikon, Aeroworks, Asahi Tech Corp, KP Bureau, Essilor, Toyota, Mitsubishi, Polycom, etc., which resulted in rapid growth in the assembly and equipment parts sectors such as electronic, mechanic, electricity components and aeronautic. The total registered capital of the companies are US$8 billion, of which US$1.6 million has been spent, US$24 million is invested by the government, US$1.27 billion by developers, and US$349 million by retail investors.

Figure 19: Share by ownership

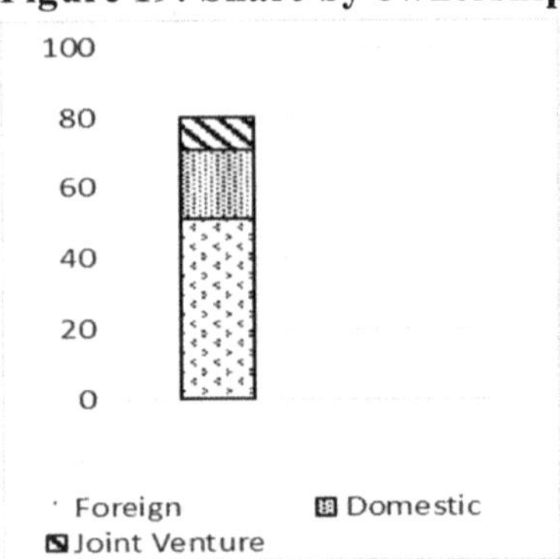

Figure 20: Share by sectors

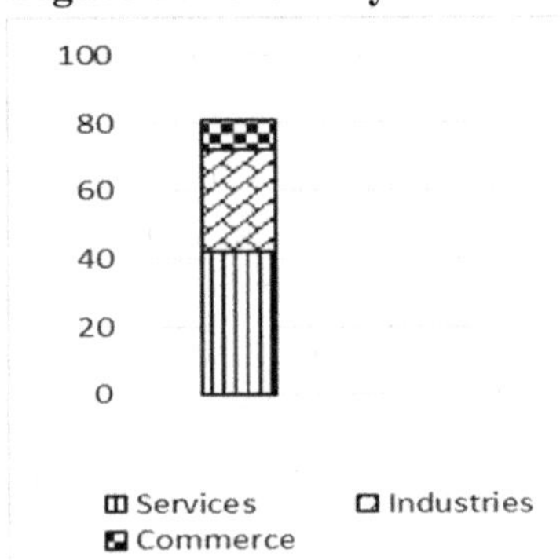

Source: Secretariat of the National Committee for Special Economic Zones.

The Figures 19 and 20 show the share of companies in SEZs by ownership and by sectors in 2015.

The total number of domestic and foreign companies is as of December 2017, 357 companies and businesses. Of these, 60 companies are privately Lao owned, 271 companies are foreign owned, and 26 are joint ventures between Lao and foreign companies. The service sector accounts for 40 percent of SEZ operations, 32 percent are industrial, and 28 percent are commercial. Jobs have been created for about 18,000 people (Lao and foreigners), of whom 8,300 are Lao nationals and 9,700 are foreign, according to the NCSEZ announcement. SEZs have yielded US$16 million for the national budget, and it is expected this figure will greatly increase in the future as many factories have been built and some are now starting production. The value of goods exported from these zones amounted to over US$400 million by companies from both Laos and overseas under the brand 'Made in Laos' produced by Lao worker[91], and the value of products imported to the zones was worth over US$1.15 billion[92].The government is given its full attention to the growth of SEZs as a means of generating more employment opportunities for local people. Enterprises operating in SEZs have been urged to advance their projects and allocate as many jobs as possible to Lao nationals so they can benefit from the upswing in industrial growth[93].

2.5 Private Enterprises and Emergence of Small and Medium-Sized Enterprises (SMEs) Contribute to Economy Growth

A new social class has emerged in Laos: merchants and small entrepreneurs. Relying on the success of decollectivization campaigns and the dismantling of cooperatives, reforms that began in the cities were extended from 1986 with the introduction of free trade and the gradual return to private enterprise.

In July 1988, the government announced new investment regulations that widely opened the economy to foreign investment. Private enterprises are the core of the "new system of economic management," and the concepts of profit, profitability, and productivity have been rehabilitated. Gradually, individual and often young entrepreneurs emerged from the nationalized system and went into business with the blessing of the state. War veterans and their families, and a few individuals close to the leadership, became pioneering merchants and began to export goods and capital equipment from Thailand to Vietnam via Laos, which was under embargo in the 1980s. Then other traders came in: small food distributors; suppliers of essential commodities, building materials, bicycles, and scooters; and import-export businesspeople. Afterward, foreign companies in partnership with the state or with Lao companies made their debut in the economic landscape through joint ventures. Until then, there had been only a few state-owned businesses. Private restaurants and entertainment premises began to open in the early 1990s, followed by a proliferation of boutiques, grocery stores selling a greater variety of vegetables and fruits whose quality improved from season to season, pastry shops, tailors, cafés, hairdressers, and so on. These enterprising people seized on all kinds of deals and developed their businesses, changing the urban landscape[94]. The Lao Constitution of 1991 protects state, collective, and private forms of ownership.

During the 1990s, an active legislative program laid the foundations for developing market-based rules and institutions to support private sector development. Therefore, the role of the private sector in Laos is growing as the country opens up and is strongly encouraged by the government.

The government's economic reform program has resulted in a transformation of Lao society within the last decade. Thus, the new generation of entrepreneurs and merchants, men and women, rushed into the opening of the market and have contributed to the emergence of an urban middle class.

The big transformation came in the mid-1990s with the sale of state assets and the privatization of public enterprises. From 1996, the state transferred its assets to individuals or private companies: buildings, factories, companies, restaurants, and hotels. These transfers were either in the form of private management, partnership with a private company (i.e., the state often being a minority shareholder), or direct sale to individuals or private companies. Furthermore, the Party allowed and encouraged state officials to leave their positions to engage in business. And in 1997, many civil servants, diplomats, teachers, and senior officials as well as some deputy ministers and army officers resigned and created their own trading businesses, import-export companies, and consulting firms. As a result, today agricultural production and most manufacturing production are in private hands and SOEs only cover one percent of employment. Nearly 98 percent of manufacturing units are small (less than 10 employees). Of the medium and large units, 35 percent are privately owned by Lao citizens and 55 percent are joint ventures with foreigners. The remainder is owned by the government, according to a recent statement by the Ministry of Commerce and Industry. Indeed, though in the 1990s Laos privatized many state firms, the government still controls roughly 130 companies with more than US$5 billion in assets. Among these are the biggest and most powerful corporations in Laos such as EDL, BCEL, Lao Holding State Enterprise (LHSE), Lao State Fuel Company (LSFC), Lao Airlines, Agro-Industrial Development Company (DAFI), Bolhisat Pattana Khet Phoudoi (BPKP), Lao Import-Export Trading Company Pharmaceutical Factory n° 3, and Bridge Road Construction n° 13 Company.

The results of the economic transformation were immediate. In early 2000, Laos had already recorded a growth rate of 6.8 percent. Driven by this collective enthusiasm, urban residents, mainly the generation born in the late 1960s, went into "business or commerce". The most visible in this transformation was the emergence from the mid-1990s of genuine Lao construction companies. True entrepreneurs of the "after-1975 generation" have taken the financial risk to support the national development program; they build schools, hospitals, clinics, buildings, hotels, shopping malls, roads, bridges, factories, and sanitation works in cities like drainage and water treatment facilities. Some entrepreneurs are in the processing industries and services business, including trading. This new generation of private entrepreneurs grew rapidly in number and in professional expertise. At the national level, about fifteen large companies or so emerged during the period 2006-2017 that have earned good reputations and financial standing; these companies are now able to run complex projects with foreign partners. Among the companies most often cited by the media are the Lao Krittaphong Group, Khamphay Sana Group, Dao-Heuang Group, Sèngsavanh Kosang, Douangchareun Kosang Limited, Vansana Construction, Lao Chitcharuen Company, Phousi Construction Group[95], Intra Corporation, TK Road and Bridge Construction Company, Phonesack Group, Tang Chaleun Group, Lao Freight Forwarder Co, Souvany Group, Inter Transport Company (ITC), and Phongsavanh Group, LG Consulting & Construction.

A few large Lao companies have extended their business successfully abroad and have been pleased to promote their capacity, among them a major local fuel supplier, Petroleum Trading Lao Public Company. This company is not only focused on the expansion of its market share locally; so far it has representative offices in Thailand, Myanmar, China, Cambodia, Singapore and Malaysia. It also hopes to have offices in all Asean countries to ensure regular fuel supply and connections and soon will open petrol stations in these countries. There is also Phongsavanh Group, whose banking activity now has offices in Vietnam and Thailand and expects to have service units or branches there in the very near future. Currently, Phongsavanh Bank has business cooperation and investments with service sectors in Thailand. To a lesser extent, Dao Heuang Coffee and Café Sinouk have also expanded their export business abroad, particularly for Café Sinouk, well known for *connoisseurs*. This company has tied up with distributors in Europe, the USA, Japan, and in the regional market.

At present, some Lao businesspeople of SMEs are trying to expand their business to other countries after they have done well or have been successful within the country, especially those in the trade and service sectors. Some ambitious and visionary young Lao business companies stepped out of their comfort zone of doing business in Laos to search for opportunities in the unfamiliar Myanmar, Thailand, and neighboring countries. Among them is SK Herbal, a company that produces cosmetic products and exports to Myanmar. Another is Sep Eeli noodle restaurant; after the launch of the franchise in Myanmar, this company is watching out for Sep Eeli noodle soups opening in Cambodia, Malaysia, and Vietnam in the near future[96]. Most of SMEs in Laos are managed by businesswomen; as in many Asean countries, Lao women have often played an important role in society and the economy.

The number of new businesses in Laos is on the rise, with registered business units going up by 5 percent each year since 2011. According to the National Committee for Business Development, with regard to private enterprise business units registered in Laos, 98 percent of them belong to SMEs and household (family) businesses. Most of household businesses are not registered. The government has set a plan to grow the SME sector in Laos by an average of 15 percent per annum in the years ahead and to boost private

Overall, local investments are expected to expand quickly as the number of new SMEs and household activities have increased in recent years. According to the Lao National Chamber of Commerce and Industry (LNCCI) survey, there are about 136,500 business units in Laos; this number does not include micro entrepreneurs operating in the informal economy. According to the Ministry of Finance, the number of Lao businesses (registered and non-registered) for the whole country can reach over 230,000. Interestingly to mention, micro SMEs registered firms in Laos indicate unfair competition from the informal sector and non-registered enterprises; they also say that high tax rates and difficult access to financing are their three major obstacles for business growth. In the same way, registered SMEs and large firms in Laos mention as well the inadequately trained workforce as the main constraint, followed by difficulty of access to financing.

enterprises by providing training for business entrepreneurs and organizing trade fairs and promotion.

2.6 Progress Noticeable on Social Development

Significant gains have been made in social development and the Millennium Development Goals (MDGs). Laos has made good progress so far on a number of outcomes, including reducing hunger, and improving education and health care.

After coming to full power in 1975 and more than thirty years of struggle, the LPRP has promised to improve the living conditions and the social well-being of the people. Its social agenda was constructed following largely around five points: 1) eradication of illiteracy and advancement of education and national culture; 2) expansion of health care for all; 3) promotion of gender equality; 4) protection of interests of all national minorities; 5) respect of all religions. The government is therefore obligated to put its revolution agenda, including its promises on social development, into practice on a national basis.

As a result, in Laos, the significant gains made in economic growth and social sectors over the recent years have paved the way for continual improvement in human development in the country. Between 1985 and 2012, substantial progress has been made in the main Human Development Index indicators: life expectancy increased by 19 years, mean years of schooling increased by 2.5 years, and Gross National Income (GNI) per capita increased by 310 percent. Consequently, Laos has seen steady improvement in its Human Development Index (HDI) value over time, making Laos one of the HDI growth leaders in the medium human development category, where it currently sits. Laos was ranked 138 out of 188 countries in the 2016 Human Development Index Report of March 2017.

The Five Year National Socioeconomic Development Plan 2011-2015 (7th NSEDP) focused on the achievement of the objectives of the MDGs as outlined by the United Nations, leading to sustainable development: maintaining an annual growth rate of 8 percent, raising annual per capita income to US$1,700 in 2015, prioritizing social development, lowering the poverty line, and providing universal elementary education to all Lao children.

Laos, despite still being a least developed country (LDC), has made significant progress in poverty alleviation over the past two decades with poverty rates declining from 46% in 1992 to 5.8% in 2017. Supported by the World and Asian Development Banks, the government has thus committed itself to a long-term poverty reduction program aimed at lifting the country out of its least-developed country status by 2020. Yet the country has made steady progress in the education sector, and has nearly achieved the national target of 98% net enrollment ratio for both girls and boys.

Regarding gender equality, the country has improved steadily on its targets. It was on track to realize parity between boys and girls in 2015. In higher education, however, equality is still not as prevalent, falling to 77 girls per 100 boys by the time they reach tertiary education. Women and men account for equal proportions of the total workforce, but there is a wage gap between male and female workers. Indeed, there is a notable result towards universal primary education, and the access to health services has increased steadily[97].

With regard to public health outcomes, health infrastructure that has been operational in Laos since 1976 encompasses 5 referral hospitals, 3 care centers, 16 provincial hospitals, 130 district hospitals, and 894 clinics and dispensaries. The health network now covers most populated areas. Access to drinking water, health services, and health infrastructure have generally been improved, with 83 percent of the population having access to drinking water, 61 percent having home toilets, and 57 percent of schools in rural areas being equipped with toilets.

According to the latest World Health Organization (WHO) data published in 2017, life expectancy in Laos is improving, currently averaging 64.1 years for males and 67.2 for females. Total life expectancy is 66.6, which gives Laos a World Life Expectancy ranking of 136, while life expectancy was 49.3 in 1980.

Laos has made clear progress towards implementing the MDGs, particularly in a global partnership for development; however, the challenge now is to ensure that all Lao people benefit in the country's development. But their overall success is still far from assured and will depend to a large extent on whether developed countries make good on their aid commitments.

During a meeting held in Vientiane in March 2017, the United Nations Development Program in Laos (UNDP) acknowledged the improvement of social development aspects and the achievements of the MDGs over the past six years in support of the goals of the 7th NSEDP, transition to the 8th NSEDP, and the period of the Sustainable Development Goals (SDGs). The UNDP is continuing its support program to the Lao government for National Socio-Economic Development Plan implementation towards Least Developed Country graduation, Middle Income Country Transition, and Sustainable Development achievement.

2.7 Weaknesses and Shortfalls of the Socioeconomic Development

Strong economic growth has enabled Laos to move from the ranks of low income economies to a "lower middle-income" country. However, the country's economic growth, which is heavily reliant on natural resources, has not created commensurate levels of employment, local markets, and businesses. Notwithstanding progress and results obtained by Laos over the past decade, there are a number of outstanding issues concerning the macroeconomic and social aspects. By way of summary, major shortfalls are listed as follows:

- Laos has weak legal frameworks, judicial systems, and law enforcement capabilities, although progress has been made over the years.
- The Lao economy has accumulated vulnerabilities in the form of high public debt, a progressively overvalued real exchange rate, and pockets of weakness in the banking sector.
- The number of non-performing loans issued by commercial banks has risen above the percentage set by the Bank of the Lao PDR, which will somehow impact the overall situation in the Lao banking sector.
- The economy remains vulnerable to a scenario of deterioration in the external environment (political and economic context, decline in mining revenues due to softer global demand and prices for minerals, diminishment of hydropower projects, and a sharp slowdown in the Chinese economy), a sustained deterioration in the fiscal position, or an assumption of a reversal of foreign capital flows.
- Weak revenue growth (budget deficit) has led to further increases in the public debt ratio and a deterioration of the external position. This

would have a negative effect on confidence and growth. Revenue shortfall, falling foreign currency reserves, and financial leakages will continue to pose great challenges for the economy within the Asean Economy Community's (AEC) context.

- Laos is highly dependent on external support, some of which flows into considerable technical assistance. Donor funding made up 45 percent of total capital expenditure, and grants accounted for about 11 percent of total government revenue.
- Laos has weaknesses in parts of its commercial banking system. Public banks that make up almost half the system are undercapitalized according to the WB.
- How is the government going to stabilize and create confidence in Lao kip and encourage Lao people to use kip in trade exchange, including the display of product prices in the nation's own currency?
- Structural reforms are needed for Lao entrepreneurs to conduct their business activities more efficiently and compete in friendly terms with other countries (due to low time and cost of resolving insolvency, protecting minority investors, and starting a business).
- Lack of government coordination and control over FDI on the interest of the project for the country; there is very limited communication and cooperation between local agencies.
- Poor quality of roads and rails, the absence of a sea port, poor electricity transmission lines, and inadequate and costly telecommunications services make costs to businesses higher, according to the OECD.
- Diversification and competitiveness, which aims to strengthen the private sector capacity's to improve productivity and compete in regional markets, focusing on the non-natural resources sectors, are hardly being carried out.
- SMEs in Laos are a major employer, but their productivity is relatively low and access to bank loans is restricted.
- Bureaucratic barriers and insufficient measures to enable SMEs to take advantage of Laos' increased trade openness.
- Too many Special and Specific Economic Zones (SEZs) are emerging at the same time and need to be carefully managed and coordinated in order to ensure their development.

- Corruption is a barrier impeding the Lao economy from becoming more competitive and may scare away some investors. According to the State Inspection Authority (SIA), the state lost more than 480 billion kip through corruption over the past five years, and this directly affected national development and poverty reduction efforts in Laos[98].
- The Lao economy and private enterprises do not create enough jobs and thus cannot prevent young people from migrating to Thailand to look for work.
- The benefits from high economic growth are not equally distributed and translated into inclusive and sustainable human development. Widening gaps between rich and poor, women and men, education, urban and rural inhabitants, ethnic groups, and residents of different regions of the country still need to be addressed.
- Low investment and little productivity in the agriculture sector remain a weak point of the economy. Laos' growth has not integrated enough the agrarian population into more productive activities.
- Weaknesses in education and training systems for young people are visible throughout the country. Insufficient of vocational schools for students who are not able to enter to the university.
- Certain MDGs remain off track, most crucially on nutrition, with an estimated 44 percent of under-five children being stunted and 27 percent severely underweight. The country still has a high maternal mortality rate and limited skilled birth attendance, and could also do more to place gender equality at the center of its national development plans.

While Laos has made steady progress towards establishing rule of law, significant challenges remain such as insufficiencies in the number and capacity of judicial professionals, weakness of the implementation and enforcement of laws, and absence of domestic legislation harmonization with a number of international legal obligation.

The foremost obstacles to economic development remain nevertheless the lack of skilled labor, poor-quality infrastructure, deficiency of national education system, insufficient and inadequate professional schools for young people, and persistent corruption[1]. Despite notable achievements made in reforms at the border, as well as behind the border, major bottlenecks to the business and trade-enabling environment remain. These include high logistics and infrastructure costs, unpredictable application of regulations, a weak private sector, non-competitive of SMEs, weak enforcement of the law, and governance issues surrounding the independence of the rules of law and legal system. Of particular importance are the weak and unpredictable enforcement of existing laws and regulations, burdensome administrative processes, and high official and unofficial administrative costs, particularly in transport and customs services. The government needs to eliminate unnecessary business barriers to pave the way for greater foreign trade and investments in Laos, and works to improve its world ranking on the ease of doing

2.8 Conclusion

The accomplishment of Laos' economic transformation is due to government policies implemented in the mid-1980s, building on economic reform and market opening. Clearly, policies of reform after 1986 were aimed at relaxing the state monopoly of industry, trade, and production. The results are remarkable in terms of economic growth driven by foreign direct investment, emergence of private enterprises, increase of trade, rapid rise of visitor arrivals in the country, and improvement in the public health sector. The health service network has been expanded, especially in remote rural areas. Success in the economic transformation was also brought by development partners and international organizations, which must be mentioned here.

Over the past thirty years of reform, economic transformation has seen tangible achievements both on economic and social development. International institutions such as the World Bank, IMF, OECD, and ADB all praised the Lao authorities for their strong macroeconomic performance and progress on poverty reduction despite economic challenges. Laos experienced rapid growth based on capital intensive investments in the energy sector. Progress has been made in achieving the Millennium Development Goals (MDGs), but poverty remains high, inequality has increased, and Laos' growth model tends to become more inclusive, in particular by integrating the mainly agrarian population into more productive activities and diversifying its industry. Public debt has risen, is mainly due to the issuances of sovereign bonds in the Thai market, higher borrowing from Thailand and China for investment in power generation projects, and the issuance of sovereign bonds in the Thai market.

Laos today is a crossroads at the center of various roads and economic corridors of development that are structured around its immediate neighboring countries. With regional integration, the country has moved indeed from a buffer state to a central position.

The Lao economy has been growing robustly in recent years, around 7.8 percent during the last decade, supported by the strong performance of the resource sector. Strong economic growth has enabled Laos to move from a low-income economy to a "lower middle-income" country. Domestic and foreign private investment focuses mainly on energy and mining, followed by the services and agriculture sectors, particularly in commercial plantation for export. To support the growth, the government has created twelve SEZs in order to attract and to develop domestic and foreign investments in a favorable business environment.

Investment and trade are dominated at present by China, Thailand, and Vietnam. There has been an upward trend in the tourism industry; from 2011 to 2017, total revenue earned from tourism increased consistently year by year. Relationship, cooperation, and trade between Laos and Asean member countries remain at the forefront and are vital for the country.

There are more than 150,000 enterprises registered today across the country, including SMEs that make up 98 percent of the total enterprises. These enterprises contribute to the socio-economic development of Laos, thus creating jobs and building a strong foundation for continuous and stable economic growth. Thirty years of economic transformation and ten years of sustained growth have changed Lao society; with the rapid growth of private sector, a new urban middle class is emerging in the country.

The 7th NSEDP (2011-2015) achieved a number of targets: transforming Lao PDR into a more open market, strengthening the private sector productivity capacity, and prioritizing the sector activities. A number of initiatives regarding social welfare aspects have been promoted and put into practice, such as minimum wage for workers in all enterprises. The social security system has been gradually improved and increasingly provides various services to the insured people and their families. At the present, the coverage of social and health security has been expanded to an equivalent of 30.4 percent of the total number of Lao citizens.

The country has enjoyed political stability, peace, social order, and broadened international cooperation, and joined the Asean Economic Community (AEC) at the end of 2015. Prominently, Laos joined the WTO in 2013 and had the honor to host many important international meetings. Laos is undergoing a sustained economic expansion, the country is richly endowed with natural resources—especially land, forestry, water resources, and minerals—and it is in the midst of a fast growing region.

Despite progress made in various fields in terms of economy and social development as mentioned above, Laos is facing many challenges in the coming years such as maintaining macroeconomic stability, monitoring budget management, building up competitiveness of its enterprises, sustaining poverty eradication, improving the quality of education, reinforcing human resources development, keeping economic reform on the agenda, developing green growth strategy, and strengthening the rule of law.

The next step for the government within the framework of the 8th NSEDP (2016-2020), and the long term Strategy 2025 and the Vision 2030 plans, is to define its roadmap on the path that leads the country's development to succeed in the AEC and beyond. For a sustainable development, Lao leaders need to consider and answer the following questions:

- How ready is Laos for the AEC? Where is Laos heading?
- What is the growth development model for Laos?
- What are the main challenges the country has to face within the AEC?
- What lessons are there to learn from the experiences of successful countries?
- How can Laos reach the Socioeconomic Development Strategy until 2025 and the Vision 2030 of the government's plans, with an aim to build a new foundation for graduating from Least Developed Country status by the year 2020 and becoming an upper-middle-income country by 203

Notes

[30] UNDP, Laos Report 2015.

[31] NA ordinary session opens to debate socio-economic performance, law making, Vientiane Times, 26/04/2017; Government mulls key improvements to boost economy growth, Vientiane Times, 26/12/2017; The Year 2017 in Review, Vientiane Times, 30/12/2017.

[32] Human Development Report 2016, UNPD; Government mulls key improvements to boost economy growth, Vientiane Times, 26/12/2017. https://tradingeconomics.com/laos/gni-per-capita-current-us$-wb-data.html.

[33] President extends Lao New Year best wishes to all, Vientiane Times, 12/04/2017.

[34] For further reading refer to Contemporary Laos by Kham Vorapheth.

[35] IMF Press Release, September 8, 2016; IMF Chief Praises Laos, Warns Of Challenges Ahead, Vientiane Times, 20/03/2016.

[36] Laos: The Great Leap Forward, July 2016.

[37] The World Bank, Laos Economic Monitor, 2015.

[38] Solid growth expected for Laos in 2017 and 2018, ADB Outlook Report, Vientiane Times, 7/04/2017; also in Government to pursue 7 percent economic growth in 2018, Vientiane Times, 12/07/2017

[39]The Year 2017 in Review, Vientiane Times, 30/12/2017.

[40] Ministry of Planning and Investment, Department of Statistics; Government mulls key improvements to boost economy growth, Vientiane Times, 26/12/2017.

[41] UNDTAC

[42] Ministry of Planning and Investment 2016.

[43] 6th, 7th and 8th NSEDP, Ministry of Planning and Investment.

[44] Ministry of Planning and Investment, Foreign Investment Promotion website.

[45] Laos, China enjoy surge in trade, investment, Vientiane Times, 26/12/2017.

[46] Vietnam Investment in Laos to grow, Vietnam News, 29/03/2016; Ministry of Planning and Investment; China reclaims top foreign investor spot in 2016, Vientiane Times, 10/04/2017; Laos becomes magnet for Vietnamese investment, VNA, Voice of Vietnam, 20/12/2017; Laos, Vietnam push for realisation of key projects, Vientiane Times, 18/01/2018.

[47] China reclaims top foreign investor spot in 2016, Vientiane Times, 10/04/2017; Vietnam government encourages bank to invest in Laos, Vientiane Times, 21/04/2017.

[48] Korean Investment in Laos, Cambodia Infrastructure, and Thailand Retail Sector – ASEAN Market Watch, 20/07/2017.

[49] Lao, US officials discuss trade, investment agreement, Vientiane Times, 25/03/2017

[50] UK Export Finance introduces financing for British businesses in Laos, Vientiane Times, 17/08/2017.

[51] Laos the Great Leap Forward, Time for Investment, Ministry of Foreign Affairs, 2016.

[52] Increased private investment boosts Lao economy, Vientiane Times, 09/05/2017/

[53] After Thailand lifted a fourteen- year ban in 1989 on the export of goods to Laos as well as goods in transit to Laos, which were designated as "strategic goods", this becomes Laos's biggest trade partner, from 2009-2013, bilateral trade between Laos and Thailand averaged US$3.76 billion a year, with annual rate averaging 35.8 percent.

[54] IMF, International Financial Statistics Yearbook.

[55] Foreign markets interested in Lao organic coffee, 06/12/2016.

[56] Laos-EU trade continues to surge, Vientiane Times, 12/01/2018.

[57] Lao, US officials discuss trade, investment agreement, Vientiane Times, 25/03/2017.

[58] Trade surplus set to increase by over 10 percent in 2018, Vientiane Times, 4/01/2018; Surge in exports yields trade surplus of US$261 million, Vientiane Times, 2/02/2018.

[59] China to buy 20,000 tons of organic rice from Laos, Vientiane Times, 16/01/2017.

[60] Laos, Thailand agree on master plan, The Nation, 25/05/2017.

[61] Laos, Thailand enjoy continuing surge in trade, Vientiane Times, 7/10/2017

[62] Laos, China enjoy surge in trade, investment, Vientiane Times, 26/12/2017.

[63] Value of Bilateral Trade between Laos, Vietnam falls, Lao News Agency, KPL, 26/09/2016.

[64] Laos, Japan push for greater economic cooperation; Asean, S. Korea trade value set to rise sharply, Vientiane Times, 12/06/2017.

[65] The Observatory of Economic Complexity is a tool that allows users to quickly compose a visual narrative about countries and the products they

exchange. It was Alexander Simoes' Master Thesis in Media Arts and Sciences at the MIT Media Lab.

[66] IMF, Laos, Country Report, February 2017.

[67] 8th five-year National Socioeconomic Development Plan (2016–2020), June 2016.

[68] Lao PDR 40 Years 1975-2015.

[69] Excluded Russian debt of US$1,456 in 1999.

[70] IMF Staff Country Report, Laos, 2002.

[71] The World Bank, Lao People's Democratic Republic, Lao Economic Monitor FY15-16, May 2016.

[72] Statistic Department, Ministry of Planning and Investment, 7th NSEDP.

[73] Lao PDR 40 Years 1975-2015.

[74] Laos to focus on cement exports, environmental protection, Vientiane Times, 03/01/2018.

[75] Ministry of Planning and Investment statement.

[76] The government planning to irrigate 160,000 hectares of crops, Vientiane Times, 04/01/2018.

[77] Coffee exports by Laos set to exceed US$112 million in 2017, 9/10/2017.

[78] More power plants fuel energy generation, Vientiane Times, 09/01/2017.

[79] Laos to export electricity to Myanmar, more for Vietnam, the Nation, 03/02/2016.

[80] Trade surplus set to increase by over 10 percent in 2018, Vientiane Times, 04/12/2018.

[81] State Holding Enterprise on track, half-year meeting hears, Vientiane Times, 21/08/2017.

[82] An Investment Guide to the Lao PDR, Opportunities and Conditions, United Nations, 2010

[83] Phu Bia Mining hands over Q4 dividend, profit tax, Vientiane tax, 29/12/2017.

[84] 8th Five-Year National Socioeconomic Development Plan (2016–2020), June 2016.

[85] National Statistical Centre, 2005.

[86] China confirmed also that the Laos-China railway will contribute US$40 billion to a Silk Road Fund aiming to finance the construction of infrastructure projects to connect markets across Asia.

[87] Four Foreign Companies Ink Deals for Use of Lao Satellite, Vientiane Times, 9/01/2017.

[88] The Data center in Vientiane is part of a demonstration project by Japanese's New Energy and Industrial Technology Development Organization. One unit houses multiple servers in a container, and it consumes about 40% less energy than a conventional Data center.

[89] Tour operators eye rise in bookings, Vientiane Times, 03/01/2017.

[90] ASEAN – Turning Vision into Reality, Laos the Great Leap Forward, Lao Foreign Affairs, 2016.

[91] Government amending SEZ decree to spur investment, Vientiane Times, 27/12/2017.

[92] Investment grows at SEZs, Vientiane, 19/09/2016.

[93] Government urges investors to allocate more jobs to Lao nationals, Vientiane Times, 15/01/2018.

[94] Refer to Contemporary Laos, book by the author.

[95] Phousi Group is listed in the Lao Stock Market in 2017.

[96] Lao companies prove they can keep pace in other markets, Vientiane Times, 25/05/2017.

[97] UNDP, Country Report, 2015.

[98] Corruption causing major loss to the nation, Corruption causing major loss to the nation, Vientiane Times, 18/12/2017.

CHAPTER 3

Quick Overview of Laos' Statistics Compared to the Overall Level of AEC

3.1 Laos' Figures and Rank in ASEAN Community

This section proposes to appraise Laos' position and rank during the period 2007 to 2015 in categories including country profile, socio-demography, economy, international trade, inflows of foreign direct investment into the region, and other developments in the AEC characterizing the regional economy (i.e. information and communications technology, infrastructure, connectivity, and tourism). It needs to be regarded as a reference for the Lao government development plan, so that the years to come can serve more as a benchmark of progress for the Lao leaders.

The latest Asean Statistical Year Book 2015 and Asean Economic Community Chart Book 2016 may inspire Laos to deliver further efforts in improving its performance in order to be able to hook onto the AEC's locomotive in motion.

The Tables and Figures below show Laos's country profile and socio-demography statistics compared to Asean member states.

Table 4. Country Profile in 2016

	Land area (sqkm)	**Population** (000)	**Population Density** (per/sqkm)	**Inflation** Rate (%)
Brunei	5,769	417.2	72.3	(1.0)
Cambodia	181,035	15,405.2	85.1	2.8
Indonesia	1,913,578	255,461.7	133.5	3.4
Laos	236,800	6,902.4	29.1	0.9
Malaysia	330,290	30,485.3	92.3	2.7
Myanmar	676,577	52,476.0	77.6	10.3
Philippines	300,000	101,562.3	338.5	1.5
Singapore	719.1	5,535.0	7,697.1	(0.6)
Thailand	513,119	68,979.0	134.4	(0.9)
Vietnam	330,951	91,713.3	277.1	0.6

Source: ASEAN Statistical Leaflet Selected Key Indicators 2016.

Except for Brunei and Singapore, Laos has the smallest population in the region and its density is also the lowest and very sparse throughout the country. The inflation rate is under controlled, with less than 1 percent in 2016, which was considered as good macroeconomic performance for the region (see Table 4).

Table 5. Socio-Demography 2016

	Youth 15-29 years (000)	Urban Population (%)	Below National Poverty (%)	Unemployment Rate (%)	Adult Literacy Rate (%)	Net Enrollment Primary Edu (%)	Infant Mortality (per 1000)	Life Expectancy (years)
Brunei	109.5	78.7	NA	0.9	97.2	97.4	7.6	77.4
Cambodia	4,815	23.0	16.0	0.5	80.7	97.0	33.0	66.6
Indonesia	64,354	53.3	11.1	6.2	95.2	96.2	27.2	70.1
Laos	2,033	38.0	23.2	1.9	79.0	95.2	58.7	65.4
Malaysia	8,551	74.0	1.7	3.2	94.2	97.3	6.3	74.9
Myanmar	14,191	30.0	23.6	4.0	89.5	86.4	35.3	65.6
Philippines	28,112	44.0	25.2	6.5	95.4	93.8	23.0	70.4
Singapore	778.1	100.0	NA	2.8	96.8	100	1.7	82.7
Thailand	15,606	49.0	13.2	0.8	96.1	93.1	6.6	74.1
Vietnam	22,561	33.1	8.4	2.3	94.8	96.6	14.9	73.2

Source: ASEAN Statistical Leaflet Selected Key Indicators 2016.

Table (5) above shows that Laos had almost all the economic weakness indicators compared to other Asean member countries, particularly for adult literacy, infant mortality, and national poverty rates. These three indicators created major handicaps for the country's development; Laos has to improve its socio-demography performance in order to be competitive and attractive for investors. The Philippines has the highest unemployment rate among the members of the association. The largest economies in the region, however, maintain low unemployment as their strong economic performance has a positive impact on labor markets.

3.2 Nominal GDP Annual Growth Comparison Between ASEAN Member States

In 2015, the region's GDP grew at 4.7 percent, lower by 2.1 percentage points from 2007. Laos' growth in 2014 and 2015 was among the highest in the region[99]. GDP growth in CLMV (Cambodia, Laos, Myanmar, and Vietnam) remained higher than in the whole Asean during the same period (Figure 21).

Figure 21. Annual GDP Growth in Percent, 2007-2015

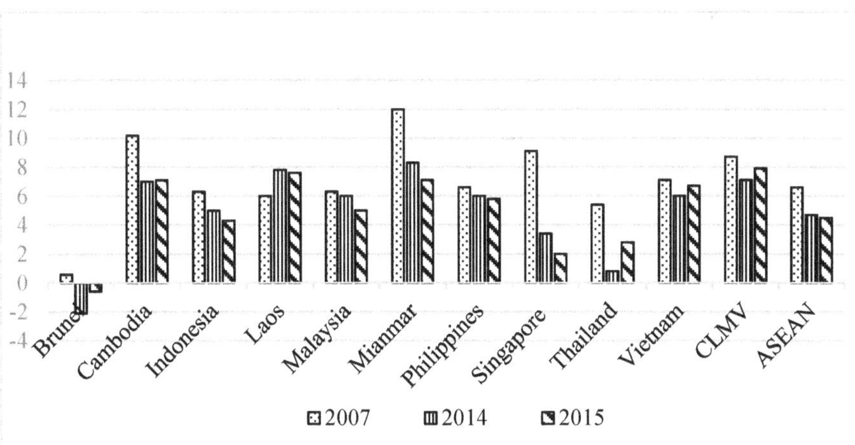

Source: ASEAN Secretariat 2016.

3.3 GDP Per Capita, at Current Price: Laos Compared to Asean Member States

Figure 22 shows that member states' GDP per capita varied widely. In 2015, GDP per capita in Singapore and Brunei reached more than US$50,000 and US$30,000 respectively; while GDP per capita in Laos, Cambodia, and Myanmar stood at US$1,831, US$1,198, and $1,246, respectively. Indonesia, Malaysia, Philippines and Thailand's GDP per capita ranged from US$2,800 to US$9,600.

In addition, the nominal GDP per capita of Laos was among the lowest, just above Myanmar and Cambodia in 2015. Moreover, its GDP per capita showed also great discrepancies between different regions of the country. In contrast, the GDP growth of Laos was the highest amid the Asean countries, as shown in Figure 21 above.

Figure 22. GDP Per Capita, at Current Price

(In US dollars)

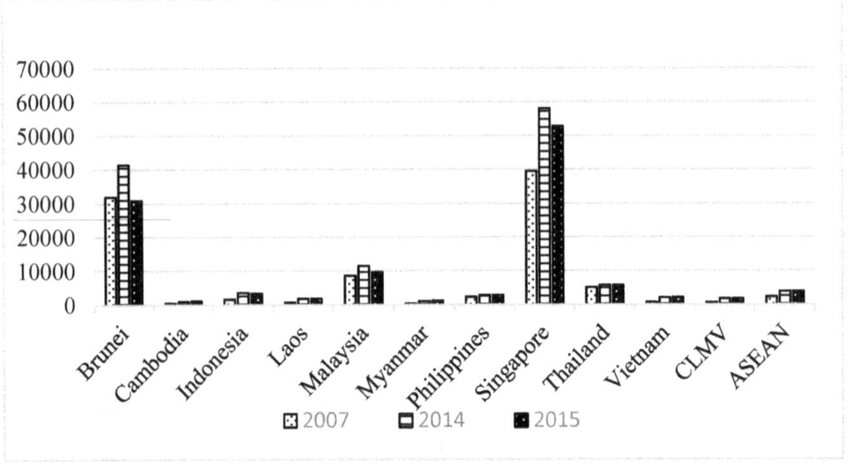

Source: ASEAN Secretariat 2016.

3.4 Total ASEAN Trade in Goods

In 2015, the region's total trade in goods fell by 10 percent from US$2,529 billion the previous year to US$2,270 billion; both extra-ASEAN and intra-ASEAN trade in goods were down by about 10 percent (Figure 23).

Figure 23. Trade in Goods, 2007-2015

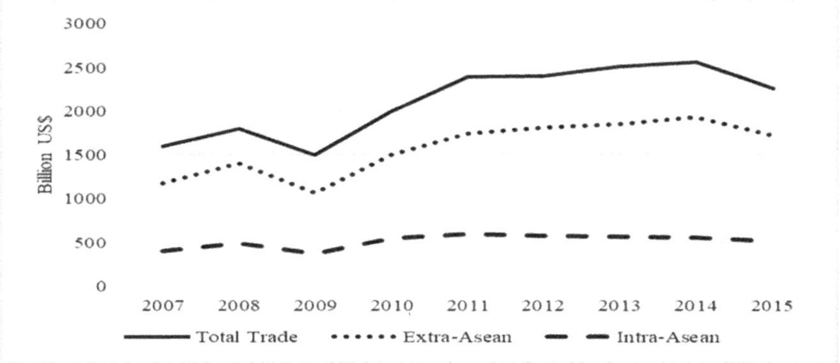

Source: ASEAN Secretariat 2016.

3.5 Intra- and Extra-ASEAN Trade in Goods

In 2015, intra-ASEAN trade in goods remained stable at approximately 24 percent of the region's total trade in goods. Nevertheless, extra-Asean trade remained predominant (Figure 24). Laos' intra-trade and extra-trade with Asean represented more than 63 percent in 2015 (Tables 6 and 7). Asean remains Laos' most important commercial partner and supplier. But this trend could be reduced in the future because trade with China will grow in importance.

Figure 24. Intra- and Extra-ASEAN Trade in Goods

(In percent share)

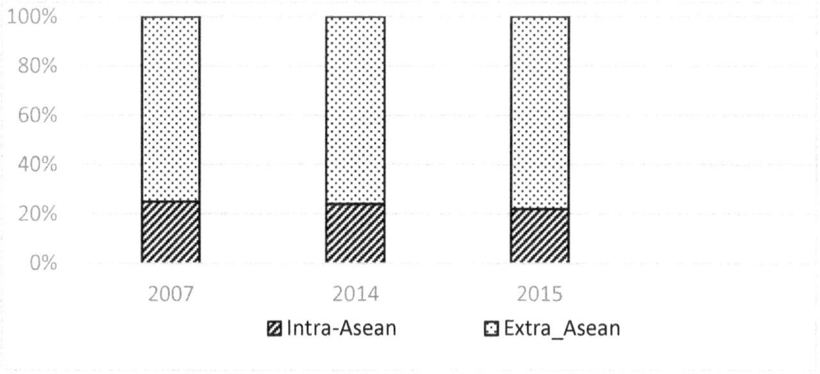

Source: ASEAN Secretariat 2016.

3.6 ASEAN Member States Exports of Goods by Destination, 2015

Table 8 below shows that within the Asean, the exports of Laos to Thailand and Vietnam are predominant (72 percent); these were important for its trade balance. Laos exported 28 percent more of its products within commodities outside the Asean (e.g., the EU, Japan, South Korea, China, Russia and the US). With the occurrence of the AEC, Laos expects to improve and expand its trade within the Asean member countries; infrastructure works (roads, bridges, and railways) are being undertaken by the Lao government, and several outcomes indicators suggest improvements in the time and cost to trade (cross-border check point facilitation, customs modernization, and the harmonization and standardization of trade and customs procedures).

Table 6. ASEAN Exports of Goods by Destination, 2015

(In percent share)

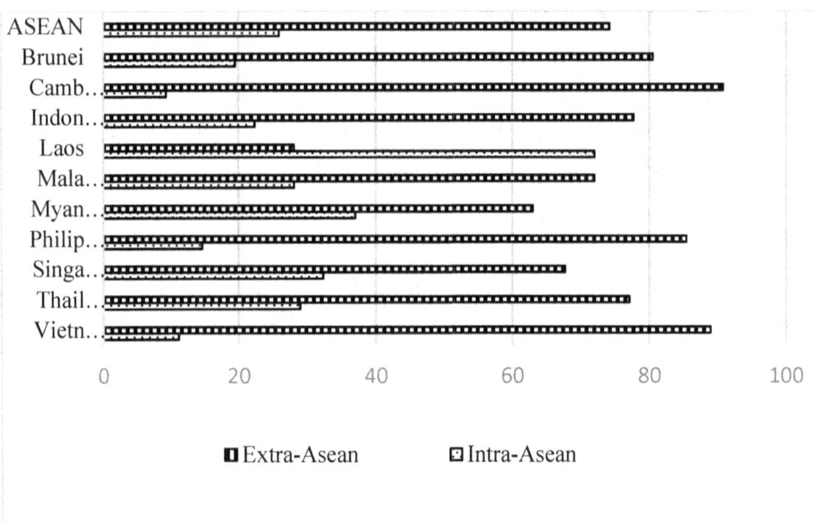

Source: ASEAN Secretariat 2016.

3.7 ASEAN Member States Imports of Goods by Origin, 2015

It is interesting to note that Brunei, Lao PDR, and Myanmar purchased nearly 50% of their commodity items from within the region; while Vietnam imported the least from the Asean countries (Table 7)[100]. The imports of Laos were mainly from Thailand: foods, mineral fuels/oils, electrical and mechanical equipment, steel, and cement. The remaining import products were from China, Vietnam, Japan, South Korea, and the EU.

Indeed, large quantities of goods are exported to and imported from neighboring countries, especially Thailand and Vietnam, along the Mekong River. These countries remain Laos' top trading partners within Asean. But while the value of trade between Laos and Asean countries is increasing, the value of trade between Laos and Europe and the US is decreasing.

Table 7. ASEAN Imports of Goods by Origin, 2015

(In percent share)

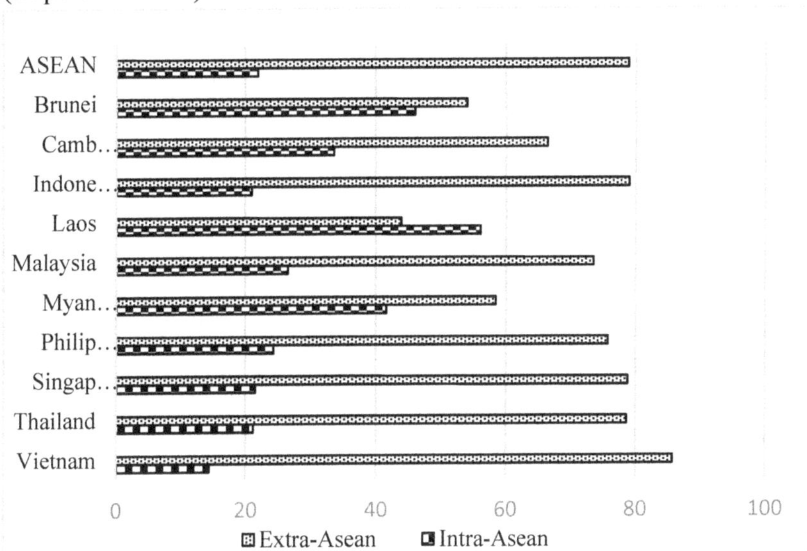

Source: ASEAN Secretariat 2016.

In summary, according to the recent Ministry of Industry and Commerce report, the total value of goods traded between Laos and Asean exceeded US$4.85 billion in the first nine months of 2017, while the export of electricity remained the top income earner for Laos, according. Among other strategic Asean trade partners, Thailand was Laos' top trading partner with the value of exports to the neighboring country valued at over US$1.73 billion of which US$935 million came from electricity in the first nine months of 2017.

The total value of Lao products exported to Asean neighbors reached US$2.29 billion in the first nine months of 2017, while the value of imports from Asean countries stood at US$2.56 billion. In 2016, the value of imports was US$3.12 billion and exports were worth more than US$2.60 billion. In 2015, exports were valued at US$2.23 billion and imports were worth US$2.98 billion, according to the report. The combined value of goods traded with Asean was more than US$5.22 billion in 2015 and US$5.78 billion in 2016.

Thailand has a dominant trade and investment role in the Lao economy, but the participation of the eight other Asean members too is considered significant and Vietnam ranked second in terms of trade with Laos over the first nine months of 2017, with exports worth more than US$520 million and imports worth almost US$400 million[101].

3.8 Foreign Direct Investment (FDI) Development and Multinational Enterprises (MNE) Activities in ASEAN

In 2015, FDI flows in Asean declined by 8 per cent to US$120 billion as shown in Figure 24. Despite the decline, Asean remained a major destination of FDI flows among developing economies, receiving some 16 percent of the world FDI flows to such economies. FDI in manufacturing rose, equity capital financing of FDI activities was at an all-time high, and regional investment expansion by MNEs remained strong, as did intra-Asean investments. FDI flows to the CLMV countries in general rose significantly.

Figure 25. FDI Flows in ASEAN, 2010–2015 (Millions US$)

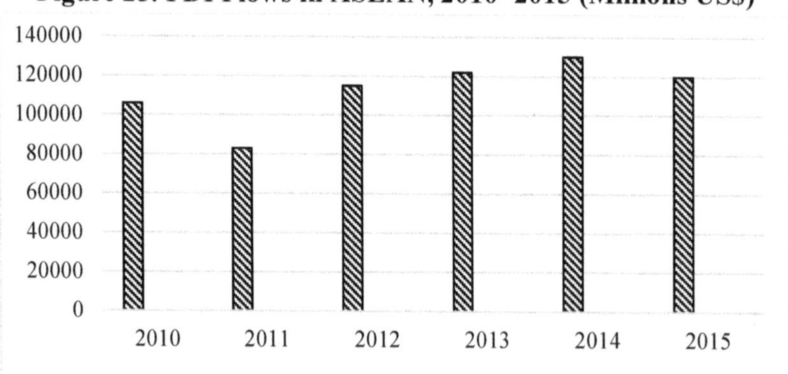

Source: ASEAN Secretariat, ASEAN FDI database.

3.9 Foreign Investments in ASEAN -6 Countries, 2007-2015

Figure 26. Net Inflows of FDI by ASEAN-6

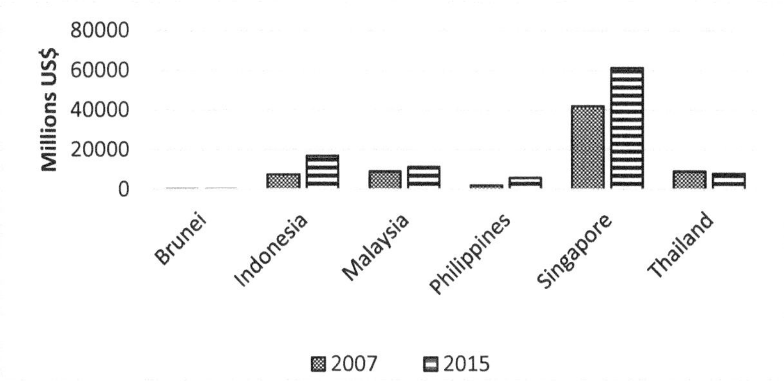

Source: ASEAN Secretariat 2016.

Figure 26 above shows that Singapore remained the highest recipient of FDI among the ASEAN-6 countries, with inflows amounting to US$61 billion in 2015.

3.10 Foreign Investments in ASEAN Member Countries (CLMV), 2007-2015

The CLMV countries witnessed a stronger growth in FDI flows, which increased by 38 per cent, to $17.4 billion in 2015 (Figure 27). On average, investment increased in manufacturing, finance, and infrastructure

As far as Vietnam is concerned, in 2015 FDI inflows grew by 28 percent, reaching US$11.8 billion. Meanwhile, investments in Myanmar expanded threefold at US$2.8 billion from US$946 million in 2014, posting the highest growth among all ASEAN member states. Laos received the least investments from FDI; however, in 2015 it reached almost twelvefold at US$1,079 million from US$95 million in 2007 (Figure 27). These inflows came mainly from hydropower plant projects and mining sector.

Figure 27. Net Inflows of FDI by ASEAN Members Countries (CLMV)

(In million US dollars)

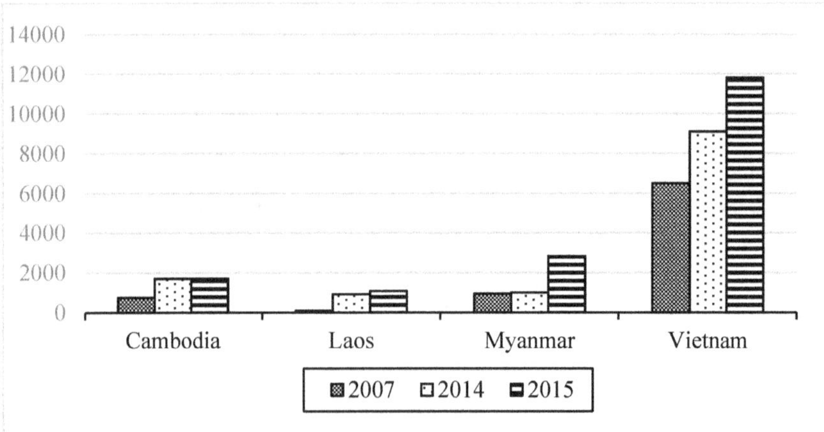

Source: ASEAN Secretariat 2016.

Since the beginning of 2017, the Lao government has being drafting a new flexible investment law and business friendly environment that could attract more investors in the years to come, after having already introduced several incentive FDI measures in the early 2010s.

3.11 Intra-ASEAN Net Inflows of FDI, 2010-2015

Intra-ASEAN investment remained the largest source of FDI flows, rising marginally by $15 billion to $22.1 billion in 2015 (Figure 28). The total FDI in 2015 in ASEAN represented 18.4 percent of the rest of the world; percentage increased from 14 percent in 2014.

Amongst these inflows, Indonesia received the largest share of intra-ASEAN investment, followed by Singapore, Malaysia, Myanmar and Vietnam. The share can be split as shown in Figure 28 below. Laos' share was modest compared to Vietnam, Myanmar, and Cambodia.

Figure 28. Intra–ASEAN Investment flows, 2010–2015

(In millions US dollars)

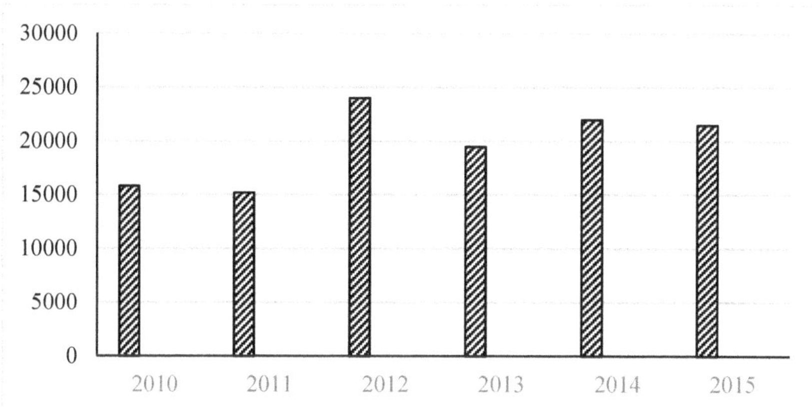

Source: ASEAN Secretariat, ASEAN FDI database 2016.

Table 8. Intra-ASEAN Net Inflows of FDI, 2015 by Country

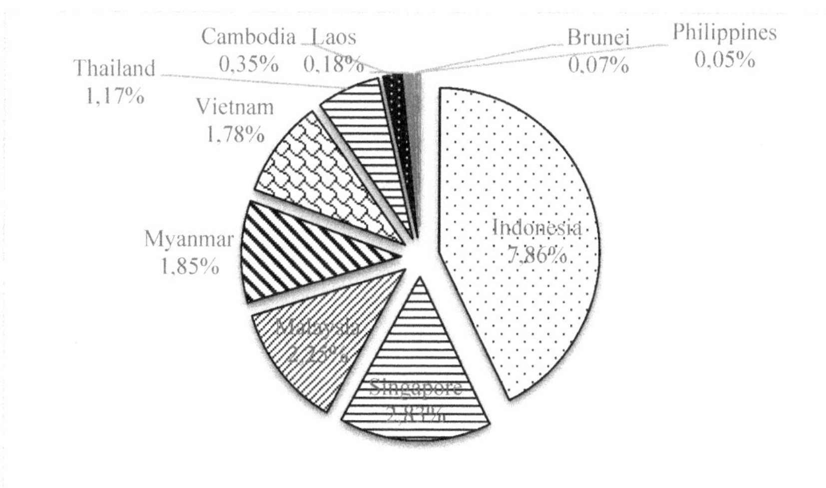

Source: ASEAN Secretariat 2016.

Table 8 above shows that Indonesia received in 2015 the largest source of FDI followed by Singapore, while Laos attracted only 0.18 percent.

3.12 Ratio of Paved Road to Total Road Length in the AEC

There is a marked improvement in Myanmar's road condition as shown by the increase in the ratio of paved road to total road length from 24 percent in 2013 to 43 percent, and in the Philippines as well during 2015 (Table 9).

Table 9. Ratio of Paved Road to Total Road Length (In percentage)

	2010	2011	2012	2013	2014	2015
Singapore	100	100	100	100	100	100
Brunei	82	82	90	90	90	90
Philippines	76	80	81	83	86	90
Thailand	80	80	80	84	85	85
Malaysia	80	82	78	78	80	80
Indonesia	57	57	56	56	57	57
Vietnam	53	51	53	53	54	54
Myanmar	21	22	21	24	36	43
Laos	15	15	15	15	19	20
Cambodia	8	9	10	10	10	11

Source: ASEAN Secretariat 2016.

Laos, Cambodia, and Vietnam did not much increase their paved roads by much. The ratio of paved road to road length remained poor. This reason could be because these three countries were heavily involved in the "Vietnam War" and suffered intensive bombing in their territories. Laos has commenced the construction of many new roads and upgraded existing ones, but more infrastructure work and investment are needed from the government and international donors to develop both the paved road and the quality of its network with a view to facilitate regional integration.

3.13 Tourism: Other Developments in AEC

Figure 29 shows that tourist arrivals in Asean grew by 3.6 percent, reaching nearly 109 million in 2015 from 105 million in 2014. Thailand was the favorite tourist destination in the region, with a share of 27 percent of total visitor arrivals, followed closely by Malaysia (24 percent) and then Singapore (14 percent). Laos, Myanmar, and Cambodia were at the same level of tourist arrivals from 2007 to 2015. Laos is enjoying more and more visitor arrivals in the country, 4.6 million in 2015, with an annual growth of about 8 percent. Nonetheless, tourism has continued to drop following a decline of some 10 percent recorded in 2016[102]. Foreign tourist arrivals for the whole of 2017 are expected to fall by 11.2 percent compared to 2016.

Figure 29. Visitor Arrivals

(In thousand persons)

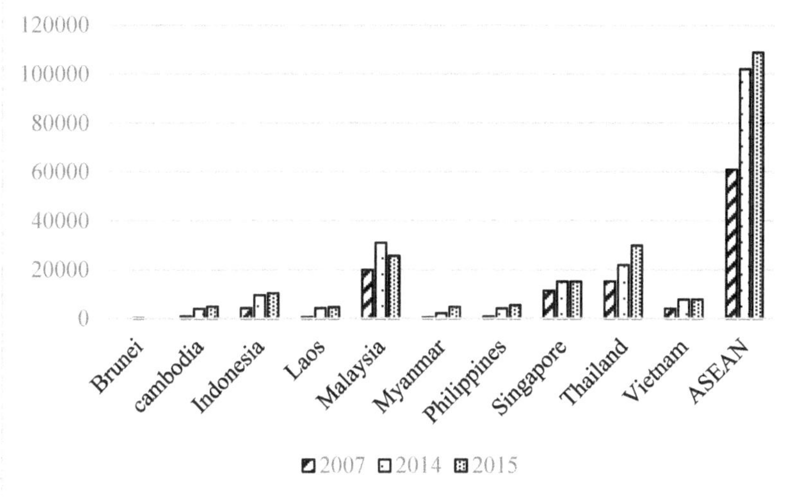

Source: ASEAN Secretariat 2016.

What can one conclude from all of this? The statistics given in the Tables and Figures above aim to measure how Asean countries grow, attract investors, develop social aspects, advance in road infrastructure, boost high levels of their education, and retain talent, in view of creating a resource for governments and decisions-makers to develop strategies for identifying and enhancing their national economy's resources and competiveness. Who are the top-rankers and bottom followers? Undeniably the top rankers are the six founders: Singapore, Malaysia, Indonesia, Thailand, Philippines, and to some extend Brunei. The new comers such as Laos, Myanmar, and Cambodia have to make considerable effort to catch up on infrastructure development, and the education system, to accelerate poverty eradication, to improve the purchasing power of their population, and to gain further export markets. Laos needs to show greater adaptability and life-long learning to continue and succeed in the competition, while Vietnam is in a good position to move up from a middle high ranking to a developed nation within the Asean.

Laos is a lower-middle-income, land-locked country that has achieved high and persistent economic growth, with its real gross domestic product (GDP) averaging about 8% per annum during the last decade. Much of the growth was the result of foreign direct investment, which transformed Laos into a provider of natural resources consisting mainly of energy and minerals. The country maintains a significant trade deficit. Despite a slow start, increasing economic integration remains the most likely driver of change in the country, where integration pressure will become stronger with the arrival of the AEC[103]. The Lao government is confident that Asean will play a significant role in the domestic economy over the next few years as the value of bilateral trade continues to surge.

Notes

[99] ASEAN Statistical Leaflet, Selected Key Indicators, 1016.
[100] ASEAN Statistical Year Book 2016.
[101] Laos, Asean benefit from surge in trade, Vientiane Times, 10/01/2018.
[102] International visitor arrivals to capital down, Vientiane Times, 10/07/2017.
[103] ADB Evaluation: Lao People's Democratic Republic Country Partnership Strategy Final Review Validation, 2012–2016.

CHAPTER 4

Laos and the Asean Economic Community (AEC)

4.1. Integration of Laos into the Regional Economic Community

The Asean Economic Community is a major milestone in the ongoing regional economic integration agenda of Asean. "AEC 2015" is no longer a refrain but a reality that the region's governments, businesses, and people are embracing. Inaugurated on 31 December 2015, the open-economy initiative among the ten Asean countries is taking shape; it aims to strip away trade and tariff barriers, facilitate a more free flow of services, goods, and high-skilled labor, and also facilitate the freer flow of capital in the regional bloc. The Asean Economic Community proposes to consolidate the economic integration of the region. The AEC is ultimately designed to create a single market and production base within Asean.

In 2007, the Asean Leaders decided to accelerate the implementation of the Asean Economic Community by 2015. The AEC is the "pillar" under the Community that is most relevant to foreign investors interested in establishing operations or trading in the region.

In order to achieve this, Asean created the AEC Blueprint. It serves as a "master plan" for the implementation of the AEC, outlining targets and timelines for specific reforms. In broad numbers, the AEC constitutes a huge potential marketplace for investors. As a bloc, the ten Asean member nations are a $2.3 trillion market, with average GDP growth of 6% per year in the last 15 years.

The AEC Blueprint 2025, adopted by the Asean leaders at the 27th Asean Summit on 22 November 2015 in Kuala Lumpur, Malaysia, provides broad directions through strategic measures for the AEC from 2016 to 2025. It succeeded the AEC Blueprint (2008-2015), which was adopted in 2007, and is built on four interrelated and mutually-reinforcing key economic pillars as illustrated in the sketch below[1]. The two bases, human resources development and research and development, are essential and form the foundation of the Asean Economic Community.

As an integrated community, Asean aims to be a region where there are simplified rules, lower tariffs, harmonized standards and closer regulatory cooperation, greater transparency, a talented, well-educated pool of workers, and a large lively consumer base. The AEC Blueprint and the four economic pillars are illustrated as below:

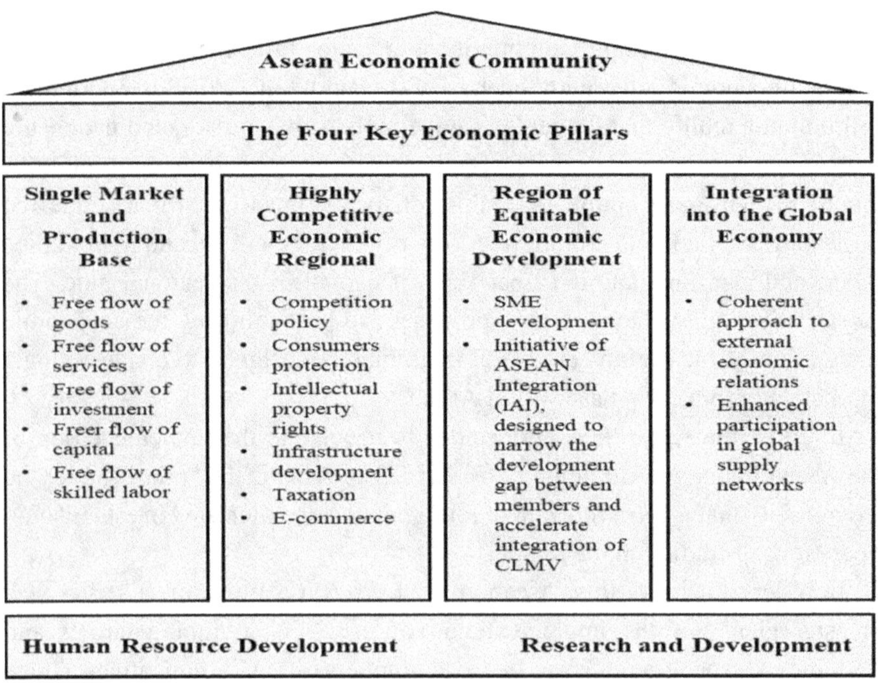

Source: From A Blueprint for Growth ASEAN Economic Community 2015.

Yet, Asean is well advanced on its roadmap to formally implementing the AEC since the end of December 2015, as it has achieved almost all its targets in the reduction of trade duties. To present all the work that has been completed and to inform Asean economies and businesses, the Association of Southeast Asian Nations has produced the report "Thinking Globally, Prospering Regionally – Asean Economic Community 2015" that highlights the achievements towards the AEC and its vision for the future.

The association seeks today to promote political and economic cooperation and regional stability in order to create a common market among its members. Since its creation, Asean has overcome various difficulties and faced the challenges arising in the region. It has become one of the most important regional intergovernmental organizations among developing countries worldwide. It has been able to stay committed to its fundamental aims by contributing to the preservation and promotion of peace and stability as well as cooperation for development.

The AEC presents new opportunities for Laos, but it also points out significant challenges. The country has long had potential, given its natural resources and geographic proximity to China and the other Asean states.

The goal of the AEC is challenging: integrating Southeast Asia's diverse economies into a single market, similar to the European Economic Community five decades ago. Asean as a single market is forecast to become competitive both for its intra and extra trade. In 2016 alone, intra-Asean trade was worth more than US$2 trillion, covering over 20 to 25 per cent of the total trade value of Asean. It is projected that its trade value will continue to rise over the years to come, according to the Secretariat of ASEAN. Meanwhile extra-Asean investment stood at US$22 trillion, equal to 17-18 percent of the total value of Asean investment in the same year.

Admittedly, the AEC will not have an immediate impact on Laos, as nothing noteworthy is going to happen for some time yet; the full realization of the AEC needs to take many years before the country can enjoy all the advantages. Nevertheless, this will likely enhance the country's international reputation, although the tangible effect will only emerge in the medium to long term[104].

"Laos will be the first country, in cooperation with the Asean member states, to turn the Asean Community Vision 2025 into reality. We will continue the integration process, enhance connectivity, and redouble efforts to narrow the development gap among member states", says Prime Minister Thongloun Sisoulith[105].

As a connectivity node of the North-South and the East-West economic corridors, Laos hopes to take full advantage of the AEC to develop its economy and pursue the "Ten-year Socio-economic Development Strategy (2016–2025)." The four key pillars of the AEC may help the country to contribute towards elevating Laos from the Least Developed Country (LDC) status by the year 2020, through continuous, inclusive, and sustainable growth. In addition, it allows Laos to take the shortcut and accelerate its development to become an upper-middle-income country by 2030 in the region. In this context, Laos is seeking within the AEC the opportunities for greater connectivity to tackle persistent development gaps and disparities between rich and poor; the country expects to attract more investors to do business and generate jobs for its people.

In conclusion, the establishment of the AEC would undeniably have its pros outweigh its cons and is indeed a stimulating period for the region and the world economy. Integrated economic blocs ensure certainty in procedures, and given Asean's consolidated influence on the world economy, the AEC is likely to be a great success. Laos is striving to seize all the advantages and opportunities to attain its sustainable development.

It is worth recalling that Asean has recorded great achievements over the past half a century, ensuring regional economic growth and stability. However, one has to acknowledge that an array of difficulties is facing the group such as the development gap between member countries, and the differences in development goals, laws, institutions, and the awareness of people and the business circle.

4.2. What Does the AEC Mean for Laos and What Are the Impacts?

4.2.1. The AEC Is Salutary for Lao's Economic Transformation

The need to find alternative sources of assistance, combined with the ideological vacuum following the collapse of Soviet Union, obligated the Lao leadership to accept the kind of market-oriented reforms advocated by the donor community, especially the IMF and the World Bank. Adhering to Asean is then a logical and salutary path for Laos, its development, and its security.

Being part of the AEC demonstrates an important determining factor in the transformation of Laos into a successful market economy and regional integration.

Laos is an economic "dwarf" compared to its Asean partners. Its market is narrow and its economy remains vulnerable; its population is insignificant, with fewer than thirty inhabitants per square kilometer; and the country is landlocked, with none of the modern infrastructure or communication networks that are necessary for the country to transact rapid economic exchanges with its neighbors and the outside world for the time being.

The Lao economy is very dependent on international aid, growth is limited, and industry is almost nonexistent due to a lack of private investment in domestic markets, and its businesses have little experience or no international networks. The country is hardly able to develop its productive tools. However, Laos has numerous assets: energy and mines, tourism, and agriculture. The country's fertile land has not yet been fully exploited.

Increased Asean integration means it will open opportunities, including transport, trade, and enlarged participation in value chains and tourism for Laos. Integration helps generate sustainable trade and investment, and creates the conditions for improved access to economic opportunities and higher incomes across Lao society. Obviously, one can notice today that trade between Laos and Asean is on a fast rise.

Besides, the AEC is beneficial to bring in new technologies, methods, and innovation in many fields into Laos, such as upgrading construction standards and levels of development. But meanwhile, it will boost the Lao economy and strengthen the cultural connectivity of all member countries. Importantly, the AEC will also encourage the Lao people to produce more goods on a commercial basis rather than just for their families. Commercial production will help to improve their living standards.

So what does all this mean for Laos? As an emerging economy in a dynamic region, it is absolutely vital that Laos is well prepared to meet the challenges of this inter-connected trade world. As with the WTO, the AEC has a series of rules, duties, constraints, and procedures to enable free trade between the ten Asean member states with some special provisions for the least-developed members. The key point, though, is that these rules and procedures will be applied across the ASEAN bloc.

Taking into consideration Laos's context, the Lao government has quite successfully managed the integration process, and has improved the regulatory and procedural environment for regional trade and investment, but much remains to be done. It is obvious that the implementation of the AEC opens promising prospects, but also brings many constraints for the regional economy, especially Laos. Indeed, the liberalization of trade and industry has allowed the appearance and enrichment of a middle class in the country, as well as an urban elite; what can be observed today is that Laos has a small but growing middle class concentrated mostly in the capital and larger provincial cities.

4.2.2. Duties and Constraints Imposed on Laos

Laos is still facing many duties and constraints in the process of economic development to comply with the Blueprint 2025, a series of the AEC's measures outlining targets after its integration. Among them are a high poverty rate, growing inequality, insufficient infrastructure, and low production base. Moreover, the Lao private sector participation in trade to benefit from AFTA and ASEAN+3 is very limited. There are many restrictions to overcome this deficiency.

As a result, the Lao government is committed to fulfilling reforms such as cutting tariffs; developing greater investment in infrastructures; streamlining and simplifying trade regulations; reducing by half, or less than 100 days from today's 245 day average, the time per shipment on documentary compliance for exporters in Laos, and implementing standards for industry and food products[106]. Moreover, Laos is aware that to remain attractive and competitive, immediate reforms are needed to modernize and simplify trade regulations of its administrative procedures for border-crossing and shipping as well.

Another priority for the Lao government in the AEC implementation means making logistic improvements to boost Laos in Asean trade. Logistics in this country faces many problems, not only the infrastructure but also the knowledge and practices in this sector of industry in which Lao enterprises have no competencies. Transportation is also an importance challenge for the government to accelerate the economy and integration with the Asean nations[107]. These two challenges are in the Lao authority's chief agenda.

Overall, since Laos joined the World Trade Organization in 2013, it has endeavored to liberalize trade by cutting tariffs and subsidies, and by opening the country to new investment opportunities, which it hopes will be increased and offered by the AEC.

With regard to tariff cuts, at the present time, Laos has abolished more than 8,000 commodity items out of a total of 9,558 under the Asean Harmonized Tariffs Nomenclature (AHTN) after the country integrated in the AEC at the end of 2015. Those 8000 product items include seafood, animal insides, and some processed agricultural products, according to the Ministry of Industry and Commerce. About 697 goods items such as vehicles, petrol, drinking products, and spare parts will be postponed and tariffs will be removed in 2018, while 265 items including unprocessed agricultural products will be reduced to between 0 to 5 percent after 2018. Indeed, Laos along with Myanmar, Cambodia, and Vietnam, the four less-developed members, benefit from flexibility (e.g. 2018 is their extended deadline for Non-Tariff Barriers (NTB) to be eliminated). Laos is currently still collecting about 5 to 40 percent tariffs for the remaining import goods from Asean member states for which tariff removal has been postponed[108].

Despite the country combining with the AEC, Laos is not ready to cut all import tariffs from Asean member states as some of the postponed products represent main sources of revenue for socio-economic development. However, the country will abolish these remaining items when the end date for full compliance with integration comes. It is worth mentioning that Laos considers tariffs as a major source of income. In the past, 11 percent of state income was sourced from import tariffs. Today, the impact of tariff cuts makes the government impose consumption taxes (VAT) so that it can generate enough revenue to replace the income lost. With the reduction of non-tariff barriers, Laos may also possibly gain the most from the AEC, through increased liberalization and competitiveness.

Existing constraints also represent burdens for Laos' finances, which appear in many aspects: handling environmental issues, reinforcing competitiveness of its SMEs, improving production efficiency, getting approval of certification and testing of the products, upgrading the education system, accelerating training of the labor force, and combatting corruption that helps secure the promise of equitable development and greater transparency. In addition, public systems such as finance, banking, and commerce, including education, are also likely to improve as the government seeks to comply with the Asean agreement and attract FDI.

The current global context means that Laos will have to work harder to maintain the high levels of growth it has experienced over the past decades. This is translating into an expanding fiscal deficit, and thus the government seeks to maintain investments from all sources.

With respect to duties committed to the AEC, Laos is speeding up reforms in several fields. The priority is for Laos to transform itself into a 'land-linked' rather than a land-locked country. To do so, it needs to invest in both policy reform and infrastructure connectivity. A transformative regional railway initiative is currently underway extending from China through Laos' capital, Vientiane, and connecting through Thai train networks to the port of Singapore; construction of the project commenced in December 2015 and is expected to be completed in 2021. There is also the extension phase of the Laos-Thailand railway under construction. The Ministry of Transport, Railways Department, gave in August 2017 a presentation on Laos' plan for a rail network, explaining that four additional railway lines have been planned to turn Laos from a landlocked country into a land link within the region. There lines are as follows: Savannakhet-Lao Bao, Vientiane-Thakhek-Mu Gia (Vietnam), Thakhek-Savannakhet-Pakse-Vangtau (Vietnam), and Pakse-Veunkham (Lao-Cambodian border)[109].

The Lao government has also since 2016 undertaken several reforms to improve the economy and create a friendly commercial environment with more flexible laws for foreign investment. Engaged in the long-term development of Laos and integration in the global economy, the Lao government is committed to developing trade. It therefore created in 2015 an online trade portal, available in English, to help businesses and people in their trading operations in and out of Laos. This portal also gathers a lot of information on customs, news, publications, articles, events, job vacancies, etc. The website was created via a loan from the Asian Development Bank as part of government efforts to promote SMEs in Laos alongside the theme of 'Enhance SME Access to Asian Market Through E-commerce Platform'. The e-commerce platform will provide more opportunities and environments for SMEs to access domestic and international markets. The website will be a promotional channel for Lao businesses, and they will learn more about the benefits of Free Trade Agreements (FTAs), according to the Ministry of Industry and Commerce[110].

Still, another area that needs to be improved is English language instruction. English is the most common language on the Internet, in academia, and in the business sector. Furthermore, English will be the common language of the Asean Economic Community. An increasing number of multinational companies now use English as the common corporate language in an effort to improve communication and performance across geographic borders. In order for Laos to be competitive in Asean and the world, English language has to be considered a necessity. Therefore, within the AEC's perspective, it also means that English in high school, universities, and private tuitions will become important to prepare the young Lao to work with Asian businesspeople in an international environment.

Furthermore, the AEC will mean there will be no protection for local products. The AEC offers an opportunity for intra-Asean trade and allows member states to refocus their trade efforts with one another. Consequently Laos is aware of its weakness and endeavors to strengthen its competitiveness, and so the Lao government is supporting its enterprises and deploying efforts to modernize both its industry and human resources development.

Additional constraints to trade can be significantly reduced if Laos and individual nations focus on developing their National Single Window (NSW)—and connect it to the Asean Single Window (ASW). The full implementation of the AEC includes instituting a NSW and eliminating other Non-Tariff Barriers (NTB). The NSW and ASW systems expedite trade in goods and services by standardizing forms and documents at the national and regional levels. Hence, Laos needs to focus on developing its NSW project: a one-stop shop where trade of goods and services can be standardized and therefore expedited. The one-stop shop customs model between Vietnam and Laos was first implemented in 2015 at the Dansavan-Lao Bao international border checkpoint. Under this model, Lao and Vietnamese customs personnel together check all people and goods at one point only[111]. The new model will be a remarkable step in local authorities and other countries expanding business exchanges at international border gates across the East-West economic corridor, as well as other key corridors in the Greater Mekong Sub-region (GMS). This will also help complete the commitments made under the GMS Cross-Border Transport Facilitation Agreement by the Lao government.

Similarly, the AEC obliges Lao authorities and enterprises to use and accommodate international practices for trade transactions, accounting systems, international laws, and all communication. The above will be a big change for the Lao business community and the government's determination for a great leap towards modernization.

While acknowledging that there are tremendous hurdles in the integration of the AEC, the Lao government believes that businesses are thriving in the region with the growth of intra-Asean trade and investments, and thus bets on the success of its long-term development strategy goals.

4.2.3. Impact on the Labor Force and the Lao Economy

The ten Asean nation states are now committed to create the AEC as a means to support the free flow of labor across Asia, and to benefit all economies falling within the AEC by sharing human resources.

At the present, big development gaps between the region's richest and poorest countries represent hurdles to forging a single economy; preferably, allowing skilled and unskilled workers to freely move from one AEC member state to another would benefit the whole region. It would allow the exchange of experience and skills. For Laos, mainly skilled youth, nurses, dentists, doctors, engineers, and architects would benefit by having the opportunity to gather work experience abroad.

Since there will be free flow of goods and labor, Laos would have at the same time a big outflow of farmers and other unskilled laborers, as well as educated professionals. Laos would see positive impacts in terms of labor movement. As a matter of fact, after gaining experience and know-how abroad, the returning Lao workers could contribute to the development of their country thanks to the competencies acquired in Thailand or Indonesia in various professions such as road building, bridge construction, electrical maintenance, welding, plumbing, maintenance of mechanical equipment, and the hotel-restaurant industry.

Also, the AEC will bring new labor flows to professions that require high skill labor inside Laos. In other words, skilled workers from Asean member countries will enter Laos, filling the increasing demand for higher skilled positions that the development of the country demands. This means that enterprises in need of skilled workers within Laos will be able to hire them more easily than at present because the market will be larger and more promising. Laos, at its stage of learning by doing, is in a position to capture skilled labor and other professional competencies from Asian member countries.

Yet many Asean employees are now working at hotels, restaurants, and other service sectors in Laos. Not to mention that in the coming years Laos will need more talent from Asean countries, particularly engineers, accountants, computer experts, qualified technicians, business lawyers, medical doctors, surgeons, logistics experts, project managers, and financial experts.

By creating a more integrated economic community, the AEC would encourage high-cost production countries such as Singapore and Malaysia to move its production to lower-cost ones like Laos, Cambodia, and Myanmar. This would allow Asean countries to leverage each other's competitive advantage and ensure that efficiency is being optimized as much as possible. With the current satisfactory trade volumes, the AEC could potentially maintain the competitive situation by ensuring that production costs are kept to its lowest possible levels in the region. Then, Laos can gain from the integration thanks to the low labor cost. Thus, in order to strengthen the labor market in the AEC, the number one priority must be to better train and educate Lao students. This is the only way Laos can compete and keep its talent.

Being part of the regional economy integration, this will also impact the day-to-day business activities of people and enterprises, particularly in terms of communication, profitability, productivity, efficiency, training of personnel, transparency, marketing, proactivity, international approach, strategy, and vision of their business. The impact on the old mindset will be great, for businesspersons have to learn to work effectively and fast as a team to cope with the new era of economic competition.

A step forward for Laos towards the AEC raises many hopes for this country seeking to break out of its cycle of underdevelopment and engage in modernization, but such a course requires the country to comply with a number of obligations, both economic and social as described above. It is a positive stage to achieve Asean's regional economic integration agenda.

However, the opening of the labor market and immigration can also create in the long run racial tension for Laos, given the small population of the country. It is up to the Lao government to control the flow of immigration and put in place a rigorous employment policy on the immigrants and their stays in Laos.

4.3. Where Does Laos' Awareness State Stand and What Progress Has Been Done to Improve It?

Is Laos ready for the AEC? Does everyone understand what that represents? And what will the real impact be? Several business and political leaders have stated that Asean nations will require some more time beyond 2015 to fully realize the vision of the AEC. Two years now after Laos entered into the AEC, general Lao awareness of the AEC seems small. AEC impacts are little understood, with the AEC preparations limited only to certain groups of entrepreneurs, Small and Medium Size Enterprises (SME), business people, government organizations, provincial officers, and students[112]. There are a lot of sceptics who question whether the AEC can deliver anything tangible for Lao businesses.

We see today that a few businesses in Asean nations have expanded their operations to Laos, but only a very small number of Lao businesses have set up shops in other Asean countries[113]. The government has to acknowledge that some Lao businesses may not survive and others may struggle just to survive in this era of competition, which today is not in favor of Lao enterprises. Admittedly, the Asean Economic Community is driving growth of the business sector in Laos, which is helping to generate job opportunities for local people, but the pace of business and economic growth has not been as high as expected, according to a senior economist at the National Economic Research Institute, Dr. Leeber Leebouapao[114].

Despite the efforts of the government, seminars, and working sessions provided by the Lao National Chamber of Commerce and Industry (LNCCI), IFC, ADB, and other business associations including assistance from Germany (GIZ), Korea (KOTRA), Japan (JICA), Singapore, and Malaysia, family enterprises and most SMEs are still not sensitive to the arrival of the AEC; moreover, interest in the AEC is low amongst the population. The AEC can be a major catalyst for national growth, but few Lao businesses have grasped the concept of its importance.

The big difficulty is that the general public and businesses do not understand well what the AEC is all about, so they don't know how to benefit from the common regional market. There has been a lack of preparation on the part of Lao businesses and insufficient information provided by relevant organizations to them. This lack of understanding and awareness may obstruct Lao entrepreneurs from seizing the opportunity or the chance offered by the AEC, leaving them unprepared and unable to face the impact of the AEC at the right time.

If one thinks about the short term, Laos is definitively not ready yet for the AEC. Nevertheless, for the long term, things might change. To address this conversion, Lao businesses have to learn how to compete and to partner with regional businesses, and importantly the government should have the right arguments to attract Lao and foreign investors and to create a friendly environment for business. The Lao government needs to continue economic reforms, paying heed to concerns of the business community. Local businesses should also have the urge to connect and the professionalism to cooperate with Asean economic community.

4.3.1. Perception of Laos' Advantages and Disadvantages by the Public and Business Community

This section proposes the assessment of the current situation of Laos in relation to its geography, market, and ease of doing business, business environment, politics, and administrative issues. It suggests to highlight the existing advantages and disadvantages of the country compared to those of the Asean countries. The selected topics are: understanding and awareness; geographic location; familiarity with neighbors; development level; size of the domestic market and land; resources; economic relations with Asean; association with the global economy; convenience in doing business; business costs; political and administrative problems; and cooperation with government bodies. The evaluation of Laos assets' perception is given in Figure 30 below, based on the analysis of Laos' economic and business environment, and interviews that the author had with major stakeholders.

1. **Geographic location**: Laos is located in the center of the region, with its borders connected to four neighboring Asean countries. The position of Laos in relation to its neighbors offers today great potential as a land-link and a location to build further trade connections. Natural disaster risks are relatively low or almost nonexistent compared to

neighboring countries (flood, typhoon, earth quake). The country is turning from landlocked to land-linked.

2. **Development level**: Laos has a low development level in the region with its weak basic universal education, poorly skilled workers and few qualified personnel, weak quality of public education system, and poorly developed infrastructure, especially roads and public transports. Furthermore, services, IT, and manufacturing sectors remain greatly behind because of its underdeveloped human capital. Moreover, Lao law, institutions, and other facilities are still in the process of developing. Lao's kip currency is not accepted by neighbors in border trade transactions yet.

3. **Domestic market's size and land area**: Lao's economy is the smallest in the Asean region. The GDP per capita is one of the lowest (US$2,400 in 2016). The domestic market is tiny with a population of less than 7 million. However, a small urban middle class is emerging today. The country has enough land area for development and future investments.
4. **Resources**: Laos has abundant natural resources: copper, gold, coal, iron, hydroelectricity, and timber. Much of it remains unexploited, although many foreign firms are already in the country. The sector accounts for over 70 percent of exports. FDI inflows have a high concentration on the hydropower and mining sectors. Non-natural resources such as agriculture and tourism are potential sectors and not yet fully exploited.

5. **Economic relations with ASEAN**: Laos' trade with Asean was about 65% of the total Lao trade, with Thailand and Vietnam as the main suppliers and customers. Intra-Asean trade with Laos in 2014 reached US$3.7 billion; the intra-Asean share in total exports with Laos represented 54%, while the intra-Asean share in total imports hit 74%. Laos will further benefit from the AEC, particularly in terms of expanding exports to Asean. Singapore and Malaysia have also committed to purchase electricity from Laos. Intra-Asean relations are experiencing greater cementing of neighborly bonds with cultural, trade, and commercial exchanges.

6. **Association with the global economy**: The Lao economy is linked to international trade particularly in the resources sector; foreign investments are present in hydropower plants, mining, commercial agriculture, and tourism. Trade within Asean is important, while trade with the EU, Japan, and Australia is decreasing. However, there is still room for Laos to deal with the global economy.

7. **Understanding and awareness**: Lao people lack awareness about the AEC as to its importance, impact, and need for readiness, except for some large enterprises, SOEs, or organizations already involved in business with foreign countries. Indeed, few people understand the AEC's aim and its mechanism. The main task of the authorities is to raise awareness of the AEC's opportunities to the public.

8. **Knowledge of the neighbors**: Lao people are not competent in English, which is an international language. They lack knowledge about their neighbors and are therefore unfamiliar with them. The Lao education system does not facilitate study options on the languages, cultures, and economies of neighboring countries. Facilities are also non-conducive to trade, investment, or tourism in neighboring countries, although some progress has been made in the past few years. However, Laos is very familiar with Thailand and has a good understanding and knowledge of Vietnam.

9. **Doing business**: Although the World Bank's Doing Business ranking has ranked Laos 141th out of 190 countries in 2017, some factors are real obstacles to doing business in Laos according to businesspeople. They are: 1/ Starting a business: investment or conducting business in Laos involves having to contact many government agencies, with multiple processing steps, which are individually time-consuming. 2/ Receiving credit: SMEs have credit access restrictions and financial costs are still high. 3/ Taxation: a 24% profit tax rate applies to both domestic and foreign businesses. Taxes in Laos are among the lowest in the region: a low corporate income tax, a low progressive income tax, and a low VAT make the country attractive for business. The Lao taxation system is quite simple and straightforward to encourage

investment in the country and help develop its burgeoning economy. The country is the most open in the region for foreign investment, with no restriction for repatriating the dividends.

10. **Business costs**: Laos has the lowest labor cost among Asean countries. Its energy on average is competitive compared to the others. Therefore, investment in the world is likely to flow into the new emerging economies, such as Laos, Myanmar, or Cambodia. But the costs of transportation and logistics are very high, associated with high global oil prices. Therefore, Laos is likely to lose its investment attraction. Trading across the borders is a long process and time consuming, but this is going to be improved.

11. **Political and administrative problems**: Laos offers political stability and peace to investors. However, the development of Lao's economy is sometimes slow or occasionally restricted due to political and administrative problems. The political interests of the nation take precedence over the economy; furthermore, corruption brings high hidden costs in the business sector, not to mention the poor performance of government agencies and the slowness of the bureaucracy.

Comparing Lao's assets to those of other Asean countries, one can see some advantages from many angles, giving Laos an opportunity to become a regional economic, trade, and investment place of interest. Advantages such as political stability, abundance of natural resources and non-resources, low wages, emergence of an urban middle class, strategic location, and land, including fertile land, are available. However, some assets show weaknesses such as the business environment, high costs for transport and logistics (up to 70 percent), and the small size of its domestic market.

Taking into account the above analysis of strong and weak points of Laos' assets, people may question whether Laos is yet prepared to cope with economic integration. The answer is yes; it seems clear given Laos' engagement in the Asean arena. Overall, the above assessment is rather positive, and it shows that the country has tangible strengths.

Figure 30. Perception of Laos' Assets

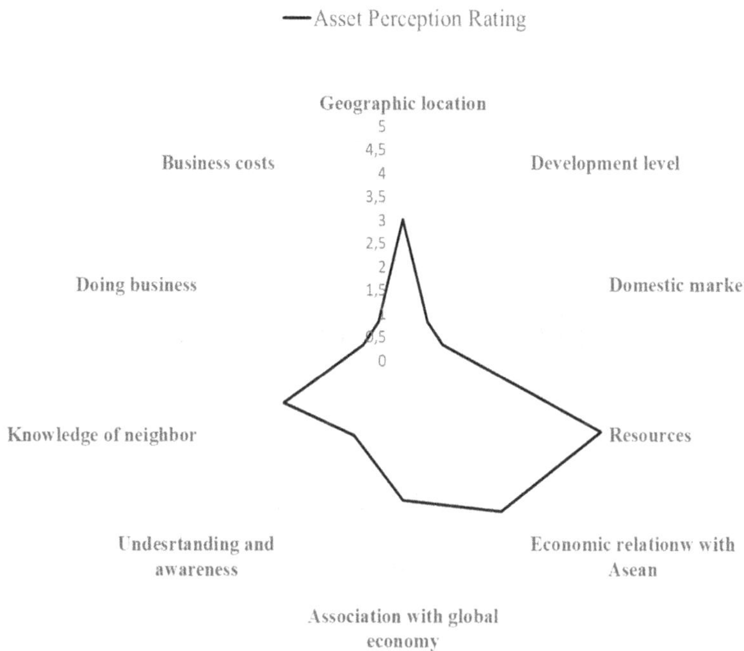

The graduation of the perception rating in Figure 30 goes from 0 to 5. With 1 rated as insignificant and 5 very well perceived.

In summary, Laos' direction has been forced by circumstances to follow the AEC's path and agenda. Nonetheless, the success of Laos in the AEC depends on how the concerned professional associations, state agencies, the Lao National Chamber of Commerce and Industry (LNCCI), SOEs, and private enterprises are supported effectively by the government and policy makers; additionally, the quality of government organizations' involvement in the negotiations both internal with all stakeholders and external with Asean state members should be constructive and fair. The Ministry of Industry and Commerce and their ongoing work in Asean trade negotiations seek to get the best deal they can for Laos. Besides, government agencies and businesses should be proactive and provide more promotion instruments in order to "sell" the attractiveness of Laos to Asean businesses and investors through partnership and alliance.

4.3.2. What Progress Has Been Made to Improve Information and Understanding on Economic Integration?

Taking into account the complex nature of AEC integration and the large number of stakeholders involved, the Ministry of Industry and Commerce is partnering with the Regional Economic Integration of Laos into Asean, Trade and Entrepreneurship Development (RELATED) project via the Lao-German Development Cooperation to assist various government agencies to steer, coordinate, communicate, monitor, and evaluate this whole process. It also aims to raise awareness about the AEC and to intensify related dialogue processes between public and private sector stakeholders.

To address the lack of awareness and understanding by businesses and people regarding the AEC, the Ministry of Industry and Commerce, Ministry of Finance, the LNCCI, international institutions, and donors have conducted many training courses from 2013 to present, covering more than several hundred participants who are company CEOs, small and medium-sized entrepreneurs, managers, bankers, farmers, educators, government officials, and the general public. Through a network of a few government agencies and the LNCCI, numerous working sessions have been held for more than one hundred participants in all the sectors of business, covering various aspects of trade. But there's still more that needs to be done to fully capitalize on the opportunities that come with regional integration. According to Lao economist experts, less than 10 percent of Lao enterprises have knowledge about the community.

With the Asean Policy Blueprint for SME Development, Asean launched a number of support initiatives for SMEs in Laos. The Asean SME Agencies Working Group (SMEWG) is the Asean body responsible for SME development and promotion. It cooperates and works on various issues with the LNCCI and other government agencies to increase awareness and the development of SMEs.

Since the Lao government pointed out the need for businesses to understand opportunities and challenges following the birth of the AEC, conferences, meetings, seminars, and workshops have taken place in Vientiane and provincial capitals throughout the years of 2016 and 2017, which offered an opportunity for government officers, researchers, students, and enterprises to seek ways to help the business circle bring into full play the opportunities and cope with the challenges.

Importantly, Laos has stepped up cooperation with other member countries and participated more deeply in the global value chain, as reflected through its engagement in the AEC Blueprint 2025. There has been significant progress regarding the AEC's initiatives since 2016. As a matter of fact, at the ASEAN Summit 2016 held in Vientiane, Asean leaders have adopted "ASEAN Connectivity 2025" and "Initiative for ASEAN Integration (IAI) Work Plan III," which are deemed as supplementary to the completion of "ASEAN Community Vision 2025."

Shortly after the AEC came officially into effect, some major actions have been taken and progress has been made in various areas towards businesses to fulfill the AEC Blueprint 2025 obligations. Through negotiations with ASEAN Secretariat and Asean member states, the following are key achievements that Laos has contributed:

- Three priority sector Mutual Recognition Arrangements (MRAs) have been established for medicinal products and cosmetics, as well as electrical equipment and electronics to standardize the safety and quality standards of such products across the region. The Blueprint 2025 also sought to create a level playing field through the adoption of harmonized legal and regulatory frameworks in the areas of competition, consumer protection, and intellectual property policy.
- To encourage cross-border labor mobility, eight MRAs have been concluded for services including engineering, nursing, architectural, and medical, giving skilled workers in these fields the flexibility of having their qualifications or certificates recognized in different Asean member states.
- Asean member states have concluded and opened a tariff portal site (tariff-finder.asean.org) and a trade service portal (Assist.asean.org) to help business people realize the real benefits the AEC provides. It has also established a system to monitor and evaluate the AEC for the effective implementation of AEC 2025. The Asean member states came up with implementation plans for various areas, such as small- and medium-sized firms, customs clearance, faster trade flows, and intellectual property rights. They also revealed a comprehensive implementation plan encompassing all sectors in 2017.
- The 36th Asean Air Transport Working Group and other related meetings took place in Vientiane in September 2017, during which

they made a commitment to enhancing cooperation on air transport services. Asean member state countries have worked to build up the Asean Single Aviation Market, which is seen as one of the key milestones in developing the road map for the establishment of the AEC. It expects to fully liberalize air travel between member states in the Asean region, allowing Asean countries and airlines operating in the region to directly benefit from the growth in air travel around the world, and also freeing up tourism, trade, investment, and service flows between member states[115]. Meetings with a related Asean group of experts are ongoing to finalize the Asean Open Sky Agreement. Laos is already to some extent building up the Asean single market and liberalized the air market to the region.

- Asean is working to enhance cooperation between member states in the area of cultural heritage protection by adopting the Asean Vision 2015, following new guidance from the bloc's leaders. Asean heads of state and government expressed concern about the increasing threats to tangible cultural heritage as a result of illicit trafficking in cultural property.
- Asean ministers under the Asean Socio-Cultural Community (ASCC) have voiced their continued support for the realization of the Community's priorities this year, welcoming a series of activities in 2017. In their joint statement, the ministers acknowledged the progress of implementation of the ASCC Blueprint 2025 and the development of work plans for the various sectoral bodies of the ASCC, including cross-cutting initiatives and community building issues. The ASCC's goals are to build a people-oriented and people-centered Asean; peace and stability in the region; maritime security and cooperation; inclusive, innovation-led growth; and Asean resiliency; and to create Asean as a model and a global player. The ministers committed to support the finalization of the Asean instrument to implement the Asean Declaration for the Protection of the Rights of Migrant Workers.

In addition to the above meetings between the Lao government's ministries and those of Asean member states, many workshops are given by Lao government agencies, international organizations and institutions, and professional associations, to the business sector. A few examples of seminars and workshops are listed below:

- The Vientiane Economic Forum, organized by the Ministry of Industry and Commerce, the Europe Chamber of Commerce in Laos, and the LNCCI[116]. More than 100 entrepreneurs from Laos, European and regional countries met in January 2017 to debate trends and opportunities in the Asean market in Vientiane. The conference on "Business Transforming Trends in the AEC" is the first of a planned series which the organizers labeled as the "Vientiane Economic Forum".
- In May 2017, more than 200 government employees and SME operators discussed opportunities and challenges to capital market access in AEC at a seminar. The seminar on "Opportunity and Challenges for Lao SMEs to Capital Market Access in AEC" was held in Vientiane and organized by the Vientiane Industry and Commerce Department in collaboration with the Vientiane Chamber of Commerce and Industry and Lao Securities Exchange (LSX).
- The LNCCI and the Lao Young Entrepreneur Association held frequent meetings in Vientiane with business sectors from various provinces. The objectives aimed to discuss how to strengthen the capacity of local entrepreneurs so they do not become victims of regional economic integration in order to reinforce the capacity of Lao businesses to benefit from the AEC.
- It should also be mentioned that the Foreign Trade Policy Department of the Ministry of Industry and Commerce organized an Advanced Training Course in its Training of Trainers Program on "Enhancing Capacity on Trade Policies and Negotiations". The training course was co-hosted by the United Nations Economic and Social Commission for Asia and the Pacific (UNESCAP) and supported by the RELATED project. The objective of the course was to prepare 12 Lao trainers to be qualified to offer courses on trade policies and negotiations to students in the country. At the end of the program, Laos will boast a dozen highly qualified experts who can lead training courses on trade in goods policies and negotiations for officials.
- To be pointed out also was setting up the first SME Service Centre (SSC) in Laos aimed at improving the environment for SMEs to do business in Laos as well as easing access to their markets. It was established under the joint efforts of the SME Promotion Department of the Ministry of Industry and Commerce, the LNCCI, and supported by the RELATED project. This center inaugurated in February 2017

provides advice, information and training for SMEs preparing to do business in the AEC. Speaking at the opening ceremony, Oudet Souvannavong, President of the LNCCI said "Small and Medium Enterprises cover 98 percent to 99 percent of all enterprises in Laos. That is the reason the government is trying to promote SMEs by outlining the decrees on SME promotion in 2004. In 2011, the decree has been upgraded into the Law on SME Promotion in a bid to strengthen SMEs in Laos[117]"

- A seminar co-organized by the LNCCI and the Japan International Cooperation Agency (JICA) drew about 100 representatives from business units, as well as students from various colleges and the National University of Laos (NUoL) in August 2017. The LNCCI, on behalf of the government, was looking to encourage more new startups by entrepreneurs from among the ranks of SMEs. The startup seminars offered the opportunity for people with a business idea to find a path to success and to grow. The government continues to work with partners to encourage the up and coming generation as they join a new wave of regional entrepreneurs ready to take their chances and risks amid numerous opportunities and challenges in an era of enhanced cross-border competition in the AEC[118].

To date, as mentioned above, energies have been deployed both by the government and its agencies to raise firms' awareness about the AEC and its opportunities for investment, trade, and private sector development, in order to motivate deeper private sector and business people's involvement in the AEC. It is a long process, and the results will come through continuous training and education to be provided to all stakeholders. Actually, according to the AEC Scorecard, Laos has done well in meeting milestones. The country's performance has been above average in meeting various indicators leading to the full implementation of the AEC. Achievements to date are attributable partly to the openness of the Lao economy and Laos' 2013 accession to the WTO, which requires Laos to put in place rules and regulations in compliance with international trade laws. The high-level policy commitments also partly explain Laos' willingness and preparedness for the AEC.

4.3.3. Progress Towards the AEC Blueprint 2025 for Laos: What Are the Remaining Challenges?

There is so much that still needs to be done versus what was promised when Asean leaders collectively agreed to accelerate the establishment of the Asean milestones.

The complex set of initiatives to promote greater economic interaction in the region poses significant challenges for the capacity of Laos' institutions and the country's private sector. The reason is simple: most public institutions in Laos are characterized by a lack of financial and human resources, uneven coordination vertically and horizontally, and a lack of sufficient knowledge to perform tasks effectively.

Progress towards achieving the AEC Blueprint has been made, but according to the AEC Scorecard, a monitoring and evaluation metric developed by Asean, considerable challenges remain (see the summary below):

1. **ASEAN Trade in Goods Agreements (ATIGA)**: 90% tariffs in Asean have been eliminated, but certain parts of the 10-nation economic bloc including Laos is lag behind others in full implementation of the ATIGA. The leaders of Asean adopted September 2017 the Asean Framework Agreement on Facilitation of Goods in Transit and the various sectoral work plans relevant to trade facilitation. They also endorsed the Asean Harmonized Tariff Nomenclature 2017 and its implementation towards a simplified uniformed classification of goods. Current status: well advanced.

2. **Non-Tariff Barriers (NTB)**: Non-Tariff Barriers are seen as discriminatory measures for less advanced countries, they are: red tape, diverse pro duct standards, import bans, import licensing, additional import requirements, and technical barriers to trade. Behind the-border interventions have also increasingly emerged as a new form of protectionism since the recent global economic crisis. Little progress has been made to address the above sensitive issues. Current status: ongoing.

3. **Rules of Origin (ROO)**: Non-Tariff Barriers are seen as discriminatory measures for less advanced countries, they are: red

tape, diverse pro duct standards, import bans, import licensing, additional import requirements, and technical barriers to trade. Current status: Behind the-border interventions have also increasingly emerged as a new form of protectionism since the recent global economic crisis. Current status: in progress.

4. **Trade Facilitations Agreements (TFA)**: Trade facilitation aims at simplifying and harmonizing custom procedures, streamlining product standards, ensuring transparency, as well as providing transport and logistics services, in order to reduce trade costs. Asean member state launched a multitude of initiatives in this area. A wide gap still exists in terms of the number of days needed to carry out exports and imports, with the highest number registered in Laos (45 days) and the lowest in Singapore (3 days), according to World Bank data on cross-border trade. Major obstacles for realizing the AEC remain: customs procedures and modernization. Current status: in progress but slow.

5 **ASEAN Single Window (ASW)**: The ASW is an initiative to provide an integrated platform between government agencies and end-users (economic operators) to expedite cargo clearance and release in the AEC. No tangible results yet. The ASW is an attempt to standardize the customs clearance process, simplify and standardize documentation requirements, and expedite clearance times throughout the region. Current status: ongoing. At the present, National Single Windows in four states are operational, while two others are being developed including Laos

6 **Harmonization and Standardization**: Achievements on many products and technical procedures are still far of expectation. Current status: in progress, few results noticed.

7 **Intellectual Property Rights (IPR)**: Some efforts have been made at IPR protection and harmonization at the Asean level, registration and enforcement remains at the national level. Asean has established an ASEAN Working Group on Intellectual Property Cooperation (AWGIPC), comprised of the IP offices of the 10 member nations, which focuses on regional harmonization of IPR enforcement issues.

Current status: consultations with members are ongoing. To date, it is difficult to see how IP related elements of the AEC Blueprint will be implemented.

8 **ASEAN Framework Agreement on Services (AFAS)**: Free Flow of Services is one of the key features of the Single Market. Liberalization Services is negotiated under the ASEAN Framework Agreement on Services. AFAS is committed to reduce or eliminate restrictions on providing services and establishing a commercial presence for service suppliers across the region. Asean member states have been gradually increasing Market Access and guaranteeing National Treatment for services suppliers from other Asean. AFAS is aiming to eliminate restrictions to trade in services among Asean countries in order to improve the efficiency and competitiveness of Asean services suppliers. Current status: negotiations are ongoing on many issues. Implementation of liberalization commitments is slow. Liberalization of Trade in Services in Asean is almost at the beginning.

9 **Financial Integration under ASEAN**: Under the AEC Blueprint, Asean seeks to achieve a well-integrated and smoothly functioning regional financial system, characterized by more liberalized capital account regimes and inter-linked capital markets. Under the financial sector integration vision for 2025 encompasses three strategic objectives, namely financial integration, financial inclusion, and financial stability, and three cross-cutting areas (Capital Account Liberalization, Payment and Settlement Systems, and Capacity Building). With integrated capital markets in Asean, Asean leaders can expect improved access to capital markets, establishment of necessary market infrastructure, lower transaction costs, and more efficient business processes. Current status: 7 rounds of negotiations of Financial Service Liberalization including Banking Integration have been completed. The Asean Banking Integration Framework (ABIF), which expresses that Asean member states will work towards allowing entry of Qualified Asean Banks in the region. Laos has not yet been approved.

10 **Capital Market Development (CMD)**: ASEAN also focuses on developing, interlinking and deepening the region's capital markets by building capacity and laying the long-term infrastructure to achieve integration of capital markets in ASEAN. Current status: this will be implemented through harmonization of domestic laws and regulations and linkage of market infrastructure.

11 **ASEAN Open Skies**: The ratification of the Asean Open Skies agreements is not fully completed with all members yet. Current status: Ongoing discussion.

To conclude, Asean economic integration has advanced from AEC 2015 to AEC 2025, with many of the tasks under the earlier Blueprint yet to be implemented. Despite the promise in the new Blueprint to deliver comprehensive sustainable growth and development, the pace of AEC implementation is going to slow down significantly in the face of increasing challenges. While almost all of the AEC 2025 commitments are met, many will simply pave the way for future actions, and the rest will remain, too sensitive to be adopted at the national level in the stipulated time-frame, such as the liberalization of people, NTBs, and facilitation of free flow in services.

4.4. The Single Market and Production Base Do Not Offer an Advantageous Impact for Laos in the Short Term

The first AEC pillar seeks to create a single market and production base through a free flow of goods, services, investment, skilled labor, and freer flow of capital. Cumulatively, these aim for a more liberalized market that provides its population with greater opportunities to trade and do business within the region, with reduced trade costs and improved investment regimes that make Asean a more attractive investment destination for both international and domestic investors. Through the AEC, Asean is marching forward with a new roadmap toward 2025 by a common aspiration based on "One Vision, One Identity, and One Community." The prospects for Asean growth will still remain strong, at around a respectable 5 percent growth. But there is still much room for further expansion. Enhancement of Asean growth naturally would translate into higher GDP growth for member states[119]. Laos will certainly take advantage of this move, making Asean a highly integrated regional market and regional production base.

Under the goal of creating a single market and production base are the central themes as mentioned above. For goods, the aim has been no less than to eliminate trade bottlenecks; that has involved the discouraging task of removing tariffs, reducing paperwork, and cutting the waiting times of getting products to market, with the added benefit of reducing risks associated with consigning goods.

Notable progress has been made on the AEC's first pillar, far more compared to other pillars, which is fundamental to developing a single market and a production base in goods. Tariffs have been substantially reduced: to date, the ASEAN-6 have virtually eliminated their intra-regional tariffs, with 99.2% of tariff lines at 0%. For the CLVM, the figure stands at 90.86%, giving an Asean average of 95.99%. These developments will encourage intra-Asean trade in manufacturing and agricultural goods. Although progress has been made with the signing of Mutual Recognition Agreements (MRAs) in eight professions such as engineers, nurses, surveyors, medical professionals, architects, dental professionals, accountants, and tourism professionals, implementation of the trade in services agreement is much slower. They constitute an important step towards the free movement of skilled labor. Thus, Laos will be able to hire skilled labor and technicians to satisfy the need of its economic growth.

Asean has endorsed three main agreements in order to create the Single Market: the ASEAN Trade in Goods Agreement (ATIGA) in 2010, the ASEAN Framework Agreement on Services (AFAS) in 1995, and the ASEAN Comprehensive Investment Agreement (ACIA) in 2012. Under ATIGA, tariffs have been reduced to 0-5% for 96% of products in Asean. Under AFAS, Asean member states liberalized services trade and allow for up to 70% of foreign equity investment in most service sectors. Finally, with ACIA, Asean countries adopted a modern investment agreement that eases investment restrictions in most sectors, grants investor protection, and provides dispute settlement mechanisms. ATIGA allows a transition period for CLMV countries. Indeed, Asean-6 (the founder countries) should have completed the reduction of customs tariffs by 2015, while Laos is allowed to complete this task by 2018. Admittedly, ATIGA was essential for many developing countries including Laos that are dependent on exports (electricity, mining, and timber). This helps Laos very much to be included in the international supply chain among Asean countries and to diversify its export items and export destination away from only resource products to Thailand, Vietnam, and China.

It is shown that tariff elimination alone, however, does not create an open market. Benefitting from intra-regional trade preferences can be made easier, among other factors, with continuous simplification of Rules of Origin (ROO) as well as the ASEAN Self Certification Project. As a matter of fact, Laos' trade is still facing cross-border transaction hurdles and the high costs of border tolls with Thailand and Vietnam.

However, tariff elimination is not a clear-cut process that guarantees the free flow of goods, as member states reserve the right to increase specific taxes that act as tariffs. Laos has already increased taxes on tobacco, alcohol products, spare parts, and some building material, which distort competitive pricing on imports. It has been said that trade barriers for the export of agricultural products to neighbors have been stalled by stringent sanitary and phytosanitary regulations despite ATIGA aiming to reduce them. While other Asean products, especially from the advanced economy member states, are flooding the Lao market, the flip side is that there is a serious deficit for Laos because it does not produce much. Importantly, most commodities are primarily exported raw for processing outside of Laos, thus denying Laos of crucial value added if the products were processed in the country. Non-tariff barriers are still in place in a few countries despite the fact that on paper they are supposed to be eliminated. In that sense, reducing restrictions on trade in services and monitoring NTBs are priorities under the first pillar.

Since the AEC has come into effect, the objectives such as free movement of skilled labor, free movement of capital, and investment are still far from being achieved. In terms of investment and services, liberalization of 154 sectors was scheduled to be completed. So far, only some sectors such as retail, wholesaling, and transport have been opened while banking and insurance have not been opened widely yet. In these sectors of business, Lao enterprises are little present and competitive. Furthermore, Lao businesses are still confronted with many administrative and technical problems when exporting their products to Asean member countries. For example, businesses have to deal with several issues when it comes to the export of goods to neighboring was scheduled to be completed. So far, only some sectors such as retail, wholesaling, and transport have been opened while banking and insurance have not been opened widely yet. In these sectors of business, Lao enterprises are little present and competitive. Furthermore, Lao businesses are still confronted with many administrative and technical problems when exporting their products to Asean member countries. For example, businesses have to deal with several issues when it comes to the export of goods to neighboring countries, because product labelling will have to be in the language of the importing country. That is another challenge for the Lao government. In contrast, products imported into Laos from neighboring countries do not have to carry labels in the Lao language, one of several disparities between Laos and other Asean countries that need definitively to be addressed if the principle of one single market and production base is followed. There are also regulations that have to be complied with in regard to sanitary and phytosanitary measures, Rules of Origin, and other measures. Also, in the AEC agreements, more than 120 service activities are categorized as being eligible to be traded between Asean countries under the ASEAN Trade in Services Agreements. The trade services areas that will most affect Laos are logistics, tourism, and banking services, due to the lack of know-how and insufficient preparation of staff to overcome the challenge

However, under the Free Flow of Capital framework, Laos will be able to integrate its financial market into those of other Asean countries. The financial market integration will facilitate access to capital for socio-economic development of the country and help businesses to enter into Lao capital market and regional finance for their growth. Moreover, under the Free Flow of Investment framework, more intra-Asean investors and extra-Asean investors are expected to increase their investments, especially in potential sectors such as energy, mines, agriculture, tourism, and real estate; the investment will be an important capital source for the socioeconomic development of Laos[120].

The solidarity and enthusiasm shown by Asean members in trying to meet the AEC goals are notable. Visible progress has been achieved in implementing the first pillar (particularly in reducing tariffs for goods trade and implementing single windows for better trade facilitation). Finally, Asean integration will have a positive impact for Laos as the country works to attract more business. With the reduction in tariffs, the creation of a single market, and the improvement of infrastructure, investors will look for countries with a favorable regulatory environment that serves the Asean market. Laos already has this environment, particularly with the implementation of its numerous SEZs as well as a proven track record of working with businesses from intra-Asean and extra-Asean countries.

4.5. What Benefit Will the AEC Create for Laos?

The goal of regional economic integration would both establish Asean as a more dynamic and integrated regional organization. In the AEC Blueprint 2025, the Asean is already set to become highly integrated and develop an interconnected economy over the next decade. It is also expected to rise globally as one market with each member gaining from each other's strengths, thus increasing its competitiveness and opportunities for development.

Without tariff barriers, the ten Asean nations are becoming a single production base and attracting trade, investment, and tourists from the rest of the world. Businesses operating in one Asean nation can export to the rest of the group.

Based on the results of the study "Realizing AEC: a Comprehensive Assessment[121]", the AEC should lead to a 5.3% increase in regional welfare (US$69 billion) due to elimination of NTBs, lower trade costs, and anticipated increases in FDI. Additional likely benefits (e.g. free movement of skilled labor, standardization and harmonization, best practices, and greater macroeconomic stability) will increase. Potentially, Laos stands to gain substantial benefits due to the liberalization and reform efforts to improve efficiency and competitiveness, for example by leveraging the AEC to undertake politically sensitive domestic reforms (business transparency, corruption, fiscal leakage); improving access to Asean capital, investment, technology, technical assistance from Asean countries, development experience, and best practices; encouraging greater participation in global production networks and value chains; and finding greater leverage in regional and international negotiations. Furthermore, for Laos is a Least Developed Country (LDC) in Asean, the EU allows Laos to use inputs from Asean member states, except Brunei and Singapore, to produce goods in Laos and export to the EU market duty free and quota free. Goods like garments, shoes, and electronic assembling in Laos are examples of these benefits. Also, Laos, like other new Asean member states (Myanmar, Cambodia, and Vietnam) has benefited from technical assistance provided by ASEAN-6 and other ASEAN Dialogue Partners like the US, the EU, Japan, China, Korea, and Canada in terms of funding, hardware, capacity building programs, study visits, and training courses.

Indeed, the AEC opens more regional cooperation and improves the scale efficiencies, dynamism, and competitiveness of Asean members. It enables easier movement of goods, services, investment, capital, and people. Ultimately, it is offering new ways of coordinating supply chains, or access to new markets for established products. The benefits that Laos will gain from these advantages are slow, but in the medium term they will be substantial. Asean countries are seen by foreign investors as a potential market, a single market of over 610 million consumers. Asean remains committed to the global economy at the regional level thanks to Free Trade Agreements with China, Japan, Korea, India, Australia, New Zealand, and Hong Kong[122]. These countries have already invested in Laos, particularly China. The AEC will reinforce undoubtedly trade relations between Laos and the global economy. SMEs accounted for 96% of enterprises and between 50-85% of domestic employment across Asean. The Singapore government fully realizes the challenge and the opportunity that the AEC will represent to SMEs and is putting both the planning talent and the resources to better support their SMEs. Laos SMEs accounted for 98%; integrating these SMEs and supporting them in the initial period will be a challenge throughout Asean. The tourism sector is also a great hope for Laos and could benefit Asean's travelers. Laos will benefit from Thailand and Singapore's assistance to upgrade both facilities and services, since Laos has little experience in this industrial sector. Healthcare is one of the sectors to be internationalized, a sector from which Laos can benefit under the AEC. Today, international and regional patients travel from one country to another seeking better care at lower cost. Laos is partnering with Japanese medical doctors to set up an international hospital to attract such patients. There is also a plan to establish a nursing home for elderly people, particularly for Japanese senior citizens. Thai hospitals and other Malaysian and Korean investors are also expected to step up the pace of joint ventures in Laos to help give them a better platform to better take care of developing AEC opportunities.

The advent of the AEC will give a boost to infrastructure in Laos: construction of new roads to comply with regional standards, upgrading the existing national road network, and building railway lines to facilitate transport and connectivity throughout the country and the region. As a matter of fact, to increase intra-regional trade among Laos, China, and other countries of Southeast Asia, a railway connecting Laos with China is under construction. Another railway project from the Savannakhek to Vietnamese border is in the pipeline. There was also talk to erect a 500 KV transmission line to supply electricity to Malaysia and Singapore via Thai power grids. Similarly, the financial sector companies stand to gain from the increase in trade and investment flows, providing business opportunities for financial institutions. Thus, the AEC will benefit Laos because the country is between three huge markets that deal and trade and carry transport across the country. As Laos is a node of connectivity between Thailand-China-Vietnam, logistics companies could see greater opportunities with the freer flow of goods. One has seen some logistic companies setting up in joint venture with Lao companies in the SEZs (Thakkek, Savan-Seno, and Boten) and are positioning Laos as part of the global supply chain. Regarding Lao consumers, they are the majority that benefit from access to a cheaper and wider range of imported goods and services, a more competitive domestic market environment, and consumer protection.

As far as business is concerned, a young generation of Lao entrepreneurs and young professionals will come up with new mindsets and will be exposed to a regional way of doing business. Importantly, SMEs stand to benefit from larger market access and lower input and transaction costs through elimination of tariffs and NTBs on goods and improved regulatory environment on services; improved trade facilitation such as customs, logistics, transportation connectivity (ASEAN Highways Network, Air Service Transport), and ICT infrastructure; and rationalized rules of origin, product, and technical standards.

In the end, what benefits will the AEC bring to Laos and how? Integration with other Asean economies will offer new prospects for Laos, which was previously limited by a small domestic market. As a matter of fact, the Lao economy has started to reap the benefits of increased integration within the region. Singapore had shown an inclination to relocate its businesses to developing regions like Laos, as Singaporean President Tony Tan Keng Yam urged Singaporean firms to "move quickly and seize first-mover advantage in developing markets like Cambodia and Laos". Singapore has also recently signed pro-business policies like the Avoidance of Double Taxation Agreement with Laos, which aims to boost Singaporean investors' confidence in Laos' economy by eliminating the double taxation relating to the cross-border transaction between the two countries.

Obviously, a fully integrated Asean will provide opportunities to attract domestic investment that will in return create jobs for skilled and unskilled workers within Laos.

A small number of Japanese, Malaysian, Chinese, Thai, Vietnamese, and Korean companies are already set up their manufacturing and assembly factories particularly in Savannakhek SEZ. The Special Economic Zones have also successfully attracted manufacturers from Europe and North America. The Lao government is continuing to attract foreigner production units from Thailand to its SEZs and benefit from the cheaper labor and production costs.

Benefits from the Asean economic integration will not arise inevitably for Laos. The economy will face increased competition in almost all sectors. Lao companies will need to adapt, to modernize and to become more efficient and productive in order to compete with stronger producers from the region. The simple reason is that many of the world's leading electronics producers and spare parts manufacturers have already established factories in the neighboring countries; these industries would not move easily and switch their production bases to a country that does not have the necessary tools and skills. For many Lao enterprises and people, given the fact of Laos' low level of economic development, it would likely benefit less than most other Asean members from the formation of the single market.

In the end the AEC will be in all ways beneficial for Laos, because Laos is a country without significant industry, deficit in human resources, small population, and a tiny market. Laos will continue to enjoy the Asean's engine.

Taking in consideration of the above, the first priority of Laos is to produce more skilled or professionally trained workers in industrial sectors as the demand of markets for these skills remains high. Admittedly, Asean is set to be one production base, but Laos will go slower according to its progress and pace. This depends on the government's determination and the speed at which it organizes its industry base and human resources development in order to enjoy all the benefits given by the AEC. Asean is working hard to implement a single market and a production base, hence bringing opportunities to all of its member countries and residents, according to Prof. Hidetoshi Nishimura, President of the Economic Research Institute for ASEAN and East Asia (ERIA).

4.6. Obstacles and Challenges for Laos

The AEC has allowed an increase in business transactions across Asean. Intra-Asean and extra-Asean trades have seen a higher mobility of capital, labor, and goods and services within the Asean region, and these have resulted in more opportunities in neighboring Asean countries. As a consequence, the AEC stimulated many firms in Asean to invest in other countries within the area, such as in Laos. With the current rising Laos economy, many countries globally are interested in investing in the Laos market. Investors also are interested in entering into this market. Conversely, some Lao enterprises may also thinking about expanding their business out of the country.

Although the Asean Economic Community (AEC) has resulted in increased economic activity between Laos and other regional bloc countries, Laos still faces numerous challenges to benefit from regional economic integration.

This section proposes to identify the obstacles and the challenges that will face Laos in the regional integration's context, several of which Laos needs to promptly address so it can continue to benefit from the AEC.

Among some of them, Laos has already stressed its concern about the Non-tariff Barriers (NTBs), considering them as discriminatory when promoting trade in services to some of the most advanced economies of Asean member states, as the country is at an early stage of economic development and transition and will not be able to fulfill any additional import requirements, inefficient customs documents, and local ownership regulations[123]. NTBs are a form of restrictive trade set up using quota systems, embargoes, sanctions, or exorbitant fees that replace tariffs and typically take the form of protectionist policies, as explained by Jayant Menon[124].

While tariff rates have come down substantially across Asia and the Pacific, non-tariff barriers remain significant, adding that these are the "real impediments to trade". These policies are detrimental to long-term trade growth, especially across the economic corridors of the Greater Mekong Subregion (GMS), an area that includes Cambodia, Laos, Vietnam, Thailand, Myanmar, and Yunnan province in southern China. For Laos, the problems still arise when larger countries use protectionist non-tariff barriers that generally leave out poorer countries because they have not reached the same level of transparency and efficiency. Protectionist sentiment in some member countries, where powerful local industries are reluctant to open up to competition, is also a problem and obstacle, therefore making it difficult for Laos to enter these markets. For example, non-tariff barriers to trade are still used widely in the form of licenses, although countries are required to scale down and totally remove them under the Free Trade Agreement (FTA). Another example of a NTB in use is inconsistent and unreasonable labeling and packaging requirements that impedes free trade across Asean. And while on paper eight groups of professions will enjoy easier access to regional talent through Mutual Recognition Agreements (MRAs), local barriers and regulation mean that there will be no overnight changes. Thailand, for example, recognizes the qualifications of foreign doctors, but they will still need to obtain a license by taking examinations in Thai; this is also the case for Lao doctors who want to practice the profession in Thailand. Laos still faces various barriers in promoting trade in services as the country is not yet well developed. Among the identified sectors with entry barriers are healthcare and tourism. The Ministry of Industry and Commerce was working with concerned stakeholders on trade in services and on developing strategies for leveraging the potential for regional cooperation to reduce barriers to trade in services.

As far as challenges are concerned, according to the Secretary General of the LNCC, Phouxay Thepphavong, at a workshop on ISO standards, when looking to expand their output, Lao SMEs are finding the cost of international standards certification a major challenge. The cost of ISO certification is very high for the budget of most enterprises, which is a major hurdle for SMEs. Presently, accessing affordable finance is a significant challenge for SMEs that forms another barrier to ISO application. On the other hand, SMEs have the duty to improve their capacity to develop products to world standards. With Laos sharing a border with China, one of the world's biggest markets, SMEs have a good opportunity to improve their production standards in response to customers' requirements and broaden their international market. Besides, it is necessary for the governments to make all-out efforts to narrow development gaps within Asean as well as between Asean and other regions, and to promote economic integration to improve the SMEs' competitiveness and enhance infrastructure connectivity, which are huge challenges for Laos during the next ten years.

Among other challenges to address is the abnormal situation such as why large Thai trucks are carrying goods to Laos, but Lao trucks cannot enter Thai territory? Lao goods need to be transferred to Thai trucks when being transported in Thailand. Access to loans for SMEs is another big issue for most businesses, without forgetting to mention that the practice of English language is today a challenge for businesses and people to deal with in the international market. Lao enterprises are facing a lack of competencies, international recognition, and financial credit compared to Asean countries.

We summarize in Table 10 below the main obstacles or barriers and challenges that Laos has faced depriving the country to benefit from regional economic integration. To be successful, survive, prosper, and lead in a more competitive environment, Lao business people may require some changes in their way of thinking and doing business, paying more attention to and caring more about human resources, and having support from the government and it agencies.

Table 10. Main Obstacles and Challenges for Laos

Obstacles/Barriers	Challenges
▪ Import license ▪ Protectionism ▪ Equity limitations ▪ Local laws ▪ Embargoes on products ▪ Administrative Sanctions ▪ Technical specifications ▪ Labelling-Packaging ▪ Communication ▪ Compliance standards ▪ Slowness border crossing	▪ No seaports ▪ Tiny domestic market ▪ Competitiveness ▪ Transport Logistics ▪ Internet access ▪ Human resources ▪ International network ▪ Weakness of SMEs ▪ Capital financing ▪ English language ▪ From Landlocked to Land linked transformation

Notes

[104] What the AEC means for Laos, East Asia Forum, 1/01/2016.
[105] Laos the great leap forward, published in Foreign Affairs, Laos, November-December 2016.
[106] World Bank Doing Business. 2013, www.doingbusiness.org/rankings.
[107] Logistic improvement to lift Laos in Asean trade, Vientiane Times, 02/06/2017.
[108] Laos cuts import tariffs after AEC integration, Vientiane Times, 4/02/2016.
[109] Plans put in action to turn Laos into a land link, Asian editors told, 29/08/2017.
[110] Nation's SMEs circle in on market opportunities through online portal, Vientiane, 31/08/2017.
[111] Viet Nam- Laos officially open "one-stop-shop" customs model, Vietnam News, 6/02/2015.
[112] 50 Informal interviews carried out in May-June 2017 with government organizations, business people, SMEs, provincial officers, students, and shop owners in Vientiane, Savannakhet, Oudomxay, and Pakse.
[113] In August 2017, Phonsavang Insurance (APA) Co., Ltd. has signed a partnership agreement with an international reinsurance operator, Hannover Re SE Malaysia Branch, to mark the progress of APA and the insurance industry in Laos as a whole; At the same time, APA Co. Ltd. has also signed a business cooperation and development agreement with a major Thai insurance operator, Bangkok Insurance Public Company Limited, and its branch office in Laos. Another Lao Logistic Group Company Limited signed an agreement on August 2017 in Vientiane in partnership with the Linfox International Group (Australian company with strong base in Asean) aiming to develop the logistic system in Laos to better improve logistics connectivity to neighboring countries in the region. These two joint-ventures are not directly with Asean companies, but with foreign companies already have strong business in the region.
[114] AEC driving Lao economic growth but at slower pace, Vientiane Times, 1/04/2017.
[115] Asean members give further boost to single aviation market, Vientiane Times, 5/09/2017.
[116] Entrepreneurs debate trends and opportunities in Asean, Vientiane Times, 26/01/2017.
[117] SME service centre to promote regional business integration in Laos, Asia News Network, 21/02/2017.

[118] Entrepreneurial efforts bridge small businesses, start up gaps, Vientiane Times30/08/2017.
[119] Key message delivered by Chief Minister of the State of Selangor, YAB Dato' Seri Mohamed Azmin bin Ali, during the Selangor-Asean Business Conference, held in Malaysia on September 11-12-2017.
[120] Opportunities and Challenges of Lao PDR's Integration into ASEAN Economic Community (AEC) by and after 2015, Dr. Leeber Leebouapao.
[121] Study made by Professor Michael G. Plummer from the Johns Hopkins University and Ms. Chia Siow Yue from Singapore Institute of International Affairs in 2009
[122] Asean signed the FTA with Hong Kong on November 2017.
[123] Indonesia is the country the most protectionist among the Asean member states.
[124] Jayant Menon, lead economist for ADB's Office for Regional Economic Integration.

CHAPTER 5

Lao Market Prospects in the AEC

5.1. Laos as a Market

5.1.1. Market Overview

Laos is small in terms of economic size and population among the ten Asean countries. The country is sparsely populated with a total population of around seven million people, of which the urban population represents about 38.6 percent, and the power purchase of the population is low compared to its neighbors. On the one hand, although Laos is a relatively small market and among the poorest in terms of per capita income, it has recorded higher GDP growth than many other Asean countries. The country has a small but growing middle class concentrated mostly in the capital and provincial capitals.

Despite the high level of sustained GDP growth, its economic structure remains narrowly-based and the agriculture sector is dominated by labor-intensive, low-value added production of farming and cultivation products. Moreover, lying along the bank of the Mekong River, Laos has benefitted enormously from this abundant water resource. Hydropower production has made a large contribution to national output. The country's economic growth is heavily reliant on natural resources.

The rich resources of the country make the economy robust. The per capita possession of natural resources is relatively high with abundance of mineral, hydropower, and land resources. Today, the urban middle class with high income provides stronger local purchasing power, and the urban population has grown at a rate of 5.3% annually since 2001, with more than two-thirds of the population growth in Vientiane Capital in recent years caused by net in-migration. Indications are that most migration is rural to urban, primarily to Vientiane Capital[125].

According to the United Nations analysis report, Laos has the distinction of having the highest total fertility rate among Asean member countries, with one of the youngest populations in the region, more than half under 20 years of age and 70 percent under 30. The country is projected to benefit from the "demographic dividend" to the economy in the medium term. In addition, strong economic growth over the past decade has enabled Laos to move from the ranks of low income economies to a "lower middle-income" country[126].

The country is becoming a market of increasing interest in a range of resource and non-resource sectors. Several resource sectors include copper, gold, coal, tin, bauxite, potash, timber, gas, and granite. As mining is one of the most important sectors in the economy, proper management will deliver sustainable, inclusive growth in the future. To that end, the government is working to optimize the mining of the country's mineral resources through the geological approach. With the geological approach, the government aims to generate income and accumulate capital and resources that it will then channel into the country's socioeconomic development to raise living standards and make Laos a vital member of Asean.

The government recognizes that growth opportunities in these industries are limited, and has prioritized the development of high-value agriculture and light manufacturing, while continuing development of a range of energy resources and improving electrical transmission capacity to neighboring countries. Therefore, reinforcing agriculture, preventing deforestation, regenerating forests, and encouraging commercial development is the government's direction today. The government is also actively encouraging people to get involved in reforestation and tree-planting activities. The private sector has steadily shifted its activities toward wood processing and is planting commercial trees such as eucalyptus, teak, agar wood, and rubber.

In tandem, Laos is diversifying its economy to lower its reliance on resources and hydropower exports. Tourism is a new economic driver, with rapid growth in arrivals and receipts.

The notable growth in the economic sector, coupled with political stability, has undoubtedly provided the country with great opportunities to invigorate its social, domestic market and development of the private sector. Laos also is a market of a variety of goods. The country is producing quality craft and silk products, furniture, food processing, and traditional medicine. Laos is becoming increasingly a market for import products such as cell phones, notebook computer, tablets, computer accessories, electronics, cars, building material, and home decoration and equipment. In Purchasing Power Parity terms (PPP), Laos' per capita income is about the US$ 6,290 in 2017[127]; at that level there is typically rapid growth of the urban middle class and consumption of all sorts of goods. More of Laos' population in the future is moving to the provincial capitals and in the SEZs to become shopkeepers, contractors, or employed in the manufacturing and service sectors, and thus accessible to retailers; furthermore Laos' construction sector with a range of commercial and residential projects and consumer markets should exhibit significant growth.

5.1.2. Market Profile and Major Indicators

Table 11. Major Economic Indicators

	2015	2016	2017*
Population (000)	7,029	7,163	7,299
GDP (US$ billion)	12,561	13,790	14,671
Real growth (%)	7.5	6.9	6.9
GDP per capita (US$)	1,787	1,925	2,472
Inflation (%)	1.3	2.0	2.3
Exports (US$ billion)	2,769	3,020	5,015
YoY growth (%)	4	9.1	
Imports (US$ billion)	5,233	4,720	4,978
YoY growth (%)	22.5	-9.8	
FDI inflows (US$ million)	1,118	890	1,230
Average exchange rate kip/US	8,131	8,129	8,212

*Source: WB, IMF, Bank of LPR, UNCTAD; *Estimate 2017 Ministry of Commerce and Industry.*

Table 12. Development Indicators

Development Indications	2006	2015
Employment (% of total labor force)	1.4	1.40
Female labor force participation rate %	78.7	77.7
Official Development Assistance (ODA) (% of Gross National Income)	11.2	4.00
Import duties collection (% of tax revenues 2008-2014)	11.7	10.0
Total debt services (% oft total exports)	16,7	10,9
Human Development Index (0 to 1)	0.51	0.59

Sources: WB, World Development Indicators; UNDP, International Human Development Indicators.

Table 13. Export Values by Regions 2013-2014

	Export Values (Th. US$)		Share of Total Export (%)	
Regions	2013	2014	2013	2014
Intra-ASEAN	**1, 233,908**	**1, 009,148**	**47.59**	**52.98**
Brunei	-	69	-	0.00
Cambodia	642	4,263	0.02	0.22
Indonesia	13,271	16,988	0.51	0.89
Malaysia	668	4,556	0.03	0.24
Myanmar	3,082	142	0.12	0.01
Philippines	57	10,020	0.00	0.53
Singapore	2,994	682	0.12	0.04
Thailand	890,364	687,166	34.34	36.07
Vietnam	322,831	285,261	12.45	14.98
Extra-ASEAN	**1, 322,366**	**895,758**	**51.00**	**47.02**
Australia	721,195	102,348	27.82	5.37
Canada	635	3,412	0.02	0.18
China	363,404	695,876	14.02	36.53
EU 27	202,885	51,973	7.82	2.73
India	514	428	0.02	0.02
Japan	24,424	18,510	0.94	0.97
Korea	1,969	2,990	0.08	0.16
New Zealand	629	1,026	0.02	0.05
Pakistan	97	-	0.00	0.00
Russia	131	22	0.01	0.00
USA	6,483	9,920	0.25	0.49
Rest of the World	36,536	9,254	1.41	0.00
Total	**2, 592,810**	**1, 904,905**	**100**	**100**

Source: Department of Economic Statistics, Lao Statistics Bureau, Ministry of Planning and Investment the data based on Department of Customs, Ministry of Finance.

As shown by Table 13, Thailand and China remain Laos's main export partners following Vietnam in 2014. This trend is still valid in 2017.

Table 14. Laos's Import Values by Regions 2013-2014

Regions	Import Values (Th. US$) 2013	2014	Share of Total Import (%) 2013	2014
Intra-ASEAN	**2, 494,955**	**3, 158,955**	**75.79**	**79.75**
Brunei	-	6	-	0.00
Cambodia	136	62	0.00	0.00
Indonesia	7,208	11, 315	0.22	0.29
Malaysia	8,730	6,875	0.27	0.17
Myanmar	-	426	-	0.01
Philippines	913	811	0.03	0.02
Singapore	6,224	9,200	0.19	0.23
Thailand	2, 182,895	2, 754,164	66.31	69.55
Vietnam	288,849	375,465	8.77	9.48
Extra-ASEAN	**778,672**	**780,407**	**23.65**	**19.70**
Australia	15,507	15,343	0.47	0.39
Canada	316	1,595	0.01	0.04
China	511,213	537,706	15.53	13.58
EU 27	37,460	36,628	1.14	0.92
India	14,274	17,055	0.43	0.45
Japan	94,833	79,422	2.88	2.01
Korea	91,188	76,753	2.77	2.01
New Zealand	292	332	0.11	0.11
Pakistan	665	609	0.02	0.02
Russia	3,055	318	0.09	0.01
USA	9,869	14,017	0.30	0.35
Rest of the World	**18,412**	**21,440**	**0.56**	**0.54**
Total	**3, 292,089**	**3, 960,170**	**100**	**100**

Source: Department of Economic Statistics, LSBs' calculation based on Customs Department's data, Ministry of finance.

Laos' main import partner is Thailand (69 percent) in 2014. Other import partners include China and Vietnam (Table 14). The trend has not much changed in 2017.

Figure 31. Goods Trade to GDP Ratio

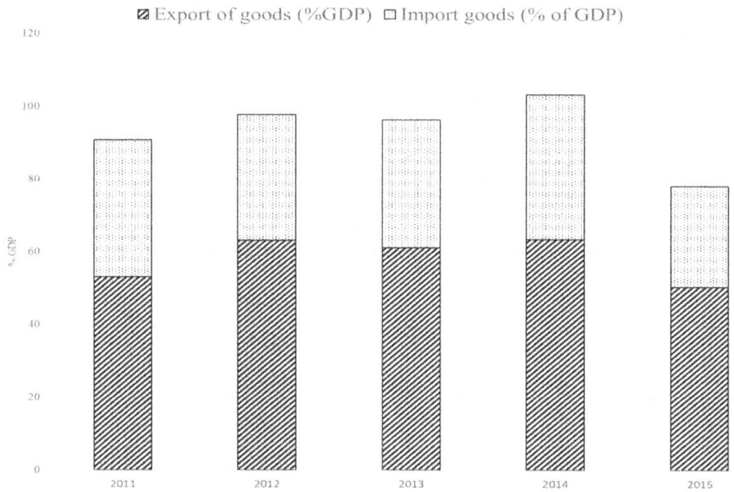

Source: ITC Trade Map (Trade); World Bank (GDP).

Figure 31 shows the evolution of the total exports and imports of goods for Laos.

Figure 32. Services Trade to GDP Ratio

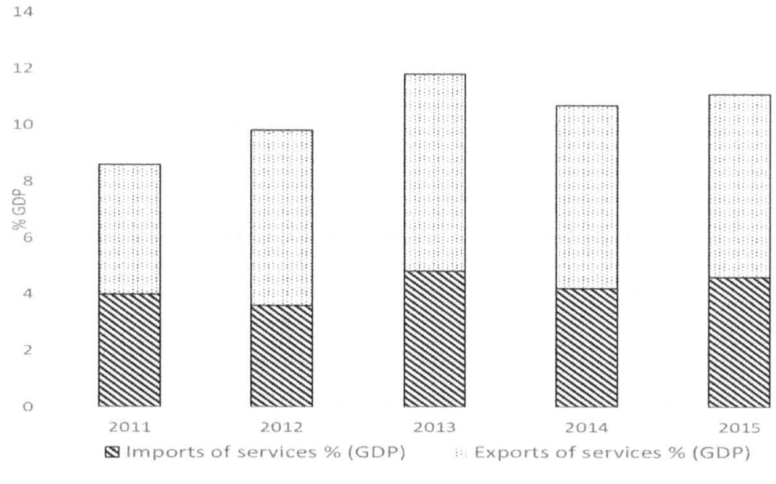

Source: ITC's calculations based on IMF's of payment; WB (GDP).

The Figure 32 above shows the evolution of the total exports and imports of services for Laos.

Table 15. Laos' Top 10 Exports 2015

Rank	List of Products	Export values (Th. US$)	% of total Trade
1	Wood and articles of wood; woof charcoal	957,988	24
2	Mineral fuels, mineral oils and products of their distillation bituminous substances	608,893	15
3	Copper and articles thereof	522,303	13
4	Ores, slag, and ash	321,702	12
5	Electric machinery and equipment and parts thereof; sound recorders and producers, TV	321,707	8
6	Articles of apparel and clothing	165,037	4
7	Fertilizers	164,327	4
8	Rubber and articles rubber thereof	114,517	3
9	Cereals	96,235	2
10	Coffee, tea, mate, and species	92,385	2
Total		**3,517,829**	**87.1**

Source: ITC.

Laos's top 10 exports accounted for over four-fifths (81%) of the overall value of its global shipments. Based on the nominal GDP of US$13.7 billion in 2016, exports represent about 25.5 percent of total Lao economic output. From a continental perspective, 92.7% of Laotian exports by value were delivered to other Asian countries including China, Japan, South Korea, and India, while 5.3% were sold to European importers. Laos shipped another 1% worth of goods to Africa with 0.9% going to North America, according to World's Top Exports statistics. Agricultural products and natural resources account for the bulk of Laos' exports. Laos' main exports are wood, clothing, coffee, electricity, metals, corn, and rubber.

Clothing and accessories was the fastest growing among the top 10 export categories, for the 5-year period starting in 2012. In second place for improving export sales was electrical machinery and equipment, followed by beverages, while the spirits and vinegar category posted the third-fastest gain in value led by water and malt beer. However, the leading decliner among the top 10 Laotian export categories was copper, which was down by -56.4%.

Table 16. Laos' Top 10 Imports 2015

Rank	List of Products	Import value (Th. US$)	% of Total Trader
1	Mineral fuels, mineral oils, and products of their distillation bituminous substances, mineral	984,179	15
2	Vehicles, parts, and accessories thereof	954,344	15
3	Electric material, equipment, and parts thereof; sound recorders and reproducers, TV	731,365	11
4	Machinery, mechanical appliances, boilers, and parts thereof	635,095	10
5	Articles of iron and steel	514,591	6
6	Iron and steel	236,843	4
7	Natural and cultural pearls, precious or semi-precious stones, precious metals, and metals clad	189,595	3
8	Aircraft, spacecraft, and parts	183,595	3
9	Plastics and articles thereof	154,767	2
10	Meat and edible meat offal	154,051	2
Total imports		**4,639,476**	**71% of Total**

Source: ITC

Laos' growing reputation and improved foreign relations within the international community has opened channels for foreign corporations and investment groups to target this new frontier. This recent development has driven the local market to demand more quality goods and international standards when it comes to workmanship and finishing. The country mainly imports oil, machinery and equipment, vehicles, iron and steel, telecommunication equipment, beverages, and cement.

Table 17. Logistics Performance Indices (1 to 5), 2017

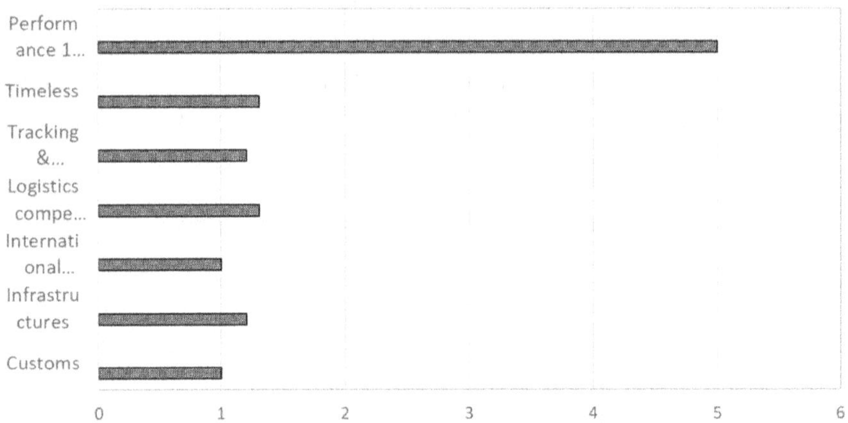

Source: WB Logistics Performance Index (LPI)

Table 18. Trade Facilitation Indicators (0 to 3), 2017

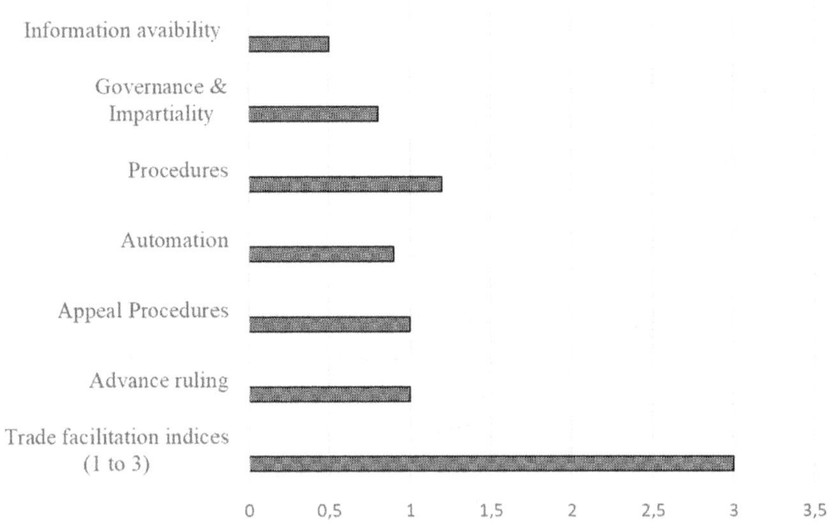

Source: OECD Trade Facilitation Indicators

In terms of logistics performance indices (Table 17), Laos is far from the performance of the Asean countries. This poor performance translates into non-competitive exported goods from Laos. Table 18 shows the trade facilitation indicators, where Laos is a quite complicated place to trade.

5. 1.3. Laos's Domestic and Regional Economies and Markets

The Lao market economy has grown at 7 percent for the last three years and is heading into a new phase of regional and global integration after the AEC was put in place on January 1, 2016. The country has many handicaps due to its tiny market size and income inequality between the various provinces.

This small domestic market is aggravated by its extremely fragmented character. The low purchasing power is reduced much further by the fact that the population is distributed over a relatively large area. The average population density over the whole country is less than 30 persons per square kilometer. The share of urban population has increased to over one-third of the total population in 2015, but this is still well below the global average of 50 percent. In addition, 70 percent of the population depends on agriculture for their livelihoods. The fragmentation of the domestic market is augmented by the underdeveloped transport network in place over what is often mountainous land. The lack of internal communications means that the country is effectively split into three economic sub-regions: the northern region with Phongsaly, Luangnamtha, Oudomxay, Bokeo, Luangprabang, Huaphanh, and Sayabouri provinces; the central region including Vientiane City, Vientiane province, Xiengkhouang, Borikhamxay, Khammouan, Savannakhet, and Xaysomboun provinces; and the southern region comprising Saravan, Sekong, Champassak, and Attapeu provinces. Uneven economic and social sector development between provinces makes the domestic market's growth unmatched with the market demand and existing infrastructure. Discrepancies exist between urban and rural areas, and between northern and central regions. Among the wealthiest provinces, there are Luangnamtha, Bokeo, Sayabouri, Vientiane, Borikhamxay, Oudomxay, Luangprabang, Khammouan, Savannakhet, and Champassak.

While around Vientiane Capital and Vientiane province are concentrated many light industries, agriculture farms, and processing industries, the northern, central, and southern regions are more devoted to commercial plantation including cement, bauxite, potash factories, and coffee processing units. Tea is cultivated in Phongsaly province, and coffee is mainly grown in the south at the Bolaven Plateau. Cassava plantations are mostly in Borikhamxay, Sayabouri, Champassak, and Vientiane provinces.

In the absence of inter-connected markets, inter-provincial and inter-city trade were often limited to non-damaged products and a few specialized goods, due to a lack of sufficient infrastructure linking the various city and provincial economies together into a coherent whole.

Overall, domestic market and transports are currently a big constraint on trade. These handicaps prevent facilitation of trade and discourage investors, increase the production costs, and spoil the goods. But things started to change with the Lao government's policy to reverse the situation and improve the infrastructure development. Infrastructure construction (including for hydropower, modernization of roads, building highways, and the Laos-China railway under construction), forestry, and services are the main contributors to this growth. Since the adoption of the market reforms only in the late 1980s, Laos has attempted to promote trade within the Greater Mekong Sub-region (GMS) and to attract foreign direct investment (FDI) to support its infrastructure development and economic growth.

Laos is facing the challenges of rapid urbanization and inadequate infrastructure. The infrastructure has impaired its manufacturing and industrial potential and does not make it easy to do business. The transportation costs that weigh heavily on business profitability could be reduced if the government accelerated all of its ongoing infrastructure development programs, which include building the roads that would improve national trade and regional connectivity and, by the same token, the efficiency of business activities and trade with Asean member countries.

However, between 2011 to present, the domestic market has continued to open and is developing gradually. The value and volume of trade have risen annually by 6 percent. The development of regional markets and infrastructure has been increased across the country. In addition, investment capital was put into building markets and shopping centers in the form of concessions based on the contracts made between domestic and foreign investors and the government and provincial authorities.

Today, with the AEC referring to the single market and one production base, barriers to trade and investment between Laos' neighbors will be eliminated, and trade will be improved and further increased for Lao economies. Indeed, through the AEC, Laos will make optimum use of opportunities to exploit projects on infrastructure, serving economic development and enhancing the connectivity with Asian member countries, the CLVM (Cambodia, Laos, Vietnam, and Myanmar) particularly, and other partners. The CLMV principle consists of six areas of cooperation, namely trade and investment, agriculture, industry and energy, transportation, tourism, and human resource development. Laos will also have more opportunities to attract foreign direct investment from Asean and other partners through improving and increasing the attractiveness of its market. Simultaneously, if Lao businesses are well prepared they will also have a greater chance to expand their investment to Asian member countries. Most importantly, the cooperation within the CLV will allow Laos' southern province markets Attapeu, Sekong, and Champassak to expand their potential in terms of trade, agriculture, industry, and tourism. Indeed, the establishment of the CLV cooperation represented efforts to meet the requirements of the Mekong Subregion and ASEAN regional integration.

Furthermore, in order to facilitate entry into the Lao market, the Lao Trade Portal, established in 2012, provides information for exporters and importers. Also, the Lao Electronic Gazette is a source of all Lao legislation and offers the public the opportunity to comment on proposed legislation. Though most information is in Lao, many laws have been translated into English as well.

Over the next several years, one would expect to see some movement towards the development of a national economy in the south of Laos through the CLV. The national highway Vientiane-Pakse is under final appraisal and other rail projects including the Pakse-Cambodia border will later start knitting the economy together. Moreover, the upgrading of the 111km Road No. 18 that links Attapeu province to southern Vietnam is under ongoing consideration in order to allow heavy trucks and increase the tonnage per axle to 11 tons[128]. The strategy of the Lao government for growth is to develop road and energy infrastructure, enhance value chains, improve access to markets and social services, and forge stronger rural–urban linkages. Moreover, sustainable growth in rural areas is supported through improved natural resources management.

Efforts to integrate the economies of the southern region of Pakse-Champassak SEZ, the Savannakhet SEZ, and other SEZs will continue and reinforce the integration. The Southern region initiative with the CLV and Thailand is likely to evolve into a national test case for the creation of the linkages between provinces and the one single market and production base between the four countries that is necessary to create national markets in Laos. The government hopes therefore to increase exports of agriculture, manufactured goods, and electricity to its more industrialized neighbors.

5.2. Evaluation of Potential Sectors

Laos's resource and non-resource sectors consists of three major sectors, namely agriculture and forestry, industry, and services. Each sector comprises several sub-sectors as illustrated below:

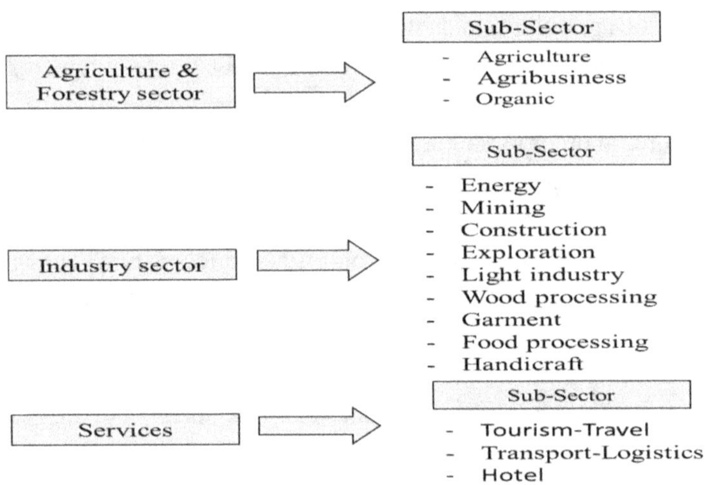

The market potential and the sub-sectors growth are shown in the matrix below. The rapid economic growth of the country has been driven by the exploitation of natural resources and development of hydropower, with both sectors largely led by foreign investors. Mining and energy are considered as growing sectors followed by the potential of the tourism sector. The light industry market is quite low due to a lack of local investments and consumer preference for imported products. Agriculture sector growth does not translate its potential due to poor mechanization, a limited market, lack of financial support from commercial banks, and insufficient irrigation system. However, organic agriculture and agribusiness have both good market potential; the growth of the organic sector is currently quite slow but very promising for the future with high demand from Japan, China, the US, and the EU. The garment sector will remain stable, and the growth is fast and has good potential for Laos since investors will likely move their factories partially from Thailand to the SEZs. The chart that shows the market potential versus the sector growth is illustrated below.

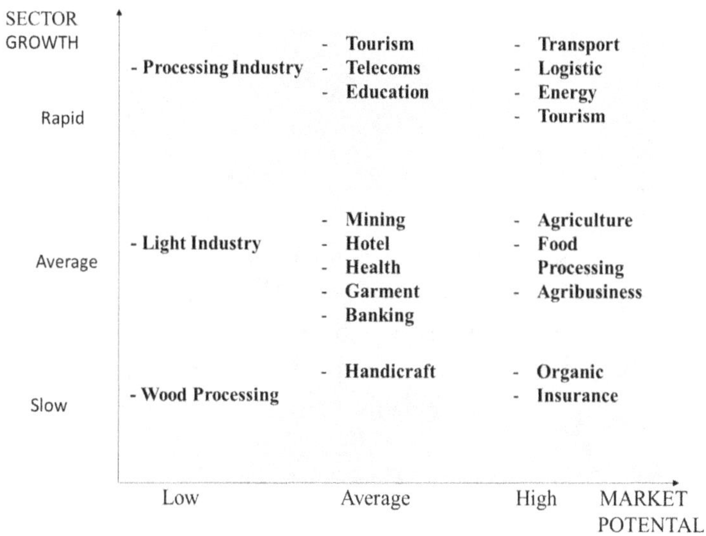

The transport and logistics sectors will have the most potential, and their growth is rapid; these markets require Lao businesses to tie up with foreign partners. The tourism and travel sector is the most attractive and high potential for Lao and foreign businesses; it is expected to have a rapid growth, with many Asian member countries and China expected to tap into this market. Furthermore, the insurance industry has a high potential to grow in Laos due to the awareness of people to have an insurance coverage for their property. In addition, banking and micro finance sectors also have a good potential and the growth is in line with the economy development.

If we use the S-Curve as a model to describe the growth of one variable in terms of another variable over time, and apply Lao's business sectors today and the potential for value creation, we obtain the following curve:

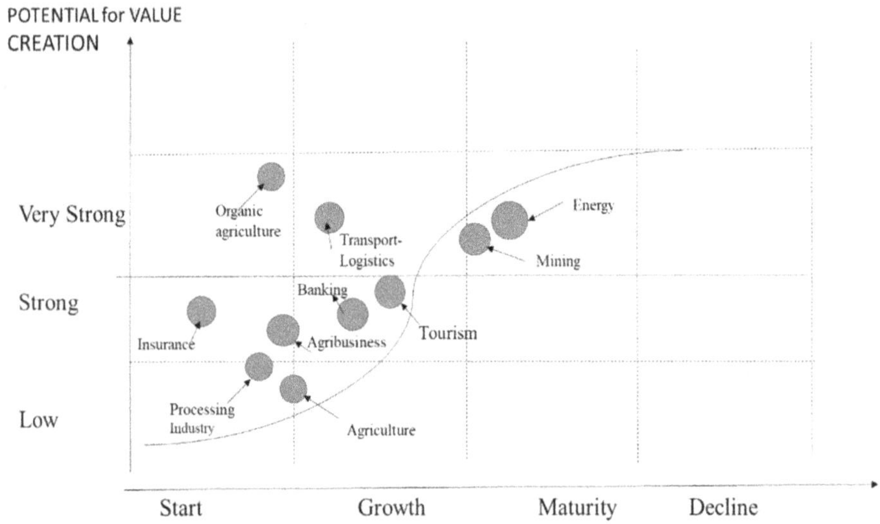

The energy sector is almost at the beginning of a mature phase, followed by the mining sector. Investors have realized so far a good return in investment, and the government earned more than one billion dollars from dividends, taxes, and royalties. These sectors have also employed thousands of local people and have created value for Laos.

Energy: Laos has considerable potential for renewable energy, particularly hydroelectricity. The country as of September 2017 has a total of 46 operational power plants with a total installed capacity of 6,444 MW that generate 35,000 GWh per year. Fifty-four more power plants are currently being built; the government and private energy developers expect to complete and commission them by 2020. Therefore, by that time, Laos will have a total of 100 power plants with a total installed capacity of 13,062 MW and power generation of 66,944 GWh per year, according to the Ministry of Energy. The policy of the government is to develop its electricity industry to make sure that it can contribute to the socioeconomic development of the country, and to promote foreign investment in the hydropower industry. Laos is aiming for a total installed capacity of about 12,000 MW by 2025. The abundant water resources of the Mekong River and its tributaries give Laos the potential to produce more than 25,000 MW of electricity, according to official analysis[129].

Mining: Although exploited and operated successfully (copper and gold) by two major companies, namely MMG-LXMC at Sepon and Phu Bia Mining, which managed the Phu Kham copper-gold mine, and although both companies have been operating for over ten years, this sector is still under-developed. Mineral deposits present numerous opportunities for investment: tin, lead, zinc, iron ore, copper, gold, gypsum, lignite, sapphires, and gaz. Importantly, concessions are granted to foreigner investors without restriction[130]. Potential exists for this sector, which contributes to more than 10% of GDP. It is one of the priority sectors in the country's socioeconomic development experiencing rapid growth, driven by domestic and foreign investment. Several forms of investment are proposed: business cooperation by contract, joint-venture between foreign and Lao companies, and 100% foreign owned or domestic owned. Currently, 61 local and foreign companies are conducting mining construction, exploitation, and mineral processing, of which 12 are foreign, 14 are local companies, and the remaining are joint-venture companies. Therefore, there is still room for other newcomers in the sector[131].

Transport and logistics: This will be certainly the most interesting sector, owing to regional integration. Prime Minister Thongloun Sisoulith has stressed for land to be the main focus of transportation development in the country. He also said "From the geographic specification of our country we have to focus on land transportation as the key to the heart of transportation, traveling and tourism.[132]" Since Laos is in the center of the Greater Mekong Subregion (GMS) countries, and with the increase of transports due to the rise of population, volume of agriculture products, particularly commercial crops like coffee, vegetable, cassava, bananas, sugarcanes, fruits, and herbs, transport and logistics are playing a predominant role.

Agriculture and organic crops: Laos is primarily an agricultural economy. Although gradually declining in terms of its contribution to GDP in recent years, agriculture continues to play a major role in Laos' economy. In

2017, the sector contributed to an estimated 15.7 percent of GDP. The growth is 2.8 percent, and it absorbed around 75 percent of the total workforce. Laos achieved rice self-sufficiency around 2000, a major milestone in the history of the country. Although Laos is one of the least densely populated countries in the region, agricultural land is by no means abundant. Only 10 per cent of the land is considered to be suitable for (permanent) agriculture activities[133].

Most households in rural areas are near-subsistence farmers engaged in rice-base agriculture, collective forest products, and raising livestock. The sector is still dominated by smallholders engaged in low-productivity rice production and characterized by low-level use of purchase inputs such as improved seeds, breeds, and fertilizers. The greatest amount of rice is consumed in the farm households that produce it, with around 10 percent marketed. Agriculture-based products made up around 15 percent of total exports in 2007, the main commodities being timber, coffee, corn, and non-timber forest products[134]. This proportion has declined rapidly from 24 percent in 2004 to around 10 percent in 2016 as a result of the increasing diversification of the export sector, such as minerals and energy. However, today, 72 percent of the total cultivated area is dedicated to rice; Laos has now a surplus of rice production and is becoming a small rice exporter. Most of the provinces that are deficit in rice are surplus maize producers. Other important economic crops include coffee, sugarcane, cassava, sweet potato, and industrial tree crops (such as rubber, eucalyptus, and acacia). Laos is a country rich in biodiversity. It is estimated that biological resources contribute over 66 percent to GDP. Furthermore, they provide indispensable benefits for the rural poor as agro-biodiversity is a source of food, nutrition, and income. In the area of forestry, for instance, some non-timber forestry products (NTFP) such as animals, bamboo and rattan shoots, fruits, greens, honey, and khem grass are sold in local markets and some are traded internationally. The major export products from Laos' agricultural sector are timber, lumber, plywood, and coffee, while major agricultural imports are sugar, condensed milk, and long-grain rice[135].

Since 2006, the domestic organic market has grown rapidly, according to the report from the International Trade Center's project "Support to Trade Promotion and Export Development in Lao PDR." In 2011, there were 1342 farmers with 5,989 ha (plus 16,786 ha for wild harvest). By the mid-2000s, the organic market was introduced as an opportunity for organic agriculture once poverty eradication became apparent. In 2006 the first organic certification of tea was obtained by Lao Farmer Product, a company founded by Dr. Sisaliao. The Lao government with several international organizations including a few NGOs have supported the sector. The organic market is becoming promising and the growth is rapid. Most organic products are so far for export markets. China has recently committed to buy 20,000 tons of organic rice. In addition, fair trade regarding agro-processing products is a potential market as well for Laos, it needs government strong support and NGO's network for export.

However, some severe issues regarding deforestation, forest degradation, aquatic resource degradation, and loss of biodiversity have been observed. They are due to increasing commercial agriculture, intensive hydropower plant construction, and excessive mining exploration in the country. In addition, flooding and droughts might damage the economy of the sector.

Agribusiness: Agriculture production is becoming increasingly commercialized. Currently, 33 percent of farmers are producing mainly for sale. This sector takes a little more advantage of agriculture, which is in fast expansion, mainly driven by interests and market demands, supported by Lao government policies and farmers' initiatives. Investors are mainly from China, Thailand, and Vietnam. A variety of crops are being cultivated on concession land and through contract farming. Industrial tree crops, in particular rubber, teak, eucalyptus, and agar wood, are among the most popular. Sugar is another important cash crop, while recently maize and cassava have emerged as increasingly important crops. To date approximately 1.1 million hectares, or roughly five percent of the country's territory, have been approved for concessions and leases. The government is now promoting contract farming instead of granting concession over large areas of land for agriculture and tree plantation, and gives special support to the people for growing commercial crops because it is one way to help villagers escape the clutches of poverty. The commercial crops are becoming increasingly important to improve the living standards of the farmers.

Tourism and travel sector: The Lao government has placed tourism as one of the 14 national priorities for 2017 under the National Socio-Economic Development Plan for 2016-2020, which covers the Millennium Development

Goals and Sustainable Development Goals[136]. The sector has grown annually around 22 percent since 2006 and contributes to the country's socioeconomic development; it is today a major contributor to the state income (7-9 percent of GDP) and employment. Importantly, the implementation of the open door policy and the one single market and production base measures of the AEC boost cooperation with foreign nations and investors in various fields such as travel agents, hotels, entertainment centers, restaurants, guesthouses, resorts, professional training, tourism, and hospitality training centers. Furthermore, the Lao government will develop a high quality tourism industry and aims to become a preferred destination in Asean and in the global travel markets. Investors from China, South Korea, Singapore, and the Philippines have expressed interest for Champassak SEZ to develop business activities and tourism facilities to drive the growth of tourism in Laos. This would include hotels, restaurants, a trade center, recreational park, and other tourism-related businesses.

Processing and light industry: The sector in 2017 is growing at an estimated rate of 9.1 percent and contributes to 30.7 percent of GDP. There is not heavy industry in Laos. Industries in this country comprise: mining (copper, tin, gold, and gypsum), timber, electric power, agricultural processing, rubber, construction, garments, cement, and tourism. The production industrial growth rate in 2010 was 17.7 percent; it is around 23 percent in 2017. Garments have now overtaken timber as the main Lao export. The largest foreign income earners are tourism, sales of hydroelectric power, logging, and textile exports. So far, a lack of adequate transportation links and its distance from the sea prevents Laos from exploiting its cheap labor to promote industry as countries like Cambodia, Myanmar, and Bangladesh have. The current situation is going to change when the railways for the East-West Economic and North-South Economic Corridors become operational in a few years.

For a long time Laos had no major industries or manufacturing. Most industry is still done on the village level: weaving, blacksmithing, carpentry, and boat making. Today, many factories are set up, among them textile, shoe factories, and motorcycle assembly plants. There are low and medium voltage transformer factories, along with several small metallurgy and steel factories in Laos. Although Laos imports most of its consumer goods from China and

Thailand, it produces its own bricks, cement, soft drinks, beer, and cigarettes. The Lao government has built two special economic zones in Savannakhet and Khammouan where bridges linking Laos and Thailand have opened. Other important manufacturing activities include the production of agricultural tools, animal feed, bricks, cigarettes, detergents, handicrafts, insecticides, matches, oxygen, plastics, rubber footwear, salt, soft drinks and beer, textiles and clothing, and veterinary products. Local business contributions to the growth of the country's economy in this sector are significant. Some manufacturing activities such as beer, tobacco, and plastics have also foreign participation in the form of joint-venture with Lao businesses. Most industries are focused around Vientiane, Luang Prabang, Savannakhet, and Pakse.

Services: The service industries of Laos were under government control until the late 1980s. The state still owns most of the banking sector, but privately owned banks are widely encouraged. Besides, there are joint-ventures between state-controlled Lao corporations and foreign investors. The retail sector is not yet well developed outside Vientiane. This sector is totally open to foreigners; Thai, Vietnamese, and Chinese communities are very active and present in commerce.

The tourist industry is for the time being not yet well structured in Laos compared to neighboring countries. It needs foreign cooperation, investments, and professional competencies to upgrade the standards and the tourist infrastructure.

Insurance: The insurance industry has a strong potential of growth in Laos as more people have a better understanding of insurance. At present the market for insurance is narrow and the regulatory framework remains largely basic. However, the number of insurance companies opening offices in the country was increasing every year, she said. Over the last six years, the number of insurance companies has increased from less than 10 to 24 companies today. Most insurance coverage applies to non-life insurance (homes, health, vehicles, property, and construction) and only a small proportion of the Lao population has coverage. Therefore, the market is attractive and numerous insurers have established operations in Laos[137].

Labor market: The current situation in Laos with regard to the labor force in the industry and construction sectors is in deficit, particularly of skilled workers. The total labor force is estimated at 2.9 million. According to the Ministry of Labor and Social Welfare, in the first six months of 2017, the number of Lao workers in the domestic and foreign markets reached 69,352 and is expected to reach 143,230 people by early 2018[138]. The government has also improved workers' skills to supply the needs of the domestic and foreign markets, with the number of skilled workers at the present estimated at 12,800 and expected to reach over 131,000 by 2018. Currently, the industrial sector is not able to recruit workers in line with the industry's targeted contribution to GDP, so many workers have had to be brought in from overseas. As more foreign companies set up factories in special and specific economic zones (SEZs) in Laos, the government anticipates that several thousand job opportunities will be created for Lao nationals in the coming years.

5.3. SWOT Analysis of Lao Market

What, in general, can be said about the Laos market in terms of its strengths and weaknesses?

In terms of **strengths**, there is no doubt that Laos is in a good geographic location and could become a hub between its richer neighbors, the rest of Asean member countries, and China. Furthermore, it facilitates trade and exchange between Laos and markets outside the country. The political stability has also helped to create a fairly good macroeconomic picture, leading to strong GDP growth and foreign investments. The peaceful country has also greatly contributed to its development. In addition, the existence of ancient royal capital, Luang Prabang, designated a World Heritage site by UNESCO, and several other sites such as the Plain of Jars, an archaeological landscape, and the Vat Phou, a ruined Khmer Hindu temple complex in southern Laos, also named a World Heritage site, have allowed the development of major tourist attraction with a total annual influx for these three sites approaching about 2.2 million tourists in 2017, while the total tourist arrivals are estimated at 4.8 million. It is worthy to mention that Laos is one of the most flexible and open markets in the Asean countries; labor wages are among the lowest and the electricity fees are very competitive compared to other Asean countries. There is almost no entry barrier for foreign investors. Importantly, reforms on business laws are ongoing to encourage investment, including the establishment of businesses in the SEZs. Laos has seen recently the emergence of a small middle class mainly in large cities; this middle class has a high purchasing power and can afford to buy and consume imported products, participating in the development of the country as well.

Several **weaknesses** are obvious. Laos is one of the countries in the world with high GDP growth, but the GDP per capita is amongst the lowest. Even after decades of foreign aid, crop yields and health and education indicators remain low, despite progress being made. The labor force is in constant deficit and workers do not meet the requirements of the industry and construction sector. Light manufacturing industries are scattered and do not reach a profitable and critical size. Furthermore, it is difficult for SMEs to grow due to the small size of the domestic markets and the lack of adequate financing. Owing to poor infrastructure, though improving, and the absence of a sea port, high costs in shipment make the products not competitive. Most enterprises have no international experience and knowledge of marketing tools, although many workshops and seminars have been provided by the LNCC recently with the assistance of the Technology Promotion Association (Thailand-Japan) (TPA) to improve the access to highly productive and skilled labor for the Lao business community. Additionally, Lao and foreign businesses agree to say that doing business in Laos is rather complicated, and although the government has set up the "one stop shop" for business registration, red tape and bureaucracy hinder the entrepreneurial spirit.

Looking forward, what advantages or **opportunities** does the Lao market have? There are many. Natural resources come in the first place. Hydroelectricity has a great but not unlimited potential for local and foreign investments. Opportunities exist for imported electrical and mechanical equipment manufacturers and high-grade cement companies. The mineral resources sector is still under-exploited and offers interesting opportunities, as this market is widely open to investors. Similarly, agricultural and forest products are not yet produced and cultivated professionally, and require competencies, assistance, and investment from foreigners. Besides, with limited industrial and production bases, and a lack of qualified engineers, technicians, and skilled workers, all this suggests that it will be useless for Lao businesses to compete with the well-established regional companies in several fields. Laos is not capable, for instance, to engage in a big garment or sneaker factory employing 3 or 5 thousand workers, or produce agriculture products to compete with well-known foreign brand names. Taking into account the fact that the domestic market is small, the export market is very competitive, and the entry barriers make Lao products unattainable in some Asean countries, so foreign investors have little interest to produce food processing or industrial products for the Lao market. Therefore, Laos has to go to "niche" markets. The most likely niche markets could be organic agriculture, handicrafts, hydroelectricity production, and mineral products[139]. As far as construction and building material are concerned, cement, bricks, steel rods, aluminum sheets, and similar products could be produced for domestic demand. However, Laos can take over some activities from Thailand for the light industry of subcontracting work, which would benefit from the abundance of electricity and young labor for the manufacturing of special steel parts, aluminum parts (cutting), mounting devices, and the assembly of electronic, electrical, and mechanical products in the SEZs. There is a promising private sector with the emergence of SMEs in Laos. Today, more than 150,000 SMEs are registered and constitute 98 percent of the total enterprises in the country. They are still in the stage of learning how to reach a professional enterprise level and produce competitive and quality products to meet Asean member states' standards. Currently, Lao businesses are seeking support from the government for their expansion; most are looking for opportunities for partnership or alliance with those of Asean. This approach is also beneficial for foreign businesses wishing to enter the Lao market. Tourism development remains a real possibility and has become one of the top government priorities. This sector is considered a niche market for Laos, which needs to be reinforced by becoming professional. In 2017, tourists who have visited Laos are estimated at 4.8 million, and the country is now working hard to improve infrastructure at tourist sites as well as collaborate with its neighbors Thailand, Vietnam, Myanmar, and Cambodia. Moreover, Laos has reached a cooperation agreement on tourism with the aim of jointly promoting the tourism potential of the two countries and implementing Asean's connectivity plans. According to Lao's strategic plan, the ministry plans to draw 7.51 million tourists by 2025 through collaboration with Thailand, Cambodia, Myanmar, and Vietnam. Transport and logistics are crucial to connect GMS countries, thus joint-ventures between Lao companies and foreign are ongoing to strengthen this sector with the government's support. To maximize all the opportunities, infrastructure development is essential, including urban services, irrigation, rural electrification, and land transport. Obviously, domestic markets close to the South China province of Yunnan will expand in various sectors of business. Additionally, the CLVM countries will boost Laos' economy development in agriculture, tourism, and industry, expanding its domestic market to neighboring countries. It will also increase Lao's private sector operations and mobilize more private sector resources to help the government implement the eighth National Socio-Economic Development Plan 2016-2020. It is worth mentioning the greater market access for Laos through the Generalized System of Preferences (GSP) to the EU, Canada, and other developed and developing countries, as well as preferential market access in ASEAN and ASEAN+1 FTA with China, Japan, South Korea, Australia, New Zealand, and India. In the present context of the AEC, Laos can also play in the future a significant role as a node of communication between the East-West Economic Corridor and the North-South Economic Corridor, thanks to its central geographic position and the railway network plan. Indeed, Laos has taken steps to pursue its plan to build a railway network that will connect the landlocked country with its neighbors, the rest of the region, and the world. According to the Director General of the Railway Department, Laos' plan for a rail network comprises six lines that have been planned to turn Laos from a landlocked country into a land link within the region. Some of these projects are already under construction. The six railways are as follows: Lao-Thai Project (extension phase under construction), Laos-China Railway Project (under construction), Savannakhet-Lao Bao, Vientiane-Thakhek-Mu Gia, Thakhek-Savannakhet-Pakse-Vangtau, and Pakse-Veunkham (Lao-Cambodian border). Concerning the 220 km Savan-Laobao railway connecting central Savannakhet province to the Vietnamese border, the railway would link with Thailand's rail network on one side and access Vietnam's Dongha Port on the other side. A prefeasibility study of the 455 km Vientiane-Thakhek-Mu Gia track linking Vientiane with Vietnam's Vung-Ang port was completed in 2011. A draft report of the project has been completed and the final report will be finished by the end of 2017. In addition, a feasibility study of the 345 km Thakhek-Savannakhet-Pakse-Vangtao railway is to be carried out. This would connect Thakhek district, the capital of central Khammuan province, with the Thai border at Vangtao via Savannakhet and Champassak provinces. The 150 km railway linking Pakse, the capital of southern Champassak province, to Veunkham on the Cambodian border, is also on the preliminary phase of discussion[140]. The above rail plan clearly shows that Laos has the ambition to become an important place for Asian connectivity.

Ironically, the "opportunity" of abundant and rich resources could also pose a potential **threat**. As a matter of fact, the risk comes if the market focuses essentially on this sector and investments go massively to hydroelectricity and mining. This case will dissuade the government to support other sectors and investors to neglect agriculture, light industry, and traditional handicrafts. As the energy sector is not unlimited, alternative sectors should then come up and be encouraged by the government, otherwise FDI will decline and challenge Laos' sustainable development. Most importantly, if Lao consumers are reluctant to buy products "Made in Laos" because of its expensive price and would prefer those cheaper products manufactured by other countries, then Laos will become only an imported and trading market, and the country will lose then its manufacturing and production base. This means also that in the long run, more people might lose their job and create social instability. What of other threats? **Waste and corruption**. These are the big issues for the country's economy and the competitiveness of the market. Corruption is a serious problem in Laos and appears to be growing alongside the economy. Waste occurs when an unnecessary and inappropriate investment is made. Therefore it increases the amount of projects and government expenses and disturbs the market. It would create a loss for the Lao economy and people. Often waste and corruption are combined. In that case, those few people involved who are able to profit from a particular bad project derive a benefit, but society still loses. Domestic and international firms have repeatedly identified corruption as a problem in the business environment and for the further development of the Lao economy. Laos has signed and ratified the UN Anticorruption Convention. Laos is not a party to the OECD Convention on Combating Bribery of Foreign Public Officials in International Business Transactions. Although the Lao government has developed several anti-corruption laws, enforcement remains weak. Corruption must be fought, but it exists in almost all societies and countries. Also, it is worth mentioning that small and medium-sized enterprises are cautious of the possible negative impacts of the integration on them, fearing the AEC will beef up competition and threaten their viability and existence.

Based on the above analysis of the Lao market, several identified strengths and weaknesses of Laos, along with future opportunities and threats, are summarized in the matrix below.

Table 19. SWOT: An Overview

STENGHTS	WEAKNESSES
▪ Centrally located in the GMS ▪ Peaceful country and political stability ▪ High and steady economic growth rate ▪ Cheap labor costs ▪ Low entry barriers ▪ Emergence of small middle class ▪ World Heritage sites attraction	▪ Small market and low mass purchasing power ▪ Deficit in labor force and skilled labors insufficient ▪ Current poor infrastructure and equipment ▪ High costs (transport, logistics, finance) ▪ Little industries ▪ Lack of business management experience and international markets and practice ▪ Complexity in doing business
OPPORTUNITIES	**TREATHS**
▪ Organic agriculture ▪ Sub contracting and Light industry ▪ Connectivity ▪ Emergence of Private sector and SMEs ▪ Growing tourist industry development ▪ China proximity and LCVM connection ▪ Free Trade Agreements to Europe, North America	▪ Products "Made in Laos" do not find buyers in their own country ▪ Lack of competitiveness ▪ Strong competition from ASEAN member countries ▪ FDI declining ▪ Persistent of waste and corruption ▪ Lack of economic diversification

5.4. Laos: What Attractiveness for Businesses?

The results in Table 20 are based on several informal interviews with business people, leaders from construction companies, SMEs, food processing centers, small industries, and foreign based companies. These results are non-exhaustive and incomplete, and need further investigation, but they give a fair idea of the attractiveness of Laos for investors based on their business sector.

Businesses have strong attractiveness for Laos and high interest in the five following sectors: energy, construction, and mining including minerals, telecoms, and tourism. Light industry, agriculture, and agribusiness also showed good interest for businesses, but with average attractiveness. Businesses have low attractiveness for Laos and little interest for wood and food processing, education and health, handicrafts, and organic agriculture. Although international demand is increasing for organic agriculture, attractiveness for the country and interest for this sector are low. This is due to too numerous constraints and limits important investment for this sector. Education and health, wood processing, and food processing have little interest for enterprises because of the small market size, with an exception for handicrafts. Regarding the wood processing industry, Lao-made furniture is at present lacking the design of creative, innovative, and ecologically friendly furniture for the Asean furniture and western markets. Private investment is an important part of the education sector development today, due to private tuitions from elementary schools to colleges including vocational schools. Interest for businesses is fairly good and profitable, but the attractiveness for the country is low due to the difficulty of finding teachers and professors, owing to the small market. Similarly for the health sector, it dissuades for the time being investors to tap in the market, as most doctors and nurses would prefer to go to Thailand, Malaysia, and Singapore to practice their profession. Nevertheless, in the medium term, with the rise of the middle class, the increasing urban population, and the people that want to be more educated and increase their well-being, the education and health sectors should be potential for investors.

Table 20. Attractiveness for Laos vs Business Interest by Sector

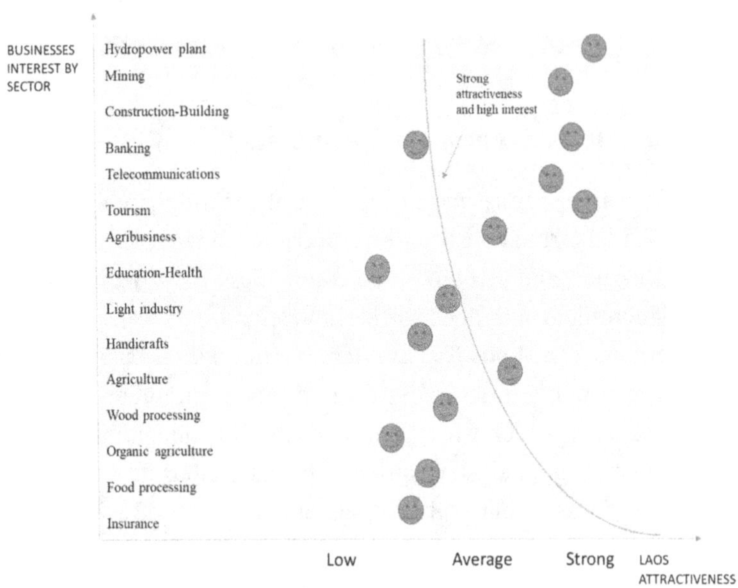

5.5. Growing Role of the Private Sector and their Fragility

The private sector is driving economic growth in Laos. It is considered an important force in economic and social development, playing an irreplaceable role in job creation, technical innovation, economic growth, and other aspects of that development. The Lao government supports and fosters regular and sustainable dialogue with the private sector, both at the national and provincial levels. A main objective of the country's private sector and industrial development efforts is to attract sustainable foreign and local investments. The government seeks to reinforce the special economic zones (SEZs)[141] to mobilize substantive foreign and domestic investments in non-resource-based sectors by building upon its small and medium enterprises (SME) strategy and investment laws and regulations. The main government agency supporting the SME is the SME Promotion and Development Office (SMEPDO) under the Ministry of Industry and Commerce. The Government recognizes that by offering the necessary infrastructure and services in strategic geographic areas for manufacturing and industry, SEZs can attract foreign investment, spur employment, boost the development of new technologies, diversify the economic base, and enhance entrepreneurial and technical capacities.

Moreover, the LNCCI participates actively with the Lao Business Forum (LBF)[142] to seek and eliminate impediments that hinder the competitiveness of Lao enterprises in the international market.

The role of the private sector in Laos is expected to grow rapidly as the country opens up and is part of the AEC. According to the LNCCI, the number of registered Lao enterprises in 2017 is over 150,000, and they are in all business activities, including agriculture, trading, and services. Key players in this sector consist of some larger companies in construction, transport and logistics, agriculture, and food processing factories; smaller companies are individual and family companies, small agriculture farms, services and travel companies, and industry processing factories. In Laos about 98% of total enterprises are SMEs and account for 16 percent of GDP and 63 percent of employment. Most of them are services and manufacturing companies and are still supplying domestic markets[143]. Today, agricultural production and most manufacturing production is in private hands, and SOEs only cover around one percent of employment. More than 98 percent of manufacturing units are small (less than 10 employees).

In the Asean region, SMEs cover about 96 percent of total enterprise and provide about 50.85 percent of employment. In Laos, SMEs are weak in terms of competencies, business management, and marketing, and the quality of their products remains low compared to international standards. Furthermore, most SMEs can barely borrow from commercial banks and access markets. According to a recent report by the Young Entrepreneurs Association of Laos (YEAL), membership in the association was continuing to grow annually, up from 208 companies in 2010 to over 500 companies in 2017, but Lao SME expansion is at a lower rate than in other countries in the region.

The total number of large Lao enterprises is estimated at less than fifty. They are professional and are able to handle medium projects in construction and processing industries sectors, but most of them do not have enough funding to expand and take on larger projects, which might be a reason behind their hesitation in actively joining the AEC.

The big issue today for SMEs is the fact that they lack the financing and technology to grow. Moreover, compared to other Asian member countries, the level of Lao SMEs is low in terms of skilled labor, productivity, assiduity, and performance, which will have an impact when producing goods for export or even for domestic markets. This has led to Lao enterprises missing out on export opportunities and stiffer competition in the domestic market from neighboring investors. The critical situation today is the fact that the rural SMEs hit hard by various distresses. SMEs in rural provinces are in dep trouble as they suffer a double whammy from a lack of innovation and unenthusiastic consumer demand. They have to adapt a lot, otherwise they won't survive. Rural SMEs have been coping with lower sales volume and access to broader domestic market, in contrast with SMEs involved in supply chain businesses, where growth still prevails due to global demand. Rural SMEs or farmers need to incorporate business innovation, technological production and marketing strategies in order to raise their growth prospects. This is also valid for other SMEs, because they are all fragile and have in common the same root of weakness.

The Lao Chamber of Professional Accountants and Auditors (LCPAA) reported that half of SMEs lack access to finance, which directly hinders their growth and sustainability. The Chamber suggested the government should focus on SME development by setting up priorities to create an enabling environment for them, including improved access to financing. This would also create opportunities in the region for SMEs to be more competitive, innovative, and able to utilize the regional economic initiatives and incentives that would add to their sustainable growth[144].

To improve the quality of products to meet international standards and to expand markets globally, SMEs will need more cooperation and assistance from the relevant government sectors as well as international organizations and other development partners. As Laos has now integrated within the AEC, it will provide opportunities and challenges for SMEs to improve their business operations in order to meet international requirements. In that sense, the Lao government, the LNCCI, the international institutions (IFM, ADB, WB, OECD), and other business associations have provided seminars, workshops, and training to SME leaders and managers. Recently, the Vientiane Industry and Commerce Department in collaboration with the Vientiane Chamber of Commerce and Industry and Lao Securities Exchange (LSX) have organized a seminar with the objective to increase understanding of SME operators in regard to the access of capital markets and the opportunities and challenges to capital market access in the AEC.

Laos does not have a well-developed capital market; its capital market (LSX) is still very small compared to regional peers, about 12.6 percent GDP in 2016. The LSX was established in 2010, and over the past seven years it has seen steady growth, notably increasing the number of listed companies from two in 2011 to seven companies in 2017. These listed entities are EDL-Gen, BCEL, Lao World Public Company, Petroleum Trading Lao Public Company, Souvanny Home Centre Public Company, Phousi Construction and Development Group, and Lao Cement Public Company is the seventh firm that has been listed on the LSX in late December 2017. All those listed companies are very large and well established. Domestic investors hold 87 percent shares in the LSX against 23 percent for foreign investors. Among investors, 87% of shares are held by individuals and 4% by institutions. Lao companies do not have yet the culture of buying shares in the stock market.

5.6. Business Environment and Investment Climate

Laos is an open and competitive market. Economic reforms continue to enable the country to insert rapidly into global integration. Investment laws have been amended several times to allow and facilitate businesses to move to and invest in Laos. Some businesses and international investors are beginning to use Lao production bases as an opportunity to reach the broader Mekong region, including southern China. A few investors, such as Essilor of France, have it in mind to include Laos as a radiation base in the Savan-Seno special economic zone for manufacturing and distributing their products worldwide.

5.6.1. Market and Competition

The informal sector of the economy is significant, with many regulations, laws, and taxes not fully under government control. Prices are now set by the market, the Lao kip is convertible, and profits from foreign investments can be transferred abroad without restriction. But competition operates within a relatively weak institutional and regulatory structure. The Decree on Trade Competition (2004) provides a rudimentary framework for regulating competition and monopolies, although it can often be bypassed through political contacts, and a number of top business groups depend upon political connections. However, this trend is changing in some sectors such as energy, telecoms, aviation, and transport. Market penetration and the way to do business are improving and becoming a little more transparent. The reforms undertaken by the government include the areas of regulatory and institutional reform of privatization. One observes today that the country has significantly reduced the number of state owned enterprises (SOEs), which is increasing private sector participation and encouraging more efficiency. SOEs account only for one percent of the total enterprises in Laos.

The 2010 Law on Investment Promotion introduced uniform business requirements and tax incentives to domestic and foreign investors. Foreigners may invest in any sector or business except in cases where the government deems the investment to be detrimental to national security, health, or national traditions, or to have a negative impact on the natural environment.

The Lao government also has expressed its ambition to expand the capital market. The Strategic Plan on Capital Market Development for 2016-2025 states the aim of having 25 listed companies by 2020 and 60 listed companies by 2025. Awareness-raising activities with companies and other stakeholders on the benefits of capital market access is a key component of this strategy. Additionally, the Lao authorities have expressed future plans to explore the bond market, introduce mutual funds, extend trading hours beyond the current morning session, and launch a new exchange for small and medium-sized enterprises (SME). The stock market would be a source of long-term funding for investment and business.

5.6.2 Taxes and Legal Issues

Laos has undertaken a number of important reforms in areas such as taxation, foreign exchange, investment, and import and export procedures. Unlike many other countries in the region, foreign companies in Laos can own 100 percent of their businesses, easily repatriate profits, enjoy one of the lowest corporate tax rates in Asean, and receive longer corporate tax exemptions than most other Asean countries. However, Laos needs to continue to educate investors about the country's opportunities.

The government has improved its business environment to make the country more investor friendly. Since 2009, several revised laws have been done such as the Enterprise Law, the Law on Commercial Banks, and the Law on Investment Promotion, which is a demonstration that the country is definitely committed to its reforms and policy of opening up. Furthermore, the 2009 Law on Investment Promotion, which merged the laws on domestic and foreign investors, was highly positive for the market and the country's image. There are no legal limits on foreign ownership or control of commercial enterprises, but in practice, many companies seek a local partner for practical reasons and to facilitate the daily life of the enterprises.

The fiscal system of Laos is considered among the most liberal in Southeast Asia. Foreign-owned enterprises are taxed only on their income earned in Laos. Lao-owned firms are taxed on their worldwide income, subject to double taxation agreements. The main characteristics of the fiscal tax policy are: Laos imposes a single tax rate of 24 percent on profits of both domestic and foreign businesses, except for companies registered on the Lao Stock Exchange, which benefit from a five-percent reduction of the normal rate for a period of 4 years from the date of registration with the exchange. After this period, the normal tax rate applies. There is a 26 percent tax rate on the profits of companies producing, importing, and supplying tobacco products. Two percent of the tax paid by tobacco companies contributes to the Cigarette Control Fund (Article 46 of the Law on Tobacco Control). Dividends for residents and non-residents are subject to income tax at 10 percent of the gross dividend received. Capital gains are taxed in the same manner as other operating profits[145]. Additional exceptions exist for companies that have a concession agreement with the government, which can thus benefit from a reduced profit tax as established in the agreement.

Regarding tax incentives, the government offers a wide range of such options, mostly tax holidays, to investors. Tax holidays were granted to investors operating in agriculture, industry, handicraft, and services sectors, and based on the investor's activities and their geographic location. The tax holidays were determined by geographic condition and the availability of infrastructure. In another words, these depend broadly on promoted activities based on three levels: level 1, activities with top-level promotion; level 2, activities with moderate-level promotion; and level 3, activities with low-level promotion[146]. Indeed, the determination of the level of priority will be partly based on the activity's contribution to the government's efforts aimed at poverty reduction, improvement of living conditions of the people, construction of infrastructure, human resource development, and employment, among others.

There are a few things that businesses may know. Foreign partners in a joint venture must contribute at least 30 percent of the company's registered capital. Capital contributed in foreign currency must be converted into Lao kip (LAK). Wholly foreign-owned companies are also today widely set up, and may be either a new company or a branch of an existing foreign enterprise. Throughout the period of operation of a foreign-invested enterprise, the assets of the enterprise must not be less than its registered capital. Foreign companies are able to tie up in the form of joint ventures with medium and large size SOEs.

Most laws of interest to investors will be featured on the Lao Trade Portal website, http://www.laotradeportal.gov.la, with many laws and regulations translated into English, or on the Official Gazette.

With regard to land, in Laos land belongs to the state. Under the new Law on Investment Promotion, foreign investors with registered investment capital of US$500,000 and above are entitled to land use rights for business or residential purposes. The duration shall be determined on the basis of the duration of the investment. If a concession is granted, it is for 30 years and can be extended to 50 years and finally 70 years.

5.6.3. Tax Incentives for SEZ Investment

The Lao government has already set up, as of the end of 2017, twelve special and specific economic zones in a bid to attract foreign direct investment to boost the economy and the development in rural areas. Infrastructure in the zones has begun to take shape thanks to special investment incentives. There are two types of economic zones in Laos, Special Economic Zones and Specific Economic Zones. Among the Special Economic Zones (SEZs) in the country there are two: the Savan-Seno Zone SEZ located in central Laos' Savannakhet Province – a central point of the East-West Economic Corridor; and the Golden Triangle SEZ located in the sub-Mekong region close to the country's borders with Myanmar, Thailand, and China. The rest of the economic regions are designated as Specific Economic Zones, with most of them located near the capital city of Vientiane[147]. Companies that decide to operate in these zones can obtain more advantageous investment incentives than in other areas. They also find it easier to obtain investment approval and set up processing plants due to easier import and export regulations and the availability of infrastructure. They are also given special tax breaks and all facilities: labor, electricity, water, and improved logistics.

Table 21. Incentives for SEZs

DEVELOPER	INVESTORS
▪ Tax exemption for equipment and raw materials for construction	▪ Tax exemption for equipment and raw materials for construction;
▪ Lower income tax and value added tax (compare to normal investment)	▪ Lower income tax and value added tax (compare to normal investment)
▪ Land lease exemption for some period of time (during the construction period)	▪ Get the business license and other service from economic board or management board of the zone through the modality of one stop service
▪ To be appointed as the chair or deputy chair of economic board and has some important roles in operating and managing the zone	▪ Foreign investors have been given the right to reside in Laos with their family during the time of the investment
▪ Has the right to decide the price of land lease in its zone	

Source: Lao National Committee for Special and Specific Economic Zones Secretariat Office.

5.6.3. Doing Business: More Reforms and Works Need to Be Done

Doing business in Laos has a poor rating compared in general to its neighboring countries. The World Bank Doing Business survey has scored Laos at the weakest position in the region. As for the ease of doing business, Laos comes just better than Myanmar, while starting a business Cambodia is behind Laos (Table 22).

Table 22. Doing Business in Laos and Neighboring Countries 2017

	Laos	Cambodia	China	Myanmar	Thailand	Vietnam
Ease of doing Business	141	131	78	170	46	82
Starting a Business	160	180	127	146	78	121

Source: World Bank 2017.

Laos is ranked 141 among 190 economies in the ease of doing business, according to the latest World Bank annual ratings. The rank of Laos deteriorated to 141 in 2017 from 139 in 2016. The government recognized the constant need to improve the business environment so that the private sector can effectively contribute to economic growth. For example long delays and costly procedures to establish a new business entity are one of the obstacles to new investment and entrepreneurial activity; as a result, a "one stop shop" has been set up to facilitate the entry of investors. Further improvement is undergoing to accelerate administrative process and eliminate unnecessary paper work. The government has also decided in 2017 to cancel the minimum registered capital required to set up a company.

The government is streamlining procedures in a bid to improve the ease-of-doing business climate as Laos' international ranking in this area deteriorates. The 10 indicators taken into account by the World Bank in 2017 include starting a business, dealing with construction permits, getting electricity, paying taxes, trading across borders, enforcing contracts and resolving insolvency, areas in which Laos ranks 164, 40, 149, 156, 124, 97 and 168 respectively[148]. Overall, Laos is far behind the other nations regarding the ease-of-doing business. Thus, Laos needs to make great efforts to overcome its ranking and improve the investment climate.

Notes

---

[125] Country Analysis Report: Lao PDR, United Nations, November 2015.
[126] Analysis to inform the Lao People's Democratic Republic– United Nations Partnership Framework (2017-2021).
[127] https://tradingeconomics.com/laos/gdp-per-capita-ppp. GDP per capita in terms of PPP recorded low of 1612.80 USD in 1990. In 2016 GDP per capita (PPP) was US$ 5,735. Estimation for 2017 is US$ 6,290.
[128] Vietnam asks Laos to upgrade link road, Vientiane Times, 4/01/2017.
[129] Electricity powers up exports towards a better trade balance, Vientiane Times, 28/04/17
[130] LNCCI Website.
[131] Mining activities in Laos, Department of Mines, Ministry of Energy and Mines.
[132] PM stresses land as focus for transport development, Vientiane Times 23/04/2017.
[133] UNEP, State of the Environment in Lao PDR, 2001.
[134] ADB Country Report, 2012.
[135] Food and Agriculture Organization of the United Nations (FAO), 2017
[136] Laos reviews progress on sustainable tourism development at UNWTO meet, Asia News Network, 20/05/2017.
[137] Insurance industry sluggish but potential for growth is strong, Vientiane Time, 23/12/2017.
[138] Government seeks more workers to meet needs of industry, Vientiane Times, 25/09/2017.
[139] Based on discussions with many senior officers, farmers, and Lao businesspeople including reflection papers from Dr. Sisaliao Svengsuksa, founder of Lao Farmer Products, former member of Lao Parliament, and president of the Support Association for Development to Subsistence farmer Societies (ASDSP).
[140] Plans put in action to turn Laos into a land link, Asian editors told, 29/08/2017.

[141] Lao People's Democratic Republic: Building Lao PDR's Capacity to Develop Special Economic Zones, ADB Assistance Report, November 2008.
[142] Lao Business Forum is an organization creating better business environment through private- public dialogue. It was established in 2005 with the support of the International Financial Corporation (IFC).
[143] SME center to boost startup skills, 14/07/2017.
[144] SME growth could suffer if financing remains difficult, 10/03/2017.
[145] Laos, KPMG, 2014.
[146] OECD Investment Policy Review, 190 center 2017.
[147] Understanding Laos' Special Economic Zones: Untapped Potential, Asia Briefing, October 2015.
[148] Rankings on Doing Business topics - Lao PDR, World Bank 2017.
Scale: Rank 190 center, Rank 1 outer edge.

CHAPTER 6

Impact of the AEC Towards Laos Business

6.1. Immediate Effects and Opportunities for Business

The increases in disposable income, particularly among elites with access to resource-based industries, and a slowly expanding middle class mean that the consumer and services sectors are likely to experience continued growth in the Lao market.

The AEC is predicted to increase Laos's real GDP, its exports, and private investment, according to the World Bank and ADB reports. The AEC allows for a single market and production base that liberalizes the flow of goods, services, investment, capital, and skilled labor across the region with a population of over 620 million. This in itself presents a challenge for Laos, whose population of 7 million constitutes only about 1.3 percent of the ASEAN population. Therefore, domestic and export markets expect to have good prospects. However, poor infrastructure in road, rail, and the absence of sea ports, as well as the limitations of funding for local enterprises and telecommunications pose practical problems. Bureaucratic and logistical costs currently make the export procedure in Laos lengthy and expensive. All of the above would have an impact on the market development.

The advent of the AEC presents both challenges and opportunities for the construction sector, in particular for the building materials industry. Traders now face both positive and negative impacts from this market integration. Numerous trade shows for the booming building market have been held recently in Laos and are also expected in the future. Imports of building material will rise significantly because of increasing real estate development. But local businesses related to concrete, cement, sheet iron, and steel rood won't be strongly affected by this market. Establishing a manufacturing facility and contracting companies remain potential options as the market matures. While Laos may represent a relatively small part of the overall ASEAN market, the construction sector means there are substantial opportunities for it to benefit within an integrated AEC.

The AEC represents an ideal opportunity for leading international brands, including those well-established in Laos, to strengthen their market share. While intra-ASEAN and international brands based in Asean are seeking market share in Laos, leading brands from major producers like China, Germany, India, Japan, and South Korea are also finding ways to enter this new market. Suppliers of international brands expanding to overseas markets usually develop by authorizing local dealerships to open representative offices before moving into a permanent subsidiary, and this is also the case in the construction industry and other sectors in Laos.

It's interesting to mention that General Electric now has a representative office in Laos, and the company expressed its participation to strengthen Laos's power grid network, including supplying comprehensive electrical equipment for power plants and extra-high and medium voltage substations. Microsoft has set up a partnership with Microsoft Asia and has expanded its commitment to supporting education in Laos by signing a memorandum of understanding with the Ministry of Education and Sport. The three-year agreement will cover a range of programs that will support the development of 21st century skills and employability of students[149]; in addition, ADB, Microsoft, and the Ministry of Education and Sports have also signed a letter of intent to collaborate and develop a technology platform to provide Lao youth with access to online technical and vocational training resources and employment services[150]. Schneider Electric, another leading world electrical company, has set up an office recently so that it can contribute to Laos's electricity distribution network and energy efficiency. As Laos' market is still immature, there is a lot of room both for foreign companies in many sectors and opportunities for Lao businesses to tie up with those international ones.

With the AEC in place, Laos will have greater opportunities to benefit from skills sharing, technology transfer, increased capital, and greater access to Asean markets.

However, there are some question marks over Laos's preparedness to capitalize on these opportunities. This suggests Laos will not immediately see a significant increase in foreign investment due to a relatively poor infrastructure and industrial basis, making the country less competitive than other Asean countries.

But in the longer term, Laos can realistically hope to integrate into the regional production value chain for sectors such as logistics, transport, light manufacturing, and assembling, or to benefit from its geographical location in serving as a regional logistics hub.

Laos's growing status and improved foreign relations within the international community has opened channels for foreign corporations and investment groups to target this new frontier. This recent development has driven the local market to demand more quality goods and raise international standards when it comes to workmanship and finishing, such as for the construction, transport, logistics, services, and telecommunications sectors. The demand for modern material and installation techniques has been met by SMEs, local companies along with international corporations that are now providing local architects, designers, and developers; most materials are sourced from all over the world (India, Japan, Korea, China, the US, Germany, France, and the UK). This new availability of resources is driving Laos's long-term vision to become a significant market in the ASEAN community, as a modern infrastructure lays the foundation for additional foreign investment and continuous growth.

Nevertheless, a warning to be taken into account is the competitiveness of local manufacturing products. Foreign products that enter the Lao market under an AEC framework are more attractive and competitive; the price of Lao products will fluctuate with inflation and local supply might not be able to compete with those of export products. This could dissuade enterprises to invest manufacturing locally and jeopardize SME development.

As already mentioned, Laos may also lag behind other Asean members in terms of education and skill, due to the low literacy rate and the fact that the majority of workers are still educated only to a primary school level. Many may not be able to be employed efficiently in a single job market. By allowing the labor market access to high-skilled labor, Laos believes that facilitating well-managed migration to the country can have positive developmental impacts. Furthermore, the Asian Development Bank's plans to facilitate trade between the six GMS countries will also boost an increase in migration, strengthen the domestic market, and stimulate consumption.

With its ambitions, a growing economy, and the most welcoming business, investment, and trade environment in ASEAN, along with a rich history and culture, Laos is gradually establishing itself on the business path of the region.

6.2. Key Business Success

6.2.1. How Can Local Businesses Survive Competition and Prevent the Lao Domestic Market From Becoming Only an Imported Market?

The influx of foreign import goods will cause worry to Lao enterprises and disturb the market. Whatever the reason Lao business leaders have, a more pressing fear for business in Laos is whether or not they can survive the competition. As the Laos economy will be flooded with new businesses from neighboring Asean and other foreign countries, this is harmful for local enterprises if the domestic firms and farmers are not strong enough to withstand the pressure. Regrettably, almost all Lao enterprises will be in this situation. One of the main challenges for Laos is its limited domestic production and a lack of advanced farming methods and equipment. Indeed, apart from equipment and machinery, animal feed and fertilizers are also imported, which adds to the cost of production. Critics say Laos is a country that doesn't produce enough for its own needs, with the nation importing foodstuffs and other goods from abroad and essentially from Thailand. In this context, with little protection and financial support from the government, only larger enterprises or the strongest businesses will survive. Most of the SMEs will then be in trouble or disappear.

Nevertheless, Lao enterprises can still survive in the Laos market within the AEC context. First, they need full support from the Lao government, and then both Lao enterprises and government bodies have to work on a clear industrial policy to back a strategy for the growth of the business. Second, Lao enterprises must definitively be productive, competitive, concentrate on quality, meet the Asean standards, and focus on some niche market.

6.2.2. Building Brand Name and IPR Protection for Lao Enterprises

Laos' producers and SMEs within the AEC are developing a resilient understanding of the likely consequences of enhanced regional integration for their specific sectors. For example, 2017 saw an increase in the number of Lao companies registering their brands so as to protect them from being accused of duplicating brands that exist in other Asean countries, and to ensure that they comply with intellectual property laws. Admittedly, building a local strong brand name by reputable companies is becoming a necessity and compulsory for those companies that wish to export their products to other Asean and international markets. Those companies must beforehand gain local recognition so that they can be considered legitimate and credible abroad.

Lao's capacity, know-how, and quality handcrafted products such as silver, silk, scarfs, bags, jewelry, and dresses are well recognized by tourists. All those products are from traditional artisans, driven by inexpensive prices and without Intellectual Property Rights (IPR). IPR issues, which have focused on Lao's domestic market, will become regional and international, as Lao exporters increasingly deploy appropriated artisanal know-how, trade secrets, and specific skills to build global market recognition.

At present, like any asset in the global marketplace, Lao's traditional handicrafts should be protected by IP rights. The result will be enhanced local know-how in the value chain of manufactured goods, and will provide jobs for villagers, contribute to market growth, and help with poverty eradication.

6.2.3. Strengthening National and Reputable Private Enterprises

The candidates for national and private larger Lao enterprises have come from various paths. Some were derived from intersections of institutional interest (energy sector, transport, banks, insurances, garments) and powerful support inside the Party or military elites, like several major industrial timber, mining, and agricultural enterprises. Others came from local private and once maverick enterprises that succeeded in the marketplace and built name recognition (among a few of them are Phousi Group, Phongsavanh Group, Dao Heuang, Phonesack Group, Khamphay Sana, Beer Lao, Lao Freight Forwarder Co, Vansana Construction, Souvany Group, and Inter Transport

Company (ITC). Clearly, in Laos, national and larger enterprises represent best practices in terms of strategy, product development, human resources, marketing, and better financial management. In that regard, they are at the front edge of domestic reform and appear widely in the newspaper and business media, which feature adulating interviews with successful domestic entrepreneurs and SOE managers. SOEs and larger Lao enterprises are also required to serve as pioneers in the effort to broaden the margins of Lao manufacturing concerns and increase Laos's benefits from post-manufacture value, especially in the regional market. Lao enterprises might look at Asean and overseas markets in the future for specific sectors such as handicrafts, organic agricultural products, and tourism. Over the last few years, foreign companies' targets have included primary commodities, power plants, agribusiness, logistics and transport, and retail chains.

The Lao government is encouraging SOEs and larger companies by giving them facilities and financial support. Those companies are likely in the position to partner with their Asean counterparts and in the medium term to pull in other Lao SMEs and develop the domestic Lao market.

It is fair to call the building of national and Lao larger enterprises a branding exercise, because it is perceived to have great value in strengthening their name recognition in the market share. In early January 2018, Deputy Prime Minister and Minister of Finance, Somdy Duangdy, made the comment when stressing the encouragement given by the government to the ICT sector in his address at the annual national meeting of the post and telecommunications sector. He also extolled Lao enterprises, including SMEs, and startup businesses to use ICT, and to drive the digital economy. Admittedly, the use of ICT equipment by businesses helped them turn a profit while reducing the cost of production and services[151]. This can help Laos to build a national strong image for its enterprises and develop innovation capacities.

In short, the development of Lao's internal and external markets depend on how national and larger enterprises manage to organize themselves and to ally with foreign groups in order to reinforce their competencies and financial resources. In return, these companies will be able to benefit Lao SMEs and help them to enter the Asean market and export their goods. Such a strategic marketing approach is already considered a successful scheme in many European countries for their SMEs' development in China and the Middle East.

6.2.4. Banking Credits for SMEs and Software System to Help SMEs

SMEs are a driver of the national economy. They make up over 98 percent of the total enterprises in Laos, covering mainly agriculture and farmers, processing industries, and services enterprises, and across all sectors they employ almost 90 percent of the country's work force.

Most SMEs have low management capacity and outdated technology, they lack transparency in information and feasible business plans, and do not have adequate assets for mortgages; in addition, the efficiency of SMEs is low, making them therefore ineligible for banking loans. Furthermore, they are facing long-standing difficulties in accessing loans. Credit institutions as well are reluctant to lend SMEs money for the same reasons. These problems were compounded by complex banking procedures and a shortage of appropriate loan packages for SMEs. Given the increasingly harsh international competition, the qualities that are often regarded as advantages of SMEs, such as flexibility and low operation costs, are no longer advantages.

So what can be done to facilitate Laos's SME expansion? Despite the government support already granted, lots of incentives and specific action still need to be further provided. Commercial banks have reduced recently the lending interest from 15 percent to 8 percent. But the conditions still remain restrictive and almost inaccessible to most SMEs today. In return, SMEs need to improve transparency of the information they provide to banks so that they can gain access to credit. Furthermore, it is necessary for SEMs to develop a database for credit institutions to use when evaluating lending decisions; this database should include information about total assets, equity capital, revenue, profit, and operations. Today, capital raising channels should be diversified, rather than largely dependent on banks, and raising capital from the securities market should be examined as an alternative source of financing for SMEs. Regarding farmers who cultivate rice, vegetables, and coffee, cassava, or fruits, banks should increase trust-based lending based on the efficiency of enterprises. Indeed, reasonable interest rates should be provided for SMEs to encourage their investments and expansions. More recently, the IFC, a member of the World Bank Group, and TMB Vientiane Branch of TMB Bank Public Company Limited, Thailand, are partnering to provide a US$9.1 million equivalent in Lao Kip of denominated financing via ACLEDA Bank Lao Ltd. The funding will help ACLEDA Bank Lao, a leading bank for the country's smaller businesses, bolster access to financing for the SMEs, especially women-owned SMEs, to expand production and grow business. With the local currency loan from TMB Vientiane Branch, backed by IFC's credit guarantee, ACLEDA Bank Lao aims to increase its SME lending to about US$60 million to more than 3,000 SMEs by the end of 2021.

Commercial banks along with ACLEDA and Lao Development Bank should in the near future plan to launch a software system that makes it easier for small business operators to put their business and financial plans on the digital platform, a move that will also allow them better access to the bank's loans. Indeed, the software system will formulate financial data, which is crucial for loan analysis, so SMEs will be able to simplify their business and financial plan. With the advent of digitization, banks have paid more attention to online market place, which would allow them to have access to SMEs and support them. However, conventional industries and larger companies, remain the focus of the banks, which would also support them to go to digital in order to increase business potential, productivity, cut operation costs and mange risks.

The help from bank credit will definitively give a great impetus to the small and medium-sized enterprises[152] that Laos needs. This will strongly encourage the expansion of micro and SMEs (MSMEs), since access to finance has been a major challenge for this sector.

6.2.5. Partnership-Strategic Alliance Approach

To tap into the Laos market, foreign enterprises need to allow some time for a Lao partner or associate to expand their business; it is the same for Lao enterprises who wish to earn their credentials, upgrade their competencies, gain public confidence, build up a brand name, give an international image to their company, and secure the sustainability of their business. To this end, Lao enterprises need to team up or make an alliance with foreigners. A possible scheme of partnership is described below (Figure 33). Lao companies in general are encouraged to strengthen their human and financial management in order to be ready for increased competition, but also to be able to benefit from greater business and partnering opportunities that are likely to arise from regional integration. Two recent examples of partnerships are meaningful: the

Deuan Sawanh Group Co., Ltd. (DSG) has agreed to cooperate in business with CEVA Logistics in order to improve the transportation and logistics management system for integration and enhanced overseas competition[153]. Also, the Phonsgavanh Group and Motorola Company have set up a joint-venture business aiming to supply a modern communication technology system to serve Laos' needs related to national defense and public security[154]. More recently, a Thai long-standing and well-established operator in medical services, BCH Group, and Lao private company have made a joint-venture to build a luxury eight-storey hospital at a cost of about 1,300 million baht to 1,500 million baht (more than US$40 million) in Vientiane. The planned hospital will cover almost two hectares and will be of international standards and best medical practices[155].

Figure 33. Three Types of Possible Cooperation

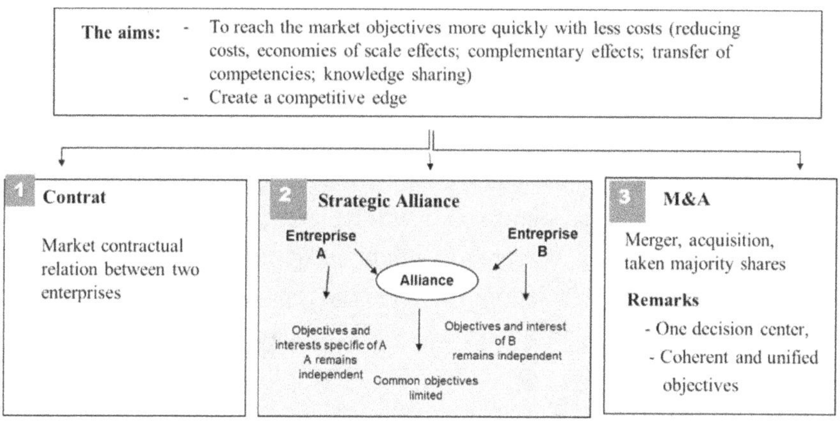

Type 1 is a contract between two enterprises. This is the most simple cooperation scheme, but local enterprises would not in this type get much transfer of know-how and financing from the partner. The Lao partner is less motivated by the business.

Type 2 is probably the most interesting for long-term cooperation between a Lao enterprise and foreign enterprise. This type would benefit both companies to lead the domestic market and also for the Lao enterprise to take advantage of the partner's reputation to tap into the Asean market. As the matter of fact, many companies from Khon Kaen, Thailand, have visited SEZs and would like to establish factories in Laos in order to boost trade and investment between the neighboring nations, according to Thai business association officials.

Type 3 is not mature enough for the time being in Laos. One cannot foresee any takeover of a Lao company by a foreign entity in the near future, because the M&A presents little interest for foreign companies in many sectors except perhaps in energy, agribusiness, and tourism.

Another type of cooperation between Lao investors or enterprises is **franchising**. This practice is the right to use a firm's business model and brand to market and sale the franchisor's products or services. For the franchisor, the franchise is an alternative to building "chain stores" to distribute goods or services that avoids the investments and liability of a chain. The franchisor's success depends on the success of the franchisees. Such a scheme is already operated successfully in Laos for coffee shops (Black Canyon, Amazon), fast food, and restaurants (The Pizza Company, Swensen, and MK). In the coming years, franchising will be certainly in great demand by local enterprises to market foreign reputable brands of products or services.

Other type of partnership to be considered by Lao enterprises is the **subcontract.** Foreign companies could require parts of their equipment or components to be assembled in Laos because of low wages and cheap electricity cost. Those assembly parts will be later forwarded to other country for final assembly. This approach might also be an opportunity for Lao enterprises to reinforce their competencies and reputation. Today, one can also observe Thai and Chinese businesses eye factories in Laos, many of them are focusing in subcontracting in clothing and electronic component factories, and establishing networks with Lao companies.

In conclusion, regardless of the type of cooperation with foreign companies: strategic alliance, M&A, franchising, or subcontract, this approach is strongly recommended for Lao enterprises. It is the best way for local enterprises to grow, acquire competencies, and learn how to produce effectively, manage the quality, and become competitive. This approach will allow transfer of technology and know-how to Lao enterprises in a "win-win" cooperation for both Lao and foreign enterprises.

6.2.6. Economic and Export Diversification

Laos must diversify its economic structure and export basket. The heavy reliance on natural resource development and export market concentration leaves the Lao economy vulnerable to external pressure on price (mineral products in particular), political dependence, and unsustainable growth. Furthermore, hydroelectricity potential also has its limit, and moreover the power plants do not employ many people during the operation and maintenance course.

It is therefore important for the government not to concentrate on the development of only the hydropower and mining sectors and rely exclusively on the export of these sources of revenue for the state. Another advantage to be pursued for the Lao economy is the agricultural sector. It shows promise, although the growth of the sector is relatively low compared to other activities.

The diversification strategy should focus on sectors that can create jobs, add value for enterprises, and impact poverty, including garments, handicrafts, tourism, Lao fashion, silk textile, and other activities such as light industry and organic agriculture. This diversification provides sustainable growth for the Lao market and economy. Organic coffee, cassava, rice, tea, and traditional medicinal plants are today amongst the export diversification goods that Laos is experiencing success with, and thus this trend shall be pursued.

6.3. Challenges for Companies in the Lao Market

In spite of the attention on Laos' macroeconomic development, the biggest challenges for companies operating in the Lao market are not macroeconomic. Overall macroeconomic growth has been vigorous during the last decade, and it is expected likely to remain healthy over the next several years. For most companies, aggregate macroeconomic growth in Laos has not been the most difficult issue they have faced over the last several years. Instead, the challenges of developing the market in provincial markets, marketing new products in Laos, convincing consumers to buy locally made products, dealing with the central government and local government agencies at all levels, recruiting key personnel and skilled laborers, achieving microeconomic development in individual sectors, and facing the ferocious competition of massive products coming from Thailand have been far more difficult.

Despite Laos' movement towards a market economy and its accession into the WTO, Laos and its market remain a challenging place from a regulation and political standpoint. While the rules and regulations are becoming clearer over time, the priority given to activity sectors is not yet well determined and coordinated consistently with the market. How they are interpreted and enforced is still subject to discussion and potential inconsistency over time and place. An example of the many SEZs in various provincial locations are confusing for companies that want to invest in Laos; the questions often asked are where to go, for what, and for which market? In addition, numerous processing industries require a range of permissions or special arrangements with provincial authorities for both domestic and foreign companies. Local companies or foreign multinational companies deal directly with the central government for large or megaprojects such as power plants, shopping malls, entertainment complexes, agriculture, tourist resorts, banking, and transport, while for other companies and in other sectors, the process of getting authorities' approval is more time consuming.

Within the AEC context, the Lao market is still attractive for companies, and the business landscape remains potentially fair for foreign companies. However, they have to compete with other global international companies in various sectors (see Figure 36). This means that it is still recommended for foreign companies to try to team up with local companies to find the best cooperation and win-win solution in which the company's investments bring some knowledge or expertise that Laos needs if they want to succeed in the country.

Additionally, among the leading challenges faced by all types of companies in Laos is the ability to compete in the Lao market with Vietnamese and Chinese companies in sectors like construction, building, and agribusiness. The political and economic influences of Vietnam and China are strong in this country. Many companies find that the competition is unfair due to the government support given to Vietnamese and Chinese companies. Dealing with this challenge involves not just an understanding of the marketplace and competition, but also of potential policy moves and political imperatives.

Given the size of the Lao market and the low-power purchasing of the population, local and foreign companies are not willing to make significant investments and take risks in some sectors such as the pharmaceutical, organic agriculture, and food processing industries.

In conclusion, despite all of the above, the Lao market will remain an interesting environment for the foreseeable future. Major challenges involve sectoral-level policies, with overinvestment in particular in the energy industry, but it is still not sufficient regarding the light processing, education, and tourism industries. In addition, the continued importance of governments at different levels in Laos's economy and market make it essential for companies to understand the nature of Laos's leadership, and the force that will influence policies going forward. This in turn requires an understanding of Laos's international relations including its Asean partners, its socio-political issues, its potential economic weak spots, the outlook of Laos's present and future leaders, and how related issues and forces can shape Laos's future market and industries. It is therefore the ability of companies and organizations to understand these forces, in addition to the nation's underlying market and economic conditions that will determine the overall performance of enterprises in Laos-related activities in the years to come.

Figure 34. Foreign Companies in Laos Versus Market Position

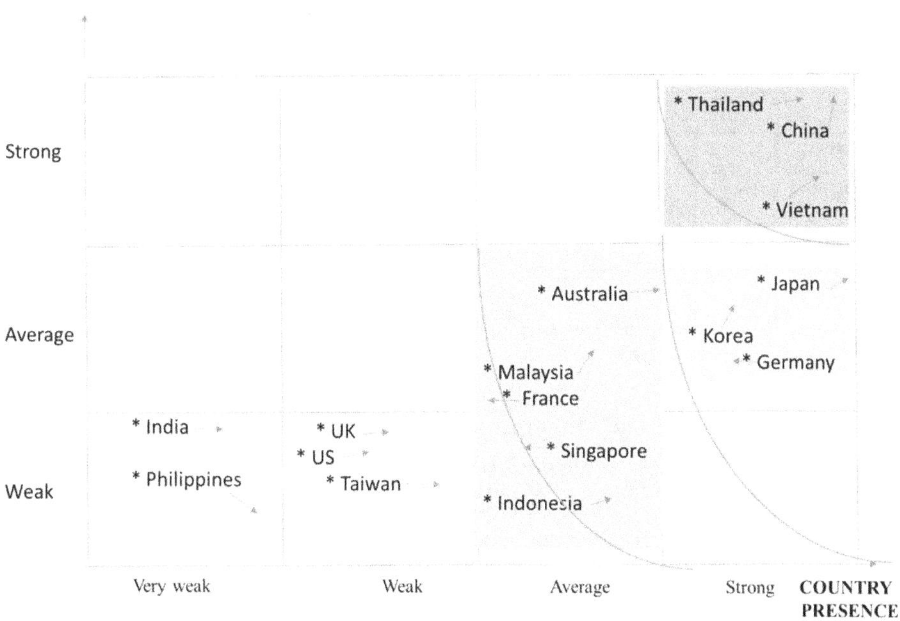

Three groups are clearly marked by their positioning: the first group is Thailand, China, and Vietnam, with a strong presence in Laos and market position; the second group is Japan, South Korea, and Germany; the third group is Australia, Malaysia, France, Singapore, and to some extent Indonesia. The UK and the US, although they are present significantly in the country, have a weak market position. France, Germany, and Taiwan have slightly weaker market positions, to the detriment of Asian countries. The US has seen its market position increase recently.

Table 23. Foreign Companies in the Laos Market

	Energy	Mines	Agriculture	Tourism	Construction	Cars	Equipment	Food	Retail
China	+++	++	+++	++	+++	+	++	++	++
Thailand	+++	+	+++	++	++	+	+	+++	+++
Vietnam	+	++	+++	+	++		+	++	++
Japan	+		+		++	++	+++		+
Korea	+				+ +	+	++	+	+
Australia		++							
India			+				+		
France	++			+					+
US						+	+		
Taiwan			+					+	+
Germany	+				++	+	++		
UK						+			
Malaysia	+			+					

- Equipment including machinery equipment and construction engines.
- Construction: building, road, bridge, and new town.
- Retail including all consumer products and electronic devices
- Graduation: +++ very present, ++ average, + weak

In Figure 33 and Table 23, assessments are not from any survey but from the author's own examination following on-site ascertainment and articles in the newspaper. Further surveys need to be undertaken to check the above findings.

6.4. Building Niche Markets

The Lao market is characterized by its small size, poor infrastructure to transport goods from one province to another, deficient logistics facilities, and absence of seaports to ease and reduce export costs. Most of the farmers are small in size and have a few hectares per family to cultivate the land; processing industries are modest units, the owners are lacking funds to expand their business and acquire new technology. Most of these small enterprises are still lacking the capacity to increase their production and to improve the quality of their products for export.

Taking into consideration the above analysis, Lao enterprises are not able to compete with established companies and well-known brand names in domestic and export markets. Thus, it will be necessary to increase competitiveness by improving the quality of products and by seeking niche markets. A **niche market** is the subset of the market on which a specific product is focused. The market niche is defined as the product features aimed at satisfying specific market needs, as well as the price range, production quality, and the demographics that it is intended to impact. It is also a small market segment.

Every product can be defined by its market niche. The niche market is highly specialized, and aims to survive among the competition from numerous large companies. Even established companies create products for different niches. In practice, product vendors and trade businesses are commonly referred to as mainstream providers or narrow demographic niche market providers. Such markets are a small area of trade within the economy, often involving specialized or specific products, goods, or services for the market. That is the case for Laos. Small capital providers as in Laos can opt for a niche market with narrow demographics as a measure of increasing their financial gain margins.

Laos has precisely a few assets to create niche markets and exploit the maximum of its potential. The following fields should be the target of developing a niche marketing strategy:

- Hydroelectricity, minerals, and mining;
- Agriculture and in particular organic agriculture;
- Fair trade for agro-processing, garments, and handicrafts products;
- Tourism industry, particularly eco-tourism; and
- Garments and textiles.

Regarding the **hydroelectricity and mining industries**, the sector is a major driver of GDP growth of foreign direct investment (FDI) and an important source of revenue for the government. This sector is performing well and remains potential and stable for another two decades or so, although mining activities have seen some drop due to the fluctuation of worldwide market prices. Indeed, the energy sector constitutes an annuity for the country. Mineral and mining industries still offer many assets for investors and the Lao economy. However, exploration and exploitation should preserve environmental concerns and national interest.

The Lao **agricultural sector** shows potential and is a priority for the Lao government under the 8th NSEDP. Traditionally, Laos has been a subsistence agricultural economy. That remains true today, though other economic sectors are growing in Laos. Land is still underutilized and not optimized in terms of crop. The low population density in Laos and large markets for agricultural goods and livestock in neighboring markets have brought many new investors to explore agricultural opportunities. There are opportunities for exports of modern harvesting, planting, processing, and other technologies that would help the sector to grow. The Thai leading food processing company CP is already well established in Laos and has no competitor. Lao small and medium business owners, instead of competing with those companies in the food processing sector, should opt for a specific segment where the others are not willing to invest yet. Specifically, organic agriculture will be a niche to be explored and exploited by SMEs. In addition, taking into consideration the transport conditions, organic products should be light, non-bulky and non-perishable, and offer high added value such as coffee, silk, and tea, for the export market. These goods may also be marketed in the country through tourists visiting Laos[156]. Crop growing and trading are booming in Laos, with several provinces focusing on agriculture as their main source of exports. Laos has the potential to grow organic crops for export to several countries and the demand is there, but agricultural business operators aren't yet able to meet the high demand. At present there are only a small number of organic farms and groups that grow crops for export. More organic farms and groups should be established as they can benefit Laos in many ways in the long term. To meet the high demand from local and global markets, the government and business operators should actively work together to transform Laos into a world-class organic garden and a green country that is a beacon within the region and will benefit Laos well into the future. Furthermore, the Lao government and NGO can help those who have invested in fair trade and are thereby trying to help farmers and producers to obtain a higher selling price of food processing to export or for local market.

The **tourism industry** and related activities are one of the industrial sectors that is growing rapidly and widely in Laos, and has contributed to the following: generated foreign currency for the country; supported related investment such as travel, hotel, restaurant, resort, transport, and souvenir businesses; created employment for people in the service and production sectors, for instance, the export of raw materials; contributed foreign currency accumulation and facilitated domestic financial liquidity; and distributed income to rural remote areas. Laos has seen a 35 percent increase of foreign visitors annually between 1990 and 2000. Since then, this number has continued to increase moderately by 15 percent every year. However, in 2016 foreign visitor arrivals witnessed a 10 percent year-on-year decrease, with 9.8 percent less foreign visits as compared to the same period in 2015.

The Lao government has dedicated its efforts to developing infrastructure such as the construction of roads to link all northern, central and southern parts. The tourism sector is today the second source of revenue and contributes to the poverty eradication of the country. The majority of tourist arrivals over the last few years were from Asean member countries and China. Laos has many assets to attract visitors like the World Heritage Sites of Luang Prabang, the ancient royal capital, and the Vat Phou Temple, ancient Khmer ruins in southern Laos. Other important tourist attractions are the Khon waterfalls in the southern region, and the Plain of Jars in Xieng Khuang province. The number of tourists has expanded dramatically up to over 4.7 million in 2017 from a few thousand in 1991. Laos has to preserve these assets, strengthen the development of tourism to become an industrial sector that generates foreign exchange revenue for the country. In doing so, it will provide more employment for people and thus participate in the promotion of cultural conservation and preserve the national heritage and customs, including the protection of abundant natural resources. This also promotes local handicrafts, silk, textiles, and sectoral products.

Based on its geographical locations, natural abundance, and historical and cultural aspects, Laos has its old special character that attracts more tourists in rural remote areas, especially those living by the protected forest, caves, rivers, well-known tourism sites, and ethnic villages. Laos is well positioned to promote eco-tourism. Several projects to protect Luang Namtha province, Phongsaly, Luang Prabang, Xiengkhuang, Vientiane, Bolikhamxay, Khammouan, Savannakhet and Champassak have proved that eco-tourism is one of the successful tourism sub sectors. Tourists come to visit those areas, which in turn provides direct and indirect benefits to local villagers. The sector also creates jobs for a number of people in rural remote areas. Eco-tourism also helps to conserve nature, reduces slash and burn practices, promotes village production, and helps to preserve the heritage and customs of ethnic people.

In short, taking into account Laos's natural landscape, tourism sites, natural resources, biodiversity, diversity of ethnic people and their unique customs and livelihood style, eco-tourism development is therefore a niche market and has been identified as a good and justified approach for Laos, which is a vital priority and has already been proven with successful results. To attract more tourists to the country, the government is trying to advertise its tourism attractions around the country, hoping to increase the number of visitors in the lead up to '2018 Visit Laos Year' to 5 million.

Regarding the **garment** sector, the Lao textile and garment sectors must be looked at from the context of the nation's status as a least developed country. This industry is important not just because of the revenue it brings in, but also because of the job opportunities for the country's small population.

While Laos is not able to develop heavy industry and compete with other Asean established industries, instead it has to develop its light industry, particularly the production of garments and textiles, which are doing well so far. Foreign direct investment and joint ventures control much of the market in that activity. FDI companies created about 30,000 jobs in 2017, and produced more than 45 million pieces (58% of the total) in the export-oriented garment sector. There are some 50 exporting factories with production mainly in and around Vientiane[157]. The garment sector is the largest manufacturing employer in Laos and makes a significant contribution to exports. The EU is by far the main destination for the country's clothing exports, though shipments to the US have grown recently, perhaps because the textile and garment industry enjoys export tax preferences from the latter. As a Least Developed Country, Laos is granted duty-free and quota-free access to certain Developed Countries under the Generalized System of Preferences (GSP), and it also benefits from preferential tariffs in many Western markets[158].

The undoubted main strength in the garment sector is its low labor costs. This is the main reason for the industry's growth, as primarily Thai, Chinese, and Taiwanese investment has looked to take advantage of this cheap labor in Laos. In view of attracting more investors in this sector, the Labor authorities has been successful in protecting the benefits and rights of workers at garment factories in recent years with the majority of workers now having access to protection. The garment factories have mainly relied on recruiting rural people who move to Vientiane but the sector is facing stiff competition for their labor from other sectors of the economy.

For all these reasons, garments remain a niche market for Laos to be carried on and maintain its competiveness. Furthermore, the country has excellent capability in producing attractive traditional textiles and handicrafts. Lao silk and cotton textiles are becoming known for their quality around the world. Those specific goods constitute a niche for the export market.

Clearly, the main opportunity lies in Laos joining with other Asean countries to offer quality products quickly as the region works as a united economy within the AEC. The Source ASEAN Full Service Alliance (SAFSA), which encourages the development of virtual vertical factories by combining downstream material suppliers with intermediate and upstream suppliers to provide buyers full service and speed to markets, hopes that manufacturers in the region will be able to form virtual vertical factories, and this has particular relevance for a landlocked country with high transportation costs such as Laos. But this would require major infrastructure investments and an ASEAN single-window agreement to ensure an efficient flow of materials and goods into and out of Laos. The garment and textile sectors as niche markets still have a bright future[159].

6.5. China Exposure and the "One Belt One Road" Initiative

6.5.1. Chinese Influence Via Economic Presence and Infrastructure

The increasing Chinese presence in Southeast Asia and particularly in Laos is obvious, but China's most remarkable advance into Laos has been via its economic presence. Bilateral trade volume has increased and at present, China has now become the biggest foreign donor to Laos, the biggest investor and the second largest trade partner.

China's investment in Laos is mostly concentrated in the mining, electricity, agricultural, and manufacturing sectors. Today, agricultural production has been highly valued by Chinese investors; the agricultural market offers great interest to China's buyers and trading corporations. Several concessions have been granted to Chinese investors, such as plantations of bananas, cassava, and rubber in northern provinces. Organic agricultural products such as rice, tea, and coffee have become Laos's premium export market to China. Chinese investors in Laos are largely concentrated in the northern areas and have focused their business on agricultural cultivation. However, most of Lao producers and farmers could not so far meet Chinese standards and delivery time.

In addition to the energy, mines, and agriculture sectors, China is widely present today in Laos in all commercial activities with various products: consumer products, food, textiles, electronics, machinery and building equipment, cars, hotels and restaurants, retail, trading, consulting services, education, health care, etc.

Laos welcomes investment by Yunnan enterprises, according to the LNCCI's announcement during the Promotion Session of Investment Projects in Laos held in Kunming in December 2017. Yunnan province enjoys geographical proximity to Asean countries, and therefore is faced with many opportunities to invest in Laos. Agriculture represents great investment potential, and Yunnan enterprises have invested in rubber and fruit plantations in northern Laos.

Today, the real estate market is expected to become a new pillar of Lao economic growth in the process of accelerated urbanization and industrialization that accompanies the increase of per capita income towards "graduation" from the least developed countries as envisaged by the Lao government. A number of Chinese construction companies targeting the Lao real estate market have gathered in Vientiane and are applying China's experience into the urban construction of Laos: building new towns, condominiums, commercial complexes, and hospitals.

In short, Chinese investors are making appropriate adjustments to the economic opening and transformation of Laos, and constantly exploring new profitable growth topics of the Lao economy beyond traditional fields. Today, Chinese enterprises eye Laos' opportunities in all sector of activities. Trade and economic cooperation between China and Laos has continuously developed in the past 20 years.

6.5.2. China's OBOR Initiative Strategy in Laos

China and Laos enjoy close bilateral economic and trade relations, as well as increasingly frequent communications between the governments and the Parties as both are socialist countries. Bilateral trade and investment have witnessed rather strong momentum in recent years, especially after China proposed the One Belt and One Road (OBOR) Initiative in 2013, in which Laos is a major partner for cooperation. Proposed by China in 2013, the OBOR Initiative refers to the Silk Road Economic Belt and the 21st Century Maritime Silk Road, aiming at building a trade and infrastructure network connecting Asia with Europe and Africa along the ancient trade routes of the Silk Road.

China pledges to strengthen ties and support to Laos under the Belt and Road Initiative through the expansion of economic and trade cooperation, investment in infrastructure, and people exchanges. As described in chapter 2, China's investment in Laos is mostly concentrated in the mining, electricity, agricultural, and manufacturing sectors. In 2017, China is the second trading partner, and main exports from Laos to China are timber, mining commodities, and hydroelectricity. Major imports from China include machinery, equipment, and motor vehicles. Chinese tourist arrivals in Laos are increasing year by year, and the number reached 545,000 in 2016 and 700,000 in 2017.

In an effort to promote industrial development, Laos established the Boten-Mohan Economic Cooperation Zone with China. The two countries signed the China-Laos Joint General Scheme for the Mohan-Boten Cross-Border Economic Cooperation Zone on August 31, 2015. The two sides have decided to establish the Mohan-Boten Cross-Border Economic Cooperation Zone in Yunnan Province of China and Luang Namtha Province of Laos in order to promote the OBOR Initiative, consolidate and develop the comprehensive strategic partnership, and enhance beneficial cooperation. This zone will focus on agriculture, biological industries, processing, logistics, and cultural tourism.[160] The Chinese government aims to develop both sides of the border into an economic hub that will help integrate ASEAN and China.

The OBOR, along with the Asian Infrastructure Investment Bank (AIIB) and Lancang-Mekong Cooperation Mechanism have brought significant changes to the structure, direction, and policy environment of Chinese overseas investment, but also created favorable conditions for further upgrades in the size and content of Chinese investment in Laos. China and Laos have begun new strategic connectivity at the government level. Following the September 2016 ASEAN meeting in Laos, Chinese Premier Li Keqiang and Lao leaders issued a joint communiqué to speed up connecting China's One Belt and One Road Initiative and the 13th Five-Year Plan with Laos' Land-locked to Land linked Transition strategy and the 8th NSEDP Five-Year Plan (2016-2020). The two countries then decided to carry forward the China-Laos Railway Project, which aims to build 417 km of railways within five years and involves a total investment of about US$5.7 billion. The groundbreaking ceremony took place in the Luang Prabang Province of Laos on December 25, 2016, marking a new phase of the railway construction. The railway has been listed as the most important project in the 8th NSEDP of Laos. Analysts believe that Laos will continue to rely heavily on China for loans and investment – especially if it is to achieve upper middle-income country status by 2030.

In a survey of participants at the ninth Asian Financial Forum (AFF) in Hong Kong, 71% said they believed the Asean region would stand to benefit from the OBOR policy[161]. The Lao government from the beginning strongly supported the China-proposed Belt and Road Initiative, and the initiative has been producing tangible benefits for the country with the construction of the Laos-China railway. As the Belt and Road Initiative progresses, more and more Chinese tourists and investors choose to travel and spend money in Laos. The OBOR changes gradually in the eyes of Lao people. Laos welcomes Chinese enterprises' investments and has now a lot of tourists coming from China. Laos is an important country along the Belt and Road, and has an increasingly close relationship with China. At present, there are around 70 flights between the two countries every week.

The Lao government hopes that infrastructure development, tourism development, and promotion of natural resource based industries will change the country from being a landlocked one to a land-linked one. It is also hoped that this will provide Laos full access to the seaports of neighboring countries and other regional networks of roads and railways. These priority sectors are expected to significantly enhance the process of economic development and poverty reduction. Moreover, the development of the ICT sector in Laos falls in line with China's Belt and Road initiative as this technology will be key for connectivity between China and countries in Southeast Asia.

It is well understood that China is fast expanding its influence within the Southeast Asian region as it attempts to win over nations by offering beneficial investment. Admittedly, Chinese influence is likely to grow even more as Laos becomes increasingly reliant on Beijing.

6.5.3. China-Laos High Speed Railway

Why build the China-Laos High Speed Railway? Who benefits from it? For China, the railway will serve as an important link in connecting countries within Southeast Asia, part of Beijing's trillion-dollar One Road and One Belt Initiative envisions a coherent trade link running from the southern Chinese city of Kunming to the island state of Singapore. The China-Laos High Speed Railway is therefore to remedy the missing link between China and South East of Asia in terms of transport railway communication (North-South Corridor).

Laos is clearly a key link for China's OBOR ambitions; the country is an important transit route for Beijing's One Belt and One Road Initiative strategy coupled with a greater integration among Asean economies. Indeed, via the OBOR Initiative, China is keen to make Laos part of its economic chain as China and Thailand have a planned cooperation pact for the flagship Eastern Economic Corridor (EEC) and Kunming's Specific Economic Zone (SEZ).

Laos has been stepping up efforts to improve its infrastructure, as it is the only inland country in Southeast Asia and it still limited transport options.

According to Lattanamany Khounnyvong, Vice Minister of Public Work and Transport: "Once completed, the railway will help facilitate people-to-people exchanges, reduce traveling time and costs. The railway will also help promote agricultural production in Laos, increase income, attract more foreign investment and provide more employment opportunities[162]." Most importantly, "the project will help Lao people to quickly escape from poverty and improve their living standards," said Lattanamany Khounnyvong.

Is the rail project worthy for Laos? Laos has currently only about 3.5 kilometers of narrow-gauge railway, which cannot meet the demand of rail passengers and the development of the local economy. When the China-Laos Railway traversing the country is completed, it will first greatly mobilize the development of the Lao economy, improving its transportation, boosting the tourism industry, and creating more jobs for the locals. Second, it will make travel between the two countries cheaper and easier compared with the expensive air flights and time-consuming coach. Third, China-Laos trains will make it convenient to transport Lao products, especially agricultural products, to China, and conversely deliver Chinese products to Laos and other Southeast Asian countries by land. Compared with costly air freight, train freight will greatly reduce the cost. This High Speed Railroad Project is the first step in building a railroad network that connects China with other Southeast Asian countries. It stands out as one of the notable landmarks in showcasing the Chinese High Speed Railway Network to the world. The China-Laos Railway will connect Kunming, the capital city of southwestern China's Yunnan Province, with Laos' capital city, Vientiane. This project is actually a section of the Kunming-Singapore Railway Project, which connects Kunming with Singapore, passing through Laos, Thailand, and Malaysia. The integration of China-Laos railway into the Trans-Asian Railway will certainly play a role in generating profits for countries along the route, but the countries involved have not yet started any discussions on the mater[163].

The train is scheduled to open by the end of December 2021, despite many challenges (unexploded land mines clearance, difficulty in logistic and transport, lack of local labors, and difficulty encountered in negotiation on land compensation). The designed speed is 160-200 km/h, and the expected duration from Kunming-Vientiane is about 10 hours. It is planned that altogether 33 stations will be built along the Kunming-Vientiane High Speed Railway. When finished, train will be the top choice to travel around Laos as well as to travel between Laos and China. With regard to the section Mohan (Boten)-Vientiane: The construction of this section began on December 2nd, 2015. The designed speed is 160 km/h and the length is 427 km. Around 162 bridges and 72 tunnels will be built along the way, accounting for about 60% of the overall length, making it a difficult project. Among the bridges, two super ones will run over the Mekong River, measuring 1,220m and 1,436m respectively. The project is jointly funded by the Chinese and Lao governments in the ratio of 70% to 30%.

Even if some critics said that the railway would lose money for the first 11 years following a feasibility study by a Chinese company, for the Lao leaders it is by far a geopolitical matter for Laos. The project will play an exemplary role in the Belt and Road Initiative and will showcase the enhanced connectivity among Southeast Asian countries, as well as bringing business benefits for local communities, according to Chinese economists and Lao authorities. The impact of the OBOR Initiative and the railway project are huge for Laos in terms of strong momentum for economic and industrial development. More importantly, it allows the Lao's government to accelerate the implementation of the "2030 Sustainable Development" agenda. "The One Belt, One Road" development strategy and framework have become a bridge connecting China and other countries around the world in several fields of cooperation including trade and investment[164].

Notes

149 Microsoft partners Laos government to develop holistic plan for education to leverage technology, Posted December 15, 2015 By Microsoft APAC News Center.
150 ADB, Microsoft, Lao PDR Collaborate to Expand Economic pportunities for Youth, News from ADB Country Office, 26/11/2016.
151 ICT businesses urged to drive economy, 25/01/2018.
152 IFC, ACLEDA Bank team up foster SME financing, 13/10/2017.
153 DSG and CEVA Logistics collaborate in business, Vientiane Times, 9/10/2017.

154 Phongsavanh, Motorola bringing modern communication technology systems to country, Vientiane Times, 14/10/2017.
155 Lao-Thai venture to build private hospital in Vientiane, Vientiane Times, 1/02/2018.
156 Based on Dr. Sisalio Svengsuksa SL-FC Conference paper, Politique agricole.
157 Garment industry commended for protecting workers' rights, Vientiane Times, 27/12/2017.
158 Laos Textile and Garment Industry, February 2011.
159 South Eas, Vienti nt Asia Textile Business Review 2009.
160 China and Laos Sign the Joint General Scheme for Mohan-Boten Cross-Border Economic Cooperation Zone", September 1, 2015, http://la.mofcom.gov.cn/article/zwjingji/201510/20151001147759.shtml, accessed on July 3, 2016.
161 The 9th Asian Financial Forum Opens in Hong Kong Global Financial Experts Gather to Discuss the Theme of "Asia: Shaping the New Paradigm for Growth", HKTDC Press release, 18/01/2016.
162 Interview with Xinhua: Belt and Road Initiative bringing tangible benefits to Laos: official, 2/05/2017.
163 China-Laos railway on track as project set to be completed in 2021, despites challenges; Global Times, 13/11/2017.
164 Railway project, a milestone in Laos' socio-economic development, Vientiane Times, 16/12/17.

CHAPTER 7

Laos Sustainable Growth Development Strategy and Vision 2030

7.1. The Growth Strategy Path in the AEC Context

7.1.1. The Achievements of the Laos Current Model

Laos' development record over the past 30 years is significant. Economic and political reforms under the "New Economic Mechanism", launched in 1986, have spurred rapid and steady economic growth and development and transformed Laos from one of the world's poorest nations to a lower middle-income country.

Laos is a small, landlocked economy that has experienced rapid growth based on capital-intensive investments in the energy sector, increasingly taking advantage of its location between its larger and more populous neighbors. The present growth model is driven mainly by strong electricity, gold, and copper exports, the construction of a couple of large infrastructure projects, and a surge in cash crop production and export. In addition, foreign aid has a strong positive impact and is the main contributor to the income level and income growth of the country.

This economic model has been opted successfully by the government over thirty years, based on intensive exploitation of natural resources and a reliance on foreign direct investments in this sector. In fact, the present model produced various positive results, mobilizing all possible resources for production and satisfying demands for food, employment, and the well-being of the population. Furthermore, the emergence of the private sector and appearance of a growing urban middle class are the most visible gains; without forgetting to mention that the agricultural sector ensured food security and an increasing volume of farm products for export (rice, coffee, and cassava). The living standard in rural areas was improved, while poverty-alleviating programs have attained significant achievements.

Since 2006, Laos' GDP growth has been among the fastest in the region, averaging 7 percent a year in the 2010s, although the GDP per capita is one of the lowest. Despite uncertainties in the global environment, Laos' economy remains resilient. The country's medium-term outlook remains favorable, with GDP recorded at a little less than 7 percent in 2017.

Progress has been made in achieving the United Nations' Millennium Development Goals, but the rate of poverty remains relatively high. However, the rate of extreme poverty has fallen to 20 percent compared to 70 percent of the population in the 1990s. The Lao population today is more educated and healthier than thirty years ago, and these advances are enjoyed across society. In average, learning outcomes are moderately high, including in primary school. Infant and under-five mortality rates have been significantly reduced in the last thirty years and life expectancy at birth is now 66.6 years, an improvement from 49 years in 1980. Significant progress was charted from 1980 to 2016. For example, as of September 2017, a total of 1,092,611 families or 94.23 percent of all households nationwide had access to the electricity grid. There were about 7,032 families with access to solar power. Immediately prior to the foundation of the Lao PDR in 1975, only 19,000 families or 3 percent of the population had access to electricity[165]. More than 51 percent of the rural population now enjoys access to sanitation facilities, and more than 55 percent have access to clean water, compared to only 11 percent and 8 percent, respectively, three decades earlier.

However, poverty gains are fragile and a significant portion of the population, particularly in rural areas and among ethnic minorities, is vulnerable to falling back into poverty. Too many inequality gaps, discrepancies, and injustices exist between different regions and between rich and ordinary people. Yet development challenges and limitations remain for Laos in the AEC context. The contribution of productivity growth is not sufficient, and a large number of informal and small and medium-sized companies have poor performance and a lack of competitiveness. The labor force is constantly in deficit; in addition, the country does not provide enough skilled laborers to accompany the economic development and needs therefore to import them from neighboring countries. Compared to Asean country members, Laos is suffering heavily in human resources and its education system is not yet up to the regional standards, which is a big handicap to its development.

At the same time, while broad macroeconomic stability remains, some vulnerabilities, including fiscal imbalances, public debt, an unstable balance of trade and payment, waste of natural resources, and unresolved asset quality problems in the banking sector, require specific attention. A stronger domestic private sector could also serve as an engine for growth, as would accelerated reforms in the SOE sector and stronger SMEs, but this is still yet to come. Human resource capacity building is another big challenge for the country for the years to come. The Lao government has thus placed priority on building its human resource capacity to address existing skills gaps in order to sustain social development and economic growth and support new enterprise. In addition to its basic education support, Australia and other countries also assist human resource development in Laos at the individual and institutional level to address existing shortages in skilled labor and to improve basic service delivery.

The 8th National Socioeconomic Development Plan (NSEDP) for 2016-2020, approved in April 2016 by the National Assembly, acknowledges the slow progress on certain policy priorities and emphasizes the need to accelerate reforms, and seeks to change the structure of production towards value-added manufacturing and service.

The present model of economic growth might not be sustainable and needs possibly to be readjusted according to the new phase of Laos' development, taking into consideration the AEC context and the country's own political and economic strategy for 2030.

7.2. Towards the 8th NSEDP, the Sustainable Growth With the Socioeconomic Development Strategy Until 2025 and the Vision 2030

The period of the 8th Five-Year Plan and the government Vision 2030 will be an extremely challenging time for Laos to undertake substantial reforms by accelerating the development of education, technology, digital economy, and innovation for its administration and private sector as key factors in empowering the development of all aspects needed to increase the country's competitiveness. Furthermore, in addition to persistent levels of income inequality, Lao citizens still lack the knowledge, skills, qualities and attitudes needed to realize the country's development to follow the pace of the AEC's path.

Laos is at a turning point, where it can turn its weakness of being a 'landlocked' country into its strength, by becoming a 'land-linked' country in the Mekong Region. The Lao government is favorable to the pursuit of new development strategies and has formulated policies to incorporate into Laos' official plans, such as the 10-Year Socioeconomic Development Strategy (2016–2025) and the Vision 2030 (2016–2030). The long-term plans: The Laos Vision 2030, the Strategy 2025 and the Main Directions for 2016–2020 are illustrated in Figure 34.

Figure 34. Three Steps of Development Path

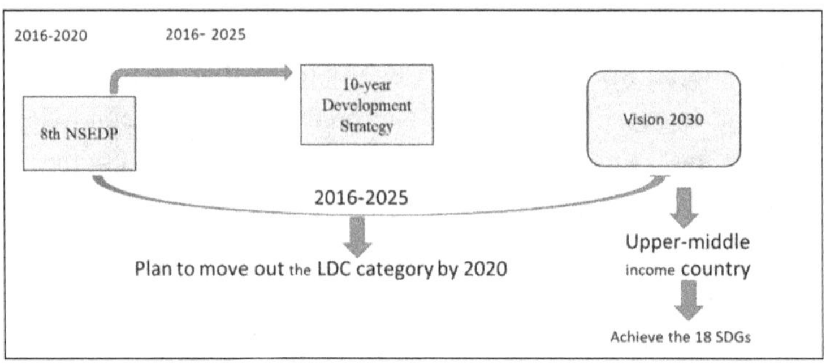

In implementing the model of intensive growth focused on energy and mining) since 1986, Laos has obtained many encouraging achievements in the past 30 years; yet this model has gradually revealed shortcomings in some aspects as explained above and in chapter 2. The next step involves changing to an intensive growth model, more inclusive, particularly by integrating the mainly rural, primarily agrarian population into more economically productive activities, promoting the quality of FDI, supporting sciences and technology and e-commerce, encouraging green development, enhancing opportunities to bring more investments, trade, and services to Laos, and boosting the private sector. This is an urgent task, and it is not easy in the current conditions in Laos. Some preconditions for a successful change in the economic growth model are necessary along with a strong political determination. In particular these require huge public and private investments, well-coordinated industrial policies, interconnected agriculture and services, better education and technology appropriation, and greater integration into the regional and global economy and its value chains.

During the period of the 8th Five-Year Plan and the 10-year Development Strategy Goals, Laos will undertake a range of reforms aimed at improving its macroeconomic indicators and social development. These reforms will take place within a global situation of rapid change and closer connectivity. Competition within the regional economy will be more intense, while the global society will be drawn closer together in an increasingly borderless world. In addition, the rapid pace of technological change will significantly affect either people's daily lives or their economic activities, particularly in service sector, banking, hospital, administration, and e-commerce. Meanwhile, Laos will face an array of fundamental strategic development factor limitations which will provide an obvious obstacle to the country's future development.

7.2.1. Laos Vision 2030

In formulating the 8th NSEDP, the Lao government adhered to the Vision 2030, this consists of the country's Sustainable Development Goals (SDGs), green and sustainable economic growth; industrialization and modernization of its economy; socialist market economy; social justice, peace and order; and as well as other reform agendas. The Vision 2030 is based on the national characteristics and context as well as the international environment and the national development priorities.

Laos is categorized as a developing country and aims to become upper-middle income by 2030, development under the 8th Plan constitutes the first five years of the implementation of the 15-year of Vision 2030, which is Laos's development long-term plan for steering the country towards security, prosperity, and sustainability. It identifies the targets for Laos's development over the next 15 years, as well as strategic issues and the main directions to be followed to achieve these targets. The 8th NSEDP in turn will be a major tool to energize the implementation of the national Vision 2030, alongside with other mechanisms and supporting instruments. The Vision 2030 will establish the main development directions that must be followed under any government in order to achieve the country's future development targets. A core objective of the Vision 2030 is for Laos to be an upper-middle income country by the end of its implementation period. Thus, both the overall targets and the sectorial targets of the 8th NSEDP are consistent with the targets of the 15-year of Vision 2030. Similarly, the subsequent National Socioeconomic Development Plan will continue to pursue the objectives and targets of the 15-year Vison 2030 after the 8th Plan period had been completed.

By taking into account the above-mentioned principles, the Vision 2030 aims to achieve the following objectives:

Ensure political and social stability;

1. Achieve per capita income in 2030 four times that of 2015;
2. Become an Upper Middle Income Country (the initiative to avoid the middle income trap);
3. Have an industrialized and modernized economy with strong supporting infrastructure;
4. Assure better living standards, human capital development, social security, and people being protected by law;
5. Ensure smaller disparity between urban and rural areas;
6. Conserve natural resources and use them efficiently; and
7. Ensure competitiveness, connectivity, and integration with the regional and global economies.

7.2.2. Key Government Direction for the 8th NSEDP (2016–2020)

The NSEDP aligns to Laos Socioeconomic Development Strategy 2016–2025, the Laos Vision 2030 and the Global Goals for Sustainable Development (SDGs). Furthermore, a majority of the 8th NSEDP targets are closely linked to the SDGs.

The development objectives of the 8th Five-Year Plan over the next five years, linked cumulatively with subsequent plans to those of the 10-year Socioeconomic Development Strategy and Vison 2030, and adopted the following core principles[166]:

1. Ensure the continued economic growth with quality and macro stability;
2. Ensure sustainable development with harmonization among economic development, socio-cultural development, and environmental protection;
3. Strengthen human resource capacity by improving workforce skills, increase the number of technical experts and specialists, enhance the technical and professional capacity of civil servants, including private industry and entrepreneurs, to enable them to compete within the country and abroad;
4. Maintain political stability, peace, and social order; and
5. Continue wide international cooperation, and enhance favorable conditions for regional and international integration.

7.2.3. The Ten-year Socioeconomic Development Strategy (2016–2025)

The 10 year Socioeconomic Development Strategy (2016-2025) consist of seven strategies described as follows:

1. Pursuing continuous, quality, balanced, sustainable, and green growth;
2. Fully graduating from LDC status by 2020, and making progress on sustainable development goals (SDGs);
3. Human resource development;
4. Sustainable and efficient utilization and preservation of natural resources;
5. Enhancing the democratic administration system according to law;
6. Global and regional integration and connectivity; and
7. Industrializing and modernizing the country.

Both the 10-Year Development Strategy and the 8th NSEDP are designed in the context of changing domestic and global socioeconomic contexts: the arriving force of the AEC and the opportunities for Laos; the increasing cooperation within the CLVM; the fall of commodity prices; the Asian Infrastructure Investment Bank (AIIB), a multilateral development bank that aims to support the building of infrastructure in the Asia-Pacific region; the One Bank and One Road Initiative (OBOR), which integrated Laos; and the increasing weight of Laos to its major partners Vietnam, Thailand, China, and

Malaysia. They also aim to become a guide to long-term development policies formulated by the Lao government. The Vision 2030 and the 10-Year Development Strategy will provide comprehensive direction for the 8th Five-Year NSEDP and beyond. This policy seeks also to improve connectivity in the ASEAN region as a whole.

7.2.4. The Outcomes of the 8th NSEDP (2016–2020)

The 8th NSEDP and the 10-year Development Strategy strive to continue the strong economic growth with the goal of graduating to a middle-income economy by 2020. The current 8th Five-Year Plan (2016-2020) of the Lao government is a continuation of the 7th Five-Year Plan. The Plan is regarded as a measure for achieving socio-economic development, industrialization, and modernization towards the year 2020. It is building the foundation from LCD status by 2020 to become an upper-middle income country by 2030. The plan presents three "Outcomes."

- Outcome 1: The Economy: A strong economic foundation and reduced economic vulnerability to levels required for LDC graduation and consolidated financial, legal and human resources to support growth.
- Outcome 2: Society: Human resources development, poverty eradication in all ethnic groups, access to high-quality education and healthcare, and the preservation and development of Laos' unique culture; development and upgrading the capacities of the public and private sectors; access or all ethnic groups and both genders to quality education and health services; maintenance of political stability, social peace and order, justice and transparency.
- Outcome 3: The Environment: Green and sustainable natural resources and environmental protection and management; preparedness for natural disasters and climate change and for reconstruction following natural disasters.

In addition, in the context of the 8th NSEDP, Laos needs to respond to the transition from the MDGs to incorporating the global development framework provided by the Sustainable Development Goals (SGDs), which contains 18 sustainable development goals for Laos, and to achieve its goal of graduating from least developed country status by 2020 through the realization of these Outcomes.

7.3. The Sustainable Development Goals (SGDs)

With regard to the Sustainable Development Goals (SGDs), at the present, the United Nations has defined the post-2015 development agenda and adopted it officially in September 2015, which also marked the day of completion of the MGDs. The Sustainable Development Goals (SDGs) provide a framework for the government to monitor and evaluate the progress in its development plan implementation and commitments. In Laos, UNDP is working closely with the government to ensure that SDG goals and targets are streamlined into national development plans. The Lao government has mainstreamed the Sustainable Development Goals (SDGs) into its eighth five-year National Socio-Economic Development Plan (2016-2020), the Development Strategy 2025, and Vision 2030.

There has been significant progress already in SDG localization, with many SDG goals and targets included in Laos' 8th NESDP. Laos is one of the first countries in the world to localize the SDGs into the national development plan. In addition to the 17 SDGs, the Lao government has adopted an additional goal (SDG 18): "Lives Safe from UXO" – unexploded ordnance[167]. The SGDs detailed for Laos are as following:

1. End poverty in all its form everywhere;
2. End hunger, achieve food security, improve nutrition, and promote sustainable agriculture;
3. Ensure healthy lives and promote well-being for all ages;
4. Ensure inclusive and equitable quality education and promote lifelong learning opportunities for all;
5. Achieve gender parity and empower all women and girls;
6. Ensure the availability and sustainable management of water and sanitation for all;
7. Ensure access to affordable, reliable, sustainable, and modern energy for all;
8. Promote sustained, inclusive, and sustainable economic growth, along with full and productive employment and decent work for all;
9. Build resilient infrastructure, promote inclusive and sustainable industrialization, and foster innovation;
10. Reduce inequality within and among countries;

11. Make cities and human settlements inclusive, safe, resilient, and sustainable;
12. Ensure sustainable consumption and production patterns;
13. Take urgent action to combat climate change and its impacts;
14. Conserve and promote sustainable use of the oceans, sea, and marine resources for sustainable development;
15. Protect, restore, and promote sustainable use of terrestrial ecosystems, sustainably manage forests, combat desertification, and halt and reverse land degradation and halt biodiversity loss;
16. Promote peaceful and inclusive societies for sustainable development, provide access to justice for all and build effective, accountable, and inclusive institutions at all levels;
17. Strengthen the means of implementation and revitalize the global partnership for sustainable development; and
18. Reduce the impacts of unexploded ordnance in Laos.

In summary, the 8th NSEDP (2016-2020) is articulated within the context of the government's long-term plan to 2025 and the Vision 2030. It enforces the goal to continue Laos' rapid growth path of recent years and graduate to an upper middle-income country by 2020. It also aims to prepare the country for post LDC graduation, and for this it recognizes the need to implement policies that will support productivity and private sector growth along with consolidation of knowledge and skills, realizing of comparative advantage, acquisition and application of science and technology, including digital economy and continued diversification, emphasizing the role of the agriculture, and tourism industries in regard. In particular, it identifies the continued need to strengthen economic integration with the region and broader economic diversification, notably by developing processing industry, organic agriculture, and tourism industries, as key strategies, and recognizes the importance of infrastructure development for achieving such objectives[168].

Notes

[165] Government investment speeds up access to electricity, Vientiane Times, 5/01/2018.
[166] 8th Five-Year National Socioeconomic Development Plan (2016-2020), Ministry of Planning and Investment, June 2016.
[167] Sustainable Development Goals spur progress in Laos, Prime Minister tells at the 71st Session of the United Nations General Assembly held in New York on September 23, Vientiane Times, 9/10/2016.
[168] OECD Investment Policy Reviews: Lao PDR.

CHAPTER 8

How to Achieve the Objectives and Targets of the Sustainable Development Strategy and Vision 2030?

8.1. Towards the Achievement of the Objectives and Targets

The 8th NSEDP (2016-2020) is the five-year Laos development plan that translates the long-term 15-year country Vision 2030 into action. Therefore, the direction of the 8th Plan, which is set within the principles of the Sustainable Development", aims to prepare and lay the foundation for Laos to be an upper middle-income country and to achieve "Political stability, Peace, and Social order". The objectives and development targets of the 8th Plan are set within the framework of the vision and targets for Laos' future, in 2030, which are incorporated in the long-term 15-year Vision 2030. The objectives and development targets of the 8th Plan are also drawn from an assessment of external and internal factors that reveals the country's strengths, weaknesses, opportunities and threats in striving to achieve the development targets of the first five years of the long-term 15-year Vision 2030. These are set to underpin the continuous effectiveness of the subsequent National Socioeconomic Development Plans' outcomes. Hence, the question is how to make progress toward achieving the SDGs as a result of realizing the 8th NESDP, the 10-year Socioeconomic Development Strategy, and the long-term Vision 2030 as described in Chapter 7.

The Vision 2030 calls for further improvements on the economic system, reforms to the role of the government in the economy, faster fiscal and financial markets, development of a modern market economy, improvements in human resources and education, improvements in income distribution and the social safety net, as well as enhanced investment in health and culture, among others. Over the period 2020-2025, Lao citizens would expect movement in the direction of "balanced development," higher "quality" growth, greater "investment in bio-agriculture," and greater "production in the processing industry". And it's best not to forget that the green economy industry will play a significant role and will take part in the country's development. This movement will be in part so that officials can show they have been acting in a way consistent with the plan and that it will be significant. These objectives should be viewed as important long-term goals of the state along with rapid economic development, preservation of national security, and assertion of national prestige.

The success of the long-term Vision 2030 will depend on how efficiently the nine stages below can be implemented and the means allocated by businesses, along with mobilizing the government, its local agencies, and donors. Laos needs to have long-term strategy in order to deal effectively with many problems and challenges faced by the country over the next fifteen years.

The diagram below proposes as a path to ensure the continuation of Laos' economic and social development goals and stability in policy formulation by successive governments. It also aims to compliment the United Nations' Sustainable Development Goals. It takes into account the "Outcomes of the 8th NESDP", aimed at enhancing national development in all aspects; strengthening national competitiveness; developing and empowering human capital; broadening opportunities to improve social equality and equity; steering toward a green economy and society; and reforming and improving public administration.

In summary, the long-term Vision 2030 sets out can be simplified in 9 priority pillars illustrated as follows:

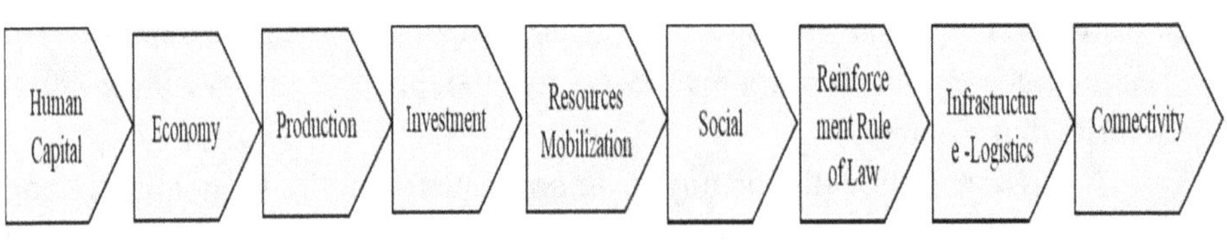

1. Human Capital: It aiming to create high potential human capital by means of human resource development in all aspects within the context of transitional changes. This is starting by improving the whole education system and upgrading the level of pupils and students. Increasing number of vocational centers and schools, and providing continuing training to skilled workforce. The Human Capital Management is essential for hiring, managing, training and retaining talented staff and high performing labor force that Laos needs for its development.

2. Economy: Maintaining economic growth at 7 percent; reducing public debt and improving taxes and revenue collection; stabilizing the Kip and controlling the inflation. Assuring the stability of the economy and growth over the next 15 years, and commencing to take part on the green economy and digital economy.

3. Production: Aiming quality and competitiveness; boosting processing industry and capacity building in farmer technology. In addition, the productivity will call for innovation, science and technology.

4. Investment: Boosting quality of investment; bringing together public sector, development partners, private investment; improving facilities and creating confidence and rust in business; providing access to financing to enterprises.

5. Resources Mobilization: Bringing all the forces of the nation: government, administration, professional association, businesses, farmers, workers, civil servants, officials, and citizens to cooperate in achieving the Vision 2030.

6. Social: Reducing inequality between region and between rural and urban population; continuing efforts to reduce poverty and providing social security to all.

7. Reinforcement of Rule of Law: Better enforcement of legislation and law; improving legal environment.

8. Infrastructure and Logistics: Improving and expanding road transports and logistics infrastructure in order to link with neighboring countries.

9. Connectivity: Becoming the regional connectivity hub in terms of communication, energy, transport, and trade with its immediate neighbors, transforming Laos from a landlocked to land-linked country. To that end, the successful achievement of the connectivity is a prerequisite for Laos' sustainable development.

8.2. What Are the Key Development Strategies to Achieve the Vision 2030?

The above nine pillars can be aggregated into four development strategies set as follows:

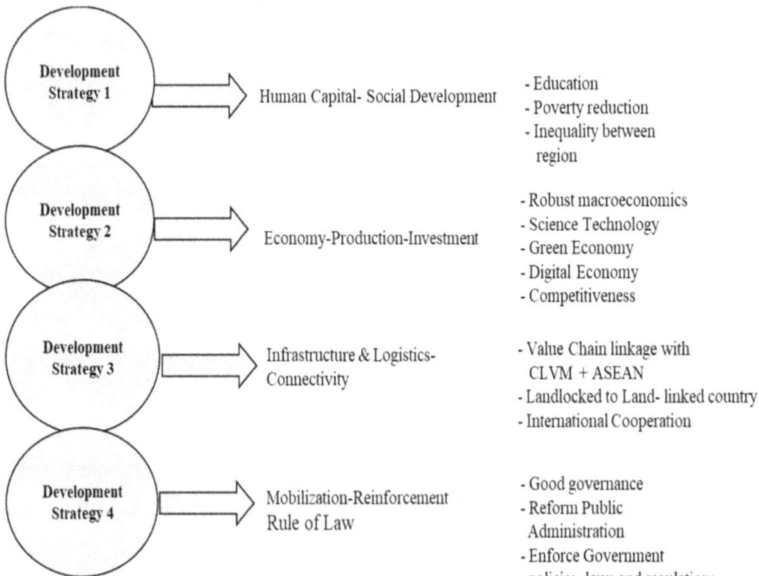

The "Laos model" has become shorthand for economic liberalization without fully political liberalization. But Laos' model of development is actually a successful, taking into consideration its own characteristics and historic features. It builds on steps designed to ensure that the LPRP remains central to economic and political policy-making. Like other high-growth Asean economies, Laos also has created highly favorable environments for foreign investment.

Yet in the Laos model, the government maintains a significant degree of control over the economy, and the path to socialism is preserved. Laos has developed a hybrid form of capitalism in which it has opened its economy to some extent, but it also ensures the government controls strategic industries, picks corporate winners, determines investments by state participation, and pushes the banking sector to support national enterprises, private sector, and particularly small and medium size companies. Furthermore, the economic reform is needed to pursue the sustainable growth in a more balanced development approach to halt the rising of inequality within Laos, between the favored urban areas and the less well-off interior rural provinces, this unbalanced wealth distribution also threatens Laos' sustainable economic growth and destabilize social institutions.

Independently of expert and research institutes' findings, the few recommendations below are the thoughts and outcomes from the discussions with business community, donors, international NGO, and professional associations.

8.2.1. Development Strategy 1: Human Capital and Social Development

Laos has made notable progress in human development and poverty reduction, however, the country's progress in poverty reduction and human development are uneven both across its regions and among its ethnic groups. Laos is going through significant moves over the next decade – immigration, urbanization, social, economical, technological, political, and environmental. These severely affect its most important resource that the country does not have: limited population and quality of the education system. Furthermore, economic strong growth has not been inclusive and the majority of Lao people have not reaped the benefits. With the population set to 7.4 million by 2020 and 8.6 in 2030, its greatest asset will be Laos' capacity to success in building its human capital development[169], improving notably the education system, creating a fair society, and reducing the inequality.

The Development Strategy 1 highlights that Laos continues to face challenges to equitable human development. The incomes have risen, but poverty reduction and consumption lag behind the GDP growth rate and inequalities are increasing.

Addressing these challenges will be essential to fulfil the country's aspirations to graduate smoothly from Least Developed Country status. In order to capture this demographic shortage, the **Human Capital Development Strategy** shall focus priority to education, skills for competitiveness and employment opportunities, accountability and voice in efficient and inclusive service delivery and social systems that ensure inclusion and social cohesion as follows:

1. Improving adult literacy rate and increasing gross secondary school ratio is the first priority, since education and skills, along with good health, raise people's employability, which in turn opens the doors to greater incomes, and reduce inequality[170];
2. Boosting the quality of the education system and lifelong learning;
3. Providing adequate infrastructure and qualified teachers to the education system;
4. Adjusting teacher training programs, with more emphasis placed on competency-based programs, professionalism, coaching skills, and the ability to stimulate learning;
5. Better teaching with more qualified teachers so that disadvantaged children (girls and boys, especially the poor and marginalized) have improved access to education;
6. Ensuring that all children finish their primary education, and giving them important literacy and numeracy skills;
7. Creating incentive mechanisms designed to attract high-potential individuals to become teachers, adjusting the teachers' academic standing evaluation method to reflect students' performance, as well as building teaching knowledge exchange networks for teachers as a platform for continuous competency development among teachers;
8. Improving the quality of non-illiteracy still a challenge to development formal education to meet the individual needs of students in rural and urban areas, including the provision of basic vocational training for adults and youths in rural areas;
9. Improving labor training centers all across the country in order to enhance and develop the competencies required by the national professional qualification framework;

10. Encouraging social institutions collaboratively to take part in strengthening the nation's development;

11. Enhancing the efficiency of public health service system management and improving the health financing system using ICT and digital infrastructure;

12. Assuring universal medical coverage for all citizens;

13. Pursuing poverty reduction and reducing inequality between region and between rich and poor as inequality is detrimental to human development, and prevents efforts to graduate Laos out of its LDC status;

14. Laos' human capital is very low, its labor force is the least literate and numerate in the Asean. In addition, the country has shortages of vocational skills. The size of Lao PDR's labor force will remain very small. The current size of Lao PDR's labor force (aged 15-64) is 4.2 million. It is projected to increase to 5.6 million in 2030, and to only 7 million in 2050. Currently, the country needs to employ foreign labor for its industry sector and in the SEZs; and

15. Building job-relevant technical skills and training centers across the country in partnership with the private sector is crucial for the development of the industry. A more strategic role of the government and the businesses in vocational skills development is required to develop policies, set standards, invest in training materials and instructors, improve public information about the training system, and carry out training evaluations.

8.2.2. Development Strategy 2: Economy-Production-Investment

The 8th NSEDP and the Socioeconomic Development Strategy (2016-2025) focus on inclusive growth in order to maintain a stable growth around 7 percent and expand the trade with neighboring countries. The Plan sets the goal of increasing economic opportunity, private sector, and quality of investment, social opportunity, and incomes of the 70 percent of the population with the lowest income. In addition, increasing productivity based on knowledge and innovation development is a crucial factor in driving the development of every sector to the next level. In moving towards the goal of being an upper middle-country by 2030, the targets of increasing income, creating a fair society, reducing inequality, expanding the middle class population group, and creating a quality society with good governance and environmental friendliness are therefore set to encourage a form of economic growth that contributes to inequality reduction and promotes greater levels of productivity.

Laos' economy centered to an energy and mining-based economy. The industry has continuously accumulated knowledge and production skills. Laos has become a significant exporter of electricity and mineral based products. At the same time, its service sector of tourism-based has grown remarkably, and to less extend handicrafts and others. However, the agricultural sector has developed at a slower pace than the other sectors because of low productivity, which is the result of the lack of use of technology, poor irrigation network, inappropriate land use, lack of financing, weakness of transport, and insufficient access to market[171].

Laos still faces problems of quality in almost all aspects, for example in terms of knowledge, skills, attitudes, virtues and ethics. There are also shortages of labor in the situation where the rapid development of the country has an urgent need. Moreover, Laos still has problems regarding the quality of public services, education, health services, ineffective law enforcement, and corruption, low basic infrastructure quality, and inefficient logistics systems, while domestic trade has not yet formed a complete network, and development in this regard is slow due to the transport deficient. Many problems remain in the basic infrastructure, such as the modes of transport have not been improved to be more efficient and meet performance targets, there is a lack of unity in management, services are insufficient and are of limited quality, have been concentrated in the urban areas. In addition, there are many laws and regulations that hinder the development of infrastructure and logistics. The development of science, technology and innovation are still slow and in an early stage. Investment in research and development is insufficient. Furthermore, local existing talents have not been used effectively to create economic or social gain.

The above complications are partly attributable to the low efficiency of public administration, lack of transparency and accountability, while development implementation has lacked continuity and law enforcement has been ineffective. Although public services, which have been provided to both the public and private sectors, have expanded, they are still slow and don't meet international standards when compared to other countries of Asean.

To ensure these pillars of cooperation are steadily implemented, it will be vital to stabilize the macro economy and achieve financial stability, coordinate development plans with the compilation of budgets, and strengthen governance.

8.2.2.1. Industry Development Orientation

According to the Ministry of Industry and Commerce, the Vision 2030 target is to ensure that commerce in Laos is open and market oriented, rule based, and in line with the ASEAN Community Vision and the World Trade Organization's framework. With regard to Laos' industrial development, a study was carried out by the Economic Research Institute for Asean and East Asia (ERIA) in cooperation with Japan's Daiwa Institute and the National Economic Research Institute from the Ministry of Planning and Investment. The country is planning in the hope that the study will help achieve the country's industrialization and modernization objectives. Actually, the research focused on eight industries that Laos can develop with sustainable growth: agriculture food processing, tourism, garment and other labor-intensive industry, transport equipment, electric and electronic machinery, small and medium enterprises, finance, and energy and transportation[172]. However, the Green Economy, the speed up development of the SEZs, and the Digital Economy are part of the Development Strategy 2025 and the Vision 2030 goals need thus distinctive attention, consensus, and support from the concerned ministries (Energy and Mines, Planning and Industry, Commerce and Industry, Agriculture and Forestry, and Sciences and Technology). ICT and digital economy will be the government priority so that to modernize its industry and improve the administration and the business efficiency.

8.2.2.2. Green Economy in the Development Strategy 2025 Plan

The Lao government is focused on the achievement of the goals in its 8th Five-year National Socio-Economic Development Plan, Development Strategy 2025 and the Vision 2030, which include green growth and sustainable development, among others, in order to attain graduation from Least Developed Country status.

The government plans to formulate a strategy for sustainable green growth that will ensure the development of the economy over the next 10 to 15 years through more effective use of national resources. More recently, Lao government officials under the patronage of the President of the Lao National Economic Research Institute and former Prime Minister Bouasone Bouphavanh, and the development partners met to discuss the project for the Green Growth strategy formulation and the establishment of a Green Growth Promotion Center of Laos[173]. The project is important for the government to be incorporated into the national socioeconomic development strategy plan as well as the national and sub-national strategy plans. "The growth strategy and green growth promotion center will become the guideline and mechanism for the harmonizing of the Green Growth strategy with the National Socioeconomic Development Plan for achieving the target of national socioeconomic development that the government decided on," said Bouasone Bouphavanh. A Roadmap shall be delivered as a guide for the implementation of green growth in Laos.

Indeed, the Green Growth Roadmap will be produced for furthering the development path to benefit the people and conserve and restore the natural capital base to continue economic growth within the limits posed by the environmental carrying capacity. In doing so, it suggests win-win situations between the economy, environment, and society to show that economic growth, environmental sustainability, and human well-being can be achieved. Adopting a full approach to development will help the country improve resilience and decrease vulnerability to climate change. Laos's neighboring countries are already well advanced in this approach, in particular Thailand.

The project of green growth strategy comes after Laos's economic growth in recent years relied too heavily on exploiting natural resources such as minerals for export, which is considered unsustainable. As a result, the extraction of finite natural resources does not constitute a sound economic base in the long-term because they will one day be ended. Nevertheless, the exploitation of natural resources is still necessary today for Laos' economic growth and national social development. For vigorous management and control of national resources and economy, it is wise to have a long-term strategy to diversify the sources of the country's revenues and to move towards the non-resources sector.

Undeniably, “Green Growth” and “Green Industry” need further and strong promotion, as it has already been done in other Asean countries. However, the Lao Department of Industry and Handicraft (DIH) is aiming tentatively to promote participation by both the public and private sectors in Green Growth and Green Industry. The “Greening” of industry will include policymaking, improved industrial production processes, and resource-efficient productivity. Laos’ green industry status is still at an early stage. The DIH is developing policies to promote high value-added products in various sectors, including agro-processing, wood manufacturing, manufacturing for the construction sector, food processing, and textile and garment manufacture. The aim is to encourage these sectors to be more efficient in resource utilization and to improve product quality, competitiveness, and the workplace environment. But the investment cost of environmentally-friendly manufacturing to produce “green”, including organic produce, is still high, calling for more tax and credit incentives to make them affordable to smaller businesses and ordinary people.

Further action is needed from government agencies to help civil society groups and communities in the country attain a better understanding of green growth, which was promoted as a new policy paradigm for emphasizing ecologically sustainable economic progress that fosters low-carbon, socially-inclusive development. It also will aim to identity stakeholders and ongoing initiatives, and to examine progress in the implementation of Green Inclusive Growth in the region. Further related initiatives will seek to facilitate dialogue between the public, private, and tertiary sectors in order to support collaboration for inclusive green growth practices and initiatives among Asean members, and last of all to encourage as well as facilitate networking between industry stakeholders across the different verticals and sectors to promote future partnerships. Laos has to a lesser extent undertaken a few measures. For example, Electricité of Laos (EDL) has two biomass plants for converting sugarcane waste into power; furthermore, small hydropower plant investors are eligible to credit Clean Development Mechanisms (CDM) or credit carbon by the United Nations Framework Convention on Climate Change" or "UNFCCC". In a recent report, the Ministry of Industry and Commerce indicated that the consumption of renewable energy at SME manufacturing factories should be increased to reach approximately 30 percent of total energy usage nationwide by 2025.

Additionally, the first of several solar power projects in Laos has been set up in Vientiane. The solar farm project has started generating 10 megawatts (MW) of solar power for Vientiane consumers in the middle of 2017, according to EDL-GEN Solar Power. The initial project will produce at 10 MW before generating 32-50 MW between 2017 and 2018 and up to 100 MW by 2020. Moreover, the US has approved a sizable grant for a 20-megawatt solar power plant feasibility study in Laos to power 30,000 households. The project supports both Laos' energy sector strategy and clean energy development in Southeast Asia.

Climate change has been recognized as a global issue putting at risk the livelihoods and security of millions of people. As a result of the 1992 Rio Summit and other summits, including the Paris COP 21 summit, Green Development has been used as a fundamental means in the world to deal with environmental challenges and play a core role in promoting a balance between development and the economy, environment, society, and culture, which are the principles of sustainable development. In the Laos context, green development is a new strategy that will ensure harmonization between economic development and environmental sustainability, and a balance between conservation and development. Currently, efforts are being made to ensure the green growth strategy is participated in by all sectors. All relevant sectors need to be ready to implement the activities of the projects supported by the World Bank, the Planning Department of the Ministry of Planning and Investment, and the National Economic Research Institute.

In response to the tendency toward global development, Laos, like other countries in Asean, is in the process of setting up a national road map on green development to contribute to the reduction of emissions that cause climate change, to take into account socially inclusive economic development, and to ensure sustainable development.

Additionally, Laos must execute a proactive strategy for creating an entrepreneurial society and intensively supporting national entrepreneurs to invest in domestic market and create potential business opportunities. The aim is also for Lao businesses to promote value chain linkages within the region, especially with CLVM.

In the recent years, Laos' overall economic development has been successful at a satisfactory level in terms of growth and economic stability. All of which has equipped the Lao economy with sound economic fundamentals and a readiness to develop further and drive Laos to be a upper middle-economy country by 2030, as set in the national reform agenda.

Development Strategy 2 as the key implementations of the agendas are as follows:

1. Further efficiency improvements in public revenue collection and budget spending are required to reduce additional fiscal deficit national budget and additional public debt.

2. Having monetary and fiscal discipline in order to achieve fiscal sustainability, more secure fiscal foundations, as well as higher international reserves;

3. Operating with more effectiveness, transparency, accountability, together with better systematic checks and balance mechanisms is recommended;

4. Revising laws and regulations to function more systematically and compliant with the economic and social structure;

5. Selection of useful and quality of investment for the country;

6. Maintaining economic stability, reinforcing and sustaining monetary and fiscal discipline, as well as developing effective monetary instruments to support capitalization;

7. Enhancing the efficiency of the financial system and financial institutions, in both the financial and capital markets;

7. Strengthening the economy by sector in order to increase the competitiveness of agriculture, industry, processing industry, services, trade and investment;

8. Providing fairness across all sectors by protecting consumers and people from being exploited, creating a competitive environment in the market as well as implementing supporting policies to facilitate Laos' ease of doing business;

9. Increasing the capacity of existing services, and creating new services, in order to drive towards a more prominent services-based economy, as well as promoting a balanced and sustainable growth of tourism;

10. Achieving more effective macroeconomic management;

11. Developing a national fiscal system that supports the competitiveness of production, services, trade and investment;

12. Enhancing Lao entrepreneurs' business skills, especially within SMEs, to increase business cooperation with neighboring countries; investing in human resources, technology, and innovation; improving the business environment and supporting the work of business associations, the LNCCI, and government agencies, under various cooperation frameworks, and providing Lao entrepreneurs with financial capital and in-depth knowledge regarding foreign production bases;

13. The Lao economic system to restructure toward a service and digital economy by supporting start-up new entrepreneurs and becoming an entrepreneurial society. The Lao economy should have robust SMEs that utilize modern instrument and digital technology in order to create quality goods and services;

14. Laos' agricultural and manufacturing product exports need to be beefed up and diversified;

15. The hydroelectricity is not limitless, Laos must prepare as the FDI in the energy sector will probably decline by 2025 and think about diversifying its economy and exports. Renewable energy such as solar energy, biomass should be carried out and developed, and investment to be planned accordingly;

16. Adopting a measured and inclusive approach based on a sound policy framework that encourages environmentally sustainable investment and promotes investment in green sectors;

17. It is essential for Laos to build understanding and enhance knowledge on green growth with a focus on a readiness program and fundraising mechanisms;

18. The organic products are increasingly in demand by neighboring and Japan, China, and European countries. Both consumers and producers in Laos are increasingly recognizing the socio-economic opportunities and healthier environmental benefits of organic agriculture and produce. However, the experience and knowledge of producing, processing and marketing of organic products remain to be at comparatively low levels in the Laos. Organic agriculture is a potential niche market and needs the Lao government's active support. Farmers need financing and technologies to grow and to increase the production. Moreover, the sector contributes to reduce rural poverty by creating employment opportunities for the country;

19. Fostering farmers to grow crops, raise livestock and fishing that is consistent with the land's potential and market demand;

20. Protecting potential agricultural land and expanding opportunities for farmers to access land for their livelihood;

21. Upgrading agricultural and food production to meet appropriate standards, respond to market demands and for healthy food consumption, in particular for export to China, Japan, and Thailand;

22. Laos cannot compete with well-established companies for industrial products in Laos and in the region, but has an advantage in a few niche market such as electricity, garments, organic agricultural products, handicrafts, ecotourism. All these items should be reinforced and targeted for exports with profit;

23. The government needs to take measures to boost the domestic economy on order to reinforce the private sector and particularly SMEs. Active promotion campaign to encourage Lao citizens to buy "made in Laos" manufactured products;

24. Improve the business environment including rules and regulations toward a fair competitive environment. Antitrust laws and tax benefits for SMEs should be improved, corporate social responsibility activities should be promoted;

25. Foster communities' capacity in economic development and strengthen microfinance based on the entrepreneurship mindset, such that communities (farmers, micro SMEs, and individual enterprises) are self-reliant and capable of managing their own land and human capital; and

26. Promoting and accelerating cluster formation for regional development in the future. The government has formed twelve Special Economic Zones (SEZ) throughout the country, private sector (domestic and foreign) have invested over US$8 billion in the delivery of manufactured goods, infrastructure and services. Federate the four southern provinces (Champassak, Sekong, Attapeu, Saravan) for example in one economic and industrial cluster can be benefit for the southern region in terms of critical size and greater potential for investors under one supervisory organization.

27. Focusing on modernizing industry, commerce, production, and services, and ensuring that they are integrated into international production chains in line with green and sustainable trends. The goals expressed in the Vision 2030 include increasing the share of exports from the processing

industry to 50% by 2020, 55% by 2025, and 65% by 2030. It also wants to see the share national gross domestic product of the processing industry and commerce to increase to 33% in 2020, 35% in 2025 and 37% five years later[174].

28. Developing the use of ICT and digitalization infrastructure throughout the country.

8.2.3. Development Strategy 3: Infrastructure & Logistic-Connectivity

The 8th NESDP strives to continue this growth path with the goal of graduation to an upper middle–income country by 2030 and recognizes the importance of infrastructure development for supporting the transition from a landlocked to a land-linked economy in order to achieve its long-term objectives. The infrastructure connectivity is crucial for Laos' economic development. Its poor infrastructure systems are a major determinant of overall costs, which in turn are among the primary causes of trade costs and jeopardize the tourism development.

The Lao government is aware the significance of the infrastructure and logistics issue and has put effort into developing its physical infrastructure in order to connect to its neighboring countries (CLVM + Thailand). Therefore, Laos must address obstacles to its socioeconomic development and has introduced regional and subregional infrastructure development projects, especially under the ASEAN framework and in the Greater Mekong Subregion (GMS) and Triangle Development Area with the financial assistance of the ADB. While Laos has enhanced its connectivity to its main trading partners through both transport and trade facilitation improvement, investment in upgrading transport network are necessary to keep pace with rapidly increasing demand. However, meeting future demand for infrastructure will require relatively large investments, besides potential additional investment needed for cross-border infrastructure projects. This could represent up to 14 percent of Lao's estimated 2010-2020 GDP.

Nonetheless, the weak infrastructure has compromised Lao's manufacturing and industrial potential and does not make it easy to do business. The transportation costs which weigh heavily on business profitability could be reduced if the government continued its infrastructure development programs, which include building the roads that would improve national and regional connectivity and, by all the odds, the efficiency of business activities.

To address the situation, the Ministry of Transport and Public Works adopted a strategic development plan for transportation and logistics in Laos and this plan was officially approved by the Lao government in 2015.

As for infrastructure development along the Thai-Lao border, the private sector of both side would be invited to invest in building the checkpoint in their territories. This would reduce the burden of the public sector and the private sector will earn income from various fees collected from transportation, warehouses, or cold storage. Moreover, local administrative organizations would be provided with the opportunity to take part in management and earn income from their management. This effort would accommodate cross-border trade, which is on the rise each year, and it would also contribute to the success of the ASEAN Economic Community.

Infrastructure (airports, seaports, roads, bridges, etc.) are all important to a country in terms of attracting investment and business and to a company when it is time to decide where to locate an investment, build a factory, establish a regional office. Conversely, the fact that Laos has infrastructure in place without providing services in logistics, the logistics operators in the regions and neighboring countries will take whole benefits in this area while Laos will reap only minor benefits with a massive responsibility of national budget spending for maintenance of the infrastructure. Therefore, implementing these logistics services in line with the strategic development plan for transportation and logistics in Laos as well as various international agreements is urgently important to consolidate goods cargo and distribution. Importantly, it will also generate real income from cross border transportation services.

The improvements of the logistics are part of the government's strategic development plan to transform the landlocked country into a regional transport hub. To do so, the Lao government has increased its budget allocation to infrastructure development and signed bilateral and multi-lateral agreements with its neighbors aimed at improving and facilitating logistics in the country – recent agreements include: the Great Mekong Sub-Regional Cross-Border Transport Facilitation *Agreement* (GMS Cross-Border Transport Facilitation Agreement (CBTA)), the ASEAN Framework Agreement on Services, and the Framework Agreement on Facilitation of Cross-border Paperless Trade for the Asia Pacific Region. These agreements aim to facilitate issues such as cross-border movement of vehicles, container customs regimes, driving licenses, road traffic regulations, licenses for transport operators, border-crossing and transit facilities and services. Besides, Laos has also become a member of United Nations Economic and Social Commission for Asia Pacific (UNESCAP) for Dry Ports, which sets aside nine locations that are assigned for international logistics parks in the country. These locations are in Bokeo, Luang Namtha, Oudomxay, Luang Prabang, and Thanalaeng in Vientiane, Borikhamxay, Khammuan, Savannakhet and Champassak provinces. Logistics improvements are underway in those nine locations, including Thanalaeng which is in ongoing negotiations for investment collaborations with Japan under a Private-Public Partnership (PPP), while Savannakhet recently opened for service.

8.2.3.1. Building the ASEAN Connectivity

Asean member states are committed to building the ASEAN Community, which is already being done. To realize this goal, a community of enhanced connectivity is essential because a well-connected Asean, from its transportation networks to its people, will contribute towards a more competitive and resilient Asean, as it will bring people, goods, services and capital closer together in accordance with the ASEAN Charter. This will ensure continued peace and prosperity for its people. Therefore, the Master Plan on ASEAN Connectivity is a key step towards achieving this vision[175]. The Master Plan is certainly an ambitious vision, demonstrating the political will of the Asean leaders. Thanks to this plan, Asean will be better connected to East Asia and to the global economy.

Enhancing intra-regional connectivity within Asean and its sub-regional groupings would benefit all Asean member states through enhanced trade, investment, tourism, and development. As all of the overland transport linkages will have to go through the mainland Southeast Asian countries of Cambodia, Laos, Vietnam, and Myanmar (CLVM), these countries stand to benefit the most through infrastructure development and the opening up of remote inland and less-developed regions. All of these efforts would significantly narrow the development gap within Asean. The state of such regional cooperation in Asean, including initiatives at the sub-regional level, are examined through the three dimensions of physical connectivity, institutional connectivity, and people-to-people connectivity.

1. With regard to **Land Transport** and **Road Infrastructure**: Asean cooperation in roads and rail aims to establish efficient, integrated, safe, and environmentally sustainable regional land transport corridors linking all Asean member states and the countries beyond. There are two flagship land transport infrastructure projects within Asean, namely the ASEAN Highway Network (AHN) and the Singapore Kunming Rail Link (SKRL).

2. For the **road infrastructure**, the ASEAN Transport Ministers (ATM) adopted a plan to develop the AHN. In particular, all designated routes to be upgraded to at least Class I standards, and the upgrading of low traffic volume non-arterial routes to Class II standards would be acceptable by the year 2020.

3. As for **Rail Infrastructure**, the SKRL flagship project was proposed at the Fifth ASEAN Summit in December 1995 and targeted for completion by 2015. It covers several routes through Singapore–Malaysia–Thailand–Cambodia–Vietnam–China (Kunming) and spur lines in Thailand–Myanmar and Thailand–Laos. Currently there are 4,069 kilometers of missing links or links which need to be rehabilitated in six member states including Cambodia, Laos, Malaysia, Myanmar, Thailand and Vietnam. Due consideration should be given to CLMV countries with regard to securing both financial and technical assistance from Asean, its dialogue partners, and other international organizations to help them in the undertaking of the SKRL project. Currently, the China-Laos Railway is under construction, and furthermore the extension phase of Nongkhai (Thailand)-Vientiane is also under construction.

In the late of December 2017, Thailand and China jointly inaugurated the construction of Thailand's first high-speed railway from Bangkok to northeastern province of Nakhon Ratchasima in the presence of Thailand Prime Minister Prayut and Chinese Premier Li Keqiang. The 253 km first phase of the railway links Bangkok with Nakhon Ratchasima province. The planned second phase of the project will link Nakhon Ratchasima (Korat) with Nong Khai on the border with Laos, which connects with the China-Laos railway in an artery railway linking Thailand, Laos and China. Thai Prime Minister said the Thailand-China high-speed railway will connect Thailand with other countries and help Thailand merge into the grand transport network under the Belt and Road Initiative[176]. Once the project Nakhon Ratchasima –

Nong Khai is finished, passengers can travel from Kunming to Singapore in ten hours, and the ASEAN Master Plan on ASEAN Connectivity (North-South) will be achieved.

4. **Asean Power Grid (APG):** Asean recognizes the critical role of an efficient, reliable and resilient electricity infrastructure in stimulating regional economic growth and development. To meet the growing electricity demand, huge investments in power generation capacity will be required. In recognizing the potential advantages to be gained from the establishment of integrated systems, Asean established the electricity interconnecting arrangements within the region through the APG under the ASEAN Vision 2020. The construction of the APG is first done on cross-border bilateral terms, then expanded to a sub-regional basis and finally to a total integrated regional system. It is expected to enhance electricity trade across borders which would provide benefits to meet the rising electricity demand and improve access to energy services in the region.

8.2.3.2. From Landlocked to Land-Linked Country

Laos is landlocked, with none of the modern infrastructure or communication networks that are necessary for the country to transact rapid economic exchanges with its neighbors and the outside world. The Lao economy is very dependent on international aid; its market is limited and lacks a significant manufacturing industry, due largely to the high logistical costs of transporting goods and insufficient private investment. The country is hardly able to develop its productivity tools. Among several other priorities, a key strategy is the importance of infrastructure development. The success of infrastructure connectivity becomes therefore a crucial issue for Laos.

With the assistance of the World Bank, the ADB, and other donors and partners, the Lao government is undertaking to strengthen road maintenance systems and improve road connectivity throughout the country. In the coming years, Laos expects to become the regional connectivity hub in terms of communication, energy, transport, and trade with its immediate neighbors. It has also the ambition to become a connectivity node between Asean member countries. Laos' strategy to become a regional transport corridor depends on substantial infrastructure links as well as a careful diplomatic balance with its more powerful neighbors. Mobilizing resources for its infrastructure needs is therefore a major challenge, as the payout from the improved infrastructure connectivity can be greatly beneficial for Laos in the long run.

Laos today is a crossroads at the center of various axes and corridors of development that are structured around China, Vietnam, and Thailand. With regional integration, the country has moved indeed from a buffer state to a central position. This new role is bolstered by Asean membership but also by Laos's contribution to the Greater Mekong Subregion, leading to the construction of transportation corridors financed by the Asian Development Bank and by private and domestic investment. (Investment can also be under a BOOT scheme[177], or a Public Private Partnership [PPP] in the case of railways or hydropower projects.).

In early February 2018, Laos' national Data Centre was underscored by the deputy minister of Post and Telecommunications Thongsay Xanxaya for the role it could play in linking China and Asean nations under the Master Plan on Asean Connectivity 2025. It is envisaged that Laos will become a hub within the region through the use of telecommunication and internet facilities and a high-speed transmission network connecting China with Asean countries under The Belt and Road – Digital Economy International Cooperation Initiative. This would doubtless overcome Laos' current disadvantage of being geographically landlocked.

Sixty years after independence and after forty two years of socialist rule, Laos has transformed its status from landlocked country to land-linked country; in other words, it is a state that has found a way to open up via high-speed rail projects and various infrastructure construction works under the GMS program. Indeed, Laos occupies a strategic position on the main transit routes designated by the GMS program (registered by the ADB in 1992), namely the north-south corridor connecting the cities of Yunnan and Sichuan Provinces in China with Bangkok on the one hand, and the east-west corridor linking the cities on the eastern and western coasts of the Indochinese Peninsula on the other. Laos is perfectly positioned as a driver of Asean connectivity. And the GMS program is transforming the Mekong River countries into a "new frontier of Asian economic growth." The opening up of Laos via these programs is a top government priority and is deemed vital for socioeconomic development; the ADB and Asean, for their part, support the strategy of creating economic corridors as a way of promoting regional connectivity. Laos' strategy to become a regional transport corridor depends on substantial infrastructure links as well as a careful diplomatic balance with its more powerful neighbors. Within the AEC framework, Laos has developed with the CLVM and Thailand measures to increase two-way trade and boost connectivity in their economies, transport, infrastructure, and energy systems.

Addressing the implementation of the Development Strategy of infrastructure, logistics and connectivity are as follows:

1. Road infrastructures are below standard and inadequate, Lao's transport sector shall deeply invest on infrastructure development and contributing to the SDG specifically Goal: 9 and 11;

2. Transport development and connectivity is an important thread to poverty eradication, hunger elimination, social integration and sustainable development. Therefore, further expansion and development infrastructure are needed in rural transport network;

3. Upgrading and developing road infrastructure for rural – urban connectivity and road linkages to neighboring countries;

4. Involving private investment in infrastructure and establishing a Public Private Partnership (PPP) legal and institution framework for project infrastructure development facility;

5. Strengthen the capacity and co-ordination across the government for planning and assessing infrastructure priorities so as to ensure infrastructure strategies are well integrated with overall national strategies;

6. Limited ICT infrastructure and use is likely to contribute to increased trade of costs, therefore improving and accelerating access and use of ICT is vital for Laos' economic and business development;

7. Transport connectivity has improved considerably in the past decade, but the quality is poor and below regional standards. The poor quality of the road network and its maintenance are an important shortcomings of economic development. Addressing those deficiencies become urgent for the government's economy;

8. Inland water transport is limited, development partners and private sector to expand and to improve the Mekong River transport are needed;

9. The goal of a seamless regional connectivity: Physical connectivity, encompassing both hard infrastructure in transport, ICT, and energy infrastructure as well as the regulatory framework and the software necessary

to deliver associated services and utilities, plays a crucial role in the process toward a more economically and socio-culturally integrated Asean region, through trade- and investment-facilitating infrastructure, potential reductions in trade-related costs, and by facilitating people-to-people contact shall be pursued in the framework of ASEAN Connectivity; and

10. Developing Land International Border Crossing Points with neighboring countries: Laos – Cambodia|- Vietnam-Thailand-China in order to speed up trade facilities and tourism.

8.2.4. Development Strategy 4: Domestic Resources Mobilization Reinforcement Rule of Law

Domestic resources mobilization refers to the generation of government revenue from domestic resources, from tax or non-tax sources (royalties, licenses, levies or other income). It creates additional space for sustainable budget expenditures, fosters ownership and reduces dependency on external assistance, according to OECD report. Domestic resources, in particular public domestic resources, are already the most important source of development finance in Laos as well as international aid through borrowing, multilateral development assistance, or both. Domestic resource mobilization has become a core priority of the sustainable development agenda for the Lao government. .

Laos needs to strengthen domestic resource mobilization efforts, including better debt management, greater profitability of state-owned enterprises, and competitiveness of SMEs, natural resources and non-resources, and judicious use of resource-rent. Moving from a sustainable development vision to implementation of the policies outlined in the 8th NESDP, Development Strategy 2025 and Vision 2030 rests on the capacity of Laos to design strategies, create political support, and mobilize the required financial and administrative resources. Domestic resources will be key for financing the eco-social turn necessary for the transformative change committed to in the 2030 Agenda for Sustainable Development.

The actual conditions prevailing in Laos indicate that the mobilization of domestic resources is a serious factor for natural development, stability, and entrepreneur participation and development. External sources of funding are also important for the country. Indeed, the Lao government revenues fall short

of the rising need for public expenditures and thus has to be supplemented through borrowing. Developing domestic resources involves first of all developing human capacities and the resources of all the people and stakeholders exploiting and using the national natural resources.
Increasing the flow of taxes and other income into government treasuries is key to achieving the ambitious Sustainable Development Goals (SDGs) [178].

Laos broadly has been the beneficiaries of ten years of strong economic growth, which has generated new revenue for the state and lifted many out of poverty. Sound public financial management is at the heart of the creation of a strong functioning government and will ensure that gains made through improved domestic and external resources mobilization are directed toward achieving development outcomes. The government revenue has to ensure that the money is directed toward the delivery of public goods. By doing this in a transparent and accountable manner, the social compact between citizens and the state will be strengthened. But this will require tremendous political will on the part of Laos, which will need to tackle the existing barriers to greater reform.

With regard to the **Rule of law**, the legal system in Laos is not fully developed and rule of law has yet to be fully implemented from a general point of view. In fact, several parallel forms of Justice coexist in Laos, producing something of a hybrid model, combining customary law and formal justice (justice of the courts.

The first Lao Constitution in 1991 has been amended twice, the first time in 2003 and the second time in 2015 in order to suit the circumstances of the era, and implies greater commitment to the rule of law through, for example, provisions that clarify the role of the different authorities and that provide for a Local People's Assembly. Laos' Legal Sector Master Plan wanted to develop Laos as a "rule of law state" by 2020. The promulgation of the 1991 Constitution as the country's fundamental law signified the country's move towards becoming a "rule of law state.

The Constitution of 2015 reaffirmed the significance of the rule of law as basis of the democratic State. It stated that, the Lao PDR is a socialist rule of law State of the People, by the People and for the People[179]. The State powers are unified and delegated to state bodies, which shall coordinate with and control one another in the exercise of the legislative, executive and judiciary powers.

Achieving the goals of the Development Strategy for Domestic Resources Mobilization and the Reinforcement Rule of Law are as follows:

1. Laos shall put emphasis on: 1) better understanding the political economy and growth implications of tax reforms to make sure that these are sustainable and support the adaptation of these reforms as appropriate; 2) addressing governance issues that undermine tax reforms (i.e. tax exemptions, corruption) to ensure effectiveness of these reforms; 3) promoting increased governmental accountability to strengthen the relationship between the authorities and the taxpayers, particularly in the management of natural resources;

2. Effective implementation of domestic resource mobilization agenda requires strong development planning institutions to strengthen tax systems, expand the tax base, address the challenges of the informal sector and fight tax evasion and avoidance;

3. Laos needs to seek advice from development partners in assisting the country to enhance the effectiveness of domestic resource mobilization agenda through providing effective financial and technical support to enhance tax capacity-building efforts and improve tax administration in priority areas defined by the country 8th NESDP and Development Strategy 2025. Furthermore, for Laos to make better use of concessional finance, there should be a greater focus on investment and trade-oriented Official Development Assistance (ODA) which can be used to unlock and leverage domestic resources to address the critical challenges hindering its small economic;

4. Greater global transparency is key to successful financing of development strategies. It needs to achieve accountable taxation, enhance the regulation and supervision of under-regulated financial markets, and reduce systemic risks of banking and shadow-banking systems. It is also equally important to ensure that investment treaties are fully aligned with long-term performance and sustainable development;

5. Foreign borrowing inherently raises the interest rate on future debt and often leads to high indebtedness. In order to service the loans and avoid falling into a debt trap, the funds borrowed from abroad by the Lao government must be invested in projects and programs that are productive and economically viable;

6. Improving compliance management is today recognized as being as important as strengthening the tools of administration. Improving data management and better analysis with the use of information technology (ICT) will help to lower compliance costs, enhance transparency, and reduce corruption and collusion;

7. To succeed the resources mobilization, Laos must create effective tax systems and, with the developed countries and institutions' help, tackle the curse of corruption, tax havens and tax evasion.

8. Adopting tax policies, following good administrative procedures, and building capacity to combat domestic and foreign sources of tax base erosion is an urgent action to be taken by government and administration;

9. Effective collection of government revenue can strengthen the social contract between citizens, companies and government;

10. Support tax reforms aimed at reducing income inequalities, improving inclusiveness, and promoting public goods such as better health and a cleaner environment;

11. Strengthening public investment, the management of public enterprises, social transfer payments and procurement can build confidence in the efficiency of public-sector expenditures. This is key to ensuring taxpayers' willingness to support effective taxation;

12. Laos has poor law enforcement, ranging from the top down to the bottom, this needs to be addressed. It needs to improve the quality of it officials at all levels, while raising public awareness about the importance of upholding our laws to the letter;

13. Expansion of rule of law to be carried out for businesses and fair enforcement of the law is a major hindrance for business operations in Laos. This in turn will help to build foreign investors' confidence in Laos.

14. Enforcement of the Law on Civil Servants and Government Employees;

15. Urging civil servants to realize the importance of state governance, public administration, money management, and political authority;

16. Improving in public administration structures at the local level, in line with the Law on Local Administration;

17. Laws and regulations are often violated, the law enforcement agencies must take proactive, decisive and strict action in a timely manner to enshrine

the rule of law and to enable the Lao people to live in a society with justice and equality;

18. Strengthening capacity of Laos to harmonize with, and transpose, international obligations and standards into domestic law and practice;

19. Improving access to justice service delivery for citizens; and

20. Increasing public awareness of legal rights and responsibilities, and confidence in justice institutions.

In conclusion, over the past twenty years, especially the last decade, Laos has taken advantage of opportunities, overcome many challenges, implemented national sustainable development projects and recorded great achievements in the economic and social fields. The outstanding achievements result from an aggregate of many factors which include Laos' strong commitment to attain sustainable development with the effective mobilization of every available domestic resources and external resources. The country has yet to exploit its resources to maximum potential and work remains to be done in achieving further success, particularly the modernization of its industry, raising the level of its education system, and improving the human resource management. In addition, Laos needs to increase its financial resources for sustainable development implementation, enhance the quality of state governance over the country's sustainable development, continue receiving the cooperation and assistance in all fields from the international community, and seek partnership with donors along the road to green growth and sustainable poverty reduction. Therefore, enabling the country to move ahead with sustainable development towards the Lao government Vision 2030.

The success of reaching the government long-term goals will also support by the growing private sector. It asserts the role of the private economy as "an important driving force of the socialist-oriented market economy."[180] The number of SMEs have been growing fast, however the big companies are still limited, but they are yet to demonstrate their leadership in innovation and driving growth. The private sector boosts trade with neighboring countries, improve and accelerate the connectivity of Laos (CLVM + Thailand). Looking at the experience from South Korea and Taiwan, where SMEs have a leading position in all activity, their governments can offer direct and indirect financial support, and providing funds to firms with good track records. Laos can follow the South Korean and Singapore path as well.

Laos must move towards international standards of economic governance, including a clear separation between regulators and market participants, a solid commitment to a judicial system that is independent of politics, public finance, and fiscal policy reforms based on clearly enounce rules and complete transparency.

Laos is moving toward becoming an upper middle-income country, which requires comprehensive structural reforms aimed at strengthening economic diversification and competitiveness to ensure sustainable economic growth with equitable redistribution of wealth. This requires consideration for a new development approach vis-à-vis expanding development opportunities and investment in new growth sectors by way of improving the necessary socioeconomic infrastructure, supply of organic agricultural products, expansion of transport infrastructure and development of logistics, education level upgrading, promotion of vocational schools and sciences education, including digital infrastructure, and institutional strengthening.

To achieve the nine pillars as proposed in this chapter, the country needs to develop a pragmatic framework that will support the implementation of the 8th NSEDP 2016-2020, Development Strategy 2025 and the Vision 2030. The 8th NSEDP's overall goal is continued poverty reduction, graduation from LDC status through realization of national development potential and comparative advantages, effective management and utilization of natural resources and strong regional and international integration and is structured around three outcomes, and to meet the country's industrialization and modernization objectives. Further fiscal reform and enforcement of rule of law should be undertaken in order to make a favorable condition for mobilizing capital for production and businesses. The Lao government needs to find some ways to mobilize extensive domestic and foreign capital to build infrastructure. Public Private Partnerships (PPP) has become today an effective methods to motivate infrastructure and logistics. PPP is a method in which the management and implementation of projects by combining the best of the public and private sectors with an emphasis on value for money and delivering quality public services. This form of cooperation will bring benefits for both Laos and private sector.

In this regard, the Lao Government has decided to adopt the NESDP in order to provide a policy framework and a specific mechanism for driving economic growth and creating jobs with focus on the manufacturing sector, agro-industrial sector, and SMEs development. In pursuance of this policy, Laos will succeed in its economic structural transformation by moving gradually from energy and mining based economy toward a processing industry, services, and agro-industry based economy, and subsequently in the final phase toward diversification in other sectors especially those that use technology and innovation.

8.3. Laos to Become a Regional Integration and Connectivity Hub

The effects of domestic and international market integration of Laos on regional development are of particular interest as described on chapter 2. This is of importance since the country's geographic character creates special challenges for the creation of an integrated national market as well as for integration with international markets. A land-locked country Laos is dependent on neighboring countries for access to international markets. As links to the outside world have gradually developed, parts of Laos have benefited from integration with regional and international markets. This is revealed in the growth of Lao exports and imports of consumer goods (see chapter 2 and 3).Today, the economic integration with neighboring economies gives an important role to local entrepreneurs who trade across the national border. Moreover, infrastructure development makes is easier for enterprises to choose the location for their activities. Increased economic integration between provinces or even between CLV and Thailand provide an environment where institutional competition could have very positive effects.

Laos, as an interconnection node today, is gearing up for greater regional connectivity and international interaction. Three economic corridors pass through Laos. These economic corridors must facilitate and liberalize trade and allow the free movement of goods and people[181]. The corridors have helped create special economic zones in the northern province of Bokeo, in Houayxay (Golden Triangle), and in Boten in Luang Namtha Province on the Chinese border. Bokeo Province allows for trade between Laos, Thailand, and Myanmar, and then to China, whereas Luang Namtha has become an important zone of southern Chinese investment in Laos. Similarly, the Savannakhet-Seno special economic zone (SEZ) is adding dynamism to that southern region, thanks to the investment of foreign companies that wish to enjoy the benefits of its location on the east-west axis and access to the sea.

Interconnectivity also means electricity to be connected to regional power grid. Most importantly, the government's strategic plan for energy development is not only aimed at bolstering coverage for domestic power consumption but Laos' export of electric energy is also set to link with Asean power grids. Indeed, electricity is to be supplied to Vietnam, Thailand, Cambodia, and Myanmar, Singapore, and Malaysia via Thai Power grid.

In 2017, fifteen foreign companies had already established themselves in this SEZ. Additionally, the Savan-Seno SEZ is expected to become part of a planned cooperation pact between Thailand and China, linking the former's flagship Eastern Economic Corridor (EEC) and the latter's Kunming SEZ. Connecting these zones will establish a supply chain and production hub for Asean, according to Thai Industry Minister Uttama Savanayana. "China has confirmed its plan to link its Kunming SEZ with Thailand's EEC, and it also wants to add Laos' SEZ to the project," he said. China believes the SEZ in the southern part of Laos could play a key role as a production center. The Kunming SEZ and the EEC are designed to accommodate high-tech industries and embrace the digital economy, while the Savan-Seno SEZ is geared toward heavy industries, Uttama Savanayana added[182].

The past decade has seen the fruits of various projects close "missing links" in road, rail, waterway, air, and energy networks in the Greater Mekong Subregion. Today, the China-Laos railway under construction is a paramount project expected to be in operation in 2021. It will further reinforce the dynamics of regional connectivity, and will connect southern China to neighboring Laos. Once finished, the high-speed line will be Laos' most expensive infrastructure project ever, representing nearly half of the small country's current GDP. Additionally, another high-speed railway was also planned, the 220-kilometer line from Savannakhet to Lao Bao on the Vietnamese border. Other rail projects are to be finalized by the Lao government, such as Vientiane-Takkhek-Vietnam border and Savannakhet-Pakse-Cambodia border (see chapters 2 and 4).

Also, Laos is aware that it must not only be a transit region; it must not be a follower, but an active player who participates and contributes effectively to the development of connectivity networks, and manages the transport flow (i.e. both passenger and freight) in order to strengthen its economy and develop its business interests. The government is trying to take advantage of Laos's position in the GMS and to cooperate fruitfully with its Asean partners in the ASEAN Economic Community already in place. Further afield, Laos's increased access to sea transport (through Thailand and Vietnam) will facilitate its exchanges with European countries particularly in the areas of investment, trade, transportation and logistics, tourism, and services.

More recently, the design of the fifth Lao-Thai Friendship Bridge across the Mekong River between Borikhamxay province and Bung Karn province in Thailand is now complete. The 1,350-metre bridge will be built 10km north of the town of Pakxan and will be about 2.5km from Road No.13 South. The bridge will serve as a key transport route, facilitating trade, investment and tourism between Laos and Thailand. It will connect north-eastern Thailand to central Vietnam and the route will serve as an economic corridor for the whole region, it is envisaged that the new bridge will lead to an increase in the amount of agricultural exports between Laos and Vietnam. The construction of the bridge is expected to cost 975 billion kip (3,900 million baht) and will be co-financed by the governments of Laos and Thailand[183]. For Laos the most important development goal is to improve its infrastructure and connectivity, particularly roads that facilitate the transport of goods between Laos, Vietnam and Thailand.

Furthermore, Laos and some experts have studied the issue of navigability of the Mekong River, which runs all the way from China to the southern part of Laos and then Cambodia. In December 2016, the Thai cabinet of Prime Minister Prayut Chan-o-cha agreed "in principle" with a plan to dredge stretches of the Mekong and demolish rocky outcrops that are hindrances to easy navigation. The international Lancang-Mekong River navigation improvement plan for 2015-2025, conceived by China, Myanmar, Laos, and Thailand, aims to the make the river more navigable for 500-ton cargo ships sailing the river from Yunnan to Luang Prabang, a distance of 890 kilometers. China has been the driving force behind the demolition plan as it aims to expand trade in the area with larger cargo ships.

In early January 2018, the leaders from the Mekong Lancang Cooperation (LMC) countries adopted four documents on cooperation in the upcoming year at their second summit held in Phnom Penh. The leaders of the six LMC member countries also endorsed the five-year plan of action (2018-2022) to enforce cooperation and development projects, focusing on development goals, basic principles, working structure, practical cooperative work and supporting systems: LMC cooperation framework on connectivity, cooperation on production capacity, border-crossing economic cooperation, water resource cooperation, and agriculture and poverty reduction[184]. The regional integration and connectivity are the Lao government's highest importance so that its objectives and targets of the Sustainable Development Strategy and Vision 2030 are attainable.

More recently, the Laos-Vietnam Inter-Governmental Committee took place in Laos on February 2018, following the meeting, Prime Minister Nguyen Xuan Phuc of Vietnam and Lao Premier Thongloun Sisoulith have agreed to accelerate the cooperation development of the Vung Ang port – a cooperation project in Vietnam's central Ha Tinh province which will enable land-locked Laos to access sea trade routes. An agreement document is expected to be signed soon, leading to the establishment of a joint-venture company to develop the seaport. The two countries to seek funding for key projects, such as the 725-km Hanoi-Vientiane highway and a railway connecting Vung Ang, Tan Ap, Mu Gia (Vietnam) and Thakhaek, Vientiane (Laos), according to the Voice of Vietnam (VoV). A number of joint projects on transport infrastructure and connectivity have also been undertaken between the two countries and within the region[185].

8.4. What Are the External and Internal Forces That Could Affect Laos' Sustainable Development Strategy and Growth?

Following are five forces that could threaten Laos' sustainable development to which the government and businesses should pay attention:

1. The **barrier entry** to Asean member countries' markets: Laos might face capital requirements, regulating limitations, standards, distribution channels, recognition of Lao brand names, and the limited size of Lao enterprises.

2. The threat to Laos from **insufficient production**: lack of industrial and manufacturing bases to cope with the market demand, and a competitiveness far behind neighboring countries. Lao producers may not be able to produce at the lowest possible average cost. This may be because of the failure to apply technology to production, or because of the inability to achieve economies of scale. Opening up the economy to free trade may help reduce this type of inefficiency, and encourage know-how and technology transfer.

3. **Regional and international competitors**: new entrance of competitors with attractive and competitive goods and services in Laos. This could

jeopardize local manufacturing goods and services and dissuade Lao people to buy local made products. In the long run, export of Laos' hydroelectricity might be in competition with solar or wind energy as substituted energy supply within Asean member states.

4. **Internal obstacles** to sustainable development: Human resources, competitiveness, market imperfections, lack of external investors, internal disorder, corruption, and maximum attainment of hydroelectric resources by 2030.

Human capital development requires investment in education. Education is a merit good, and the long term benefit to society is often considerably under-perceived, and therefore, under-consumed. For Laos, the return on human capital development is uncertain compare to the immediate return from employment on the land. Therefore, there is little incentive for human capital development to continue in full-time education. The solution is to reduce information failure by promoting the benefits of education and using the market system to send out effective signals to encourage people to alter their behavior. Laos is lack of capital, it does not have sufficient financial capital to engage in public or private investment. There are several reasons for this, including the following: Growth is not sufficient to allow scarce financial resources to be freed up for non-current expenditure; a general lack of savings is often seen as the key reason why financial capital is in short supply; in the case of public sector funding, spare public funds are often used to repay previous debts, so there are less available funds for capital investment by government; Laos suffers from corruption in many different sectors of its economies, corruption comes in many forms, including the theft of public funds. Bribery is also alleged to be a persistent threat, and tends to involve the issuing of government contracts, this seriously weakens the operation of the price mechanism.

5. **The lost advantage of the niche market** would vanish the potential of Lao SMEs' profits. As a result, many enterprises would withdraw from the domestic and regional market. Indeed, there are a number of advantages and disadvantages of niche marketing. Understanding the market means the company able to identify the unique needs of its customers, provide new and compelling products, tailor its products in the right way, communicate

efficiently with the target group and identify how the company will position against the competitors. Niche market is generally a smaller market, it makes difficult to enjoy a larger profit margin in the market. Among the advantages and disadvantages of niche marketing is that there is limited growth because there is a small group of customers to buy products.

The non-control of these forces can hurt the Lao economy and the modernization of its industries. Consequently, the 8th NSEDP and the Sustainable Development Strategy could thus be in question, then the objectives of the Lao's government Vision 2030 will not probably be attainable.

We can transpose and apply Porter's five forces model to illustrate the threats that could curb Laos' sustainable development in the following chart (see Figure 35). This model is widely used in enterprises as marketing strategic study.

Figure 35. The Five Forces Analysis to the Sustainable Development

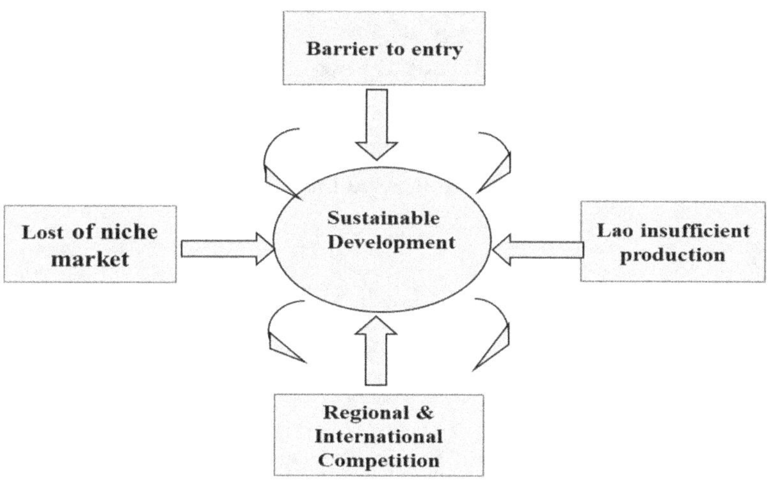

Similarly, Laos should focus its strategic choice to achieve success in the sustainable development plan and the Vision 2030. There are three generic strategic model available to organizations for gaining competitive advantage. These are: Cost Leadership, Differentiation, and Focus Strategy:

The Cost Leadership Strategy develops the "edge" that brings Laos attractiveness and takes it away from other Asean countries. The fact that Laos provides cheap labor and electricity is an advantage to proceed to the leadership strategy.

The Differentiation Strategy involves making the products or services different from and more attractive than those of competitors. Laos has a unique product to sell to its neighbors, the hydroelectricity. This is a huge asset for the country to be preserved, capitalized, and served to a broad market.
The Focus Strategies are used to concentrate on particular niche markets and, by understanding the dynamics of that market and the unique needs of customers within it, develop uniquely low-cost or well-specified products for the domestic and Asean markets. Because they serve customers in their market uniquely well, they tend to build strong brand loyalty amongst their customers.

Cost Focus Strategy is positioned on the advantage of the regional connectivity provided by Laos and its several SEZs set up around Thailand, Vietnam and China. While **Differential Focus Strategy** is focused on a small segment or narrow and specific market, a niche market. Laos has a few niche markets to develop and to promote: hydroelectricity, garments, silk textiles, handicrafts, bio agriculture, fair trade, and tourism (see chapter 6).

Laos' development growth depends on how the country is able to overcome the external and internal forces that could threaten the sustainable development plan, and also how the government and businesses are able to cooperate and coordinate their interests in order to focus on strategic choices and strengthen the modernization of the country's industry. Although overcoming and addressing these forces are numerous, following are a few ideas that might help: The drive to conduct strategic path must be supported by the government's leadership. This sends a strong signal of the level of importance of the process, which often improves the level of acceptance for stakeholders; communication process and effective change management are important to allow a clear strategy for the industry and agriculture sectors to continue without significant loss of productivity; having a visible marketing strategy also boost the dynamic of the production and competitiveness, including priority segment of organic agriculture products to be privileged for exports; partnering with foreign enterprises allows to catch up technology and know-how; anticipating for an alternative source of energy to hydroelectricity is to be undertaken; and investing in human resources development, for example, loans, grants and aid can be made conditional upon funds being allocated to provide 'free' education and books, or to fund teacher training, or to raise the wages of teachers so that more will train in the future.

Notes

169 https://www.livepopulation.com/population-projections/laos-2030.html.

170 UNPD, Graduation From Least Developed Country Status Graduation From Least Developed Country Status Lao PDR 2017 National Human Development Report Lao PDR, 2017.

171 OECD, Structural Policy Country Notes Lao PDR, 2013.

172 Laos plans industrial development strategy for next 15 years, Vientiane Times, Business, 31/03/2016.

[173] Government, development partners discuss green growth strategy development, 27/07/2017.
[174] Industry and Commerce Visualizes Modernizing Industry, Commerce, Production, Services, KPL, 22/08/2016.
[175] Master Plan on ASEAN Connectivity, ASEAN, 2011.
[176]China, Thailand inaugurate construction of high-speed railway in Thailand, Xinhua News, 21/12/2017; Bangkok Post, 21/12/2017.
[177] Build, Own, Operate, and Transfer.
[178] United Nations Development Programme Lao PDR and Ministry of Justice, 'The Law-Making Process in Lao PDR: A Baseline Study,' (Vientiane) November 2015, 1.
[179] See Country Constitution 2015.
[180] Read more at http://vietnamnews.vn/economy/377671/how-the-private-sector-can-drive-vns-growth.html#84GKHpZd5VPfj2PZ.99.
[181] Christian Taillard, "Le Laos à la croisée des corridors de la Région du Grand Mékong," in Le Laos, doux et amer: 25 ans de pratique d'une ONG, ed. Dominique Gentil and Philippe Boumard (Paris: Comité de Coopération avec le Laos and Éditions Karthala, 2005).
[182] Asia Focus, Laos, Bangkok Post, 10/07/2017.
[183] Laos seeks loan for fifth Lao-Thai Friendship Bridge, Vientiane Times, 27/12/2017. ASEAN, 2011.
[183]China, Thailand inaugurate construction of high-speed railway in Thailand, Xinhua News, 21/12/2017; Bangkok Post, 21/12/2017.
[183] Build, Own, Operate, and Transfer.
[183] Christian Taillard, "Le Laos à la croisée des corridors de la Région du Grand Mékong," in Le Laos, doux et amer: 25 ans de pratique d'une ONG, ed. Dominique Gentil and Philippe Boumard (Paris: Comité de Coopération avec le Laos and Éditions Karthala, 2005).
[184] Leaders endorse plans for Mekong-Lancang cooperation, Phnom Penh Post, 11/01/2018.
[185] Vietnam PM to visit Laos for inter-governmental meeting, Vientiane Times, 1/02/2018.

CHAPTER 9

The Twelve Future Key Challenges

9.1. The Main Challenges

The twelve challenges are all almost at the same level of difficulty that Laos has to face to attain the targeted sustainable development goals described below. It is understood that the identified challenges listed here are not exhaustive.

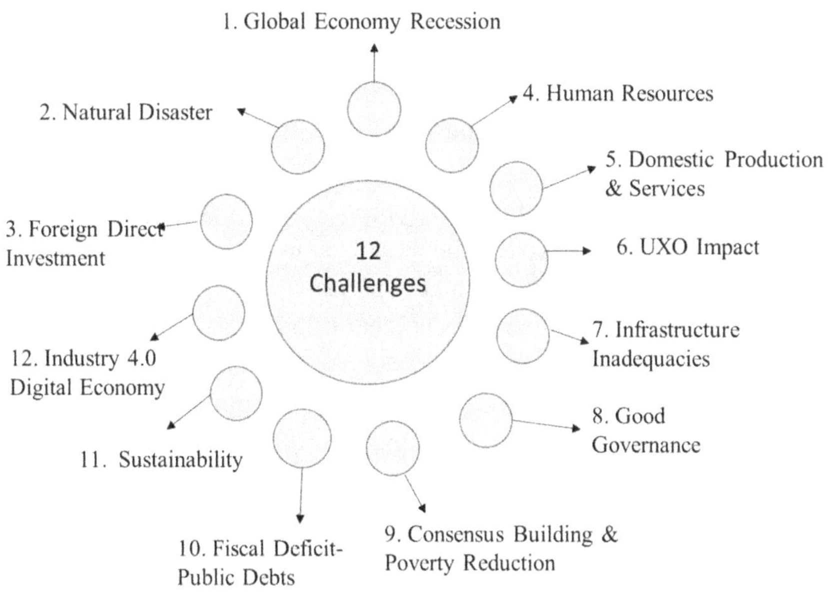

Three challenges are outside the control of Laos: the global economic recession, natural disasters, and foreign direct investment:

1.The **global economic recession** if happens will impact less private investments in Laos, domestic production will also decline with an increase of unemployment; falls in export revenues due to lower demand (and falling prices) for agricultural products and a sharp reduction in demand for mineral goods; recession will cut export prices; a recession in global tourism, which is a significant share of GDP for Laos; rising food prices will create a huge problem of food poverty. Overall the recession would deteriorate Laos' prospects for Laos meeting the SDGs. Thus the national economic growth will suffer, the economic uncertainty will threaten social stability, and that could lead to social unrest and political instability.

2. Natural disasters influence the weather, and consequences for the country could have the following effects: typhoons, floods, droughts, rodent and pest attacks, and animal disease epidermis. Unsustainable livelihoods, including the chopping down of protective forests for agricultural production and building houses near streams and rivers, have increased risks of natural disasters according to experts.

The negative impact for businesses and agricultural production is huge; natural disasters will deteriorate the country's infrastructure and cause huge losses in farmers' revenue. Likewise, ensuring environmental sustainability and addressing vulnerability to natural disasters will be central to a sustainable and better future.

The Lao government and the European Union Civil Protection and Humanitarian Aid have implemented a community-based disaster risk management projects across the country to prepare people to know more about disaster risk, therefore to reduce the national calamity and train villagers in emergency disaster countermeasures.

3. Foreign direct investment could move to other more competitive and attractive countries, as companies are looking for profit before anything else.

FDI flows to Laos are likely to decline in the future because of the lower expectation of profitability by investors. Moreover, after 2030, the potential for hydropower might have some limits and investment in the sector will slow down. Also, on the wider economic landscape, a sustained reversal in the momentum of fiscal consolidation driven largely by Laos' weak revenue growth could lead to further increases in the public-debt ratio and a deterioration of the country's external position, with potential flow-on effects for investor confidence.

Thus Laos will suffer from a significant decrease in foreign investment, and this could jeopardize its economic growth. Therefore, the policies to promote FDI in many sectors and the policies that attract stable FDI inflows should be promulgated by the government in order to secure long-term investment planning. Investing for the long-term is vital for Lao economic growth and social well-being. Whether it's building new infrastructure or maintaining what already exists, funding is vital to maximize the economic benefits that flow from it.

Then come the nine challenges that the Lao government and businesses can control and determine the destiny of the country:

4. Human resources are the most critical challenge for Laos' development. Apart from Myanmar, Cambodia and Laos are the lowest ranked country in the region regarding education. Laos also underperforms in primary education and delivering high-quality in higher education and training. While the enrolment rate has increased, the sector is still plagued with numerous challenges. Lao university and its faculties are lack learning and teaching resources and facilities, and qualified academic staff are in short supply, although great improvement has been achieved. However, higher education programs are largely driven by commercial interests, focusing on a few business-related courses; while engineering and science subjects are lacking. Soft skills training is missing and research activity is limited in Laos today.

Unless Laos enacts comprehensive, effective and timely polices to improve its education system, it will lose the competition, affecting its long-term development. Therefore, first, enhancing human development and addressing low primary school completion are key goals of the 8th NSEDP (2016–2020). Second, in the framework of the AEC, human resources will require addressing the gap in the supply of skills and qualifications in the workforce to meet the changing demands of the economy. Without strengthening the foundations for quality basic education, reinforcing technical vocational schools, training of workforce, and providing continuous training for employees, Laos might have a hard time catching up to its neighbors.

5. Domestic production and services is one of the most significant factors for Laos to drive the economy and be resilient to external impacts. The productive capacities of the country are essentially a matter of what Laos is able to produce efficiently and competitively an increasing range of value added goods and services increase. This process occurs through expanding investment – in physical, human, social and environmental capital – and also through know-how acquisition and innovation.

Currently, Laos' industrial production is weak due to a lack of competencies, skilled laborers, and technicians. Services provided to customers are not professional. SMEs are already an important part of the economy of Laos and employ a large part of the population, but they are not well structured and organized yet. They are lacking the financing, know-how, and marketing tools to expand, with no access to long-term credit, which makes it difficult for SMEs to grow and compete against other SMEs in Asean.

Therefore, Laos will need to address its weak institutional capacities and the financial constraints to the growth of SMEs. Furthermore, promoting SMEs will be especially beneficial for women, as women make up more than half the owners of newly registered enterprises. In addition, today there is not a law yet or a tool to protect domestic producers in Laos against the negative impacts of imported foreign goods. Such producers are affected by imported products due to international economic integration, and this prevents them from working harder and putting greater effort into developing themselves.

6. UXO impact destabilizes the country's capacity production today. UXO remains a challenge for the progress of development in Lao PDR. An estimated 80 million cluster sub-munitions remain unexploded. UXO limits safe access to agricultural and land for development projects and makes construction of transport and power infrastructure, schools, hospitals, and water supply facilities much more costly and dangerous. UXO is also a major humanitarian threat. Over 50,000 casualties were reported from 1964 to 2012[186]. Despite the challenges, the past few years have seen a number of achievements.

The 8th NSEDP has made a start in this regard, in an attempt to integrate UXO into a national development framework. Even so, UXO continues to be a stand-alone area. Therefore, mobilize world opinions and support to clear the unexploded ordnance (UXO) and help its victims are a huge challenge for

Laos. Though UXO is a legacy of the "Vietnam war." Reducing the impact of UXO is Laos' own national Sustainable Development Goal. By committing to Goal 18 as a part of the global 2030 Agenda for Sustainable Development, Laos holds itself accountable to advancing the reduction of UXO impact and contributing to many other goals at the same time, e.g. Goal 1, Ending Poverty. An integrated approach is crucial for progress across the multiple goals.

7. Infrastructure inadequacies are one of the constraints on sustainable and inclusive growth. Laos needs to continue to speed up the improvement of roads, quality of the electricity network and distribution[187], telecommunication, connectivity, and upgrading the skills of its people to take full advantage of its central location. The poor infrastructure has impaired Laos' manufacturing and industrial potential and does not make it easy to do business in this country.

The country is currently handicapped by the relatively high costs of accessing international gateways caused by inadequate infrastructure in cross-border secondary cities and localities. The transportation costs which weigh heavily on business profitability could be reduced if the government continued its infrastructure development programs, which include building the roads that would improve national and regional connectivity and, by the same token, the efficiency of business activities.

Laos has put much effort into developing its weak physical infrastructure but this needs further investment to address obstacles to its socioeconomic development. As a prerequisite for structural change, infrastructure should be given greater priority in public investment programs. Significant amounts of ODA have to be earmarked for infrastructure development in Laos, desirably by creating dedicated funds. Domestic capital and inflows of FDI have to be guided to development of physical infrastructures in the country. Different forms of PPP, such as build–operate–transfer (BOT) may be more purposefully practiced to expedite development of physical infrastructure.

8. Good governance is not yet fully satisfactory. Despite some improvement, there is slow progress on regulations and governance. The issue concerns especially macro-management. Coordination and cooperation between ministries and central and local agencies are weak. Service delivery does not respond to citizens' needs in terms of quality and timeliness.

Moreover, there are complaints by the people about the corruption and pressure exercised by officials on ordinary and business people. Different levels of education and the public interest awareness of officials exist between those of the capital and the provinces. The gap is important and needs to be addressed. Moreover, the rule of law has not yet been strongly enforced. Strict compliance by the authorities and the people has not yet been adequately enforced either. Governance work now recognizes the importance of the relationship between states and society in general, thus leaders and high ranking officers should have a good behavior and demonstrate exemplarity[188].

Despite the assistance given by the United Nations Development Program (UNDP), the United Nations Capital Development Fund (UNCDF), and the Swiss Agency for Development and Cooperation (SDC) to create the capacity of administrative work and promote sustainable development, especially at the local level, tangible results have not yet been achieved. The government has now implemented stronger measures to enhance transparency and governance, exposing corruption and thereby contributing to an improved investment climate in the country.

9. Consensus building and poverty reduction are important in today's interconnected society because many problems exist that affect diverse groups of people or governments with different interests. In Laos the reform process has focused exclusively on economic reforms. There is no political actor within the country who advocates the opposition to the Party. However, there is a consensus among the main actors to move towards a form of market economy. This is considered necessary to improve the real incomes and living standards of the population and thereby the legitimacy of the regime. The Lao government has committed itself on repeated occasions to the notion that Laos is a multiethnic state. This is also formally acknowledged in the 1991 Constitution. The law enforcement, access to justice, and people-centered justice delivery remain as important challenges. Indeed, the government has adopted the Sustainable Development Goals (SDG16) in recognition of a number of core principles that are essential for good governance in order to serve as a catalyst for development. These principles are partnership, participation, transparency, accountability, improvement of public financial management, and strong anti-corruption measures; all are prerequisites for inclusive, equitable, and balanced nation-wide growth. National consensus building must be reached to continue reducing poverty. However, today, poverty reduction has been accompanied by rising inequality, as income disparities of farmers have widened today. Rural livelihoods are also under threat as the conversion of agricultural lands to cater to the needs of foreign direct investment leads to the displacement of populations away from their traditional sources of income. Inequality can also lead to the misallocation of human capital. Those with little wealth or low incomes are unable to invest in their human capital or wealth and remain caught in the vicious cycle of poverty. At the same time, inequality restricts the access of the poor to basic infrastructure services, utilities, and sanitation, which in turn affects their health and well-being. Higher poverty reduction in Laos can be achieved by creating better economic opportunities for the poor and non-poor in strengthening the consensus building between business stakeholders and the government to create jobs, increase productivity, and improve the quality of jobs in the non-farm sector. Despite the government initiating a process of decentralization in 2000 to strengthen regional self-empowerment, poverty still remains in Laos. Today, reinforcing the social protection system is important to ensure sustainable poverty reduction.

10. Fiscal deficit and Public Debts are a recurring problem in Laos. The economy has accumulated vulnerabilities in the form of high public debt, a progressively overvalued real exchange rate, and pockets of weakness in the banking sector. With few buffers to address shocks, the economy remains vulnerable to a rapid deterioration in the external environment, a sustained deterioration in fiscal position, or a rapid reversal of foreign capital flows. The current account deficit is expected to widen slightly, reflecting higher imports to support the construction of hydroelectric and railway projects, financed by private capital inflows, but is expected to narrow in 2021 as project-related imports fall and electricity exports come on line. The current account deficit is projected to widen to around 19 percent of GDP in 2017 due to the execution of large infrastructure projects with foreign direct investment, and reserves are expected to remain at around 2 months of imports. According to IMF recent release, on current trends without the resumption of fiscal consolidation, the fiscal deficit is expected to remain at around 5 percent and the public debt could rise to around 70 percent of GDP. Risks are on the downside. A failure to consolidate the fiscal position and bring down public debt could undermine confidence in the government's macro policy framework, raise public debt further and worsen the external position. The economy is also exposed to external shocks, notably a further regional growth slowdown and a deterioration in terms-of-trade and capital inflows. Financial risks could also present risk to macroeconomic stability, particularly the growing foreign currency debt financed by foreign borrowing, and the existence of balance sheet currency mismatches in the private non-bank sector[189].

11. Sustainability. Laos' resource-based economy is driven by forestry, agriculture, hydropower, and minerals. The over-exploitation of hydroelectricity in the long run will have a negative impact on the ecology and environmental issues, in particular with respect to the management of the Mekong River, which is increasingly in peril in part due to dam construction on the upstream river. While Laos is one of the most biodiverse countries in the region, mining development poses threats to environmental and human health. The environmental impacts of mining, especially in terms of longer-term waste accumulation, are a serious threat for Laos. Forest cover has decreased significantly over the past decade (44 percent in 2017). The main drivers of forest degradation are unsustainable wood harvesting from illegal logging and poorly regulated harvesting, and shifting cultivation. Deforestation is largely due to agricultural expansion (including rubber and sugar cane plantations), hydropower, mining, infrastructure, and urban expansion. Furthermore, Laos is vulnerable to climate change and will need to plan accordingly. The country is seeing an increased frequency and intensity of extreme weather events, such as droughts and floods. The majority of floods occur in the central and southern parts of the country along the Mekong Plain.[190] As a result, the rice harvest is hardly meeting the farmers' expectations. The four areas of national resource management that should be of concern are forests, land management, mining management, and hydropower production. Natural resource wealth, if managed properly, can greatly benefit Laos' economy as it can raise average income. Therefore, ecological management should be ensured so that there is sustainable economic growth and poverty alleviation.

12. Fourth Industrial Revolution or Industry 4.0 is today industrial jump in transformation the business and industrial in digital world. The digital economy is on the move. Developed countries are already in this step of process. With innovation and technology fast changing the development and growth horizons, society and enterprises need to always be prepared for the fast coming future, where industry 4.0 is now moving in every level of industry. Some Asean countries are quite advanced in the industrial revolution 4.0 while Laos is just at the early stage and has just moved gradually to phase 3.0. A digital economy creates ample opportunities for a country like Laos to jump up from industry 3.0 to industry 4.0. The AEC will provide greater chance for Lao's industries to go faster in the digital transformation and the modernization of its businesses. The government and Lao's business sector should not miss this digital economy and overcome the challenge; therefore private sector has to start preparing to build the capacity and human resources, increase staff knowledge and skills, and adapt themselves in order to stay competitive.

Amid strong economic growth in Laos, buying and selling online both domestically and internationally has increased. The value of online shopping in Laos will grow steady due to consumers' use of smartphones and the provision of online payment infrastructure by the public and private sectors, as well as the benefits gained from expanded coverage of high speed Internet across the country. However, the growth in the digital economy may be concentrated in few businesses types, such as online shopping and online financial services. To facilitate and respond to this growth, it is important to make payments easy for businesses and trade partners. The banking sector in particular needs to improve and change to keep well-informed of developments in this field. To respond to changing needs in its services, the Bank of the Lao PDR in collaboration with the relevant ministries has improved its payment methods and the management of these new systems. These have become necessary due to the rapid growth of the economy and the increase in trade using electronic methods[191]. However, negative factors including the threat of cybercrimes, legal constraints on online shopping, consumer concerns over the fake goods and services, the limitation of IT infrastructure coverage and a lack of knowledge of technology among many entrepreneurs.

Today, the Lao government, its administration, and the Ministry of Sciences and Technology also embark gradually on an e-government service and the expansion of the Internet infrastructure to remote communities. Recently, the National Social Security Fund (NSSF) also asked to improve its health service information system. Currently, the country has a few Lao ICT consulting enterprises capable to handle projects for the government and its administration. Among them are CALAT ICT Co., LG ICT, Lao First Solutions, Datacom, and APIS. These companies have all worked successfully for the Ministry of Finance, Ministry of Public Health, Ministry of Public Works and Transport, and the World Bank. CALAT ICT for example has developed for the Ministry of Finance the system for land tax collection namely Land Tax Information System, they have also developed an international and acclaimed Open Source health information system dubbed GNU Health for one of the largest hospitals Mahosot Hospital in Vientiane. The GNU Health system allows the hospital to manage all patient activities and within departments as well, this includes: Electronic Medical Record (EMR); Hospital Information System (HIS); Laboratory Information System; Health Information System; and Financial/Accounting. With regard to APIS, this company has designed the architecture of the Civil Registration and Vital Statistic System for the Ministry of Home Affairs, while LG ICT has developed the social security information system known as Benefit Claim Management for the Ministry of Labor and Social Welfare. The system related to sickness, maternity, death, accident, survivors, disabled, retirement, and unemployment management through Internet application across the country.

At the present, digital technologies have been transforming the global economy. Yet many countries have yet to experience the full developmental benefits of digital technologies, such as inclusive and sustainable growth, improved governance, and responsive service delivery. Laos has the opportunity to learn from the experience of frontrunner countries while designing policies and applications that meet its own needs and fit the local context. Mastering the digital transformation process demands solid managerial and technical skills, leadership institutions, policies and regulations for a digital economy, it calls on stakeholders to define clear roles and cooperation between government, business, local ICT companies, development partners, and to build competent institutions to lead the transformation process. Promote Local Innovation and Utilization of Science, Technology and Telecommunications and Management, and Application of ICT is among the Lao government Development Strategy 2025 goals.

These are only twelve of many complex challenges Laos grapples with on a daily basis. Concerted, coherent global efforts will be needed if Laos is to tackle these issues – and make the development of the country history.

Now it's the right time for Laos to focus on improving its competitiveness to sustain long-term economic and social development. If Laos gets this right, it would be on track to fully part of the AEC. The Lao authorities are in the process of implementing the new NSEDP to address the remaining bottlenecks to meet the Sustainable Development Goals. The authorities note that economic expansion needs to bring a durable reduction in poverty and substantial improvements in socioeconomic conditions, and are committed to maintain macroeconomic and financial stability, promote sustainable and inclusive growth, and stand ready to implement any measures deemed appropriate. Mindful of the challenges ahead, efforts will be intensified to improve efficiency of public service delivery, reform public financial management, modernization of the industries, strengthen the banking regulatory and supervisory framework, and enhance the business environment. In addition, strengthening institutions, modernizing infrastructure would contribute to improving innovation and Laos' overall competitiveness. More needs to be done to create an enabling environment to support national private sector, particularly SMEs. Laos must make an effort to remove bureaucratic and regulatory obstacles to entrepreneurial activities, which can asphyxiate business spirit.

First, Laos needs to improve the quality of its higher education and increase greatly vocational schools across the country. Higher education plays a vital role in building up a competitive and skilled workforce for the country. Improving the quality of higher education would ensure that Laos meets its current and future human capital needs, and allow the country to benefit from the AEC. Laos needs financial resources to improve education infrastructure, update the curriculum and teaching methods, and recruit well-qualified teaching staff with reasonable wages. Research should also be promoted, and internal quality assurance should be the top agenda for all higher education institutions. Local talents should not be neglected and should contribute to state's needs in all government's sectors and administrations.

Second, Laos needs to invest in key infrastructure such as roads, railways, transport and logistics, expand the connectivity, quality of internet access, and digital infrastructure. It needs to rehabilitate high-priority road networks and bridges to facilitate the growth of agriculture, tourism and trade in rural areas. Laos' existing infrastructure around its SEZs and airports should be efficient enough to handle forthcoming increases in production and trade.

Third, the priorities and development objectives are guided by the Vision 2030, the ten-year Socio-Economic Development Strategy 2016-2025 and 8th five-year NESDP 2016-2020.The Vision 2030 aims to transform Laos into an upper-middle income developing country with innovative, green and sustainable economic growth. The development is focusing in all sectors of the industries: agriculture food processing, tourism, garment and other labor-intensive industry, transport equipment, electric and electronic machinery, small and medium enterprises, finance, and energy and transportation. The objective is to transform the modernization of Laos industries and commerce.

Fourth, Laos should take action to ensure that state institutions function effectively. The government's anti-corruption strategies and agencies need to be strengthened to minimize rent-seeking and abuse of power. The judicial system should be made fully independent to conduct objective evaluation and enforcement of the law.

Notes

[186] National Regulatory Authority (NRA) 2010, and updates from the NRA for the 2013 MDG Report.

[187] In Vientiane, enterprises and expat residents complaint the very often blackout of electricity, it sometime lasted many hours. Critics say electricity is one of essential requirements of the investment sector. Without sustainable power supplies, it would be difficult for people to do business. "Tackling power blackouts key for growth of business sector" Vientiane Times, 28/10/2017.

[188] Limits of good governance in developing countries, by Hirotsune Kimura

[189] IMF, Lao PDR, Country Report 17/53, February 2017.

[190] World Bank, UNISDR et al., 2013.

[191] Bank staff beef up on electronic payment methods, Vientiane Times, 19/12/2017.

CHAPTER 10

Laos Into the Future

10.1. The Dynamic that Will Define Laos' Future

President Bounnhang Vorachit, after his election as General Secretary of the Lao People Revolutionary Party (LPRP) in 2016, reiterated that Laos continues on the path of socialism. This has been repeated on various occasions by the top Lao leaders. As former President Choummaly asserted: "The trust of our people in the new regime and future of the nation has been lifted to new heights." This emphasis on confidence and national consensus building will be placed on the solidarity between the Party-State and the "Lao multiethnic people" for the goal of future prosperity. Yet it can be expected that the ruling Party will maintain its discipline, provided that the economic growth remains strong around 7 percent over the next ten years, the foreign direct investment continues to flow into the country, and the external geopolitics do not come to disturb the country's course of development. Undoubtedly, the economic growth is essential. And the government has promised a great deal for the next ten years to come. In April 2016, the National Assembly approved the country's 8th Five-Year National Social Economic Development Plan, for 2016-2020, as well as a 10-year plan and a 15-year plan. According to the shorter one, GDP per capita will be $3,190 by 2020, taking Laos out of its Least Developed Country status. The national poverty rate will also be cut to below 10 percent of the population within four years.

Laos' future will be certainly different from its past. Despite greater market-orientation, the government will continue to play an immensely important role in Laos' economic and social life. For its development, Laos will not simply follow the path suggested by others; it will trace its own way. For businesses in Laos, rapid economic growth requires in the future a match between the government's long-term plan and investment focused on the quality of the projects.

Laos has embarked on a transformation of an unprecedented scale of its modern history and scope. It has shown itself capable, distinctive, resilient, and adaptable. Laos' future will be a confluence of forces rather than a simple master plan. These forces will come from the government, business sector, international institutions, the AEC, regional powers, and the Lao community.

Along with growing regional recognition is the fact that, for the first time, Laos' leadership is encouraging Lao enterprises to become "capitalist", making profits, and looking for Asean markets in the framework of the AEC. In parallel, with its domestic economic imperatives, the Lao government believes it is critically important for Lao companies to take more active action in investing in technology, know-how, and acquiring competencies to be competitive and produce good quality products for domestic and regional and international markets. The government has already supported SOEs to join with foreign reputable companies for its sustainable development in regional markets. Just as with other Lao imperatives, the target of the Asean market for Lao SMEs must be seen as a political as well as a business initiative. The SME Development Plan of the Ministry of Industry and Commerce shall also pledge to support and promote Lao entrepreneurs and SMEs to invest in Asean member countries.

China, Thailand, and Vietnam will remain in the future Laos' main suppliers and buyers. The trend will continue due to the huge need of the country for its infrastructure development and trade with those neighbors. Vietnam will keep a political ascendency as in the past on Laos; this will not change, but China will have a stronger grip on the country's economy. China's active investment and diplomatic efforts have resulted in Laos as its market of choice and as its preferred friend. The fact that Chinese investment, aid, and accompanying diplomatic support has come without the human right conditions often claimed by traditional international donors has made China a virtual ally of Laos. At the same time, Laos has become increasingly part of the AEC and also adept at leveraging bilateral relations with regional powers, the EU, Russia, and the US, in order to keep a balanced positioning. But given its track record of diplomacy, one can be sur that Laos knows well how to play the game of geopolitics.

Today, under the "Second Generation" leaders with transition to the "Third Generation" leaders coming up, Laos has continued the basic path of development set out by their predecessors from the "First Generation", but with some new wrinkles of their own. Laos has continued to make progress in opening its economy, consistent with its commitments under its World Trade Organization (WTO) accession agreement. Inward flow of FDI has remained high, the financial sector has been opened to a significant extent, and progress has been on a certain number of fronts. On the other hand, foreign critics claim that Laos has not moved ahead rapidly enough on the application of the rule of law and other political issues; for example, the state exerts tight control over the media, owning all newspapers and broadcast media. The "Third Generation" leaders are starting to emerge with younger cadres that are more elitist and technocrat, having international exposure, and this might bring novelty and momentum to the country and the way politics shall be conducted in the new era of competitiveness and in the Asean community context.

Predicting the exact path of Laos' development is an impossible task; nobody can foresee what would happen within the next fifteen or twenty years in Laos. The LPRP is still in the process of transitioning from a revolutionary party to a ruling party, and there will probably be a more pragmatic approach to openness and a leaning towards a new model of political system, for example the Singaporean model, but without abandoning socialism. If the regime calls itself socialist, the economy, however, feels very capitalist. The overall picture that emerges from an analysis of the transformation process towards a market economy over the past thirty years is rather positive; however, reforms in politics are still to come. Of course, the change of political orientation, if it will happen, depends very much on the international political context, the regional economic environment, the macroeconomic stability of the Lao economy, and the Laos' internal Party evolution. But most importantly, Laos' destiny depends fundamentally on how Vietnam's policy itself will evolve, in what time frame and in what form.

Each generation of Laos' leaders has made its own imprint on Laos' policies. The present one is to plan a long-term vision for sustainable strategic development until 2030, focused on modernization of the industry, social and political stability, achievement of a per capita income in 2030 four times that of 2015, and becoming an upper middle income country. The next generation might focus on the competiveness of Lao enterprises, its effective incorporation into the Asean community, and taking advantage of all the opportunities of Laos' location at the crossroads of the regional and subregional market integration offered by the AEC and the GMS. But greater accountability, transparency, effective rule of law, and public participation will also be taken into account by the future leaders. The prospects for Laos to develop a market-based democracy in the long term could not be unlikely; again it will be conditioned by external forces.

What development is in the future for Laos? Based on the 8th NESDP, the 10-Year Development Strategy, and the Vision 2030, the future is expected to call for more "balanced development," an emphasis on the "quality" of economy growth rather than the "quantity" of growth, greater "investment in bio agriculture", and greater "production on processing industry". "Balanced development" is a motto used to mean the development that limits the economic disparities across regions and between the urban and the rural economies. Attempts will be made to raise the efficiency of agriculture and improve public services to rural areas, many of which are hardly touched by public services at present. Since Lao manufacturers are not able to compete with well-established foreign companies, the Lao government wishes therefore to foster niche market sectors such as garments, handicrafts, silk textile, organic produce, the processing industry, and tourism. Most importantly, commercial agriculture along with light industry manufacturing should be beefed up; furthermore, the objectives of the SEZ must be met in order to attract companies to invest there. Energy and mining sectors will continue to be encouraged by the government but while respecting the environment and biodiversity. These sectors will be an integral part of the green economy industry.

The fourth industrial revolution or digital economy will bring opportunities in some segments of industry for Laos (manufacturing, agriculture, health, transport and many more sectors are already being transformed, e-government, and e-commerce). Smart objects are equipped with sensors, processors and software, enabling them to collect data and operate autonomously. Keeping pace with the changing world, the Central Bank of Laos has launched several new initiatives over the years to help transform the banking system. Indeed, technology and application programming interfaces

(APIs) are becoming critical in the context of digital banking today. In a digital banking world, technology is becoming a key and primary driver, the ability to handle changes quickly in a cost-effective manner, keeping pace with global changes and to enable technology-driven financial inclusion. A workshop jointly conducted recently by the First Lao Solutions and Fiorano Software Inc., to educate the bankers in Vientiane about how "APIs & Digital Banking" can be handled seamlessly and governed efficiently, thereby creating a real-time banking environment for Laos. Several banks are already part of the "Lao ATM Pool Switch" (LAPS). In the future, all banks operating in Laos will have to be part of the LAPS.

When combined with technologies such as digital infrastructure and cloud computing, they can automate entire business processes and government administrative management. But the drivers for growth in the next decade for Laos would still be energy, mining, FDI, construction, agriculture, tourism, and services with digital application to be more and more present.

The Vision 2030 also calls for further improvement on the economic system, reforms to the role of the government in the economy, faster fiscal and financial markets, development of a modern market economy, improvement in human resources and education, improvement in income distribution and the social safety net, as well as enhanced investment in health and culture, among others. Over the period 2020-2025, Lao citizens would expect movement in the direction of "balanced development," higher "quality" growth, greater "investment in bio-agriculture," and greater "production in the processing industry". And it's best not to forget that the green economy industry will play a significant role and will take part in the country's development. This movement will be in part so that officials can show they have been acting in a way consistent with the plan and that it will be significant. These objectives should be viewed as important long-term goals of the state along with rapid economic development, preservation of national security, and assertion of national prestige.

The success of the Vision 2030 will depend on how efficiently the domestic and external resources mobilization can be implemented and the means allocated by private sector, along with mobilizing the government and its local agencies. In particular, attracting international institutions, organizations, and regional stakeholders to help Laos form a common understanding about the opportunities and challenges related to investment promotion will be important, along with financing and partnership for cross-border production infrastructure development within the broader framework of Asean connectivity. Thus, attracting public and private investments and promoting south-south and triangular cooperation to finance infrastructure development will be one of the top priorities endorsed by the 10-Year Development Strategy Plan 2016-2025. This local infrastructure development in border areas will serve as "gateways" for inclusive development, acting as external linkages with wider domestic and regional production networks and global value chains, and it will help Laos to become a regional logistics and transport hub and open steady up markets with neighboring countries.

To pursue the growth within the AEC, Laos should simply follow its own path and pace of development. Laos has shown itself willing and able to chart its own path in many fields. There is no compelling reason for it to adopt a foreign model of economic growth or suggestions provided by various external consultant services. Nevertheless, Laos shall take what are the best from western's or other nations' practices and management tools, and adapt them in the country. On a whole range of issues, such as the role of government in the economy, the role of investors, economic openness, outlooks toward trade facilitations, cross-border trade, the role of markets in allocation of natural resources, and on basic issues of governance, Laos should seek to develop what would be the suitable model for itself. Furthermore, Lao's enterprises have great opportunities today to take a shortcut to catch up on it development in several aspects, such as technology, marketing strategy, processing industry competencies, finance, quality control, project and factory management, international trade practice and law, human resources management, and capital market by learning from the experiences of successful countries.

Today, Laos' got talent from its entrepreneurs, researchers, consultants, and senior retired experts, but doesn't develop it or doesn't use it satisfactorily. Who knows Laos better than the Lao people themselves? This lack of talent in the key skill of talent development, if not overcome in double-quick time, will be the game-stopper in attempts to achieve Laos Socioeconomic Development Strategy 2025 and the Vision 2030. Laos should therefore initiate the industry modernization in the country into more value-added, innovative and creative sectors by the Lao people and with the assistance of external competencies if necessary: processing industry, bio-agriculture, digital infrastructure, basic and support industries, and high-value services.

Another factor that can boost Laos' development are the migrants, they are a catalyst for Laos long-term strategy development plan. Migrants can and should play a vital role in the realization of the Laos Vision 2030. Migrant investors form the backbone of many of Laos' export-oriented industries, local dynamic commerce, and wealth. Their overall contribution to the economy is undeniable. With regard to migrant workers, their contribution may become even more crucial in Lao's economy. There are several reasons for this. The first is demography. Laos faces few population, migrants will therefore play a key role in compensating for shortage of Lao labor and skilled workforce, and will continue to do jobs that few Lao workers are willing or able to do. The 8th NESDP, the Development Strategy 2025, and the Vision 2030, for example, call for large scale infrastructure projects including express ways, railways, power plants, bridges, roads, SEZs, buildings, and commercial complexes to be built, all of which are likely to be constructed with migrant labor. Laos should consider migration as a viable solution that can complement efforts to address any shortfall in skilled labor.

Laos' also requires technical expertise and a growing pool of skilled workers to drive modernization economic transformation to come. Preparing the Lao workforce for the future envisioned in Laos Vision 2030 will require investments in education and vocational training schools in partnership with employers and local authorities, such as the Champassak provincial technical and vocational college in southern Laos, this college will play a key role in supplying workers to the Pakxe-Japan SME Specific Economic Zone. There is also the private Xaysombath Technology College in Savannakhet that supplies graduated students for the SEZ and the Pakpasak technical college in Vientiane supported by Luxembourg Development Cooporation.

Effectively managed migration and boosted investment in building vocational technical centers and schools across the country in partnership with private sector and donors have the potential to boost all the pillars of sustainable development in Laos: economic, processing industries, social, and environmental. The return in this investment will be a major contribution to the success of Laos Vision 2030.

10.2. Milestone: Looking To the Future

In assessing Laos' future prospects in this time of the AEC, only one prediction can be made with assurance: the future as has been the case with the past, will be dominated by a balanced relationship between Laos-Vietnam and Laos-China, while Laos also manages the delicate balance between Vietnam and China.

On the political front, despite its shift toward a little greater openness, for the foreseeable future, Laos will remain an authoritarian system and the country keeps maintaining the socialist ideology with Lao characteristics. Finally, Laos' domestic politics are being increasingly influenced by the combination of rapid domestic growth and expanding international intercourse. The cooperation within the Asean continues to have a benefit impact on Laos' economic and political development. Laos' friendly relations with the two super powers, the US and China, and other regional powers are essential to preserve peace and social order for the country. Almost certainly, this will continue in the years immediately ahead, constituting rising challenges to Lao's leaders. On balance, Laos' position in the region is more positive and more stable than at any time since the founding of the Lao PDR. The regional integration of Laos and its inter-connectivity, including the government energy policy as electricity provider, make the country that matters to Asean, and this is of significant benefit for Laos.

As it mentioned above regarding talents, there are Lao talents not only in Laos, but also around the world. However, all of them are now living and working abroad. For some of them, it is a loss for Laos. Therefore, should Laos be more active in the process of pulling back talents, the country will have the right to expect a promising future.

Definitively, Laos has been changing and developing comprehensively in terms of economic, social, cultural, and international dimensions. Economically, Laos still maintains a stable socio-economic environment, ensuring confidence among foreign investors in the context of a volatile international economic and political situation, like oil price fluctuation, falling price of raw material (gold and copper), and political uncertainty. Looking to the future, with its central position in the region, Laos may become an attractive destination of foreign investors. Laos in the future will have a dynamic and open economy, offering its citizens an improving standard of living and opening its markets to imports and attracting investment. Laos has a modest part to contribute to regional stability and security, and to be an "electricity" provider for economic growth in this region.

Socially, it is no doubt that Laos' reform process has been a driving force in promoting a stable process of industrialization and modernization. The Lao government has tried its best to innovate its regime. Improving the living standards of the people, and narrowing the gap between urban and remote area have been the heart of government's policies. Additionally, it will be important for the government to balance it regional development. It means that efforts to be implemented to create activity and commerce in remote areas so that people can live from their agricultural and crafts products. This will prevent them to move to the urban overpopulated areas and at the same time allowing the reduction of the poverty in their region. It is a long process and needs government strong determination and political will. The long-term objective of Laos' social policy is a secure, stable, prosperous, and open Laos. Laos' goal in the future is to implement the Sustainable Development Goals (SDGs) set by the United Nations, including reducing the impact of UXO, this is Laos own national Sustainable Development Goal. By committing to Goal 18 as a part of the global 2030 Agenda for Sustainable Development.

As described above, the educational background of the present third transition and the following generation of leaders is significantly different from their predecessors' and their training in politics, duty of historical memory, management, and economic will stand them in better stead to deal with new challenges to come than the current leadership of trained political cadres and officials.

In brief, these are some of the main factors upon which the future of Laos will be built. Clearly, both Laos, Cambodia, Vietnam, and Thailand will play a vital role in that future in terms of cross-border trade and connectivity. The external influences of these three countries and doubtless a growing role for China will be decisive. These trends are already evident. In addition, because of its modest economic size, low political weight, and small population, Laos is not an intimidating presence; it does not threaten any of its neighbors, and it is indeed forced to be on friendly terms with all the states with which it interacts. Laos does not compete with any member of Asean, and it must maintain friendly trading relations with all members simply to keep its head above water as it is doing so far. Politically, Laos works as it always did to make its non-alignment position be accepted by all super and regional powers. Based on the above principles Laos will succeed in achieving its growth objectives, political stability, and social order. Hence, tremendous challenges await present and future leaders.

Laos is likely to undergo unpredicted difficulties and setbacks as it strives to diversify, modernize its economy, and establish more close commercial links with other Asean member countries. However, with the Lao government's implementation of necessary regulatory changes, improving the ease of doing business index, and the setting up of the AEC, Laos will experience further and sustainable economic growth. A dynamic Laos' economy is an outcome that not only Laos, but all Asean countries should collectively strive for, since an economically thriving Laos will not only reduce the development gap within Asean, but will also lead to higher volumes of intra-regional trade and investment, benefiting Asean as a whole. Moreover, Laos is committed in promoting friendship and enhancing its further open-door policy and is looking forward to continued support and assistance from international institutions and donors, and increased foreign direct investments. Laos Vision 2030, Strategy 2025 as well as its 8th NSEDP aim at advancing the country towards attaining green economy and sustainable development goals, which demonstrated the Lao government's will to fulfill its international obligations as member of the international and regional community. Unless all the challenges and obstacle are addressed and lifted within an effective framework for an improved business environment and progress toward economic integration in the region, Laos will have difficulty completing the needed transformation for sustainable and inclusive economic growth. While it is impossible to predict the future of Laos, it is certain that this small, developing country will play a strategic role in economic development and foreign relations in Southeast Asia well into the 21st century.

CHAPTER 11

What lessons are there to Learn from the experiences of successful countries?

Is there anything Laos can learn from the experiences of successful countries? This part of the book proposes to outline a few models of topics that six countries have developed effectively in their country. Some examples include a landlocked country, developed rich country, and developing country with many resources. The pattern of success described here can inspire Laos (government, local agencies, and the private sector) to catch up its industry development and help the sustainability of SMEs, as well as for western donors and international institutions to consider it. It is understood that Laos would have to take into account its own specificities before anything else: geographic, cultural, economic, regional integration, and political consideration.

11.1. How Does the French Government Help Its SMEs?

As in many other European countries, SMEs are the backbone of the economy in France. SMEs dominate mostly in the retail and wholesale trade, transport, and the hotel and restaurants sectors; they are also numerous in some manufacturing industries as well as construction.

Better conditions for access to various sources of financing are offered to SMEs, such as a decrease in the cost of credit for small businesses (for loans under €1 million), which is about 11 % higher than for larger enterprises (which generally need loans of over €1 million). The commercial banks participate to give competitive loans to SMEs. In addition, the government has implemented the "Competitiveness and Employment Tax Credit" (CICE) measures to reduce labor costs and business taxation, improved margins, and low financing costs for SMEs[192]. The French government supports SMEs thanks to various allocated funds spread to several agencies through the Ministry of Economy, Industry, and Employment (Ministry of Economy) and its Office of Competitiveness, Industry, and Service (DGCIS). Also working under the Ministry of Foreign Affairs to support exporting SME activities is the international business development agency Business France (a merger since 2014 between former Ubifrance and French International Investment Agency)[193], which provides foreign market information and accompanies French firms on international trade missions. Business France was set up by the French government and acts as a link between French SMEs and foreign markets. As a result, potential exporters have access to research and reliable advice on selecting their markets, making the right contacts, and identifying sources of funding. Other key agencies are:

- Coface, a private multinational financial services company to provide trade credit information and trade credit finance and insurance worldwide. Coface also provides trade credit guarantees to French firms on behalf of the French government. Coface's main mission is to insure businesses – from SMEs to multinationals - against unpaid invoices, which can undermine their profitability.
- OSEO, an agency jointly managed by the Ministry of Economy and the Ministry of Higher Education and Research, was established to support innovation and growth in French SMEs. Its main goal is to provide loans to French SMEs to support innovation and development.
- The Union of French Chamber of Commerce and Industry Abroad (UCCIFE) network, which represents 114 French Chambers of Commerce and Industry (CCIF). Both UCCIFE and CCIF assist French companies in foreign markets by providing a variety of services, such as foreign mark analysis and business to business matchmaking. One of the main activities of the CCIF is to identify export-ready SMEs and to send them to Business France for export-related commercial service.

Direct government support to help finance French SMEs exporting activities includes two programs by Business France:

- Export development loans: For up to 6 years to cover the tangible and intangible costs of goods and services needed for French SMEs to establish an international presence.
- SIDEX program: Short term aid for SMEs export project finalization for a maximum period of 15 days for French businesses located in France.

OSEO also provides several financial programs for SMEs:

- Export investment guarantees and financing to expand production and expand production capacity in order to export.
- Credit guarantees for pre-export financing and export credit risk guarantees.
- Loans for export for up to 6 years for SMEs to develop exports or set up a business operation in another country.
- International development contract loans for up to 6 years for SMEs in business 3 years or longer seeking to export for the first time or already exporting a product. Loans cover intangible project costs such as localization of products to foreign markets, attending foreign trade fairs, relocating materials, and creating a foreign branch office.

Furthermore, there are a wide range of programs to promote exporting varieties by French SMEs, provided mainly by the French Business Agency. For example under Business France responsibilities, all government bodies abroad participate along with Business France to strengthen the export position of SMEs; the VIE (International Company Volunteers) program is aiming to send freshly graduated students for 6 to 24 months to work abroad to assist SMEs without any cost for them; Business France's "Label France" program offers reduced costs for eligible SMEs to participate at international trade fairs; Business France's managerial capacity building program for SMEs provides coaching and training in all aspects of international export issues, commercial export negotiation, and international business cultures; and also the large companies are encouraged by the government to assist SMEs to tap into foreign markets.

The French government and business community have also set up the French "pôles de compétitivité", clusters serving business and job growth for SMEs. The goal of clusters is to build on synergies and collaborative innovation projects in order to give partner firms the chance to become first in their markets, both in France and abroad. In 2013, SMEs received 67% of the financial support granted to companies by the state fund dedicated to collaborative R&D projects[194].

> Four important ideas picked up from the above that could help Laos' SMEs: 1. To have a government financial structure to back up SMEs. 2. To have a strong appropriate international investment agency to accompany the SMEs abroad. 3. To pull large companies and SMEs to work together, and the important thing is that SMEs have to cluster with one another to be competitive and solid in terms of finance, production, and innovation. 4. To have Lao large enterprises act as a driving force for SMEs in tourism, agro-products, processing enterprises, and other business sectors.

11.2. How Has the Small Principality of Andorra Become So Attractive for Tourists?

Andorra is a small independent European coprincipality situated among the southern peaks of the Pyrenees Mountains and bordered by France to the north and east and by Spain to the south and west. It is one of the smallest states in Europe, and the capital is Andorra la Vella. The total area is 468 sq. km with 78,000 inhabitants in 2017. The literacy percentage of the population age 15 and over is 100%, and the GNI per capita in 2016 was US$ 47,500. The urban population in 2017 was 84.1% of the total population.

Although not a member of the European Union, Andorra has used the euro as its de facto primary currency since 2002. In July 2011, Andorra concluded a monetary agreement with the EU that made the euro its official currency, though the Andorran government was not granted the power to issue its own euro banknotes. No railway system exists, but good roads link Andorra with France and Spain. The University of Andorra was established in 1997; it has faculties in nursing, computer studies, virtual studies, and continuing education. Virtually all Andorrans are literate.

With only a tiny proportion of Andorra's land cultivable[195], the traditional economy is centered on the pasturing of sheep and the harvesting of modest quantities of tobacco, rye, wheat, olives, grapes, and potatoes. Industry is limited to processing these products and to handicrafts.

How does the economy work and why is it so successful? Andorra has a developed economy and a free market. Tourism, retail sales, and finance are the mainstays of Andorra's small economy, accounting for more than three-quarters of GDP. Andorra has a duty-free status and low or nonexistent taxes for some products. Andorra has become an important international center of retail trade that has attracted millions of shoppers from all over Europe with its duty-free imported consumer goods, including alcoholic beverages, electronic devices, tobacco, and clothing. Tourism is another of Andorra's leading industries, and the area has excellent opportunities for summer resort and winter sports. According to the government statistics, the number of tourists arriving in 2016 in Andorra was 8,057,500, an increase of 2.6 percent compared to 2015[196]. The construction industry flourished in response to the increase in tourism. The banking sector is also economically significant.

Could Laos take the same path as Andorra? Why not emphasize one of its SEZs (for example the Savan-Seno special economic zone or Thakkek specific economic zone) and focus on making it a duty free import hub, and market luxury international brand name products such as perfume, cosmetics, alcoholic beverages, clothes, bags, luggage, jewelry, cigarettes, cigars, wine, and electronic devices. Additionally, Lao SMEs also could take the opportunities at the same time to sell their locally made products such as organic produce, tea, coffee, handicrafts, silk textiles, food processing, and jewelry. This approach could bring in regional shoppers and tourists and accelerate local livelihoods and bring prosperity to the region.
By creating inside a special economic zone a duty free status for imported luxury goods, this will attract regional tourists with high purchasing power to spend their money in Laos and will also help locally made products.

11.3. Norway Is Richly Endowed With Natural Resources, So How Does the Country Manage Its Wealth?

Norway is one of the world's most prosperous countries. It saves a large portion of its petroleum-sector revenues, including dividends from the partially state-owned Statoil and taxes from oil and gas companies operating in Norway. The total population in 2017 was estimated at 5.2 million with GDP per capita reaching US$73,450. Norway is a welfare state. Since World War II, successive Norwegian governments have sought to broaden and extend public benefits to its citizens in the form of sickness and disability benefits, minimum guaranteed pensions, heavily subsidized or free universal healthcare, unemployment insurance, and so on. Public policy still favors the provision of such benefits. Norway practices a mixed economy with both privately and publicly owned enterprises. Most of the economy is based on natural resource exploitation, including fishing, petroleum, and hydroelectric power.

The economy of Norway is a developed mixed economy with state ownership in strategic areas. Although sensitive to global business cycles, the economy of Norway has shown robust growth since the start of the industrial era. The country has a very high standard of living compared with other European countries, and a strongly integrated welfare system. Norway's modern manufacturing and the accumulation of assets from hydrocarbon production, particularly in North Sea oil, has provided a cushion for fiscal stimulus[197].

With the financial reserve produced by exploitation of natural resources, Norway has the best welfare system in the world for its population. It also has the lowest income inequality in the world, helped by a mix of policies that support education and innovation. It also channels the world's largest sovereign wealth fund, which manages its oil and gas revenues into long-term economic planning.

How does the Norwegian government manage its wealth for the benefit of the country? The government manages the country's petroleum resources through extensive regulation. It allows itself to use up to 4% of the fund's value, its annual expected real rate of return, to help balance the federal budget each year. In anticipation of eventual declines in oil and gas production, Norway saves the state revenue from petroleum sector activities in the world's largest sovereign wealth fund, valued at almost $900 billion as of early 2017. To help balance the federal budget each year, the government follows a "fiscal rule," which states that spending of revenues from petroleum and fund investments shall correspond to the expected real rate of return on the fund, an amount it estimates is sustainable over time. In February 2017, the government revised the expected rate of return for the fund downward from 4% to 3%. The government has expressed willingness to increase public spending from the sovereign wealth fund to help prevent a recession.

> The Norwegian Sovereign Wealth Fund model has been widely regarded as a success to manage the resources from the petroleum sector. This could be considered by the Lao government based on the establishment of an energy and mining fund to prudently manage revenues from the sector, stabilize government revenue, and shield the economy from variations in prices and production. The fund will be structured such that transfers to the government cannot exceed a maximum estimated sustainable income without approval by parliament. This reserve could also be served to invest in innovation for Laos' enterprises, improving their productivity and competitiveness as well.

11.4. How Can We Explain Switzerland's Extraordinary Economic Success, in Spite of Its Small Size and Lack of Natural Resources?

Many Lao' officials, business leaders, students, and people in the street have a great admiration for Switzerland, for the success of its economy and the well-being of its citizenry; the Lao people often compare the similarity of Switzerland with their country. Indeed, both are landlocked countries, small in terms of surface area (41,284 km^2), a total population 8.4 million, and several ethnic and religious groups in their respective countries. Is there anything that Laos can learn from Switzerland? This question has often been wondered by Laos' officials.

Switzerland is a success story, as James Breiding points out in his remarkable book[198]. Medieval Switzerland was an impoverished mountain society whose main export was soldiers who fought as mercenaries in other people's wars, and where households were habitually so poor that they sent their children off to work as quasi-serfs in more prosperous homes in Germany and elsewhere. Modern Switzerland is a highly prosperous society, and is also more resilient than its neighbors to external shocks. Switzerland has produced so many remarkable innovations, ideas, and products. Areas of Swiss innovation are: textiles, tourism, food, engineering, medical technology, chemicals and pharmaceuticals, trading and insurance, as well as banking, architecture, construction, and watches.

Openness is a crucial quality for the Swiss. Many of the most dynamic figures who shaped their iconic global brands came to Switzerland from other countries, fleeing political oppression as much as poverty. This openness to foreigners has worked the other way, too. The country is poor in minerals, the soil is not fertile, and the land is not suitable for agriculture. Only water is plentiful: for domestic or industrial use, as ice or snow for recreational use, or as a source of energy. Switzerland is mountainous and has no direct link to the world's oceans. Conversely, the transport corridors through the Alps give Switzerland an important strategic position between the great mercantile regions and those of northern and southern Europe. In language, culture, and political and religious persuasion, Switzerland was, and is, heterogeneous. This heterogeneity has been reinforced by the arrival of immigrants from many cultures from an early date. Almost a third of today's population consists of immigrants or the descendants of immigrants. In the past, many of them arrived as political refugees, taking advantage of Switzerland's long-held policy of neutrality. More recently, immigration has reflected the country's needs.

What are the features of Swiss success? In short, it can be summarized as follows: taking into consideration its small size, Switzerland has always been a neutral country and has pursued an open policy to immigrants. The entrepreneurship and industrial success are another characteristic of the whole country, and the success of immigrants is the result partly of the Swiss environment and partly of the immigrant mentality. The Swiss have always had a high work ethic and a high value placed on professionalism throughout the working population. This is expressed in, among other things, an education system that still allots a central place to traditional vocational training (apprenticeships) alongside university education. The country also focuses on the best quality of products: milk, chocolate, cheese, watches, food, and medicine, including machinery and machine tools. Tourism also attracts millions of visitors annually in summer as well in winter for the skiing. Swiss powerful multinational companies are ranked among the top globally in the world and in every business sector: banking, food industry, insurance, machinery, electronic, textile, chemical, pharmaceutical, aeronautic and aerospace, hotel industry, and tourism. No other country of or near its size holds leading positions in so many industries, notwithstanding the pressures of globalization.

One important element to be mentioned is the confederation structure of Switzerland. Swiss cantons have great autonomy, much more than American states or Canadian provinces. And within cantons, municipalities have considerable autonomy. Decision making happens at the lowest practical level. Public expenditure is decided largely at the community and state levels, and taxes are raised locally and voted upon. This results in highly localized government administration and taxation. The Swiss believe that this structure imposes self-discipline on each level.

Are there lessons for Lao enterprises and policy makers in Laos to learn from what might be called the "Swiss Way"? While Switzerland is in "splendid isolation" with its big businesses and high technology and industrialized firms, Laos, a tiny market with almost insignificant industry, has huge natural resources and potential in the tourism sector, among others, and should take an example from Switzerland to become a "small is beautiful" country. Laos is an ecological country; it has succeeded to avoid the deterioration of four basic elements of agricultural productivity: water, soil, seeds, and biodiversity, which are now being degraded at an alarming rate in developed countries. While organic farming is now a highly sought-after practice in developed countries, it remains a reality and a natural practice as always among many Lao farmers and villagers. Laos's agricultural production still uses natural methods. As the trend in many countries around the world is to return to natural agricultural practices, Laos has the potential to serve as a positive example and trendsetter. Despite some already mentioned disadvantages, Laos is "blessed by the gods"; the country expects to be a primary producer of electricity within Asean. The Lao people are indeed still poor, but not miserable, and nature serves them well. Many people in rural areas have preserved a traditional way of life in harmony with nature. Laos has turned all the disadvantages of a small state into numerous benefits; the country has particularly taken advantage of significant financial aid from foreign donors earmarked for economic growth and social development. Yes, Laos can become a "small is beautiful" country and the best country to live among the Asean countries for its climate, ecological environment, organic food, peace, leisure resorts, green parks, and friendly atmosphere of the people. The country is wide open to the outside world and committed to pursuing the connectivity with Asean member countries.

Make Laos an enchanted, peaceful, ecological, and safe country. Produce top quality Lao-made goods and promote innovation culture in all enterprises by reinforcing the Lao processing industry, including its building capacity in bio-agriculture and handicrafts. Promote Laos as the best tourism destination in Asean, particularly for eco-tourism. Organize more activities in several amazing sites for international tourists and preserve cultural heritage. It's also a challenge to lure people to spend larger sums of money and attract higher-spending groups of tourists. Boost the tourism industry and make it more professional. This stimulates the growth of businesses, particularly airlines, hotels, restaurants, buses, and other operations, which create job opportunities for local people and serve as revenue sources for the country. By doing so, the government has to strengthen and invest in a better education system for young people, prepare the country for the Industrial Revolution 4.0, and transform Lao society and business sectors into digital ones. Promote, encourage, and stimulate students to choose technical studies and vocational training, including apprenticeship. To achieve all the above targets, Laos needs before anything else to make the quality of human resources development its top priority.

11.5. How Does Finland's Forest Industry Manage the Country's Resource?

Finland has a highly industrialized, mixed economy with a per capita output similar to that of other western European economies, but slightly lower than Sweden. The largest sector of the economy is services at 72.7 percent, followed by manufacturing and refining at 31.4 percent. Primary production is 2.9 percent. The total population in 2017 was 5.5 million and the GDP per capita was US$43,090. The surface area of the country is 338, 145 sq. km. The forest covers 72.3 % of the territory, while arable land only covers 7.4 %.

In Finland, forest ownership is mostly based on the possession of private individuals. 60% of Finland's forest area is private property and almost 14% of Finns are forest owners. For many people, forestry is a profession and source of livelihood[199].

The **forest industry in Finland** is one of the world's largest producers of pulp, paper, and cardboard, and one of Europe's largest producers of sawn timber. Forests are Finland's most valuable natural resource; it directly and indirectly employs approximately 160,000 people in Finland. Forestry, an important export industry, provides a secondary occupation for the rural population. The forest industry employs 15% of industrial workers in Finland. Most of the products of the Finnish forest industries are exported, and it is the main source of income for many regions in Finland and accounts for approximately 20 percent of all Finnish exports, consisting of timber, paper, and pulp.

Forestry, paper factories, and the agricultural sector are important for rural residents, so any policy changes affecting these sectors are politically sensitive for politicians who are dependent on rural votes.

Forests play a key role in the country's economy, making it one of the world's leading wood producers and providing raw materials at competitive prices for the crucial wood-processing industries. As in agriculture, the government has long played a leading role in forestry, regulating tree cutting, sponsoring technical improvements, and establishing long-term plans to ensure that the country's forests continue to supply the wood-processing industries.

The forest sector is a key player in promoting sustainable development in Finland. Indeed, the ongoing structural change in the forest industry focuses not only on improving existing products but also on developing new biodegradable products and energy solutions based on forest resources and wood. In the wood product industry, the use of wood in construction in particular is expected to be a significant growth area, since wood is a low-energy, renewable construction material throughout its life cycle while providing long-term carbon sequestration. Product development and research, especially regarding forest fibers, is forward-looking and gives the opportunity to achieve remarkable environmental benefits, such as replacing plastics and other environmentally burdensome materials.

Sustainable forest management, however, is becoming a more and more complex question of balance. It includes the balancing of private and public interests, present and future generations' needs, and environmental and economic benefits, to mention just a few examples. Forestry must address increasingly complex demands from a growing number of users.

The profitability of Finnish forestry is based on the good timber production capacity of forests and demand for Finnish wood. In addition to wood production, today's forest management focuses on the preservation of natural values, landscape management, and recreational needs. Finnish forests are managed so as to promote their biodiversity. Ecologically valuable trees, including dead and decaying trees, are left in the forest during logging, and care is taken to preserve valuable natural features including the habitats of endangered species.

Finnish forest politics has been carried out with the aim to manage forest resources in a sustainable way, maintain the biodiversity of forests, and ensure the effective regeneration of forests, as well as the overall growth of forest resources. After harvesting, according to the law, forests have to be reforested. Failure to do so results in the offender being sanctioned. It is fair to say that the Finnish have the most progressive forest legislation in the world, since they are one of the most forest-rich countries in the world. In Finland, the total amount of forests and trees has been growing over the course of centuries, whereas in many other European countries forests were deforested long ago[200].

Today, Finland promotes wood as building material. In Finland, wood accounts for about 40% of all building materials. Nearly 80% of detached houses have a wooden frame. Wood as renewable raw material provides a long-term carbon sequestration potential, and thus is promoted in Finland for use in construction, above all for building blocks of flats in wood. This is an idea that Laos could take for inspiration. Laos needs to use forest resources responsibly and sustainably to create employment and well-being for Lao people as the Finns do.

As far as Laos is concerned, the country is highly dependent on forest products due to its low population density and high forest cover. Forest products serve a wide range of subsistence needs and provide opportunities for income generation. More than 500 plants and animal products are reported to be used. Forestry is also the second largest economic sector, after agriculture, and a crucial source of export income. Forest cover has recently been estimated at 44 percent.

The Lao economy depends on its existing natural forest resources. As one of the fastest growing sectors in the overall economy, the forest sector has provided a vital source of material, jobs, and financing for both public and private sectors. However, this sector has been claimed as one of the major causes of rapid deforestation from overharvesting of natural forests. Even if the policy is vigorously enforced, Laos will still face difficulties in managing its forests in a sustainable manner, because forests and forestlands are among the few valuable resources existing in Laos and there is competition between different ministries and bureaus over their use. Little coordination exists between various ministries, and each defends its own interests and way to manage sustainable forest development, according to experts and international organizations reports.

The government is aware of the risks of deforestation, and thus sustainability is the key thinking in planning, implementing, and monitoring processes. Practicing sustainability in forest management has become necessary at national, provincial, and district levels, and is promoting collaboration with domestic and international players in several focal areas including plantation development, wood processing, non-wood forest products (NWFPs), forest resource conservation, and ecotourism.

Above are Finland's few best practices that have successfully managed its forest resources. Therefore, the Lao government could take inspiration from and promote actively the use of wood, since it is expected to be more in demand in the production of renewable forest energy, biofuels, new bio economy products such as clothing, fiber packages, composites, pharmaceuticals, cosmetics, and in wood construction. Laos must encourage enterprises and architects to use wood as a noble building material for construction of houses and villas. In order to manage the forest resources in a more sustainable manner, efficient forest management, rehabilitation of poorly growing forests, drainage, increasing the density of forests, and fertilization will be necessary to increase the forest stock growth. In addition, since slash-and-burn cultivation, extensive tar production, and cutting timber for domestic use, charcoal, and fuelwood are also major causes of deforestation, these should be banned.

Improving the forestry law enforcement system cannot necessarily save the forest. Laos has implemented several decrees but they so far do not have tangible results. Particularly, the main law related to forestry in Laos is the 2007 Forestry Law. It seeks in particular to ensure and control that timber and timber products exported to the EU come from legal sources. The agreements of Forest Law Enforcement, Governance & Trade (FLEGT) also help timber-exporting countries stop illegal logging by improving the regulation and governance of the forest sector. Analysis of the enforcement approaches which Finland and other countries have taken indicates that a successful policy must be a blend of regulatory, market-oriented, and consensus-oriented approaches. Concerted action needs to be taken at the national and international levels to protect the world's forests. Action will be successful only if it takes into account the interdependence of the economic, social, and cultural factors that bear on the management of forests. The Lao government should obligate enterprises to cut timber and set up wood processing factories in Laos and have at least 30 percent of local added value before being authorized to export it, at the same time boosting and modernizing the wood industry.

11.6. Why Germany's Dual System of Vocational Education and Training (VET) Is Highly Acknowledged and Performant?

With the lowest youth unemployment rate in Europe, the Germany's dual VET system is highly recognized abroad for its performant. The majority of Germany's workforce received its high qualification through the dual VET-system. The dual VET-system is an integral part of the general education and training system in Germany. Furthermore, the German apprenticeship system is called a "Dual System" because training takes place both in the companies and public training schools. With dual education, the German companies turn apprentices into customized specialists at low net costs through in-house training. The Germany's apprenticeship system provides 344 certified trained jobs, designed by the government and industry. The key success factor of the German dual apprenticeship system is the close partnership among all social partners. The dual VET-system is strongly integrated into the German economy and society. This dual VET-system has a long tradition and is constantly revised. In higher education, dual study programs are on the rise[201].

Vocational training in Germany, how does it works? One way of training for young people's future job in Germany is by pursuing a dual vocational training programme. Such programmes offer plenty of opportunity for on-the-job training and work experience. Programmes usually last between two and three and a half years and comprise theoretical as well as practical elements. The students graduated from high school will spend one or two days a week, or several weeks at once, at a vocational school where they will acquire the theoretical knowledge that will need in their future job. The rest of the time will be spent at a company. There young students get to apply their newly acquired knowledge in practice, for example by learning to operate machinery. They will get to know what their company do, learn how it operates and find out if they can see themselves working there after completing their training.

This combination of theory and practice gives young students a real head start into their job: by the time they have completed their training, they will not only have the required technical knowledge, but they will also have hands-on experience in their job. There are around 350 officially recognised training programmes in Germany, so chances are good that one of them will suit his interests and talents. They can find out which on that might be by visiting one of the jobs and vocational training fairs which are organized in many German cities at different times in the year. Employment prospects for students who have completed a dual vocational training programme are very good. This is one of the reasons why this kind of training is very popular with young Germans: around two thirds of all students leaving school go on to start a vocational training programme[202].

In addition, in Germany many young people enter the labor market over the apprenticeship system. Over 500,000 new apprenticeship contracts are concluded every year. The system developed historically out of the medieval guild system. Its base is the concept of "occupation" or job, a dual system based on school learning and practice in enterprises. The dual system is firmly established in the German education system. The main characteristic of the dual system is cooperation between mainly small and medium sized companies, on the one hand, and publicly funded vocational schools, on the other. This cooperation is regulated by law. Trainees typically spend part of each week at a vocational school and the other part at a company or they may spend longer periods at each place before alternating.

In Germany apprenticeship in the dual system is (still) the main pathway into employment for young people (after 9 years schooling). Depending on the occupation it is also a widely accepted option for young people with university entrance qualification. Many companies consider training as a social task and take pride in being a training company. The relatively smooth transition into employment and the resulting low youth unemployment are seen as important strengths of the system. Because of the importance of apprenticeships for the economy the German government puts a high emphasis on the promotion of the system. It addresses the challenges through initiatives and programs.

Businesses that take part in the dual training scheme consider vocational training to be the best form of personnel recruitment. Companies which provide training not only save on recruitment costs but also avoid the risk of hiring the wrong employee for the job. Investment in first-class training is a key factor for success in an increasingly competitive world. The main benefit for apprentices is that they receive market-relevant training that improves their chances on the labor market which is constantly evolving and upgrading skills in response to the latest innovations of the digital age while simultaneously broadening their social and democratic participation.

Laos can inspire from the above practices considered as the best system known in Europe and enhance vocational technical schools and set up apprenticeship in partnership between private sector and Lao education authorities to supply graduated students to SEZs and other SMEs and services sectors.

> The Germany's dual VET and apprentice system could be a good example for Laos to follow. Authorities and enterprises should work on a "win-win" plan. Make a dual system between public schools and enterprises a compulsory cooperation in the education system. Encouraging large enterprises (Lao and foreign) to participate on the dual education and training system for young people. Promoting internship for graduated students in enterprises, this could be a best form of future recruitment for businesses and for students. Supporting and enhancing apprenticeship in the dual system for young people in each provincial capital under the regional education authorities in connection with business and professional associations based on the needs of the industries.

Notes

[192] Government, SMEs and Entrepreneurship Development: Policy, Practice R. Blacbum; https://www.gov.uk/government/publications/overseas-business-risk-france/overseas-business-risk-france.
[193]http://export.businessfrance.fr/organigramme-businessfrance-accompagne-les-PME-a-l-export.html.
[194]http://competitivite.gouv.fr/les-brochures-de-presentation-des-poles/french-poles-de-competitivite-clusters-serving-business-and-job-growth-787.html
[195] https://www.worldatlas.com/webimage/countrys/europe/ad.htm
[196]http://www.actua.ad/fr/news/le-nombre-de-visiteurs-en-andorre-encore-augment%C3%A9-en-2016-et-d%C3%A9passe-les-8-millions
[197] http://www.heritage.org/index/country/norway.
[198] Swiss Made: The Untold Story Behind Switzerland's Success.

[199] https://www.forestindustries.fi/statistics/
[200] http://www.fao.org/docrep/c3200e/c3200e03.htm.
[201] Vocational Training "Made in Germany" Germany's Dual System of Vocational Education and Training (VET), German Trade &Invest.
[202] http://www.make-it-in-germany.com/en/for-qualified-professionals/training-learning/training.

Conclusion and Recommendations

A meeting of the "Round Table Implementation Meeting" took place with the presence of the Deputy Prime Minister Somdy Duangdy and the UN Resident Coordinator and UNDP Resident Representative Kaarina Immonen in late November 2017 under the theme "Greater Partnership for Implementation of the 8th NSEDP Which Covers the Period 2016–2020: Realizing the Least Developed Country (LDC) Graduation and the Achieving of the Sustainable Development Goals (SDGs)." As the main outcome, the Lao government and its development partners have committed to closer cooperation to realize Laos' graduation from LDC status and achieve the SDGs. Participants attended the meeting, including senior government officials, development partners, and representatives of the private sector as well as national and international non-profit organizations. The discussions focused on four key areas: Graduating from LDC status and integrating the SDGs; realizing the quality of private sector investment for sustainable development; investing in skills and labor force for the development of human resources; and enhancing the south-south cooperation and triangular cooperation[203]. Several keys areas which were not discussed during this meeting are, however, taken into consideration in this book. Participants stressed the importance of the private sector as a key partner in development, and for the government to understand the needs of businesses and for businesses to recognize the government's priorities. Many representatives of international development partners have contributed suggestions in relation to the way the government can achieve the Sustainable Development Goals (SDGs) and reduce the gap in income-earning ability between urban and rural people. The meeting had a great meaning for Laos as it was where all of participants gathered to discuss Laos' preparedness for LDC assessment by the UN Committee for Development Policy in 2018.

The 8th NSEDP will be in line with the longer-term national strategy that is almost concurrently being developed, which looks at Laos becoming a lower mid-income country by 2030. It lays a strong foundation for the achievement of the National Strategy on Socioeconomic Development 2025 and the Vision 2030 as well as the Sustainable Development Goals. The Vision 2030 and Strategy 2025 are seen as crucial to strengthening the national economy, which depends heavily on agriculture, industry, services, investment, and trade; hydropower and mining are other important sectors for resource mobilization. It is also seen as essential to diversify the Lao economy, and to identify and overcome the obstacles and brakes that can slow down its growth momentum.

Laos has been successful in attracting so far various profiles of investors, particularly in the energy and mining sectors, including agriculture, which has resulted in an economic growth rate that has been one of the highest in the region, even in the years when many similar countries have not been successful in maintaining high rates of economic growth. However, both the Lao government and international development partners (bilateral and multilateral) recognize that human resources, including the whole education system, social development, productivity, infrastructure, transport and logistics, and skilled labor have not performed satisfactory. Despite the government's efforts to address the gap and change for a better situation in the 7th NSEDP, there remains room for improvement. Hence, the 8th NSEDP, the 10-Year Development Strategy (2016–2025), and the Vision 2030 (2016–2030) will need to pay particular attention to all the above non-performing of the economy, rather than focusing disproportionately on achievement in a few sectors such as exhaustible mineral resources and energy.

Laos faces several serious challenges for the next decade in order to ensure robust and stable economic growth. Among a few challenges to overcome are strengthening the enterprises' building capacity, developing the competitiveness of its manufacturing industries, reinforcing the SMEs, enhancing the doing business climate, ensuring the attractiveness for businesses, improving good governance, struggling against corruption and eradicating waste, boosting the growth of organic agriculture, becoming a center of connectivity for the region, managing the country's deficit, and narrowing the current development gaps between and within regions in the country.

This book has attempted to provide some inputs for Laos' economy and industrial development. It includes concrete recommendations that can contribute to further the sustainable development and economic growth of Laos. The author believes that Laos can turn its numerous handicaps into strengths, provided that the government, private sector, and international development partners have a common vision. Laos' economic and manufacturing industries development strategies should also give particular consideration to improving infrastructure in order to transform the country from being landlocked to one that is connected with other nations in the Great Mekong subregion under the Master Plan on Asean Connectivity 2025, and China's "One Belt, One Road Initiative". The Lao government is committed to maintain macroeconomic and industrial development, promote sustainable and inclusive growth, and stand ready to implement any measures deemed appropriate. Hence, Laos takes further steps toward industrialization and modernization to enhance the well-being of the people and the prosperity of the country in order to achieve the ranking of an upper middle-income country by 2030.

Thus, to achieve Laos' path towards the long-term strategy development goals within the framework of the AEC, the conclusion of this book makes some general recommendations and highlights key future challenges as below; this in addition to the specific actions and recommendations proposed in chapter 8. The importance of moving on to concrete actions to realize industrial policies is timely for Laos in the frame of regional integration.

1. General Recommendations on a Selected Few Issues

Issue	Recommendations
Laos Should Be a Leader and Not a Follower	A "West is Best" concept should not be a creed today. Laos has to follow its own path and pace of development. Lao people should truly ask whether they should also begin to think for themselves. The country needs to choose the "Lao way" for its economic development that best fits Lao conditions and needs. Lao people have to ask more fundamental questions about whether the western or foreign model of real economy and practice best fit their own

	domestic conditions. Today, many projects and studies shall be handled by local young talent or senior experienced Lao people instead of calling on foreign consultants or other external organizations. Laos is in a position to require know-how and technology transfer whenever they are possible from foreign partners, and to privilege sharing agreements for any future energy and mining projects. Only by utilizing local resources and learning by doing will Laos become knowledgeable and economically efficient and competitive. It is time to take a step forward and think for the Lao people themselves.
Constraints	Laos needs to transform the economy from subsistence–oriented to a commercially and regionally integrated economy. To remove constraints to Laos' development, the country needs to improve its educated and skilled human resources; strengthen and develop its financial sector; build up suitable connectivity between rural and urban areas; reinforce governance; fortify competitiveness in the non-resource sector; control and enhance nutrition and food security; and reduce the gap between regions throughout the country.
Human Resources	The whole education value chain has to be reevaluated, commencing at the bottom. Teachers, educators, instructors, and professors should be qualified and must have an honorable salary. Teachers need to improve their skills by providing training courses to them. In turn, they will be accountable for the success of their mission and also have to identify problems and create solutions in a bid to reduce the number of students failing at all levels from primary to college. Continuing training should be provided to staff and employees. Public and private sector partnerships must be called upon for developing and increasing the number of vocational schools across the country. Laos has to encourage more young people to study in professional schools that the country needs for its

	industry. Specific training has to be provided for young people to become skilled laborers, to facilitate university graduates to take internships in enterprises, to set a target to raise significantly the country's education system, and to establish a high standard for the next decade to come. Number of Skills Development Centers, including educational equipment to respond the demand for teaching and learning materials shall increase for the young in local communities for the continuation of their studies at vocational schools.
Poverty and Inequality Reduction	Although significant progress has been realized over the past decade on the reduction of the poverty, inequality between regions, and gender disparities, Laos is still lagging behind on a number of Millennium Development Goals (MDGs). Laos needs to overcome several issues, which require the country to invest further in remote areas: Increasing the number of primary schools and dispensaries, improving sanitary conditions, constructing rural infrastructure, allowing access to clean water, providing basic healthcare, and providing electricity, particularly for inhabitants of the northern part of Laos. These goals will assist upland people to cultivate commercial crops, handicraft products, and organic vegetables and fruits. Promoting ecotourism in the villages can help and improve livelihood of the rural population. The priority attention is to accelerate education access, retention, and literacy/ numeracy skills among the poor, including technical and vocational education and training. Therefore, with jobs created locally, they live from their work and do not feel the utility to find work and live in the plain around the cities. The financial sources can be obtained from various donors, institutions, and international NGOs to help reduce poverty and inequality for poor regions and for different ethnicities, including struggling children and maternal mortality, and malnutrition. Local authorities need to

	join private sector partnerships to achieve and speed up the implementation of the above goals.
Wastes and Corruption	- Waste occurs when an unnecessary and inappropriate investment is made at a cost to the state and taxpayers. Additionally, dishonest officials committed financial deception by embezzling state funds and assets, including money that should have been used to fund schools and improve health services across Laos. - To eradicate such wrong expenses, any projects have to be first budgeted and approved by the government; the bidding process must be fair and transparent; eliminate spending on projects that cost more than the benefits they create for national interest; identify the mis-targeted programs whose recipients should not be entitled to government benefits; stop spending on outdated, unnecessary, or duplicative programs or material; and detect then intervene on inefficiency, mismanagement, and fraud. With regard to this, the government has already taken some steps to promote austerity and cut unwanted expenses, such as banning the use of official luxury vehicles by leaders and attempting to reduce the number of vehicles used by state organizations. The Prime Minister Thongloun Sisoulith confirmed at the NA that the government would pay special attention to austerity and measures that discourage extravagance.

	- The Lao government has enacted the Anti-Corruption Law in 2006 and ratified the United Nations Convention Against Corruption in 2009. Since 2016, the government recognizes the importance of preventing and combating corruption throughout the country and is publicly committed to tackling corruption within the government organization and administration. To combat this plague it must: Sufficiently increase the civil servant salaries, include those of hospital staff, police, army, customs, and treasury officers; and carry out the decree on the declaration of assets for government officials at all levels and control with force its application. More importantly, to enforce the law effectively is essential to ensure that the corrupt are punished and to break the cycle of impunity, or freedom from punishment or loss; to reform public administration and finance management and strengthen the role of auditing agencies; and to promote transparency and access to information for the public. The State Inspection Authority (SIA) has warned it will seriously enforce the laws to counter the misappropriation of funds.
Good Governance	Major donors and international financial institutions are increasingly basing their aid and loans on the condition that reforms that ensure "good governance" are undertaken. To provide the technical and managerial competence of civil servants is an obvious factor of good governance; decisions taken by the government must be founded in law, so that private firms and individuals are protected from arbitrary decisions; government officials and public servants must ensure that their power is used appropriately and in accordance with the public interest; promoting transparency is an important aspect of good governance; and transparent decision making is critical for the private sector to make sound decisions and investments.

	Accountability and the rule of law require openness and good information so that higher levels of administration, external reviewers, and the general public can verify performance and compliance to law. The function of good governance in the public sector is to ensure that entities act in the public interest at all times. Acting in the public interest requires: Strong commitment to integrity, ethical values, and the rule of law, the exemplarity of the leaders, and openness and comprehensive stakeholder engagement. In addition, achieving good governance in the public sector also requires: Managing risks and performance through robust internal control and strong public financial management; implementing good practices in transparency and reporting to deliver effective accountability, and conducting effective public management and administration based on laws and regulations.
Building Trust	Building Trust between government bodies, donors, and businesses is already becoming an engine of success, both human and economic. Trust is built through dialogue and mutual understanding that begins with a measure of "Climate of Trust" and awareness of the "Invisible Contract."[204] - The "Climate of Trust" is constructed around the triangular government bodies-donors-private sector through the six masts that follow: Word (are commitments held?); Future (are relations well managed?); Rules of Value (are rules and values clear for all?); Pride (do government agencies relate to the partners' business vision?); Recognition (are the quality of relations appreciated?); and Cooperation (are stakeholders willing to embark on a common project?). - The "Invisible Contract" is constructed by the below elements to consider: Knowing the true DNA of each stakeholder; characterizing the performances that each partner should have; identifying the motivations that would incite partners to have these performances;

	determining the supporters, individuals, or organizations that guarantee the achievement of these motivations; and identifying key moments and events that prove that the contract is fulfilled.
Public Debt Management	Public debt has risen and has become less concessional. To improve the situation it needs a sustainable fiscal adjustment by reducing tax exemptions and strengthening tax administration. Furthermore, according to IMF reports, unifying the VAT rate between the Special Economic Zones (SEZs) and the rest of the economy would simplify VAT between administrations and improve tax efficiency, along with implementing and speeding up a better collection and control of tax revenue by means of information technology (ICT). Salaries to civil servants shall be extended to all by means of electronic payment across the country. To achieve public fiscal management, it requires reducing off-budget spending and strengthening control over expenditure. Future borrowings will mainly be on concessional terms and turn necessarily towards investments (projects and capital expenditure).
Economic Vulnerability to Shock	To address structural constraints that limit growth is vital due to Laos' economic context. It requires improving the business environment and upgrading skills and human capital that will impact investment and productivity growth. In addition, it requires boosting the diversification of exports that helps Laos to take advantage of growing export opportunities, particularly if focusing on organic agricultural products. To enhance financial inclusion will also support macro-financial stability and growth.
Private Sector	The private sector plays a key role in the economy and is already tangible; it needs to expand further and accelerate its contribution to social development, infrastructure projects, ecotourism, organic agriculture development, and boost the "green industries" and "green growth."

	However, the private sector is underdeveloped. To address the shortcomings, it needs to review the taxation system for enterprises. Lao authorities have to help SMEs to have access to formal financing, including market capital. And provide them with market information and analysis; and elevate the level of education of employees and develop the skills of the workforce, including vocational training that matches with the needs of enterprises in order to be more productive and competitive. Especially, it requires, from public and private partnerships' initiative, the construction of housing to accommodate workers in the cities. Encouraging the SMEs to use modern technology is particularly pertinent in the current era of digitalization and connectivity, with the ubiquity of computers, tablets, and smartphones to improve their administrative daily works, company management, and promote their products online. To support actively SME integration into value chains and markets, it's necessary to make SMEs more competitive with a clear market strategy approach and using updated technology and equipment. To be recognized as SMEs, all enterprises must be effectively registered; this is to avoid unfair competition and practices from family or unformal enterprises that do not pay taxes. The costs of doing business are comparatively high due to infrastructural issues related to the country's landlocked supply chain. Laos needs to improve its infrastructure, the speed of the Internet network, improve the quality of electricity, and promote the use of ICT tools.
Fourth Industrial Revolution and Digital Transformation	The Fourth Industrial Revolution or Digital transformation has today an impact on the whole economy and society. It will bring significant changes to the way people live, interact, and do business. The Fourth Industrial Revolution refers to a set of highly disruptive technologies, such as artificial intelligence

	(AI), robotics, block chain and 3D printing that are transforming social, economic, and political systems and placing pressure on leaders and policy-makers to respond. Laos has the chance and opportunities to jump to the "internet of things and services", which is becoming an integral part of manufacturing. Industry 4.0 technologies have the potential to create extraordinary growth opportunities and competitive advantages for Laos as a location for emerging business[205]. Government bodies and enterprises shall take advantage of the huge benefits this digital transformation will bring, such as empowering SMEs and creating new ways to connect citizens to healthcare. It will also ease the development of information and communications technology between the central government, its agencies, public servants, and citizens. Laos shall engage in ICT sector development, cybersecurity and program development, and provide online services such as apps on smartphone to government and private industry, such as e-services and e-Government. Laos will need a new approach to policy and governance to help it navigate these technologies, which do not recognize national borders. Furthermore, it is recommended to implement a new electronic system for road tax payment via BCEL Bank's electronic system. Indeed, it is an advantage for the government to introduce such ICT more widely to bring in similar benefits from other sectors, including land taxes and fees for the use of state property and related assets. As such, payment of all taxes and service fees (hospital running, customs, and administrative management) ought to be possible via transfers from bank accounts. If all companies, stores, shops, and individuals turn to cashless tax payment and fees systems, it will make it much easier for the government to collect due taxes and manage the money in circulation in the economy. Hence, the nation will obtain the massive revenue increases due

	from this source. These funds can accrue to the national coffers directly, with less chance of unwelcome leakages. Given these challenges, the key to Laos Digital transformation's success lies in improving human resources by drastically reforming and improving the education system while also creating new, dynamic education systems designed to produce specific workers for specific roles; encouraging creativity, innovation, critical thinking, entrepreneurship, sustainability and inclusiveness. Digitization would disrupt some business areas and at the same time create new business opportunities. With the digital trend, the banks would focus on the modernization of Lao industries, in line with the government's economic road map under the Laos Vision 2030.
SEZs and Regional Cluster	As of 2017, there were 12 approved Special Economic Zones or Specific Economic Zones (SEZs) in Laos. SEZs have played a crucial role in attracting FDI, especially non-resource-based investment, into Laos. Most of the SEZs are located in strategic locations with easy access to neighboring countries and have facilities and contact with local authorities. Boten, Savan–Seno SEZ, and Vientiane Industrial & Trade Area (VITA) Park are three of the most active SEZs in Laos today. There are too many SEZs, and this leads to an unclear strategy approach and unnecessary possible completion, which will bring limited benefits to the economy. Further strategy and priority development for SEZs need to be defined and take into account the link with other regions and the availability of the workforce. In a bid to maximize the benefits, it is necessary to strengthen the Savan-Seno SEZ and Thakkek SEZ, and create a hub and a dry port in these two SEZs to connect with Thailand and Vietnam. Besides, Boten SEZ is already well connected to the South of China.

	Given the small market, population, and few manufacturing industries, it might be useful to form three regional clusters (North, Center, and South) in order to maximize all the potential of the country in terms of competitively sharing the production resources, rationalizing investments, increasing the critical size of the region, facilitating the recruitment of workers, and continuing training of staff. Hence, the local authorities will have a better regional economic and industrial management, including a global strategic approach. For the southern region, for example, it makes sense to aggregate Sekong, Attapeu, Saravan, and Champassak provinces into one economic, industrial, and tourism cluster under one supervisory organization. The proposed cluster allows a good critical size development plan of the Cambodia-Laos-Vietnam-Thailand border and transit trade. This cluster will improve facilities and cross-country connectivity and will contribute significantly to exports and increase trade. In doing so, the Champassak Specific Economic Zone and the Khonphapheng Special Economic Zone could attract reputable foreign and domestic investors and contribute greatly to the economic development of the region. Moreover, the top exporting provinces in 2017 are Champassak, Saravan and Attapeu, which sell electricity, coffee, sweetcorn, cassava, rubber, sugar, and cattle carcasses.

2. Synthesis of Future Key Challenges

A summary table of key future challenges in industry, agricultural products, and tourism sectors are recalled below:

1. Agricultural products.

1.1. **Rice**. Situation in 2017: Production stands at 4.1 million tons, for various type of rice. About 2.1 million tons of rice will be supplied for consumption, 400,000 tons will be allocated to stockpile, some 500,000-600,000 tons will be processed, and 100,000 tons will be used as seeds. Laos exported about 400,000 tons of rice in 2017 and hopes the figure will climb to 1 million tons by 2020[206]. Rice is the main commercial crop for Laos' domestic market supply and export. Main export market: China, Vietnam, and Thailand.

Future challenges: Encouraging farmers to utilize machinery in their production processes to save labor and reduce costs; boosting productivity so that harvests are large, and improving different stages of production if growers in Laos are to supply rice for export on a large-scale and sustainable basis; focusing on export of organic rice to China; encouraging farmers to work together to market their produce in medium and large sized groups and expanding yields while maintaining quality control; helping Lao rice growers get necessary loans because of their high capital requirements for the crop; and purchasing modern equipment. Lao farmers need to meet delivery times to customers.

1.2. **Sweetcorn, watermelons, bananas, coffee, tea, and cassava.** Situation in 2017: Organic agrarian. Main crop export countries are China for cassava and bananas; Vietnam for cassava; and coffee for Japan, the EU, and the US.

Future challenges: Maintaining quality and control during the whole process. The government shall support farmers to focus on the sustainable export of commercial crops; targeting based on top quality of products to meet international standards. The export market has its own challenges and requires Laos to improve at several stages of the production process, notably in the field, technical systems, packaging, machinery, and product certification.

1.3. **Organic agriculture exports.** Situation in2017: Agriculture and organic products are faced with challenges and obstructions, due to lack of export management procedures and destinations specific requirements from Laos to international market.

Future challenges: Laos needs to focus on developing clean agriculture to have local produce certified as free of chemicals and pesticides with an eye on organic exports.

2. Industries

2.1. **Food processing.** Situation in 2017: Great varieties of vegetables and fruits, including beverages.

Future challenges: Enterprises need first to build up locally a brand name. Own a solid reputation and a strong market share in Laos before thinking to go abroad. Packaging of products is a must and needs to be carried out professionally with an attractive design. In order to access the international market Lao suppliers will need to meet challenges related to large supply volumes and consistent quality control.

2.2. **Energy**. Situation in 2017: As of December, the total installed capacity is 6859 MW with 50 power plants producing more than 7,555 million Kwh. All 148 districts of the country now have access to electricity. 85% of electricity is exported, essentially to Thailand.

Future challenges: To further export electricity to Vietnam and Cambodia within the ASEAN Power Grid initiatives. Improving the quality of the distribution network and deliver a stable power supply; seeking further reputable partners in joint investment for large hydro-power projects with EDL; maintaining an equitable share between EDL and its partners; integrating as a leading position in the ASEAN Power Grid and supply electricity to Malaysia, Singapore, and Myanmar; developing actively renewable energy by investing in solar farms; encouraging enterprises for using bio-agriculture and biomass energy and subsidizing them if necessary; and partnering with Asean member countries to develop and invest in solar and bio-agriculture energy.

2.3. **Mining**. Situation in 2017: Mining is an important source of economic growth and national revenue, and a driver for local community development and a contributor to poverty eradication. The mining industry has been growing 15 to 20% per year. Gold and copper are mature sectors and to date well exploited. The potential of the sector is great for other mineral deposits and is under exploited.

Future challenges: Laos needs to produce and improve the geological map in a bid to evaluate mining's real potential. A geological survey (details of reserves, grade of mineral deposits, and prospects) shall be conducted with Lao authorities in connection with foreign experts. Exploration licenses should be granted only to reliable investors within a limited time imposed for exploration. Mining law shall be updated, reinforced, and inspired from foreign mining countries. A sharing agreement shall be applied within a "win-win" scheme for government and investors.

2.3. **Processing industries**. Situation in 2017: Products in this category that the country can produce to supply domestic markets include foods, drinks, clothes, paper, and paper products.

Future challenges: To achieve all of its targets, authorities have to support and promote active production, agricultural processing, and industry to exploit raw materials within the country. Enterprises must produce quality products with competitive prices and build up a strong brand name. Enterprises must continue to improve the competence and ability of workers in the garment industry through a development center for this purpose. Promoting the production of high value-added wood panels with small diameter logs and lesser known timber species. The government needs to boost construction-material production by focusing on monitoring systems for quality and standards. This will apply to materials produced within the country and those that are imported. Improving wood-processing factories and increase local added value. Enterprises need to partner with foreign designers in a bid to have modern and innovative furniture that meets the western and Chinese markets.

3. Tourism. Situation in 2017: 80 % of arrival tourists are from Asia, mainly from Thailand, Vietnam, and China. In 2016, Laos received about 4.23 million tourists. The tourism industry generated US$724 million for Laos, with average spending of US$52 per person per day. The country is organizing Laos Visit Year 2018 to attract more regional and international tourists.

Future challenges: The tourism sector needs to clearly demonstrate the experiences, concepts, and tourist attractions in Laos through professionalism. Organizing many more activities to attract more tourists to Laos and to encourage them to stay longer and spend more to help poverty reduction efforts. Improving absolutely sanitation (toilets). Developing the quality of services in hotels, restaurants, and entertainment centers, including the English level of the staff. Building the tourist industry: Infrastructure, hotels, guest houses, transports (water, air, and road) to ensure the quality of welcome for tourists. Raising staff standards and provide training in vocational schools to be created in partnership between tourism authorities and industry professionals. Making the Laos Visit Year 2018 a success by promoting eco-tourism, but also preserving the unique traditional culture of the country and stimulate several economic sectors, particularly tourism-related business units.

In synthesis, besides thinking of growth, productivity, and integration, Laos needs to revamp its education system, particularly to improve creativity, rather than producing "standardized students", civil servants, and unskilled workforce. Singapore is doing great in this area, using innovative approaches to improve education and training. The disruption of companies, and entire Lao nascent industry, by new economy and technologies is another theme relevant to Laos. Change and challenges will come for instance, in transport and logistics, retail, processing industry, business, financial services, and the media.

Moving Laos's integration to an upper middle-economy country needs higher ambitions and human resources. It's not just about enjoying manufacturing sector tariff reductions and non-tariff barriers. They also have to think of how to advance social services sector, how to advance poverty reduction and gap between poor and remote region and rich urban region. Those complex issues of integration are critical and require strong political will and national mobilization of all stakeholders. Close collaboration with international development partners, stakeholders, and other identified actions, as well as talking about the way forward with the government are necessary for Laos to attain its industrial and sustainable development.

Notes

[203] South-South Cooperation (SSC) is a broad framework for collaboration between the countries of the South in the political, economic, social, cultural, environmental or technical domains. It involves the mutual sharing and exchange of key development solutions – knowledge, experiences and good practices, policies, technology and resources – between and amongst countries in the global south. Triangular Cooperation involves two or more countries in the global south collaborating with a third party, typically a traditional donor, emerging economy or multilateral organization, facilitating SSC exchange through the provision of resources.

[204] Stratorg group: Building Trust, Make senses to the Future, The Trust Management Institute, Paris.

[205] SME Lao application of Industrial 4.0 in AEC context, Sethakit News, by Ms. Santi.

[206] Laos expects to promote rice exports, Xinhua, 29/01/2017.

Recommended Reading

Asean, A Blueprint for Growth ASEAN Economic Community 2015: Progress and Key Achievements.
-------, ASEAN Economic Community Chart book 2016.
-------, ASEAN: Profile, Trade, Socio-Demography, Investment, Connectivity 2015.
Asian Development Bank, Country Partnership Strategy: Lao PDR 2012–2016.
--------, (2015), Technical Assistance Report- Lao People's Democratic Republic: Support for Governance and Capacity Development.
---------, Key Indicators for Asia and the Pacific 2015.
---------, (ADB)/Evaluation Lao People's Democratic Republic Country Partnership Strategy Final Review Validation, 2012–2016.
---------, (ADB), Development Finance for the 8th National Socio-Economic Development Plan and the Sustainable Development Goals in Lao PDR, 2016.
Bank of Lao PDR, Annual Report, various issues from 1999–2015.
Boulanger, Paul le. Histoire du Laos français: essai d'une étude chronologique des principautés laotiennes. Paris: Librairie Plon, 1930.
Boupha, Phongsavath. The Evolution of the Lao State. New Delhi: Konark Publishers, 2002.
Burchett, Wilfred G. The Furtive War: The United States in Vietnam and Laos. New York: International Publishers, 1963.
Deloitte, The ABC of AEC to 2015 and beyond, 2015.
Dominique Gentiland Philippe Boumard. Le Laos, doux et amer: 25 ans de pratique d'une ONG, Comité de coopération avec le Laos (CCL) Kartala, 2005.
Economic Research Institute for ASEAN and East Asia, Lao PDR at the Crossroads: Industrial Development Strategies 2016–2030, edited by

Hidetoshi Nishimura, Fukunari Kimura, Masahito Ambashi, and Souknilanh Keola, 2016.

ESCAP/ADB/UNDP (2015), Making it Happen: Technology, Finance and Statistics for Sustainable Development in Asia and the Pacific. Asia-Pacific Regional MDGs Report 2014/15.

EU (2009), 10 Benefits of Trade for Developing Countries, Brussels: European Commission.

FIDH - International Federation for Human Rights, Update for the 7th European Union (EU)-Laos human rights dialogue 16 February 2017, Vientiane, Laos.

Food and Agriculture Organization of the UN regional office for ASIA and the Pacific, Lao PDR Forestry outlook study, by Pei Sin Tong, Bangkok 2009.

GIZ (2014), HRDME Enterprise Survey 2013 for Lao PDR, Vientiane.

-----, (2017), Lao PDR's Way into the ASEAN Single Market.

IMF (2017), Lao People's Democratic Republic – Staff Report for 2017 n° 17/53 Article IV Consultation, Washington, D.C.: IMF.

ISEAS Institute of Southeast Asian Studies, The ASEAN Economic Community, A work in progress, 2013.

History of the Special Relationship between Vietnam and Laos, 1930–2007. 7 vols. Hanoi: National Political Publishing House, 2011.

Lao PDR, Education for All 2015 National Review.

-----------, Agriculture business investment in Laos: Opportunities and challenges for poverty reduction, 2015.

Lao Statistics Bureau (2016), Statistical Yearbook 2015, Vientiane Capital:

Leebouapao, L. (2008), 'Lao PDR Country Report', in Soesastro, H. (ed.), Developing Roadmap toward East Asian Economic Integration, ERIA Research Project Report 2007-1-1,Chiba: IDE-JETRO, pp.117-120.

------------------. (2014), LDC Graduation Progress and the Way Forwards, the Case of Lao PDR, (NERI)

------------------. (2014), How Economic Integration Can Promote Inclusive

------------------. Opportunities and Challenges of Lao PDR's Integration into AEC by and after 2015.

Ministry of Finance (various), Government Finance Statistics Annual Report, various editions, Vientiane Capital: Ministry of Finance.

Ministry of Health (2014), Health Financing Strategy, 2014–2025, Vientiane Capital: Ministry of Health.

Ministry of Industry and Commerce (2013), Diagnostic Trade Study, 2012, Vientiane Capital: Ministry of Industry and Commerce.
------------, (2013), Initial Conceptual Framework and Roadmap for Public-
Ministry of Planning and Investment, Private Partnerships in Lao PDR, Vientiane Capital:
-------------, MPI (2014), Background Document for the 2014 Roundtable Implementation Meeting Vientiane, Lao PDR, 14th November 2014, Vientiane Capital: Ministry of Planning and Investment – Department of International Cooperation.
---------------, (2015), Vientiane Declaration on Partnership for Effective Development Cooperation (2016–2025), Vientiane Capital: Ministry of Planning and Investment.
---------------, (2015), Background Document for the 12th High Level Round Table Meeting: November 2015, Vientiane Capital: Ministry of Planning and Investment – Department of International Cooperation.
---------------, 7th NSEDP and 8th NSEDP.
Nathalie Fau, Sirivanh Khonthapane et Christian Taillard (eds.), *Transnational Dynamics in Southeast Asia, the Greater Mekong Subregion and Malacca Straits Economic Corridors, Revue de la Régulation 15, Spring 2014.*
NERI (2013), Lao PDR's Macroeconomic Model: The Technical Background Paper, Vientiane Capital: National Economic Research Institute (NERI).
------, (2014), Macro-economy in 2013 and the Outlook in 2014, Vientiane Capital: National Economic Research Institute (NERI).
OECD (2014), Development Co-operation Report 2014: Mobilizing Resources for Sustainable Development, Paris: OECD Publishing.
--------, DAC, Country Programmable Aid database.
--------, Growth. Laos PDR's Experience, National Economic Research Institute
Perera, O. (2011), The Incentives for Sustainable Development: The Case of Lao PDR, Winnipeg: The International Institute for Sustainable Development.
Phommahaxay, Anitta and Vanhnalat, Bounlert, Impact of FRI on economic growth in Lao PDR, Faculty of Economics and Business Management, National University of Laos, 2015.
Porter, Michael. Porter's Five Forces – Competitor Analysis, A Harvard Business Review Book, 1979.

Shanghai Institutes for International Studies, Assessment and Prospects of China-Laos Development Cooperation, September 2016.

Singhalath, Phonethavong. Current Investment Regime of the Lao PDR, 2012, Investment Promotion Department (IPD), Ministry of Planning and Investment.

Sisouphanthong, Bounthavy, and Christian Taillard. Atlas de la république démocratique populaire lao. Paris: CNRS-GDR Libergéo/La Documentation Française, 2000.

Souvannamethy, Vathsana. Determinants of Foreign Direct Investment Flows to Lao PDR, 2016. Thesis Presented to the Higher Degree Committee of Ritsumeikan Asia Pacific University.

Stuart-Fox, Martin. Buddhist Kingdom, Marxist State: The Making of Modern Laos. Bangkok: White Lotus, 1996.

———. A History of Laos. Cambridge: Cambridge University Press, 1997.

Suvannaphakdy, Sithanonxay. An Empirical Study of Trade and Foreign Direct Investment in Laos, A Dissertation Submitted to the Graduate School of Economic Sciences in Partial Fulfillment of the Requirements for the Degree of Doctor of Philosophy in Economics, 2013.

Taillard, Christian, ed. Intégration régionales en Asie orientale: la région du Grand Mékong; un espace transnational péninsulaire en Asie du Sud-Est continentale. Paris: Éditions Les Indes Savantes, 2004.

———. "Le Laos à la croisée des corridors de la Région du Grand Mékong." In Le Laos, doux et amer: 25 ans de pratique d'une ONG, edited by Dominique **Gentil and Philippe Boumard**. Paris: Comité de Coopération avec le Laos (CCL) Éditions : Le Laos, doux et amer: 25 ans de pratique d'une ONG, Karthala, 2005.

Thammavong, Kapkeo. Break Through ASEAN, Vientiane, 2014.

Than, Mya, and Joseph L. H. Tan. Laos's Dilemmas and Options: The Challenge of Economic Transition in the 1990s. Singapore: Institute of Southeast Asian Studies, 1997.

Toye, Hugh, Laos: Buffer State or Battleground. London: Oxford University Press, 1968.

UN (2006), United Nations Common Country Assessment (CCA): Lao PDR, Vientiane Capital: United Nations Country Team, Lao PDR.

-------------, United Nations symposium on hydropower and sustainable development, Lao hydropower potential and policy in the GMS context, Beijing 2004.

UNDP (2014), Asia-Pacific Effective Development Co-operation Report 2014, Bangkok: UNDP Regional Centre – Asia Pacific Development Effectiveness Facility.

--------, /AP-DEF, "Development Finance Assessment (DFA): Linking Finance and Results to Implement the SDGs at Country Level- A Guide", forthcoming (draft of March 2016).

--------, National Human Development Report, Lao PDR, 2017.

Vorapheth, Kham. Contemporary Laos, Published by White Lotus, Bangkok 2016.

———. Laos: la redéfinition des stratégies politiques et économiques (1975–2006). Paris: Éditions Les Indes Savantes, 2007.

World Bank, Lao PDR Country Office, 2017.

---------------, (2014b), Lao PDR Economic Monitor: Managing Risks for Macroeconomic Stability, Vientiane Capital: The World Bank – Lao PDR Country Office.

---------------, (2014e), Doing Business 2015, Going Beyond Efficiency: Economic Profile 2015 Lao PDR, Vientiane Capital: World Bank CO Lao PDR.

---------------, World Development Indicators database.

Zasloff, Joseph J., and MacAlister Brown. "Laos 1990: Socialism Postponed but Leadership Intact." In Southeast Asian Affairs 1991, pp. 147–150. Singapore: Institute of Southeast Asian Studies, 1991.

Asie
aux éditions L'Harmattan

Dernières parutions

RHÉTORIQUES DE L'HÉRÉSIE DANS LE JAPON MÉDIÉVAL ET MODERNE
Le moine Monkan (1278-1357) et sa réputation posthume
Rappo Gaétan - Préface de Philippe Borgeaud
Le moine Monkan fut un personnage influent du paysage religieux japonais du XIVe siècle. Après sa disparition, on le présente comme un homme extravagant et un «hérétique», charmant par des rites sexuels l'empereur Go Daigo pour obtenir ses faveurs. Cet ouvrage traite de la contradiction entre la vie du personnage et son image posthume, et permet grâce à la récente découverte d'œuvres du moine de pouvoir confronter ces deux visions.
(Coll. Japon. Etudes du fait japonais, 39.00 euros, 498 p.)
ISBN : 978-2-343-08825-9, ISBN EBOOK : 978-2-14-005247-7

CHINE
Chronologie simplifiée – Des origines à 1949
Drapeaud Pierre
Ce livre est l'œuvre d'un Occidental curieux, amoureux de la Chine ; il est le fruit d'un long travail qui l'a conduit à faire revivre 5 000 ans d'histoire. Un ouvrage simple et pratique à consulter au fur et à mesure des interrogations.
(39.00 euros, 464 p.)
ISBN : 978-2-343-11450-7, ISBN EBOOK : 978-2-14-005053-4

THE SOUTH CHINA SEA : the Mediterranean of Asia
The geostrategic Maritime Review 9
The South China Sea is a classic Mediterranean sea-structure with a long history of populations living in the basin and taking advantage of a permanent trading activity interrupted by some dramatic war moments. The Chinese preponderance on the development and the history of the basin has been a permanent element of both equilibrium and dilemma. Political and military tensions are heating up with a sharp increase in commercial relations amongst the regional countries and the great international powers.
(20.00 euros, 158 p.)
ISBN : 978-2-343-13360-7, ISBN EBOOK : 978-2-14-005147-0

VIETNAM, LES ETHNIES MINORITAIRES DES HAUTS PLATEAUX DU CENTRE
Histoire, mode de vie, avenir
Giraud Joël
Cet ouvrage expose l'histoire et le mode de vie des ethnies minoritaires des hauts plateaux du centre du Vietnam. Ces populations qui fuyaient l'esclavage ont occupé des territoires par vagues successives de migrants Môn-Khmers et Malayo-Polyéniseins à partir de 3000 ans et 1000 ans avant J.-C. Dès 1850, les missionnaires commencent à approcher ces populations et découvrent des ethnies égalitaires entre époux et parfois la pratique du matriarcat avec des femmes chefs de

village. Victimes de génocide lors de la guerre du Vietnam, ces populations insoumises ont été intégrées par l'État vietnamien, avec la victoire du communisme, au modèle «Việt».
(Coll. Recherches asiatiques, 26.00 euros, 260 p.)
ISBN : 978-2-343-12342-4, ISBN EBOOK : 978-2-14-004789-3

ACCORD SUR LA FACILITATION DES ÉCHANGES DE L'OMC POUR LE VIETNAM
Les implications de sa mise en œuvre
Sous la direction de Ngoc Ha Nguyen
Adopté en décembre 2013 à Bali, l'Accord sur la facilitation des échanges (AFE) est récemment entré en vigueur. Il crée à ses Membres de nouvelles obligations pour faciliter les échanges. Il prévoit également les traitements spéciaux et différenciés destinés aux Membres en développement et à ceux les moins avancés. Dès son entrée en vigueur, le Vietnam est obligé de réaliser quinze mesures prévues dans l'AFE. Voici une clarification des AFE de l'OMC, et une analyse des enjeux juridiques et pratiques auxquels le Vietnam doit faire face.
(19.50 euros, 186 p.)
ISBN : 978-2-343-13003-3, ISBN EBOOK : 978-2-14-004776-3

DICTIONNAIRE NORD-CORÉEN
De Gouyon Matignon Louis
Tout a été écrit sur la Corée du Nord. Sauf cette situation, unique au monde, d'une langue parlée à l'origine par une même population sur un même territoire, et qui se trouve depuis près de 70 ans comme séparée en deux. La langue parlée au Nord, à l'écart du monde moderne, celle au Sud, résolument engagée dans la contemporanéité. Le même idiome, mais aujourd'hui deux langues, qui se différencient dans le vocabulaire, l'écriture, mais également la prononciation.
(36.00 euros, 350 p.)
ISBN : 978-2-343-12386-8, ISBN EBOOK : 978-2-14-004153-2

UNE DIPLOMATIE DU RESPECT : LE JAPON ET LE MULTILATÉRALISME
Trois cas d'étude : l'Assemblée générale des Nations unies, le PNUD et l'AIEA depuis les années 2000
Tanke Sarah - Préface de Pierre Grosser
Le Japon a mis en place une diplomatie multilatérale très active : contributions financières considérables, visibilité importante dans l'aide au développement, engagement pour le désarmement nucléaire, efforts pour obtenir un siège permanent au sein du Conseil de sécurité des Nations unies, etc. Cet ouvrage interroge donc la place que prend le multilatéralisme dans la diplomatie japonaise ainsi que son rôle dans la diplomatie multilatérale globale.
(Coll. Questions contemporaines, 25.00 euros, 250 p.)
ISBN : 978-2-343-12218-2, ISBN EBOOK : 978-2-14-004327-7

LE YOGA DE LA RAISON
Initiation à la pensée de l'Inde
Bouthillette Karl-Stéphan
Qui s'éveille à la pensée indienne sait rarement se diriger seul. La présente introduction s'adresse à ce non-initié intéressé à découvrir différents courants philosophiques indiens, tout en évitant l'écueil de l'écriture académique formelle. À travers sept tableaux, incluant le yoga, le Védanta et le bouddhisme, apparaissent autant de développements idéologiques qui ont façonné la culture indienne, auxquels s'ajoutent des éléments biographiques inspirés d'aventures personnelles de l'auteur en Inde, enracinant alors le récit dans une expérience d'apprentissage concrète.
(16.00 euros, 146 p.)
ISBN : 978-2-343-12578-7, ISBN EBOOK : 978-2-14-004280-5

LA FRANCE ET LA RÉPUBLIQUE POPULAIRE DE CHINE
Contextes et répercussions de la normalisation diplomatique (1949-1972)
Sous la direction de Françoise Kreissler et Sébastien Colin
Le 27 janvier 1964, un bref communiqué publié simultanément à Paris et à Pékin annonçait l'établissement des relations diplomatiques entre le gouvernement de la République française et le

gouvernement de la République populaire de Chine. En ces temps de guerre froide, alors que la RPC se situait depuis sa fondation en marge de la communauté internationale, les contextes et les répercussions de la décision prise par le général de Gaulle furent de nature multiple. Cet ouvrage se propose de revenir sur ces contextes et répercussions de la normalisation des relations entre la France et la RPC.
(28.00 euros, 296 p.)
ISBN : 978-2-343-12385-1, ISBN EBOOK : 978-2-14-004050-4

GÉNÉRATION HIKIKOMORI
Tajan Nicolas – Préface d'Agnès Giard –Postface de Marie-Jean Sauret
Depuis les années 1990, un phénomène très particulier touche la population japonaise. Chaque année, des centaines de milliers de personnes disparaissent. Appelé hikikomori, «retrait social», ce phénomène désigne des personnes qui, enfermées chez elles pendant plusieurs mois (au moins six), voire plusieurs années, se coupent du monde et n'ont plus aucune relation sociale. Dans une société ultra-organisée et codifiée et où prévaut le collectif sur l'individu, les hikikomori bouleversent l'idée d'un Japon uniforme, suscitent le débat et interrogent une société japonaise en perte de repères.
(Coll. Japon. Études du fait japonais, série Psychologie, 37.00 euros, 384 p.)
ISBN : 978-2-343-12356-1, ISBN EBOOK : 978-2-14-003985-0

LA PÉRENNITÉ DES SYSTÈMES DE CROYANCES OU LE FONDEMENT D'UNE UNITÉ NATIONALE JAPONAISE
Une éthique de l'autonomie
Mourtont Jonathan Jay
Les hiérarchies de valeurs, les normes ou « nomos », issues de croyances ont codifié l'organisation sociale du Japon en assurant de fait leur pérennité. Dans la société, les interactions entre les individus procèdent d'une mémoire collective transmise d'abord au sein des familles, puis par la « praxis » de la « cité ». C'est ainsi que les « autorités narratives », les institutions ont acquis leur légitimité, leur « identicité». En somme une société qui procède d'une « Éthique de l'autonomie ».
(18.50 euros, 174 p.)
ISBN : 978-2-343-09066-5, ISBN EBOOK : 978-2-14-003986-7

JACQUES DOURNES
Prêtre, missionnaire, ethnologue
Tison Brigitte
Vingt-cinq années passées sur les hauts-plateaux de l'Asie du Sud-Est, hauts plateaux situés au Vietnam, un carnet de notes sous la main, Jacques Dournes regarde, observe ce qui se passe et se vit autour de lui. Il va ainsi développer une véritable démarche d'ethnologue. Envoyé par les Missions étrangères de Paris pour établir des liens avec des populations ignorant tout du christianisme, il innovera aussi sur ce point. Cet ouvrage dévoile quelques-uns de ses dessins remis à l'auteur peu avant sa disparition, montrant alors la force de l'homme et du chercheur de Dieu qu'il fut tout au long de sa vie.
(Coll. Trajectoires, mouvements, changements, 14.50 euros, 98 p.)
ISBN : 978-2-343-12248-9, ISBN EBOOK : 978-2-14-003978-2

APERÇUS MULTIPLES DU MONDE UYGHUR
Études orientales
Wheidi Souad
Conseillers auprès de la rédaction : Françoise Aubin, Burhan Ghalioun, Marie-Paule Hille
L'ouvrage se décline en cinq parties : Le monde uyghur intellectuel, spirituel et culturel ; Le Xinjiang politique et économique ; Christianisme au Xinjiang ; Pensée islamique en Chine et Han Kitab ; Partie arabe.
(30.00 euros, 474 p.)
ISBN : 978-2-343-11760-7, ISBN EBOOK : 978-2-14-003462-6

LES DÉFUNTS À LA PAGODE
La bouddhisation du culte des ancêtres chez les Vietnamiens de la région parisienne
Gidoin Jérôme - Préface de Richard Pottier
Au Vietnam, le culte des ancêtres et le bouddhisme sont deux systèmes religieux distincts. Ils peuvent être juxtaposés et se chevaucher, mais leurs frontières restent relativement étanches l'un pour l'autre. Dans le contexte postmigratoire français, on observe un phénomène étonnant et nouveau : ces deux références religieuses sont amenées à entrer en contact. Cet ouvrage, qui s'appuie sur une enquête de terrain réalisée dans des pagodes vietnamiennes de la région parisienne, décrit les multiples aspects de ce contact entre culte des ancêtres et culte bouddhique.
(Coll. Connaissance des hommes, 21.50 euros, 210 p.)
ISBN : 978-2-343-11669-3, ISBN EBOOK : 978-2-14-003480-0

CAP SUR KARAKORUM (nouvelle édition)
Chevauchée franco-mongole sur les traces de Guillaume de Rubrouck
Alix Patrick
Suite à la lecture du livre *Voyage dans l'Empire mongol*, Pierre Létang nourrit le projet de partir sur les traces de Guillaume de Rubrouck, moine franciscain chargé par saint Louis de nouer des liens avec la cour des grands khans mongols. L'auteur de cet ouvrage a tenu le carnet de route de cette formidable épopée, tout en dialoguant avec le texte médiéval. Leur voyage, aux fins tant universitaires que ludiques, contribuera au premier jumelage franco-mongol, ainsi qu'au rayonnement culturel de la Mongolie.
(Coll. Écrire et voyager aujourd'hui, 30.00 euros, 354 p.)
ISBN : 978-2-343-11470-5, ISBN EBOOK : 978-2-14-003038-3

J'AURAI VINGT ANS DANS DEUX JOURS
Tran Thi Hao – Préface de Pierre Brunel
Lan est née à Hanoï au début des années 90, au moment de l'ouverture du Vietnam. Comme les jeunes de sa génération, elle n'a pas connu la guerre, elle ne croyait pas à la guerre, aux bombardements. Elle a 20 ans, étudiante de français dans une université de la capitale, sa vie est belle et pleine d'avenir. Pourtant une grande épreuve va frapper cette jeune fille. Lors d'une hospitalisation, elle devra être amputée des deux jambes. Que s'est-il passé dans son histoire pour être victime de ce drame ? En publiant ce témoignage intime et bouleversant, l'auteure veut aussi rendre hommage aux familles de vétérans, invalides de guerre.
(14,5 euros, 136 p., juillet 2016) EAN : 9782343096674

L'ÉNIGME CHINOISE
Stratégie, puissance et influence de la Chine depuis la Guerre froide
Sous la direction de Pierre Journoud
Préface de Hugues Tertrais – Postface de l'ambassadeur Christian Lechervy
La Chine est susceptible de devenir la première puissance économique mondiale : aucun continent n'échappe désormais à son influence. Comment interpréter l'écart entre les proclamations rassurantes sur le caractère pacifique et responsable de sa puissance, et la poursuite d'un réarmement massif, qui pousse Pékin à bousculer un *statu quo* régional qui ne la satisfait plus et à se déclarer prête à recourir à la force armée dans les disputes territoriales si on l'y obligeait ? Cet ouvrage collectif offre une analyse de la stratégie de la Chine de la fin de la Guerre froide au tournant des années 2015-2016.
(Coll. Inter-National, 36.00 euros, 430 p.)
ISBN : 978-2-343-11929-8, ISBN EBOOK : 978-2-14-003460-2

L'HARMATTAN ITALIA
Via Degli Artisti 15; 10124 Torino
harmattan.italia@gmail.com

L'HARMATTAN HONGRIE
Könyvesbolt ; Kossuth L. u. 14-16
1053 Budapest

L'HARMATTAN KINSHASA
185, avenue Nyangwe
Commune de Lingwala
Kinshasa, R.D. Congo
(00243) 998697603 ou (00243) 999229662

L'HARMATTAN CONGO
67, av. E. P. Lumumba
Bât. – Congo Pharmacie (Bib. Nat.)
BP2874 Brazzaville
harmattan.congo@yahoo.fr

L'HARMATTAN GUINÉE
Almamya Rue KA 028, en face
du restaurant Le Cèdre
OKB agency BP 3470 Conakry
(00224) 657 20 85 08 / 664 28 91 96
harmattanguinee@yahoo.fr

L'HARMATTAN MALI
Rue 73, Porte 536, Niamakoro,
Cité Unicef, Bamako
Tél. 00 (223) 20205724 / +(223) 76378082
poudiougopaul@yahoo.fr
pp.harmattan@gmail.com

L'HARMATTAN CAMEROUN
TSINGA/FECAFOOT
BP 11486 Yaoundé
699198028/675441949
harmattancam@yahoo.com

L'HARMATTAN CÔTE D'IVOIRE
Résidence Karl / cité des arts
Abidjan-Cocody 03 BP 1588 Abidjan 03
(00225) 05 77 87 31
etien_nda@yahoo.fr

L'HARMATTAN BURKINA
Penou Achille Some
Ouagadougou
(+226) 70 26 88 27

L'HARMATTAN SÉNÉGAL
10 VDN en face Mermoz, après le pont de Fann
BP 45034 Dakar Fann
33 825 98 58 / 33 860 9858
senharmattan@gmail.com / senlibraire@gmail.com
www.harmattansenegal.com

www.ingramcontent.com/pod-product-compliance
Lightning Source LLC
LaVergne TN
LVHW011156061026
849535LV00003B/760